DATE DU

Great Inflations of the 20th Century

Great Inflations of the 20th Century
Theories, Policies and Evidence

Edited by

Pierre L. Siklos

Wilfrid Laurier University
Waterloo, Ontario
Canada   N2L 3C5

Edward Elgar

Published by
Edward Elgar Publishing Limited
Gower House
Croft Road
Aldershot
Hants GU11 3HR
UK

Edward Elgar Publishing Company
Old Post Road
Brookfield
Vermont 05036
US

British Library Cataloguing in Publication Data
Great Inflations of the 20th Century:
Theories, Policies and Evidence
I. Siklos, Pierre L.
332.41

Library of Congress Cataloguing in Publication Data
Great inflations of the 20th century: theories, policies, and
    evidence / edited by Pierre L. Siklos.
        Includes index.
        1. Inflation (Finance) I. Siklos, Pierre L., 1955–
HG229.G676 1995
332.4'1'0904—dc20   95–15682
                                                                CIP

ISBN 1 85898 232 4
Printed and bound in Great Britain by
Hartnolls Limited, Bodmin, Cornwall

Contents

Figures

Tables

List of Contributors

Peter Bernholz, *Wirtschaftswissenschafliches Zentrum der Universität Basel, Switzerland*

Richard C.K. Burdekin, *Claremont McKenna College and Claremont Graduate School, USA*

Paul Burkett, *Indiana State University, USA*

Alex S. Cukierman, *Tel-Aviv University, Israel*

Pierre L. Siklos, *Wilfrid Laurier University, Canada*

Carlos A. Végh, *International Monetary Fund, USA*

Preface

Despite the largely successful disinflation record of the industrialised countries during the second half of the 1980s in particular, the problems associated with chronically high inflation and hyperinflation continue to preoccupy policy makers in many other countries. Most notable among these are the so-called 'transitional economies' which abandoned the central planning concept in favour of the market-oriented approach. Even in regions of the world, such as Latin and South America, where progress on stabilising inflation has been impressive there remain outcast countries which, despite several attempts at halting accelerating inflation, have yet to succeed in a more permanent fashion.

Amongst economists, the study of high inflation episodes has never been out of fashion since Philip Cagan's pioneering work on seven historical episodes of hyperinflation this century was published in 1956. Nowhere is this more true than with the German hyperinflation which continues to fascinate many and maintains scholars' interests. But the German example is but one of many interesting and potentially useful illustrations of the problems and policies necessary to deal with exceedingly high or protracted inflations.

For these reasons it was felt timely to collect a sampling of previously published work on high inflation. The book is divided into four parts. Two papers present general surveys of the litearure. Chapter 1 focuses on historical experiences with hyperinflation while the second chapter deals with cases of chronic inflation. In part II, the various papers explore the conditions which are conducive to generating high inflation. Despite the attempt by some in the relevant literature to argue that these are straightforward, a closer look at the historial experience suggests that a rather more complex set of characterisitcs and conditions must be present to give rise to a particular level of inflation. Part III of the book provides a sampling of studies whose focus is the link between monetary policy and inflation. Again, it is not always easy to sort out the causal role of monetary policy in high inflation countries but some of the epsiodes of hyperinflation do offer some clues in this regard. The final part of the book, Part IV, deal with a subject that continues to preoccupy policy makers in several countries, namely how to end high inflation with the smallest possible economic costs. Again, the requirements need not be simple and the historical experience, while helpful, is fraught with difficulties when one attempts to draw simplistic policy recommendations.

Almost all the papers are reprinted, with minor revisions usually, from previously published work. The first chapter, which is a survey of episodes of hyperinflation was more substantially revised in light of recent developments in the area.

I am grateful to the contributors, Peter Bernholz, Richard Burdekin, Paul Burkett, Alex Cukierman, and Carlos Végh, for agreeing to include some of their previously published work along with my own, and to the various Publishers for permission to reprint the articles in this volume. I am also grateful for financial support from Wilfrid Laurier University and the wonderful word processing talents of Elsie Grogan. I hope the volume will prove to be a useful basic source of reference for interested scholars and policy makers about the myriad of issues surrounding the beginning and the ending of high or chronic inflation.

Pierre L. Siklos
Waterloo, Ontario
Canada
December 1994

PART I

Surveys

1. Hyperinflations: Their Origins, Development and Termination[*]

Pierre L. Siklos

1. INTRODUCTION

The aim of this chapter is to summarize and critically survey research on hyperinflations. Such events have been arbitrarily classified as occurring whenever the inflation rate exceeds 50 per cent on a monthly basis (Cagan 1956), thereby highlighting the relatively few cases of excessively high rates of change in the price level that have taken place since the beginning of this century.[1]

The study of hyperinflation has fascinated economists for many years, in part because they continue to be concerned about policies required to attain price stability. The steady appearance of articles on the subject also attests to its recurring popularity as a topic of research in the area of monetary economics. Although economic and historical descriptions of the better-known episodes of high inflation this century were written several decades ago (e.g., Bresciani-Turroni 1937) a wave of articles followed the seminal study by Phillip Cagan (1956) on money demand under hyper-inflationary conditions. Cagan's device of using such unusual events as a means of testing, using econometric methods, some of the fundamental tenets of the quantity theory of money (hereafter QT) inspired considerable subsequent research.

Renewed interest in the study of hyperinflations was later prompted by the influential work of Sargent (1981, 1993, ch. 3), and Sargent and Wallace (1981, 1982; hereafter SW), who thought that there were important policy lessons to be learned from such episodes and that, moreover, these should be treated as the closest example the macroeconomist has to a laboratory-type experiment. Experiences with runaway inflation were also interpreted by SW as symptomatic of the failure of the QT as a general theory of the price level. As we shall see, neither of these two views has gone unchallenged in recent years.

While a considerable literature exists about both the development and termination of hyperinflations, relatively less research has been devoted to isolating those factors which have led to the abandonment of conventional instruments to raise government revenues and to resort instead to the almost complete reliance on the inflation tax.[2] It seems appropriate, therefore, to begin this survey in section 2 with an analysis of how hyperinflations are thought to have originated. Here the key issues revolve around the role of civil disorder and weak governments, the significance of reparations payments, and the role of central bank independence, in persuading policymakers to select a path destined to produce hyperinflation.

Section 3 of the chapter explores the issues which have received attention concerning the development of hyperinflations. Here it will be necessary to recall the fundamental contributions made by Cagan and Sargent and Wallace. Since this survey was originally prepared there have also been many developments in the area of time-series analysis which have a bearing on the interpretation and estimation of money demand under inflationary conditions. It will be useful to cover some of the relevant main points at a later stage in the survey.

Section 4 discusses economists' views about the financial and real effects of achieving price stability, and the controversies surrounding the interpretation of the end of several hyperinflations this century. Once again Sargent's work should be credited with initiating the recent considerable debate in this area.

The chapter concludes with some comments about the significance of the study of hyperinflations and the lessons to be learned from such events.

The principal goal of the chapter, then, is to describe the essentials of the analysis of the origins, development and termination of hyperinflation, while noting where appropriate the vast literature which stems from some of the key contributions noted above.

2. ORIGINS

Although it is widely accepted that hyperinflations result when there is an almost total reliance on the issue of money to finance deficit spending, there is some question about the conditions which lead policymakers to follow such a path. Borrowing from Keynes' suggestion in his *Economic Consequences of the Peace*, namely that 'even the weakest government can enforce inflation when it can enforce nothing else', Capie (1986) argues that the combination of weak governments, civil disorder and unrest, leads to conditions which facilitate the loss of fiscal discipline and to the use of the inflation tax as the overwhelming source of government revenue. Certainly the hyperinflations after the breakup of the Habsburg monarchy following World War I, the post-World War II hyperinflations in Hungary and China, the Russian hyperinflation early this century, as well as the more recent hyperinflations in, say, Lebanon, Peru, Brazil and Yugoslavia, appear consistent with Capie's hypothesis. Since economists tend to judge cause and effect or assess the determinants of a particular economic event on the basis of statistical evidence, the difficulty with Capie's hypothesis is that it is very difficult to find quantifiable proxies, especially for social unrest. Moreover, as Fratianni (1986) notes, there are almost just as many historical episodes where the existence of weak governments or civil disorder did not lead to runaway inflation (e.g., Israel).

At best, Capie's hypothesis may be applicable to the South American experience and perhaps to some countries remnant of the former Soviet Union, while it is generally the case that 20th century European hyperinflations emerged following the end of a major conflict or were the result of severe physical damage coupled with large demands for reparations. This is true, for example, of the hyperinflations after the Versailles Treaty of 1920, as well as the post-World War II Hungarian hyperinflation (Siklos 1990). Recently, and as a result of the return to fashion of political explanations of business cycles, there has been some interest in empirically assessing the reasons why some countries tend to be prone to resorting to seigniorage and, thus, to chronically high inflation, while others are not. For example, Cukierman, Edwards and Tabellini (1992) argue that political instability is synonymous with inefficiency in the tax system resulting in, for example, widespread tax avoidance or too few resources invested in enforcement of tax collection. Hence, the implication that governments are effectively constrained to select the inflation tax route. Using data from 79 countries, they find empirical support for their hypothesis. If, however, political stability is partly determined by the presence or absence of democratic institutions, the evidence appears to be less clear. Haggard and Kaufman (1989), for example, do not find that authoritarian governments are more prone to generating an inflationary bias than more democratic governments.

It has also been pointed out that inflation tends to redistribute income away from wage earners towards rentiers and as rentiers find inflation profitable, the potential exists for continued hyperinflation (Kalecki 1962). Certainly, the German and some recent South American hyperinflations could be viewed in this light (Pastor 1991; Horsman 1988)). Thus, the inflation route is viewed as facilitating the maintenance of an unequal distribution of income. Theoretical contributions about the distributional effects of inflation, which concentrates on the organization and efficiency of markets under hyperinflationary conditions, have been made by, for example, Clower and Howitt (1978), and Casella and Feinstein (1990). Burdekin and Burkett (1992 and Chapter 5 in this volume) also point out that wage-push pressure on fiscal policy and inflation is a neglected facet of the stimulus to hyperinflation, and find evidence in favour of this hypothesis using German hyperinflation data.

While the foregoing considerations can explain why some countries prefer more inflation than others it would seem irrational for governments to allow inflation to degenerate into hyperinflation unless other considerations, often external ones, are also present, such as those discussed above and a few others which are described below. Alternatively, a hyperinflation may be viewed as a means of creating conditions in which a group reluctantly accepts shouldering the economic burdens attendant on a stabilization (Alesina and Drazen 1989).[3] Again, as in the unequal income distribution explanations of inflation, heterogeneity in the population is essential. Surely, such differences as exist in the socioeconomic make-up of a particular country are always present, yet episodes of high inflation are the exception and not the rule in how policymakers deal with and implement redistributive schemes.

Instead, it is surprising that the role of central bank independence has not been more forcefully brought to the fore (see, however, Rogoff 1985; Bade and Parkin 1985; and Toniolo 1989). Yet, even a cursory glance at the literature dealing with the end of hyperinflation reveals that the introduction of an independent monetary authority is a crucial element of the long-term solution to hyperinflation.[4] Although a quantitative classification of countries according to the degree of central bank independence may be difficult to construct, an attempt to do so may provide some answers to the inflationary bias question. Such a classification would have to consider the fact that the degree of authority monetary policymakers have at their disposal may itself be a function of political stability. This is indeed what Cukierman, Kalaitzidakis, Summers and Webb (1993) conclude. Siklos (1994a), however, concludes otherwise and finds instead that the degree of maturity of the financial system and the type of exchange rate regime matter more in determining inflation rates in developing countries.

Another consideration which is often thought to loom large in explaining the origin of a hyperinflation is the problem posed by demands for reparations payments. Keynes, again in his celebrated *Economic Consequences of the Peace*, foretold the disastrous effects of reparations demands on Germany after World War I. Bresciani-Turroni (1937) also documents the burden of reparations for that country, while Webb (1989) notes that not until reparations payments ceased to be economically important was Germany able finally to terminate its hyperinflation despite four attempts to do so. Yet, even if reparations were a causal factor in a subsequent hyperinflation, by effectively eliminating a government's incentive to tax, this is not the same as stating that a hyperinflation is unavoidable in its presence. Holtfrerich (1986) doubts that reparations were as onerous for Germany as is generally believed to be the case, though the 'psychological' impact on German society from the aftermath of defeat led policymakers to resort to the inflation tax. Nor are all cases of hyperinflation traceable to demands by others for financial compensation (e.g., Greece after World War II, and hyperinflations in South America). In fact, Czechoslovakia after World War I and Finland following World War II both escaped hyperinflation altogether, despite reparations relatively more onerous than Hungary's, or Romania's in the case of Finland (Kindleberger 1987).

Nevertheless, the role of reparations payments has tended to be under-emphasized in studying the origins of hyperinflations since, except for Cairncross (1986) and Kindleberger (1987), little mention of them is made in the study of the immediate post-World War II period. This is not surprising if the principal precondition of a hyperinflation is traceable to the application of 'incorrect' economic policies even when the initial impetus may be linked to external factors. However, such a view would seem to imply a kind of irrational behaviour on the part of policymakers which economists would not expect from utility-maximizing individuals. For this reason, Cukierman (1988 and Chapter 4 in this volume) has suggested that a political economy approach to the study of hyperinflations would lead one to conclude that they emerged from a rational policy choice instead of originating from a miscalculated policy. One wonders, however, whether or not there exists some validity in the policy error thesis when comparisons between Latin American debt and reparations are made (see Webb 1988 and references therein). Overly optimistic beliefs by perhaps both creditors and borrowers about prospects for future economic growth have led to cycles of the kind where foreign debt promotes persistent deficit spending and, eventually, to hyperinflation and virtual insolvency. It would hardly seem rational for governments to engage deliberately in such behaviour continuously over time. Since political considerations, for example, are not yet fully understood nor are they easily quantified, there remains scope for further investigation of the relevant issues.

Not all the focus on the policy errors issue has been on the behaviour of domestic policymakers exclusively. Thus, Dornbusch (1992) argues that the newly formed countries emerging from the old Soviet Union share something in common with many of the Successor States of the former Austro-Hungarian Monarchy, namely the lack of structure in controlling deficits and inflation. Events in the Ukraine and Russia have proven Dornbusch correct and he raises questions about some of the early policy advice from international institutions such as the International Monetary Fund, as have other economists, most notably Jeffrey Sachs. Ultimately, as Garber and Spencer (1994) note, by also referring to the example of the old Austro-Hungarian Monarchy, it is sound fiscal and monetary policies which prevent the emergence of hyperinflation.[5]

Even if the origins of hyperinflations are traceable to a few factors such as the ones discussed above, an understanding of their role may be crucial if one is to assess properly success or failure to stabilize prices, especially as episodes of high inflation tend to be rather short in duration. Physical damage, reparations, recovery from a wartime economy, the resort to temporary market-driven measures as in China in 1949-50 (Burdekin and Wang 1994), or, as in the case of the German hyperinflation of the 1920s, the ending of subsidies financed by the inflation tax to the capital goods-producing sector (Garber 1982), are factors which imply that an analysis of conditions which lead to a termination of runaway inflation must disentangle aggregate demand influences, emanating from monetary and fiscal policies, and from aggregate supply-side changes, which follow recovery from many experiences with hyperinflation. It is partly for this reason that, as Eichengreen (1986) suggests, a complete understanding of historical events prior to the emergence of a hyperinflation, and following its termination, is necessary before we are tempted to reach dramatic conclusions about the key features of policies which can lead to its successful termination.

Having briefly explored some issues relative to the origins of high inflation we now turn to a survey of the major questions which have attracted economists' attention to the study of the process and development of hyperinflations.

3. DEVELOPMENT

The study of hyperinflationary episodes was originally attractive as a means of deriving empirical support for the QT under demanding conditions. More precisely, the objective of Cagan's (1956) classic study of seven hyperinflations this century was to demonstrate the existence of a stable demand for money function even under the severe strain of a monetary policy based almost exclusively on generating inflation. Facilitating the analysis and, indeed, one of its attractions was that the magnitude of changes in the nominal values of the money supply and aggregate prices so dwarfed changes in the other principal determinants of the demand for money, namely real income and the interest rate, that it led to the formulation not only of a simple specification but one amenable to econometric testing as well. It is not surprising, therefore, that Cagan's work became the foundation of future theoretical and empirical work.

Cagan's demand for money function has as its sole determinant inflationary expectations for reasons indicated above. Thus, Cagan's model may be written in logarithmic form as:

$$m_t - p_t = \alpha \pi_t^e + u_t \qquad (1.1)$$

where m and p are the logarithm of the money stock and the price level, respectively, and where a rise in inflation expectations $\left[\pi_t^e \right]$ is hypothesized to produce a reduction in the demand for real balances ($\alpha < 0$). u_t is the residual term which accounts for all other factors (statistically) independent of π_t^e, which may also influence the demand for money. Typically, such residuals are expected to be uncorrelated. Since this is rarely the case the modelling of the error term has, as we shall see, led to modifications in Cagan's original formulation although the functional form posited has been found to be adequate (Frenkel 1977). Note that the money stock is generally defined in terms of the domestic currency unit. Not surprisingly, currency substitution often takes place, especially under conditions of extreme inflation.[6] Since Cagan assumed that the economies under consideration operated under a regime of perfectly flexible exchange rates he was able to ignore potential difficulties with the interpretation of the domestic demand for money in the face of alternative transactions media (see also Bernholz et al. 1985). It may very well be the case that the total demand for money (i.e., domestic and foreign currencies) is unstable during high inflation (Bernholz and Jaksch 1989) but other recent evidence suggests that Cagan's assumption may be a reasonable one (e.g., Calomiris and Domowitz 1989). In addition, because severe data limitations make it generally difficult to broaden the definition of m in (1.1) above, henceforth it shall be assumed to be measured in terms of the domestic currency unit alone.

As the QT assumes that money is supplied in the economy exogenously the vicious circle of hyperinflation originates with sustained increases in the money supply (or money growth) which cause prices to rise (or inflation). Once prices rise this feeds back into price expectations. To obtain inflation rates consistent with hyperinflation requires accelerating money growth. Cagan assumed that changes in inflation expectations move only gradually to adjust to the actual prevailing rate of inflation, thereby giving rise to the adaptive model of expectations formation. Under such an approach, expected inflation is a function of both past inflation and inflation expectations and, solving recursively, it was possible to arrive at a testable model which links the current demand for real money balances to a distributed lag of past actual inflation rates. However, since the rate of inflation, which is an endogenous variable, ends up being the regressor in a transformed version of (1.1) which can be estimated using available data, the resulting estimates violate the requirement of serially uncorrelated errors (u_t). We return to a discussion of the implications of such a problem below.

It has since been pointed out, in line with changes in how economists model inflationary expectations, that it makes little sense a priori for utility-maximizing agents continually to revise their expectations based on lagged information, especially when they become convinced or recognize that the monetary policy in place is consistent with an accelerating inflation rate in the future. Therefore, in contrast to adaptive expectations, rational expectations posits economic agents' behaviour consistent with the current (monetary) policy stance. In other words, individuals are assumed to be forward looking instead of backward looking. The foregoing considerations led to the seminal work by SW (1981) who note that modifying Cagan's model of expectations formation has important implications for the demand for money under hyperinflation.

Within the constraints imposed by severe data limitations, one way in which expectations of inflation can be made rational in some sense, according to SW, is for the public to form its forecasts of inflation based on the rate of money growth which, in a QT setting and under conditions of hyperinflation, fully determines actual rates of inflation. Thus, in effect, we need to define the content of the information set used to determine π_t^e in (1.1). More formally, we write

$$\pi_t^e = E(\pi_t \mid I_{t-1}) \tag{1.2}$$

where all the variables except I have previously been defined. Equation (1.2) simply states that expectations of inflation are based on the mathematical expectation of inflation conditional on the information set I available to agents at the time forecasts are formulated which is, presumably, the period immediately preceding the time a decision needs to be made. For example, if the information set consists of money growth then expected inflation can be written as a distributed lag of money growth. Such an approach permits the money supply behaviour of the monetary authority to influence an individual's beliefs about the future course of inflation. However, the same model also assumes that expected inflation will be dependent on the past history only of money growth. Yet, if a government is intent on pursuing a policy to maintain fixed real expenditures in the face of accelerating inflation, rises in inflation must force the monetary authorities to generate future additions to the money stock.[7] Thus money growth and inflation are both, in effect, 'caused' by the growth in government debt (e.g., as in Webb 1985), and individuals, being rational, must incorporate the potential for such behaviour on the part of policymakers. To see under what conditions this would be appropriate, consider the following expression for the government budget.

$$D_t + \rho B_t = (\pi + g)M_t + gB_t \qquad (1.3)$$

where the undefined terms are D, the deficit net of interest payments, M is the money stock, B is the stock of bonds or publicly held debt, ρ is the real interest rate and g is the growth rate of output. An expression such as (1.3) has been used in criticisms about monetarists' belief in inflation being exclusively a monetary phenomenon (Sargent 1993, ch. 5).

Thus, it is impossible for the time path of money to be unaffected by deficits so long as output growth is below the growth in interest payments (i.e., $g < \rho$). In other words, a government would be unable to finance deficits indefinitely. This is the so-called unpleasant monetarist arithmetic. As a result, both the deficit and debt would grow explosively and money growth could be accommodated to finance a growing deficit which would then result in hyperinflation. The public determines the size of the money stock and, as a result, the money supply process becomes endogenous.

Therefore, the belief that deficits must be inflationary is subject to estimates of the parameters in (1.3). It has even been suggested that the current debt, load situation in many Latin American countries, for example, is more sustainable than is commonly believed (i.e., g tends to exceed ρ) and that only in the case of hyperinflations do conditions arise where the unpleasant monetarist arithmetic holds. Darby (1984) and Friedman (1987) contend that these instances, at best, represent historical aberrations.

An additional factor which may contribute to the belief that the money-supply process is endogenous and, consequently, that some inflation is inertial, is the existence of indexation. A few of the earlier hyperinflations (e.g., Germany, both Hungarian hyperinflations), as well as some of the modern episodes of runaway inflation (e.g., China, Israel, Brazil, Argentina), were characterized by the introduction of more or less comprehensive indexation schemes to protect wages and, occasionally, assets from erosion due to inflation. Although it was first believed that such a policy would remedy the problem of rising inflationary expectations it was quickly realized that, unless the government was committed to ending its reliance on the inflation tax, the only result would be further accelerations in money growth and, subsequently, in inflation which the government would resort to in an attempt to generate the desired level of seigniorage. For a recent survey of the indexation experience in Brazil and Argentina, for example, see Pereira and Nakano (1987). For the German case see Holtfrerich (1985). The earlier post-World War II Hungarian experience with indexation, and the reaction of policymakers under the circumstances, was analysed by Siklos (1991) and Bomberger and Makinen (1980). For the Chinese case, see Burdekin and Wang (1994). For a general survey, see Horsman (1988).

The difficulty posed by the potential endogeneity of money naturally suggests that one examine the direction of statistical causality (i.e., Granger causality) between money growth and inflation. Thus, SW (1981) find that, in the European hyperinflation, past inflation explains current money growth substantially more than future rates of inflation. Consequently, it may be entirely rational for current forecasts of inflation to be extrapolated on the basis of past inflation alone thereby rendering adaptive expectations in some sense rational. Nevertheless, as one cannot entirely reject the hypothesis of feedback from current money growth to future inflation, the assumption of an exogenous money-supply process is not an adequate one. In general, it is now well known that the issue of the direction of bivariate causality cannot be divorced from views about the underlying model being considered. In other words, Granger-Sims causality need not be equivalent to causality in the structural sense (e.g., see Cooley and LeRoy 1985).

Christiano (1987), for example, has reconsidered the restrictions imposed by SW (1981) and Sargent (1981), including the SW assumption that the residuals in (1.1) follow a random walk which enables one to circumvent easily the econometric difficulty, namely the spurious regression problem (Jacobs 1977), raised by Cagan's approach.[8] He argues that the SW formulation is consistent with two interpretations of how the money-supply process is affected by central bank behaviour under conditions of hyperinflation. The monetary authorities could set current money growth (time t) based on their expectations of inflation. These decisions are made at time $t-1$. Instead, SW choose to interpret monetary policy by assuming that current money growth is set by observing inflation in the same period. The reason, as noted before, is to ensure that a fixed level of real expenditures be maintained. Christiano (1987) argues that the first interpretation is closer to Sargent's stated objective but that, in any event, the choice of restrictions has significant empirical implications for the estimation of the elasticity of the demand for real balances to inflation expectations (coefficient α in (1.1)). He compares the two interpretations consistent with SW with a version of Cagan's model in which adaptive expectations are consistent with rational expectations. Though the empirical evidence presented by Christiano, using data from the German hyperinflation, rejects both the SW versions as well as Cagan's model augmented with rational expectations under which, it will be recalled, the money stock is exogenous, Cagan's model apparently best fits the data.

A further difficulty with the SW approach is the view that the aim of policymakers is to finance a more or less constant level of real expenditures. Jacobs (1977) presents evidence to the effect that real revenue fluctuated significantly during the German and Austrian hyperinflations, without, however, showing any systematic trend, while Siklos (1991b) shows the same was true in the second Hungarian hyperinflation (1945-46).

Bernholz and Jaksch (1989) have argued that Cagan's model of the demand for money represents an altogether implausible theory of inflation. In particular, the authors demonstrate that if the real debt is entirely monetized and is sufficiently large, real balances would increase over time instead of decreasing as in all known hyperinflations. Since real debt, with some exceptions, has a tendency to fall over time rather than rise it is unclear that Cagan's model is as implausible as the authors claim (see, also, Bernholz 1988).

Two other issues have also been raised about economic models which attempt to evaluate the behaviour of the monetary authorities under hyper-inflationary conditions. The first concerns the question whether central banks faced with hyperinflation issued currency in amounts which exceed the value which would have maximized real revenues from seigniorage.[9] Sargent (1981) presents estimates of the slope of the demand for money schedule which encompasses those which would have maximized the yield from the inflation tax. Alternatively, the political economy explanation put forward by Cukierman (1988) instead stresses adjustment lags between the demand for money and the money supply exploited by rational policy-makers who, for political reasons, adopt the use of seigniorage to collect the bulk of its revenues. The presence of such lags would also be consistent with recent models of government behaviour of the Barro and Gordon (1983) variety in which reputational considerations matter and can avoid the inferior outcome predicted by possible time inconsistencies in optimal policies introduced by Kydland and Prescott (1977).

There is assumed to be a cost, arising from a loss of reputation or credibility, in pursuing an inflationary policy. An inflationary bias in monetary policy results because of the incentive to inflate, in order to reduce unemployment, which opportunity exists once the public's inflationary expectations have been set. Such a bias also presupposes a short-run trade-off between inflation and unemployment of the Phillips curve variety. Thus, under these circumstances, the choice of money growth and inflation rates is essentially at the policymaker's discretion and it is, therefore, easy to see why credibility plays an important function in understanding inflation. However, as there exist fine surveys of the credibility issue the reader is referred to them for details (Cukierman 1986; Rogoff 1987; Perrson 1988; Blackburn and Christensen 1989). We return again to the credibility question in section 4 of the chapter.

A second issue relates to the apparent instability of the Cagan formulation in the final months of the hyperinflation. Cagan, among others, was forced to truncate his hyperinflation sample by excluding observations from the final months of the German hyperinflation. He hypothesized that rumours of an impending currency reform may have prompted individuals to increase rather than reduce real balance holdings (see equation (1.1)).[10] Flood and Garber (1980, 1983) propose an explanation for this apparent paradox experienced towards the end of some European hyperinflations this century (e.g., Germany, Greece, Poland) which centres around the notion of process inconsistency. The requirement for attaining process inconsistency is that individuals be unable to solve for π_t^e in an expression such as (1.2), where expectations of inflation are formed rationally. In other words, money would, in effect, become worthless in the sense that individuals would become unable to quote finite prices in terms of the domestic currency in use.[11] Thus, whenever the process by which money is supplied to the private sector changes or becomes inconsistent with the public's demand for money behaviour, expectations of an impending reform reach their peak and this appears to occur in the final stages of a hyperinflation.[12]

Combining the assumption of rational expectations with an exogenous money-supply process, Flood and Garber (1980) begin with a Cagan (1956) type model, but condition it on whether a monetary reform will or will not take place which itself is dependent upon the degree to which the process is consistent or not. Probabilities of a reform are then evaluated. Such an approach leads one to predict that process consistency would be expected to be positively related to real balances. In four of the hyperinflations considered by Flood and Garber (Greece, Hungary

1945,46, Russia and Germany) only the Greek hyperinflation provides evidence most favourable to the process consistency hypothesis. The simple correlation between the log of real balances and the computed process-consistency probabilities is 0.858. While the correlations are similarly positive, as predicted, in the other three cases examined they are rather low to be convincing (Hungary 1945-46: 0.339, Russia: 0.365, Germany: 0.197).

La Haye (1985), who also provides evidence in favour of the view that anticipations of a monetary reform may explain the seemingly paradoxical pattern of real balances in the final months of the German, Greek and Polish hyperinflations, points out that the pattern of process consistency probabilities is consistent with the anticipated number of months until reform, where such anticipations are generated from a model of expected future money growth rates. However, La Haye assumes individuals know when monetary reforms will take place. Nevertheless, as Webb (1986) and Siklos (1991) have argued, in analysing the German and post-World War II Hungarian hyperinflations, fiscal news, instead of the acceleration of money growth, may be an equally good, if perhaps better, candidate to explain the pattern of inflationary expectations. [13]

Table 1.1 lists a selection of estimates of the elasticity of the demand for money with respect to expected inflation, together with their standard errors, for the German hyperinflation. [14] With one exception, all the estimates are negative, and most models used are based on versions of the Cagan formulation of the demand for money with or without the assumption of rational expectations. Generally, the estimates do not vary as much as one might have expected given the variety of estimation methods and restrictions placed on Cagan's model. Yet, one cannot exclude, statistically, the possibility that some of the estimates are consistent with the self-generating inflation hypothesis.

Jacobs (1977) points out that the level of real expenditures desired by governments in many 20th century hyperinflations could only be sustained by ever increasing rates of note issue rendering these hyperinflations unstable, which is inconsistent with Cagan's results. A difficulty with Cagan's formulation arises because his demand for money model assumes that the money market is in equilibrium at each time period. The implication of this assumption is the possibility of runaway inflation (or, in more technical terms, dynamic instability) even in the absence of an accommodating monetary policy. If, however, some disequilibrium in the money market is permitted, explosive inflation no longer follows (see Harris 1981, pp. 386-8). Another problem occurs when, as seems clear, hyperinflation is believed to be the result of, or to occur simultaneously

Table 1.1 Selected Estimates of Elasticity of the Demand for Money with Respect to Inflation Expectations for the German Hyperinflation*

Source	Estimate	St. Error	Model Description
Cagan (1956)	-5.46	0.54	Adaptive inflation expectations. See text equation (1.1). Estimation by non-linear least squares.
Sargent (1981)	-5.97	4.62	Cagan's model with rational expectations. Demand for money residuals restricted to follow a random walk. Maximum likelihood estimation.
Jacobs (1977)	2.96	0.02	Cagan model with rational expectations. Does not assume constant seigniorage. Estimation by non-linear method.
La Haye (1985)	0.84	0.14	Cagan's model with rational expectations and expectation of a monetary reform. Maximum likelihood estimation.
Christiano (1987)	-1.76	0.71	Cagan's model with rational expectations with no restrictions on the residual of the demand for money equation.
	8.18	17.98	Cagan's model with rational expectations. Residuals follow a random walk.
	-0.07	31.00	Above model except current money growth is generated by (rationally) expected current inflation. Maximum likelihood estimation.

* *Notes*: Generally, the samples and data are similar to the ones originally used by Cagan. Differences arise due to the requirements of the analysis (e.g., La Haye 1985) or reference to a source of data other than Cagan's (e.g., Jacobs 1977). The reader is referred to the above papers for more precise details. A detailed survey of demand for money models applied to the German experience is contained in Webb (1983).

with, a fiscal policy based on deficit spending financed by money creation. The connection between fiscal policy and the demand for money is also dependent on the equilibrium condition and the assumption of an exogenous money supply, as specified in Cagan's model. Thus, under these conditions, large budget deficits can never lead to hyperinflation, as shown by Evans and Yarrow (1981). Kiguel (1989), however, demonstrates that by relaxing Cagan's equilibrium condition a policy of deficits financed through seigniorage can be hyperinflationary. Nevertheless, he assumes that monetary authorities deliberately attempt to generate an inflation tax in excess of the revenue-maximizing rate. In other words, hyperinflation is an unstable process — a view which does not generally square with the rest of the demand for money and inflation literature (see McCallum 1989 for a review) or with basic economic principles.

Hahn (1982, pp. 11-13), however, demonstrates the theoretical possibility of inflation rising without limit for a given level of money growth,[15] thereby providing the logical possibility that a price level 'bubble' can exist. The result would also lead one to object to the notion that price increases must originate from a rising stock of money (see also section 4 below). The result is a prediction whereby the steady-state rate of inflation is independent of money growth, thus allowing again for the theoretical possibility that money stock control is not a sufficient condition for the maintenance of stable inflation.

This possibility has recently resurfaced in the literature in connection with whether, empirically, money supply and output data appear to display explosive or bubble behaviour (see also Casella 1989). Studies of the time-series properties of money and prices in the German (Evans 1978) and Hungarian episodes of hyperinflation (Siklos 1990, 1990a and Chapter 6 in this volume) have generally found that the relevant series are covariance stationary in second log difference form.[16] In other words, the log change in the money stock and prices each contain a unit root so that a tendency for explosive behaviour apparently can be excluded since a constant variance representation of the series of interest can be found. However, Siklos (1990 and Chapter 6 in this volume) reports that money growth and prices are cointegrated only during identifiable policy regimes within the Hungarian hyperinflation of 1945-46. Such a result implies that a linear combination of the money growth and inflation series is not always stationary or, alternatively, that an equilibrium relationship between these two series need not exist.[17]

Consider a version of the crude quantity theory ($MV = Py$) written in regression form as

$$p_t = \beta m_t + \varepsilon_t \qquad (1.4)$$

All the variables have been previously defined and are in logarithms of the levels. If real income effects are negligible, (1.4) implies that velocity is stationary since it is, in effect, represented by the error term ε_t. Thus, if the linear combination $p_t - \beta m_t = \varepsilon_t$ is stationary the series p and m are said to be cointegrated (Engle and Granger 1987; Johansen and Juselius 1990). Otherwise, the stationarity assumption of velocity is violated and a regression such as (1.4) is a spurious one (Granger and Newbold 1974, and n. 5). Siklos (1991) examines whether money and prices data are stationary in first or second differences using weekly data from the Hungarian hyperinflation of 1945-46 and finds that the two series share a common trend in their growth rates. Similar evidence is found for the more recent hyperinflation in Yugoslavia (Lahiti 1991; and Bogetić, Dragutinović and Petrović 1994) as well as for the post-World War II Taiwanese experience (Phylatkis and Taylor 1992) and the more recent hyperinflation in Yugoslavia (Frenkel and Taylor 1993).

A difficulty with testing for cointegration is that much of the existing theory is based on series which are difference stationary or $I(1)$. The theory is more complex when series are $I(2)$ (see Johansen 1991).[18]

Taylor (1991) shows that the failure to find cointegration between real balances and inflation implies a rejection of the model summarized by equation (1.1). He then presents results which are supportive of the finding of cointegration for the Austrian, Polish and Hungarian episodes of hyperinflation. The German hyperinflation of the 1920s poses a problem, unless consumer prices are used to generate inflation. Michael, Nobay and Peel (1994) also present cointegration using a Cagan-type model but with 18 months of data it is difficult to believe that one can make useful inferences about long-run relationships between series of interest (Burdekin and Burkett 1994).

As noted earlier, however, Cagan's model under rational expectations suggests a direct relationship between real balances and money growth (see discussion under equation (1.2) or the forward premium, both of which act as proxies for expected inflation. However, rational expectations models of hyperinflation are generally rejected by Taylor.[19] Engsted (1993) shows that Cagan's model augmented with rational expectations yields two cointegrating relationships, namely one between the price level and the money-supply level and a second between real balances and money growth. Engsted finds support for the presence of these two vectors in the German hyperinflation case and concludes that, as a result, velocity is stationary and not a random walk. Hence, deviations from the hyperinflation model summarized by (1.1) and (1.2) are found to be transitory.

The possibility that u_t in (1.1) is a random walk suggests that the variance in money demand errors is either increasing or infinite which is suggestive of explosive behaviour in inflation, termed inflationary bubbles. The evidence about the cointegration properties of (1.1), however, generally rejects such phenomena even under conditions of hyperinflation. Other evidence about the possible existence of inflationary bubbles (e.g., Hamilton and Whiteman 1985) also finds that second log differences eliminate a growing mean in data from hyperinflation. For doubts and criticisms of tests which attempt to detect bubble behaviour, see McCallum (1989). Recent interest in the existence of chaotic dynamics in economic time series (for a survey, see Frank and Stengos 1988) creates the potential for applications to data on hyperinflations though the lack of sufficient observations poses a formidable constraint at present. To sum up, the restrictions imposed on a model of the demand for money of the Cagan variety may have wide-ranging implications at both the theoretical as well as empirical levels for the interpretation of monetary policies under hyperinflationary conditions.

In the following section we consider the issues and controversies surrounding assessments of the end of hyperinflations.

4. TERMINATION

There are at least two reasons why economists have viewed the study of the termination of a hyperinflation as having potentially significant policy implications for economies suffering from milder inflations. First, it has been noted (e.g., Sargent 1993) that all episodes of hyperinflation are followed by a sharp and steady rise in real balances. SW (1982) elaborated on the view that, as this appeared to contradict a fundamental prediction of the QT, a more general theory of the price level was required. Accordingly, a version of the real bills doctrine, called the 'backing' theory of money, was developed in which the QT was a special case of a more general theory of the price level. The more general theory views the government as behaving much like a firm with respect to the financing of a deficit. Following the discussion of the previous section, let the expression below represent a theory of price level determination

$$P_t = A(L)E_j M_{t+j} \qquad (1.5)$$

where P_t = price level at time t, $A(L)$ is a distributed lag term (i.e., $A(L)$ = $1 + a_1 L + ...$, where $a_1 L x_t = a_1 x_{t-1}$), and $E_j M_{t+j}$ is the rationally anticipated future path of the base money stock.[20] According to equation (1.3), deficits are inflationary if and only if the base money stock is expected to change. This can occur in one of two ways. Either, as in a hyperinflation, all deficits are virtually exclusively financed through the issue of money or, perhaps because current deficits are not expected to be sustainable without resort to the printing press at some time in the future, the public expects future rises in base money. Thus, while the expected path of base money may be linked to deficits, any such relationship is dependent upon the way in which such deficits are expected to be financed. Hence, as in the case of the termination of all hyperinflations this century, a sustained rise in real balances is made possible according to (1.3). despite initial deficits following new issues of currency[21] as the economy remonetizes itself, so long as the resulting debt is expected to be financed by future budget surpluses so that there are no expectations of future rises in base money. Thus, the QT becomes a special case of a more general theory of the price level, itself a version of the so-called real bills doctrine (SW 1982).[22]

Empirical tests and illustrations of the two theories of the determination of the price level have been conducted based on episodes of inflation in US colonial history (Smith 1985, 1985a; Calomiris 1988) and, more recently, on Taiwanese data (Cunningham 1992).[23] Laidler (1987), however, points out that the SW interpretation of the QT is a narrow one. Hence, the kind of sharp rise in real balances witnessed after high inflation can readily be accommodated in a version of the QT by, for example, allowing velocity to change because expectations of inflation are sharply reduced, which permits the severing of the one-to-one relationship between money and price movements. Yet the SW, Smith and Calomiris interpretations of the QT are not inconsistent with the positions expressed by Lucas (1980) or even Friedman and Schwartz (1982). Laidler (1987), however, describes how Wicksell and Fisher both understood that the degree to which a currency is backed would be reflected in changes in velocity. Nevertheless, the 'backing' theory does stress, as the QT does not, the fundamental role played by the viability or sustainability of the chosen fiscal policy as a crucial determinant in influencing inflation. By contrast, when most economists think about the fundamental prediction of the QT they have in mind a model in which money and price-level movements are highly correlated with each other. Incidentally, although the episodes used as illustrations of the failure of the QT are generally short in duration there is even econometric evidence disputing high money and price co-movements in the long run (Hendry and Ericsson 1991).

Nevertheless, there have been attempts to rescue, as it were, the QT. Michener (1987) allows the exchange rate regime in place to influence co-movements between the money stock and the price level. Movements in the two series need not be highly correlated at all times. Since exchange rates have tended to be flexible under hyperinflation (e.g., Germany, post-World War II Hungary) and, in most cases, fixed following the return to price stability, the paradoxical behaviour of the money-prices link detected by Sargent may be accommodated by the QT.[24] In the US colonial evidence cited above, however, Smith (1988) forcefully argues that the fixed versus flexible exchange rate distinction makes no sense in an environment in which there were no central banks or other institutional arrangements to enforce any particular kind of exchange rate regime.[25]

A second reason for analysing an economy after hyperinflation has been terminated concerns the inability to reconcile the experience of post-hyperinflation economic performance with predictions from a short-run Phillips curve-type relationship generally relied upon to explain the trade-off between inflation and unemployment in relatively moderate inflations. Historically, a sudden and drastic reduction in inflation following hyperinflation appears to have been followed by only moderate increases in unemployment. Yet, one would expect a sharp rise in unemployment following the return to price stability based on the Phillips curve model.[26] As Sargent (1993, ch. 3) points out, the only theory consistent with such events is the rational expectation version of the natural rate hypothesis, which predicts that the unemployment rate would not depart from its natural value, since this is the only theory which is able to explain a sudden transition from one policy regime, hyperinflation, to another, namely price stability, without significant adjustment costs. Wicker (1986) has reconsidered the evidence from the end of hyperinflation in Poland, Austria and Hungary, following the dismemberment of the Habsburg monarchy, and found the increases in unemployment too large to be consistent with the natural rate view. Siklos (1994b) disputes Wicker's conclusions for Hungary after World War I, while Siklos (1989 (reproduced as Chapter 9 in this volume), 1991a) found the unemployment effect of a sudden return to price stability in post-World War II Hungary to be rather small and, therefore, not inconsistent with Sargent's view (see also Bomberger and Makinen 1983), although many policy choices faced by the Hungarian government following the war would be unlikely to have arisen in more recent hyper-inflationary experiences such as in, for example, South America. Garber (1982) argues that the assumption of a constant natural rate of unemployment underlying Sargent's hypothesis is misleading in the German case because a significant portion of the proceeds from the inflation tax went to the capital goods-producing industry. When the subsidy policy was eventually abandoned the result was a structural distortion in the economy with a consequent impact on the natural rate of unemployment.[27] Siklos (1989 and Chapter 9) notes that a similar problem may exist in interpreting unemployment rates in Hungary following the return to price stability in 1946 when government make-work projects were terminated, and when a policy favouring a higher price for industrial goods relative to agricultural commodities, to encourage rapid recovery and expansion in the former industry, was abandoned.

Of course, the key element in persuading the public to modify radically its expectations must be the government's reputation and ability to convince the public of the credibility of the set of policies whose objective it is to produce more stability. Yet, several authors have questioned such a view. Sachs (1986), for example, has developed a model in which the cessation of inflation is not followed, in the short run at least, by a reduction in inflation expectations. Dornbusch (1986), Dornbusch and Fischer (1987) and Bernholz and Jaksch (1989) wonder why recent reforms produced very high real interest rates or real exchange rates following the return to price stability, if not to assist in enforcing or guaranteeing credibility. Yet, if such actions are deemed necessary they would seem counterproductive as real economic activity would be adversely affected by high real interest rates, thereby threatening the credibility of stabilization policies in the first place. Rodrik (1989), however, develops a model in which governments signal their determination to end inflation, and the likelihood that their promise will be kept, by a policy of 'overshooting'. This requires stronger medicine of the kind just noted than simply introducing those reforms such as, for example, the banning of central bank discounting of government debt and the introduction of balanced budgeting which, in the absence of concerns about credibility, would be all that is necessary for the cessation of inflation. Alternatively, Cukierman (1987) uses the example of the recent Israeli plan to end high inflation in 1985 to suggest that a reform of monetary and fiscal policies alone, without a number of other elements, such as a tight credit squeeze or other policies mentioned above, will not produce a rapid and successful stabilization (see Makinen and Woodward 1989 and Franco 1990). Resorting to high real interest rates, for example, also seems difficult to reconcile with the fear governments are purported to have towards increases in unemployment following the return to price stability. It is for this reason that Sargent warns that an accommodative monetary policy should be practised after the termination of hyper-inflation.

The above considerations have produced the view among some (e.g., Blejer and Cheasty 1987) that a so-called 'heterodox'-type end to high inflation seems preferable to the orthodox mix of policies advocated by Sargent among others. The combination of traditional monetary and fiscal policies, combined with adoption of other measures such as a wage and price freeze, is known as the heterodox solution to ending a hyperinflation (see Végh 1992 and Chapter 2 in this volume).

The evidence suggests, however, relatively little success at arresting inflation in those South American countries where the heterodox approach has been practised while the recent Bolivian experience (Sachs 1986, 1987; Bernholz 1988) appears to reinforce the view for orthodox measures to control inflation. The Israeli case (e.g., Cukierman 1987) seems to be the only good illustration of the successful application of heterodox policies, although the necessity of adopting heterodox measures has also been viewed as essential in the short term in the Brazilian and Argentine attempts at arresting inflation (Pereira and Nakano 1987).

Credibility, of course, is a difficult concept to quantify. Moreover, it has generally been assumed that reforms which lead to the end of a hyperinflation must, by definition, have been credible in the first place. This, of course, is a poor way to model credibility and its relationship with the stabilization of inflation.[28] The current state of the debate suggests that the credibility issue is a controversial one in relation to whether it is a necessary ingredient for stabilization in the short-run. Economists do not, however, dispute the necessity of credibility aimed at stemming inflation in the long run.

Although some proxies for inflation expectations have been devised to ascertain whether the public anticipated the maintenance of inflation stabilization following reforms (e.g., Siklos 1989, reproduced as Chapter 9, and 1990, reproduced as Chapter 6), for the Hungarian episode of 1945-46), a variety of criticisms have been levelled at Sargent's interpretation of history and his assessment of the degree of success of several stabilization programmes. Webb (1985, 1989) and Makinen (1984, 1986) argue that the German and Greek hyperinflations this century were both ended only after several attempts, each of them credible by the available standards and measures of credibility.[29] Eichengreen (1986), in his review of Sargent (1986, second edn 1993), also points out that a proper assessment of the successful transition to price stability requires a detailed examination of the historical experience of each country concerned in order to isolate particular factors which may have made some attempts at monetary reform credible and others not.

5. CONCLUSIONS AND LESSONS TO BE LEARNED

Sargent concluded his analysis of the end of four hyperinflations early this century (Austria, Hungary, Poland and Germany) by stating the hope that useful policy implications can be drawn from such seemingly unusual events.

The four incidents we have studied are akin to laboratory experiments in which the elemental forces that cause and can be used to stop inflation are easiest to spot. I believe that these incidents are full of lessons about our own, less dramatic predicament with inflation, if only we interpret them correctly. (Sargent 1993, p. 76).

As we have seen, it is arguable to what extent episodes of hyperinflation are laboratory-type experiments since a variety of important factors influencing both the types of policy changes as well as the likelihood of success in maintaining price stability can easily differ from one historical experience to another. Unlike in a laboratory experiment some factors which can impinge on the causes and consequences of those forces which determine inflation cannot be said to be fully controlled. It is largely for this reason that Eichengreen (1986), among others, draws attention to the need to consider all the relevant historical facts prior to reaching definitive conclusions about the lessons to be learned from experiences with high inflation.

Two other objections have also been raised about the relevance of earlier cases of hyperinflation. First, Witte (1984) argued, borrowing from the anticipated-unanticipated policy distinction popularized by Barro, among others (see Barro 1988, ch. 21, for a survey), that under conditions of high and accelerating inflation the likelihood of future policies being unanticipated is so small as to be, for all practical purposes, irrelevant. In other words, individuals become immune to the possibility of real effects from monetary policies, unlike milder episodes of inflation where there is much greater scope for such kinds of influences to take place. Alternatively, as in the monetary theory of Allais (1966, 1969), the slope of the demand for money schedule is determined by the speed of adjustment in the 'psychological rate of change in total expenditures'. As inflation becomes more intense the scope for monetary surprises falls until it reaches a point where output effects are negligible.

The second criticism centres around the view that a distinguishing characteristic of modern-day South American hyperinflations is the existence of weak governments unable to impose a credible anti-inflationary policy. Apart from the difficulties with this thesis expressed earlier in this chapter is the fact that there are fundamental doubts about how credible some of these attempts at stabilization have been (e.g., Sachs 1987; Heymann 1987; Cardoso and Dornbusch 1987; Fischer 1987). Moreover, it has sometimes been alleged that the South American experience stands apart from others considered here (e.g., Morales 1987) because of repeated experiences with high inflation which has led in the mind of the public to the attachment of a relatively low probability of success for any attempt at monetary reform. However, it may instead simply be one case where some of the fundamentals necessary to achieve a successful transition to price stability discussed in this paper were absent. Certainly, a reading of the recent Bolivian experience with hyperinflation (e.g., Morales 1987; Sachs 1986, 1987; Bernholz 1988) shows that a successful move to price stability is possible in South America despite the aforementioned difficulties. Moreover, Hungary is a nation which experienced two hyperinflations in one generation and there is little evidence that the memory from the first episode influenced the successful arrest of hyperinflation after its experience with high inflation following World War II (Siklos 1991a; however, see Jacobs 1977).

To sum up, while there are good reasons to be careful in drawing lessons from episodes of hyperinflation for milder cases of inflation it should nevertheless be emphasized that, with a proper understanding of the historical events underlying these experiences, there are a wide variety of useful implications emanating from an analysis of such events, such as the understanding of the forces which link monetary and fiscal policies to inflation, and the policymakers' role in influencing individuals' expectations.

ENDNOTES

*   Reprinted with permission from Blackwell Publishers and originally published in the *Journal of Economic Surveys*, 4 (3 1990), 225-48. Significant revisions were made to the originally published paper due to new developments in the relevant literature. Originally, the chapter was written while I was on leave at the Institute of Economics and Statistics and St Antony's College, both in Oxford, UK, and the University of California, San Diego during 1988-89. I appreciate the very helpful suggestions received from Peter Bernholz, Michael Bordo, Richard Burdekin, Carl Holtfrerich, Bruce Smith, Steven Webb and an anonymous referee. I am also grateful to participants in many seminars for their comments on my work on hyperinflation which stimulated and influenced the writing of this chapter.

1.   For a description and a quantitative analysis of an early hyperinflation, that of China in the 11th and 12th centuries, see Lui (1983). For a survey of monetary history in general, see Bordo (1986).

2.   A measure of government revenue derived from inflation. One method of calculation consists in computing the change in the money stock as a proportion of some average value of the price level for the relevant period.

3.   See also Asilis and Milesi-Ferretti (1994) on the more general question of the links between politics and sustainability of economic reforms.

4.   Horsman (1988), based on historical experiences in centrally planned economies, doubts that central bank independence is necessary for inflation control. However, as inflation in these countries is largely suppressed it would seem doubtful that there are many useful lessons to be learned from the experiences of these countries. Cukierman

(1992) documents the importance of central bank independence and its connection with inflation in an exhaustive empirical analysis of 70 countries.

5.   Santaella (1993) argues, based on an analysis of six stabilisations orchestrated via League of Nations help during the 1920s, that international institutions can provide a 'commitment technology' and that the greater the credibility problem facing a country having experienced hyperinflation the more heavily it relied on external enforcement mechanisms to stabilize.

6.   Calvo and Végh (1992) provide a comprehensive survey of the issues relative to currency substitution. Siklos (1994) considers the case of the substitution between two domestic currencies issued by the same monetary authority which took place during the Russian hyperinflation of the 1920s. Generally, one expects the presence of a substitute currency to increase inflation in the original currency (a reverse of Gresham's Law) but this need not necessarily hold either theoretically or empirically (see Sturzenegger 1994 and Siklos 1994).

7.   Such an outcome also follows from the Olivera (1967)-Tanzi (1977) effect in which any general expansion in prices will produce a deficit, other things being equal.

8.   Under this hypothesis $u_t = u_{t-1} + e_t$, where u_t is the error term in equation 1., and e_t has all the econometrically desirable properties of an error term in a regression. To do so, one simply needs to estimate (1.1) in first differences. A spurious regression arises when all variables in a regression require differencing but no linear combination exists between them which produces a stationary series (i.e., constant mean and variance). Granger and Newbold (1974) show that, under these circumstances, ordinary least squares yields misleading inferences. See also the discussion in section 3 below.

9.   Differentiating (1.2), the steady state (no income growth, $\Delta p_t^e = \Delta m_t$, Δ is the change operator) revenue-maximizing inflation rate is $1/\alpha$.

10.   Morales (1987), in a related question, observes how speculation, against an unknown but impending reform led, at first, to price increases later reversed when details of the stabilization programme were announced. This may also explain some of the seemingly unusual changes in real balances toward the end of a hyperinflation.

11.   Burmeister and Wall (1987) have also challenged the assumption of converging expectations using data from the German hyperinflation.

12.   Makinen and Woodward (1988) have used Granger-type causality tests to show, empirically, that the money-supply processes before and after reform are significantly different from each other in the German, (both) Hungarian, Austrian, Polish and Greek hyperinflations. Also, see Siklos (1990a). In a related matter, part of the difficulty in comparing studies of hyperinflation arises from the fact that Cagan, among others, treats money as a medium of exchange whereas in SW's work money is assumed to fulfil a store of value function. Since there is insufficient space here to deal with this question the reader is referred to Laidler (1987) and Michener (1987), for example, both of whom argue that what is distinctive about money is precisely its role as a transactions medium.

13.   Alternatively, as in Webb (1985), one might have examined the relationship between the acceleration of money growth and the rate of change in real balances. Flood and Garber's hypothesis predicts that expectations of a reform should be positively related to accelerations in money growth. Webb (1985, n. 60) does not find this to be true in the German case and the evidence is similarly weak in the other cases considered by Flood and Garber.

14.   The German case was selected both because it is the most widely studied episode and the one for which there is a relatively large number of observations.

15.   This possibility is not the only motivation for relaxing some of the constancy assumptions in Cagan's model. Sommariva and Tullio (1987) suggest that omission of real exchange rate influences on the demand for money in the German hyperinflation

significantly influences the coefficient estimates of the elasticity of the demand for money with respect to inflation expectations.

16. A stationary series possesses a constant mean (usually zero) and finite variance.

17. This implies that velocity growth need not be a stationary series. Money growth and inflation are usually approximated by taking first differences in the logarithm of the respective series. Yet, under conditions of hyperinflation, such a transformation can become a poor proxy for the percentage change in a series. If it is the rate of inflation that individuals are forecasting, the selection of the appropriate transformation may not be an irrelevant question. Siklos (1991a), however, finds conclusions generally unaffected, at least for post-World War II Hungary, when using proportional rates of change in money and prices.

18. Also, the Engle and Granger technique is informative about the number of cointegrating vectors. Thus, for example, when money demand in terms of domestic currency is believed to be also a function of foreign currency holdings then there exists the possibility of more than one cointegrating relationship. In such cases, the Johansen technique (Johansen and Juselius 1990) must be implemented.

19. • Cagan (1991) finds that there is a bias in forward exchange rates during the German hyperinflation which is consistent with the adaptive expectations framework. He suspects that, even under hyperinflationary conditions, there are permanent versus transitory effects of monetary policy on inflationary expectations.

20. Base money is typically defined as currency in circulation and reserves of the banking system. Moreover, it is the component of the money stock the government is empowered to issue.

21. Typically, the end of hyperinflations occur simultaneously with the introduction of a new currency though this fact is not generally interpreted as a necessary condition for ending high inflation.

22. So called because, under a real bills system, the note issue is tied to the value of titles to real assets and, hence, in theory cannot be issued to excess. Thus, in the SW analogy, if deficits are not excessive, that is, if they are expected to be financed by future surpluses, there need not be a crude QT-type link between money and price-level movements. In fact, as argued by Smith (1988), it is possible in these models for long-run changes in the money supply to have no effect on the price level.

23. Though inflation was high in such episodes it did not meet the arbitrary definition of hyperinflation. Siklos (1990, reproduced as Chapter 6) provides tests of the two theories using data from the Hungarian hyperinflation of 1945-46.

24. Michener's argument relies too heavily on evidence about the quantity of specie in circulation in US colonial times. According to Smith (1988) our historical knowledge is far too limited on this question to permit relevant inferences to be made.

25. Private correspondence between Smith and historians who have studied this period in US history also argues against the views of Michener.

26. This prediction would also hold in the short run in an expectations-augmented Phillips curve where anticipations of inflation are formed in an adaptive fashion.

27. Although Wicker (1986) considers the impact of certain policies, such as unemployment compensation, he does not interpret his unemployment data relative to possible changes in the natural rate of unemployment.

28. See Dornbusch (1991) for some preliminary suggestions about modelling credibility, and Bruno (1989) for a discussion of why it can take some time to build credibility. Delay in introducing stabilization plans has spawned work which relies on game-theoretic models (e.g., Alesina and Drazen 1989).

29. Credibility, for reasons explained above, is generally assumed to be negatively related to budget deficits.

REFERENCES

Allais, M. (1969), 'Growth and Inflation', *Journal of Money, Credit and Banking* 1, August, pp. 355-426.

Allais, M. (1966), 'A Restatement of the Quantity Theory of Money', *American Economic Review* 56, pp. 1123-56.

Alesina, A. and Drazen, A. (1989), 'Why Are Stabilizations Delayed?', NBER Working Paper No. 3053, August.

Asilis, C.M. and Milesi-Ferreti, G.M. (1994), 'On the Political Sustainability of Economic Reform', *IMF Paper on Policy Analysis and Assessment* 94/3, January.

Bade, R. and Parkin, M. (1985), 'Central Bank Laws and Monetary Policy', unpublished.

Barro, R. (1988), *Macroeconomics*, second edn., John Wiley and Sons, New York.

Barro, R.J. and Gordon, D. (1983), 'Rules, Discretion and Reputation in a Model of Monetary Policy', *Journal of Monetary Economics* 12, July.

Bernholz, P. (1988), 'Hyperinflation and Currency Reform in Bolivia Studied from a General Perspective', *Journal of Institutional and Theoretical Economics* (also reprinted in this volume).

Bernholz, P. (1988a), 'Inflation, Monetary Regime and the Financial Asset Theory of Money', *Kyklos*, no. 41, pp. 5-34.

Bernholz, P., Gartner, M. and Heri, E.W. (1985), 'Historical Experiences with Flexible Exchange Rates: A Simulation of Common Qualitative Characteristics', *Journal of International Economics* 19, pp. 21-45.

Bernholz, P. and Jaksch, J. (1989), 'An Implausible Theory of Inflation', *Weltwirtschafliches Archiv*, June.

Blackburn, K. and Christensen, M. (1989), 'Monetary Policy and Policy Credibility', *Journal of Economic Literature* 27, March, pp. 1-45.

Blejer, M.I. and Cheasty, A. (1987), 'High Inflation, "Heterodox" Stabilization and Fiscal Policy', IMF Working Paper 87/78, November.

Bogetić, Ź., Dragutinović, D. and Petrović, P. (1994), 'Anatomy of Hyperinflation and the Beginning of Stabilization in Yugoslavia 1992-1994', Working Paper, The World Bank, Washington, DC.

Bomberger, W.A. and Makinen, G.E. (1983), 'The Hungarian Hyperinflation and Stabilization of 1946-1946', *Journal of Political Economy* 91, October, pp. 801-24.

Bomberger, W.A. and Makinen, G.E. (1980), 'Indexation, Inflationary Finance and Hyperinflation: The 1945-1946 Hungarian Experience', *Journal of Political Economy* 88, June, pp. 550-60.

Bordo, M.D. (1986), 'Explorations in Monetary History: A Survey of the Literature', *Explorations in Economic History* 23, pp. 339-415.

Bresciani-Turroni, C. (1937), *The Economics of Inflation: A Study of Currency Depreciation in Post-War Germany*, Allen & Unwin, London.

Bruno, M. (1989), 'Economic Analysis and the Political Economy of Policy Formation', NBER Working Paper No. 3183, November.

Burdekin, R.C.K. and Burkett, P. (1994), 'The German Hyperinflation and the Demand for Money Revisited', unpublished, Claremont McKenna College and Claremont Graduate School.

Burdekin, R.C.K. and Burkett, P. (1992), 'Money, Credit and Wages in Hyperinflation: Post-World War II Germany', *Economic Inquiry* 30, July, pp. 479-95.

Burdekin, R.C.K. and Wang, F. (1994), 'A Novel End to the Big Inflation in China: How the Communists Used Market Forces to Restore Price Stability in 1950', unpublished, Claremont McKenna College and Claremont Graduate School.

Burmeister, E. and Wall, K.D. (1987), 'Unobserved Rational Expectations and the German Hyperinflation with Endogenous Money Supply', *International Economic Review* 28, February, pp. 15-32.

Cagan, P. (1991), 'Expectations in the German Hyperinflation Reconsidered', *Journal of International Money and Finance* 10, December, pp. 552-60.

Cagan, P. (1956), 'The Monetary Dynamics of Hyperinflation', in M. Friedman (ed.), *Studies in the Quant. Theory of Money,* University of Chicago Press, Chicago, pp. 25-117.

Cairncross, Sir Alex K. (1986), *The Price of War: British Policy on German Reparations*, Basil Blackwell, Oxford.

Calomiris, C.W. (1988), 'Institutional Failure, Monetary Scarcity, and the Depreciation of the Continent', *Journal of Economic History* 48, pp. 47-68.

Calomiris, C.W. and Domowitz, I. (1989), 'Asset Substitutions, Money Demand, and the Inflation Process in Brazil', *Journal of Money, Credit and Banking* 21, February, pp. 78-89.

Calvo, G.A. and Végh, C.A. (1992), 'Currency Substitution in Developing Countries: An Introduction', *Revista de Analysis Economico* 7, June, pp. 3-28.

Capie, F. (1986), 'Conditions under which very rapid inflation has appeared', in *Carnegie-Rochester Conference Series on Public Policy*, vol. 24, North-Holland, Amsterdam, pp. 115-68.

Cardoso, E.A. and Dornbusch, R. (1987), 'Brazil's Tropical Plan', *American Economic Review* 77, May, pp. 288-92.

Casella, A. (1989), 'Testing for Rational Bubbles with Exogenous or Endogenous Fundamentals', *Journal of Monetary Economics* 24, pp. 109-22.

Casella, A. and Feinstein, J.S. (1990), 'Economic Exchange During Hyperinflation', *Journal of Political Economy* 98, February, pp. 1-27.

Christiano, L.J. (1987), 'Cagan's Model of Hyperinflation under Rational Expectations', *International Economic Review* 28, February, pp. 33-49.

Clower, R.W. and Howitt, P.W. (1978), 'The Transactions Theory of the Demand for Money: A Reconsideration', *Journal of Political Economy* 86, June, pp. 449-466.

Cooley, T.F. and LeRoy, S.F. (1985), 'Atheoretical Macroeconomics', *Journal of Monetary Economics* 16, pp. 283-308.

Cukierman, A. (1992), *Central Bank Strategy, Credibility and Independence*, The MIT Press, Cambridge.

Cukierman, A. (1988), 'Rapid Inflation Deliberate Policy or Miscalculation', in K. Brunner and A.H. Meltzer (eds.), *Carnegie-Rochester Conference Series on Public Policy*, vol. 27, North-Holland, Amsterdam, pp. 11-76 (also reprinted in this volume).

Cukierman, A. (1987), 'The End of the Israeli Hyperinflation - An Experiment in Heterodox Stabilisation', Working Paper No. 7-87, April, Tel-Aviv University.

Cukierman, A. (1986), 'Central Bank Behaviour and Credibility: Some Recent Theoretical Developments', *Federal Reserve Bank of St. Louis Review* 68, May, pp. 5-17.

Cukierman, A., Edwards, S., and Tabellini, G. (1992), 'Seigniorage and Political Instability', *American Economic Review* 82 (June), pp. 537-55.

Cukierman, A., Kalaitzidakis, P., Summers, L.H. and Webb, S.B. (1993), 'Central Bank Independence, Growth, Investment, and Real Rates', *Carnegie-Rochester Conference Series on Public Policy*, vol. 39, December, North-Holland, Amsterdam, pp. 95-140.

Cunningham, T.J. (1992), 'Some Real Evidence on the Real Bills Doctrine Versus the Quantity Theory', *Economic Inquiry* 30, April, pp. 371-83.

Darby, M.R. (1984), 'Some Pleasant Monetarist Arithmetic', *Quarterly Review, Federal Reserve Bank of Minneapolis*, Spring, pp. 15-2.

Dornbusch, R. (1992), 'Monetary Problems of Post-Commission: Lessons from the End of the Austro-Hungarian Empire', *Weltwirtschafliches Archiv*, 128, pp. 391-424.

Dornbusch, R. (1991), 'Credibility and Stabilization', *Quarterly Journal of Economics* 106, August) pp. 837-50.

Dornbusch, R. (1986), 'Money, Interest Rates and Stabilization', *Review of Economic Conditions in Italy*, no. 3, pp. 439-53.

Dornbusch, R. and Fischer, S. (1987), 'Stopping Hyperinflations Past and Present', *Weltwirtschafliches Archiv* 122, No. 1, pp. 1-47.

Eichengreen, B. (1986), 'Rational Expectations and Inflation (T.J. Sargent): A Review', *Journal of Economic Literature* 24, December, pp. 1812-15.

Engle, R.F. and Granger, C.W.J. (1987), 'Co-Integration and Error Correction: Representation, Estimation and Testing', *Econometrica* 55, March, pp. 251-76.

Engsted, T. (1993), 'Cointegration and Cagan's Model of Hyperinflation Under Rational Expectations', *Journal of Money, Credit and Banking* 25, August, Part 1, pp. 350-60.

Evans, P. (1978), 'Time Series and Structural Analysis of the German Hyperinflation', *International Economic Review*, February, pp. 195-209.

Evans, J.L. and Yarrow, G.K. (1981), 'Some Implications of Alternative Expectations Hypotheses in the Monetary Analysis of Hyperinflations', *Oxford Economic Papers* 33, March, pp. 61-80.

Fischer, S. (1987), 'The Israeli Stabilization Program, 1985-86', *American Economic Review* 77, May, pp. 275-78.

Flood, R.P. and Garber, P.M. (1983), 'Process Consistency and Monetary Reform', *Journal of Monetary Economics* 12, pp. 279-95.

Flood, R.P. and Garber, P.M. (1980), 'An Economic Theory of Monetary Reform', *Journal of Political Economy* 88, February.

Franco, G.H.B. (1990), 'Fiscal Reforms and Stabilisations: Four Hyperinflation Cases Examined', *Economic Journal* 100, March, pp. 176-87.

Frank, M. and Stengos, T. (1988), 'Chaotic Dynamics in Economic Time-Series', *Journal of Economic Surveys* 2, no. 2, pp. 103-34.

Fratianni, M. (1986), 'Conditions Under Which Very Rapid Inflation Has Appeared: A Comment', in K. Brunner and A.H. Meltzer (eds.), *Carnegie-Rochester Conference Series on Public Policy*, vol. 24, North-Holland, Amsterdam, pp. 169-78.

Frenkel, J.A. (1977), 'The Forward Exchange Rate, Expectations and the Demand for Money: The German Hyperinflation', *American Economic Review* 67, September. pp. 653-70.

Frenkel, J.A. and Taylor, M.P. (1993), 'Money Demand and Inflation in Yugoslavia', *Journal of Macroeconomics* 15, Summer, pp. 455-82.

Friedman, M. (1987), 'Rational Expectations and Inflation (T.J. Sargent): A Review', *Journal of Political Economy* 95, February, pp. 218-20.

Friedman, M. and Schwartz, A.J. (1982), *Monetary Trends in the United States and the United Kingdom: Their Relation to Income, Prices, and Interest Rates, 1867-1975*, University of Chicago Press, Chicago for NBER.

Garber, P.M. (1982), 'Transition from Inflation to Price Stability', in K. Brunner and A.H. Meltzer (eds.), *Carnegie-Rochester Conference Series on Public Policy*, vol. 16, North-Holland, Amsterdam, pp. 11-42.

Garber, P.M. and Spencer, M.G. (1994), 'The Dissolution of the Austro-Hungarian Empire: Lessons for Currency Reform', *Essays in International Finance*, No. 191, February, Department of Economics, Princeton University.

Granger, C.W.J. and Newbold, P. (1974) 'Spurious Regressions in Econometrics', *Journal of Econometrics* 2, pp. 111-20.

Haggard, S. and Kaufman, R. (1989), 'The Politics of Stabilization and Structural Adjustment', in J. Sachs (Ed.), *Developing Country Debt and the World Economy*, The University of Chicago Press, Chicago, for NBER, pp. 263-74.

Hahn, F.H. (1982), *Money and Inflation*, Oxford University Press, Oxford.

Hamilton, J. and Whiteman, C. (1985), 'The Observable Implications of Self-Fulfilling Expectations', *Journal of Monetary Economics* 16, pp. 353-73.

Harris, L. (1981), *Monetary Theory*, McGraw Hill, New York.

Hendry, D.F. and Ericsson, N. (1991), 'An Econometric Analysis of U.K. Money Demand in Monetary Trends in the United States and the United Kingdom by Milton Friedman and Anna J. Schwartz', *American Economic Review* 81, March, pp. 8-38.

Heymann, D. (1987), 'The Austral Plan', *American Economic Review* 77, May, pp. 284-87.

Holtfrerich, C.L. (1986), *The German Inflation*, De Gruyter, Berlin.

Holtfrerich, C.L. (1985), 'Past Experiences with Monetary Reform', in J.W. Williamson (ed.), *Inflation and Indexation: Argentina, Brazil, and Israel*, Institute for International Economics, Washington, D.C.

Horsman, G. (1988), *Inflation in The Twentieth Century*, St. Martin's Press, New York.

Jacobs, R. (1977), 'Hyperinflation and the Supply of Money', *Journal of Money, Credit and Banking* 9, February, Part II, pp. 287-303.

Johansen, S. (1991), 'Estimation and Hypothesis Testing of Cointegrated Vectors in Gaussian Vector Autoregressive Models', *Econometrica*, 59, pp. 1551-81.

Johansen, S. and Juselius, K. (1990), 'Maximum Likelihood Estimation and Inference on Cointegration - With Applications to the Demand for Money', *Oxford Bulletin of Economics and Statistics* 52, No. 2, pp. 169-207.

Kalecki, M. (1962), 'A Model of Hyperinflation,' *Manchester School* 30, pp. 275-81.

Kiguel, M. (1989), 'Budget Deficits, Stability, and the Dynamics of Hyperinflation', *Journal of Money, Credit and Banking* 21, May, pp. 148-57.

Kindleberger, C.P. (1987), *Marshall Plan Days*, Allen Unwin, Boston.

Kydland, F.E. and Prescott, E.C. (1977), 'Rules Rather Than Discretion: The Inconsistency of Optimal Plans', *Journal of Political Economy* 85, June, pp. 473-92.

La Haye, L. (1985), 'Inflation and Currency Reform,' *Journal of Political Economy* 93, June, pp. 537-60.

Lahiti, A-K. (1991), 'Money and Inflation in Yugoslavia', *IMF Staff Papers* 38, December, pp. 751-88.

Laidler, D. (1987), 'Wicksell and Fischer on the "Backing of Money and the Quantity Theory" - A comment on the debate between Smith and Michener', in K. Brunner and A.H. Meltzer (eds.), *Carnegie-Rochester Conference Series on Public Policy*, vol. 27, North-Holland, Amsterdam, pp. 325-34.

Lucas Jr., R.E. (1980), 'Two Illustrations of the Quantity Theory', *American Economic Review* 70, December, pp. 1005-14.

Lui, F.T. (1983), 'Cagan's Hypothesis and the First Nationwide Inflation of paper Money in World History', *Journal of Political Economy* 91, December, pp. 1067-74.

Makinen, G.E. (1986), 'The Greek Hyperinflation and Stabilization of 1943-1946', *Journal of Economic History* 46, September, pp. 795-806.

Makinen, G.E. (1984), 'The Greek Stabilization of 1944-46', *American Economic Review* 74, December, pp. 1067-74.

Makinen, G.E. and Woodward, G.T. (1989), 'A Monetary Interpretation of the Poincaré Stabilization of 1926', *Southern Economic Journal* 56, July, pp. 191-211.

Makinen, G.E. and Woodward, G.T. (1988), 'The Transition from Hyperinflation to Stability: Some Evidence', *Eastern Economic Journal* 14, January-March, pp. 19-26.

McCallum, B.T. (1989), 'Inflation: Theory and Evidence', B.M. Friedman and F. Hahn, (eds.), *Handbook of Monetary Economics*.

Michael, P., A.R. Nobay and Peel, P.A. (1994), 'The Demand for Money During the German Hyperinflation Revisited', *International Economic Review* 35, February, pp. 1-22.

Michener, R. (1987), 'Fixed Exchange Rates and the Quantity Theory in Colonial America', in K. Brunner and A.H. Meltzer (eds.), *Carnegie-Rochester Conference Series on Public Policy*, vol. 27, North-Holland, Amsterdam, pp. 233-308.

Morales, J.A. (1987), 'Inflation Stabilization in Bolivia', paper presented at a conference on Inflation Stabilization, June, Toledo, Spain.

Olivera, J.H.G. (1967), 'Money, Prices and Fiscal Lags: A Note on the Dynamics of Inflation', *Banca Nazionale del Lavoro Quarterly Review*, September, pp. 258-67.

Pastor, M. Jr. (1991), 'Bolivia: Hyperinflation, Stabilisation and Beyond', *Journal of Development Studies* 27, January, pp. 211-37.

Pereira, L.B. and Nakano, Y. (1987), *The Theory of Inertial Inflation: The Foundation of Economic Reform in Brazil and Argentina*, Lynne Rienner, Boulder, Col.

Perrson, T. (1988), 'Credibility of Macroeconomic Policy: An Introduction and a Broad Survey', *European Economic Review*, pp. 519-32.

Phylatkis, K. and Taylor, M.P. (1992), 'The Monetary Dynamics of Sustained High Inflation: Taiwan, 1945-49', *Southern Economic Journal* 58, January, pp. 610-22.

Rodrik, D. (1989), 'Promises, Promises: Credible Policy Reform Via Signalling', *Economic Journal* 99, September, pp. 756-72.

Rogoff, K. (1987), 'Reputational Constraints on Monetary Policy', in K. Brunner and A.H. Meltzer (eds.), *Carnegie-Rochester Conference Series on Public Policy*, vol. 26, North-Holland, Amsterdam, pp. 141-82.

Rogoff, K. (1985), 'The Optimal Degree of Commitment to an Intermediary Monetary Target', *Quarterly Journal of Economics* 100, November, pp. 1169-90.

Sachs, J. (1987), 'The Bolivian Hyperinflation and Stabilization', *American Economic Review* 77, May, pp. 279-83.

Sachs, J. (1986), 'The Bolivian Hyperinflation and Stabilization', NBER Working Paper No. 2037, November.

Santaella, J.A. (1993), 'Stabilization Programs and External Enforcement', *IMF Staff Papers* 40, September, pp. 584-621.

Sargent, T.J. (1993), *Rational Expectations and Inflation*, Second Edition, Harper Collins Publishers, New York.

Sargent, T.J. (1986), *Rational Expectations and Inflation*, Harper and Row, New York.

Sargent, T.J. (1981), 'The Demand for Money during Hyperinflations under Rational Expectations', in R.E. Lucas and T.J. Sargent, *Rational Expectations and Econometric Practice*, vol. 2, University of Minnesota Press, Minneapolis, Minn., pp. 429-52.

Sargent, T.J. and Wallace, N. (1982), 'The Real Bills doctrine versus the Quantity theory: A Reconsideration', *Journal of Political Economy* 90, December, pp. 1212-36.

Sargent, T.J. and Wallace, N. (1981), 'Rational Expectations and the Dynamics of Hyperinflation', in R.E. Lucas and T.J. Sargent, *Rational Expectations and Econometric Practice*, vol. 2, University of Minnesota Press, Minneapolis, Minn., pp. 405-28.

Siklos, P.L. (1995), 'Tales of Parallel Currencies: The Early Soviet Experience', in J. Reis (ed.), *The History of International Monetary Arrangements*, Macmillan, London, forthcoming.

Siklos, P.L. (1994a), 'Establishing Central Bank Independence: Recent Experiences in Developing Countries', *Journal of International Trade and Economic Development* (forthcoming).

Siklos, P.L. (1994b), 'Interpreting a Change in Monetary Policy Regimes: A Reappraisal of the First Hungarian Hyperinflation and Stabilization, 1921-28', in M.D. Bordo and F. Capie (eds.), *Monetary Regimes in Transition*, Cambridge University Press, Cambridge, pp. 274-311.

Siklos, P.L. (1991), 'Fiscal Policy and Inflationary Expectations: The Hungarian Tax Pengo Experiment of 1946', *Journal of European Economic History* 20, Winter, pp. 615-28.

Siklos, P.L. (1991a), *War Finance, Hyperinflation, and Stabilization in Hungary 1938-1948*, Macmillan and St. Martin's Press, London and New York.

Siklos, P.L. (1991b), 'The Money Growth - Inflation Relationship Under Hyperinflation: An Illustration from Hungary's Postwar Experience', *Applied Economics* 23, pp. 1453-60.

Siklos, P.L. (1990), 'The Link Between Money and Prices under Different Policy Regimes: The Case of Postwar Hungary', *Explorations in Economic History* 27, October, pp. 468-82.

Siklos, P.L. (1990a), 'The Transition from Hyperinflation to Price Stability: Further Evidence', *Eastern Economic Journal* 16, Jan.-March, pp. 65-9.

Siklos, P.L. (1989), 'The End of the Hungarian Hyperinflation of 1945-1946', *Journal of Money, Credit and Banking* 21, May, pp. 135-47.

Smith, B.D. (1988), 'The Relationship Between Money and Prices: Some Historical Evidence Reconsidered', *Quarterly Review*, Federal Reserve Bank of Minneapolis 12, Summer, pp. 18-32.

Smith, B.D. (1985), 'American Colonial Monetary Regimes: The Failure of the Quantity Theory and Some Evidence in Favour of an Alternate View,' *Canadian Journal of Economics* 18, August, pp. 532-65.

Smith, B.D. (1985a), 'Colonial Evidence on Two Theories of Money: Maryland and the Colonies,' *Journal of Political Economy* 93, December, pp. 1178-211.

Sommariva, A. and Tullio, G. (1987), *German Macroeconomic History 1880-1979*, St. Martins Press, New York, pp. 121-59.

Sturzenegger, F. (1994), 'Hyperinflation with Currency Substitution: Introducing an Indexed Currency', *Journal of Money, Credit and Banking* 26, August, Part I, pp. 377-95.

Tanzi, V. (1977), 'Inflation, Lags in Collection and the Real Value of Tax Revenue,' *IMF Staff Papers* 24, March, pp. 154-67.

Taylor, M.P. (1991), 'The Hyperinflation Model of Money Demand Revisited,' *Journal of Money, Credit and Banking* 23, August, Part I, pp. 327-51.

Toniolo G. (ed.) (1989), *Central Banks' Independence In Historical Perspective*, de Gruyter, Berlin.

Végh, C.A. (1992), 'Stopping High Inflation: An Analytical Overview', *IMF Staff Papers* 39, September, 626-95.

Webb, S.B. (1989), *Hyperinflation and Stabilization in Weimar Germany*, Oxford University Press, New York.

Webb, S.B. (1988), 'Latin American Debt Today and German Reparations after World War I - A Comparison', *Weltwirtschafliches und Archiv* 124, no. 4, pp. 745-74.

Webb, S.B. (1986), 'Fiscal News and Inflationary Expectations in Germany after WWI', *Journal of Economic History* 46, September, pp. 769-94.

Webb, S.B. (1985), 'Government Debt and Inflationary Expectations as Determinants of the Money Supply in Germany, 1919-23', *Journal of Money, Credit, and Banking* 17, November, pp. 479-92.

Webb, S.B. (1983), 'Money Demand and Expectations in the German Hyperinflation: A Survey of the Models', in N. Schmukler and E. Marcus (eds.), *Inflation Through the Ages*, Columbia University Press, New York, pp. 435-49.

Wicker, E. (1986), 'Terminating Hyperinflation in the Dismembered Habsburg Monarchy', *American Economic Review* 76, June, pp. 350-64.

Witte, W.E. (1984), 'Ending Hyperinflation: The lessons which can be drawn', unpublished, Indiana University, August.

2. Stopping High Inflation: An Analytical Overview[*]

Carlos A. Végh

1. INTRODUCTION

> There is no subtler, no surer means of overturning the existing basis of society than to debauch the currency. The process engages all the hidden forces of economic law on the side of destruction and does it in a manner which not one man in a million can diagnose.
>
> John Maynard Keynes (1920, p. 220)

From a historical perspective, high inflation is a recent phenomenon. Prior to World War I, episodes of high inflation were mainly confined to the period of the *assignats* in France, the American War of Independence, and the Confederacy during the American Civil War (see Capie 1986). The historically rare occurrence of high inflation reflects the prevalence of convertible currencies and commodity moneys, which put a natural lid on inflationary forces. In the aftermath of World War I, however, hyperinflation burst onto the stage. Heavy disruptions and reparation payments resulting from the war caused massive fiscal deficits whose monetary financing led to hyperinflation in Austria, Germany, Hungary and Russia. Following World War II, hyperinflation erupted once again in Hungary, Greece and China. In 1985, Bolivia experienced the first hyperinflation of the 20th century not related to a foreign war, civil war, or political revolution.

After World War II, when hyperinflation had already achieved notoriety, a much less dramatic, but equally ominous, phenomenon began to emerge: chronic inflation. Some countries, particularly in Latin America, began to endure high (relative to industrial countries) and persistent rates of inflation, which in many instances have lasted up to the present day. Argentina, for example, has suffered from chronic inflation since the late 1940s and has been unsuccessful in eliminating it, in spite of eight major plans (two per decade), and countless other attempts. A similar story could also be told for Brazil and Uruguay. There are, however, success stories: Chile, Israel and Mexico managed to reduce three-digit annual inflation rates to around 20 per cent during the 1980s. Although such levels of inflation are still quite high by international standards, they are viewed as a significant achievement, considering the resilience of chronic inflation.

High inflation has proved to be fertile ground for researchers. Seminal studies by Cagan (1956) and Sargent (1982) on hyperinflation, and Pazos (1972) on chronic inflation have set the tone for much of the discussion. A reading of the extensive literature suggests that theory and evidence need to be further integrated to enhance our understanding of inflation stabilization in high-inflation countries. With this in mind, this chapter interprets the main stylized facts associated with stopping hyperinflation and chronic inflation in terms of a unified analytical framework.

The model used in this chapter, based on Calvo and Végh (1991a), provides a simple and plausible explanation of the dynamics of stabilization policy. The model relies on intertemporal substitution effects as the key channel through which stabilization policies may have real effects, along the lines of Calvo (1986). In addition, the presence of sticky prices introduces dynamic considerations that are key to an understanding of the outcome of inflation stabilization programmes. Since programmes designed to stop high inflation have usually relied on the exchange rate as the nominal anchor, the analysis will concentrate on exchange rate-based stabilization.[1]

The discussion is organized around two analytical exercises, which are used to interpret the evidence on stopping hyperinflation and chronic inflation. The first exercise considers a reduction in the rate of devaluation that is fully credible, in the sense that the public views the policy change as permanent. Under these circumstances, inflation falls instantaneously without any output costs. Sticky prices do not prevent an instantaneous adjustment because all price-setting behaviour is assumed to be forward looking. It is argued that the analytical exercise of a permanent reduction in the rate of devaluation is, to a first approximation, relevant for interpreting the end of hyperinflation. The reasons are, first, hyperinflationary processes appear to be characterized by the absence of backward-looking behaviour; and, second, programmes designed to stop hyperinflation usually command high credibility given the unsustainable state of affairs. The evidence reviewed in the chapter seems to bear out the prediction that hyperinflation can be stopped abruptly and at relatively small output costs, compared to those that would obtain in low-inflation countries.

A second analytical exercise assumes that the reduction in the rate of devaluation is not credible, in the sense that the public expects the higher rate of devaluation to resume at some point in the future. The fall in the nominal interest rate that results from the lower devaluation rate and the assumption of perfect capital mobility is thus viewed as temporary. Since the cash-in-advance constraint requires that money be used to purchase goods, the opportunity cost of holding money is part of the effective price of consumption. The temporary fall in the nominal interest rate thus reduces the effective price of consumption in the present relative to the future. Hence, demand for both traded and nontraded goods increases and leads to an initial expansion in the nontraded goods sector and a current account deficit. The slow convergence of inflation to the rate of devaluation results in a sustained real appreciation of the domestic currency, which ultimately reduces the demand for nontraded goods. As a consequence, output falls and a recession sets in. The recession may occur either before or when the programme ends. The real effects caused by a noncredible stabilization do not depend on whether the programme is eventually abandoned, as the public expected, or not.

It is argued that the analytical exercise of a noncredible reduction in the rate of devaluation can be used to interpret inflation stabilization in chronic-inflation countries, where a history of failed stabilizations, together with the ability of the economy to live with high inflation, makes any attempt to stop inflation less than fully credible. The stylized facts are generally consistent with the predictions of the model. In particular, a boom-recession cycle has characterized both failed and successful stabilizations, with the recession often setting in before the programme ends (see Kiguel and Liviatan 1992a). Furthermore, the dynamic adjustment predicted by the model, with U-shaped curves describing the behaviour of both inflation and the real exchange rate (defined as the relative price of traded goods in terms of nontraded goods), is consistent with the stylized facts. The inflation 'inertia' exhibited by the model, in the sense that the inflation rate remains above the devaluation rate, has been observed in most programmes.[2]

The chapter proceeds as follows. Section 2 discusses the stylized facts associated with stopping high inflation. Section 3 introduces the model and analyses the effects of a permanent reduction in the rate of devaluation. Section 4 discusses the evidence on ending hyperinflation in the light of the model. Section 5 examines a temporary reduction in the rate of devaluation and matches the analytical results with the evidence on stopping chronic inflation. Section 6 discusses the quantitative relevance of the lack-of-credibility (or 'temporariness') hypothesis and the role of backward-looking behaviour, and offers some concluding remarks.

2. STYLIZED FACTS OF HIGH-INFLATION STABILIZATION

This section first discusses the key differences between chronic inflation and hyperinflation, and then reviews the main stylized facts associated with ending both hyperinflation and chronic inflation.

2.1 Hyperinflation Versus Chronic Inflation

For practical purposes, the term 'hyperinflation' will be defined as in Cagan's (1956) classic paper.[3] At a conceptual level, it is useful to keep in mind the distinction between 'hyperinflation' and 'chronic inflation,' emphasized by Pazos (1972). Pazos (1972) argues that chronic inflation exhibits two key characteristics. First, it may last for long periods of time; it is not measured in terms of months, as is the case of most hyperinflations, but in terms of years. Second, chronic inflation has an intermediate intensity — higher than that of moderate inflation but much lower than that of hyperinflation — which results from countries' learning how to live with high and persistent inflation by creating various indexation mechanisms. Specifically, inflation does not have an inherent propensity to accelerate or, if it does, soon reaches a new plateau. In hyperinflations, however, the rate of inflation oscillates freely, before accelerating exponentially in the last six months or so.[4]

In order to illustrate the differences between chronic inflation and hyperinflation, Table 2.1 shows annual inflation rates and money growth rates during the last three decades for six Latin American countries (Argentina, Bolivia, Brazil, Chile, Mexico and Uruguay), Israel, and, for comparison purposes, the United States. Beyond the general notion of 'high and persistent inflation', there is no generally accepted definition of chronic inflation. Moreover, any definition would probably not withstand the test of time, since the notion of what constitutes high inflation changes over time.[5]

In spite of the lack of a clear definition of chronic inflation, some cases are beyond dispute. Countries such as Argentina, Brazil and Uruguay would be classified as chronic-inflation countries under any sensible definition. In all three countries, average annual inflation has been above

Table 2.1 Inflation and Money Growth in Selected Countries (in Per Cent per Year)

Year	Argentina Inflation Rate	Argentina M1 Growth	Bolivia Inflation Rate	Bolivia M1 Growth	Brazil Inflation Rate	Brazil M1 Growth	Chile Inflation Rate	Chile M1 Growth	Israel Inflation Rate	Israel M1 Growth	Mexico Inflation Rate	Mexico M1 Growth	Uruguay Inflation Rate	Uruguay M1 Growth	United States Inflation Rate	United States M1 Growth
1961	13.4	-7.3	7.6	18.4	33.4	51.2	7.7	...	6.8	11.1	1.6	6.8	22.7	22.1	1.1	3.4
1962	28.3	8.9	5.9	12.1	51.8	61.9	14.0	28.9	9.4	30.0	1.2	13.2	10.9	-3.1	1.1	1.6
1963	23.9	28.6	-0.7	19.6	70.1	64.4	44.1	34.1	6.6	23.1	0.6	16.1	21.3	29.0	1.2	4.2
1964	22.2	39.9	10.2	20.7	91.9	84.6	46.0	51.1	5.2	13.8	2.3	17.6	42.4	42.0	1.3	4.5
1965	28.6	25.5	2.9	17.5	65.7	76.6	28.8	21.1	7.7	16.7	3.6	5.7	56.6	102.7	1.7	4.7
1966	31.9	35.0	7.0	22.3	41.3	15.8	23.1	89.8	7.9	14.3	4.2	12.2	73.5	39.4	3.0	2.4
1967	29.2	62.7	11.2	3.3	30.5	42.6	18.7	24.9	1.7	25.0	3.0	9.2	89.3	111.2	2.8	6.5
1968	16.2	24.9	5.5	8.0	22.0	42.5	26.3	38.0	2.1	10.0	2.3	14.2	125.3	53.7	4.2	7.3
1969	7.6	21.3	2.2	5.8	22.7	28.7	30.4	35.5	2.4	9.1	3.4	15.0	21.0	61.2	5.4	3.3
1970	13.6	6.5	3.8	12.6	22.4	26.7	32.5	65.5	6.1	8.3	5.2	10.7	16.3	14.4	5.9	5.4
1971	34.7	13.5	3.7	15.2	20.1	32.4	20.0	112.2	12.0	23.1	5.3	7.6	24.0	54.0	4.3	6.6
1972	58.4	65.0	6.5	25.2	16.6	28.3	74.8	154.3	12.9	248.0	5.0	17.9	76.5	46.8	3.3	9.3
1973	61.2	72.7	31.5	34.3	12.7	47.5	361.5	322.6	20.0	33.2	12.0	22.4	97.0	80.0	6.2	5.2
1974	23.5	57.9	62.8	43.4	27.6	34.5	504.7	266.0	39.7	17.5	23.8	20.7	77.2	64.2	11.0	4.3
1975	182.9	211.1	8.0	11.8	29.0	44.4	374.7	256.0	39.3	22.0	15.2	21.4	81.4	42.3	9.1	4.9
1976	444.0	275.0	4.5	36.5	42.0	36.7	211.8	256.0	31.4	26.9	15.8	29.1	50.6	65.5	5.7	6.7
1977	176.0	115.2	8.1	20.9	43.7	38.1	91.9	86.7	34.6	38.8	29.0	31.8	58.2	40.4	6.5	8.1
1978	175.5	159.7	10.4	12.4	38.7	36.1	40.1	76.7	50.6	44.0	17.5	29.8	44.5	85.1	7.6	8.3
1979	159.5	137.8	19.7	16.7	52.7	74.9	33.4	61.7	78.3	31.6	18.2	33.6	66.8	71.7	11.3	6.7
1980	100.8	96.7	47.2	42.6	82.8	69.7	35.1	53.8	131.0	96.7	26.4	32.2	63.5	47.4	13.5	6.8
1981	104.5	70.1	32.1	19.7	105.6	82.6	19.7	-5.2	116.8	91.3	27.9	33.1	34.0	8.3	10.3	6.4
1982	164.8	247.5	123.5	228.8	97.8	68.5	9.9	12.1	120.4	109.2	58.9	62.4	19.0	39.2	6.2	8.8
1983	343.8	362.0	275.6	207.0	142.1	102.7	27.3	22.3	145.6	140.8	101.8	40.3	49.2	9.0	3.2	9.7
1984	626.7	501.6	1,281.4	1,798.3	197.0	204.1	19.9	15.4	373.8	352.3	65.5	60.0	55.3	48.4	4.3	5.9
1985	672.1	571.5	11,749.6	5,784.6	226.9	334.3	30.7	13.8	304.6	245.7	57.7	49.5	72.2	107.6	3.6	12.4
1986	90.1	84.8	276.3	86.1	145.2	330.1	19.5	44.8	48.1	112.8	86.2	67.2	76.4	82.8	1.9	16.5
1987	131.3	124.7	14.6	39.9	229.7	215.4	19.9	6.6	19.8	49.5	131.8	118.1	63.6	60.4	3.7	2.8
1988	343.0	337.9	16.0	35.3	682.3	570.3	14.7	68.2	16.3	11.3	114.2	67.8	62.2	64.3	4.0	5.8
1989	3,079.8	4,096.2	15.2	2.4	1,287.0	1,384.2	17.0	14.5	20.2	44.4	20.0	37.3	80.4	72.8	4.8	1.5
1990	2,314.0	1,070.5	17.1	39.5	2,937.8	2,335.7	26.0	17.2	17.2	30.6	26.7	63.1	112.5	101.2	5.4	3.6
1991	171.7	...	21.4	45.1	440.8	328.2	21.8	51.5	19.0	13.7	22.7	122.5	102.0	99.3	4.2	8.2
Annual Averages																
1961-1970	21.2	23.2	5.5	13.9	43.5	48.0	28.9	41.8	5.6	3.7	2.7	12.0	44.0	43.4	2.8	4.3
1971-1980	119.5	108.6	18.8	25.4	35.3	43.5	130.3	147.6	41.6	48.9	16.5	24.4	62.7	59.0	7.8	6.7
1981-1990	437.6	400.4	222.7	204.2	337.1	339.8	20.3	19.5	91.2	99.6	65.1	58.4	60.6	55.9	4.7	7.2

Sources: IMF, International Financial Statistics (various issues); except for 1988-91 M1 figures for Brazil, Central Bank of Brazil.

Note: The annual averages for Chile are for 1962-1970 instead of 1961-1970.

39

20 per cent in all three decades (Table 2.1).[6] Argentina has had triple-digit inflation since 1975 (with the exception of 1986 when, as the result of the Austral Plan, inflation fell to 90.1 per cent). Uruguay's inflation has been above 30 per cent since 1972 (with the exception of 1982 when, as a result of the 1978 stabilization programme, inflation fell to 19 percent), and above 50 per cent since 1984.[7] As one would expect — and as the averages presented at the bottom of Table 2.1 clearly suggest — the proximate cause of inflation was high money growth. Massive money printing, in turn, resulted from the need to finance chronic budget deficits.

Chile, Israel and Mexico provide cases in which, after reaching three-digit figures, chronic inflation was successfully stopped. During the 1960s and 1970s, inflation in Chile was not much different from that in Argentina, Brazil and Uruguay. However, as a result of the stabilization plan of 1978, inflation fell to 9.9 per cent in 1981, and averaged 20.3 per cent during 1981-90. In contrast, Israel and Mexico were low-inflation countries during the 1960s, with Mexico experiencing the same inflation rate as the United States. During the 1970s inflation unraveled and soon reached three-digit figures. Both the Israeli stabilization plan of July 1985 and the Mexican programme of December 1987 brought inflation down to around 20 per cent where it has remained ever since.

The inflationary processes in the six countries just reviewed (Argentina, Brazil, Chile, Israel, Mexico and Uruguay) exhibit the main characteristics of chronic inflation suggested by Pazos (1972). As already noted, inflation has been high and persistent. Moreover, inflation does not have an inherent propensity to accelerate, as best exemplified by the case of Uruguay, where inflation has been remarkably stable in the last 30 years. When inflation does accelerate, it soon reaches a new plateau. In Argentina, for instance, inflation accelerated in 1975 to triple-digit figures and remained there for 11 years. In Israel, after 9 years of double-digit figures, inflation jumped to triple-digit figures in 1980 and remained there for 6 years, until the 1985 stabilization plan.

Bolivia provides an excellent example of the explosive nature of hyperinflation. In contrast to the other six countries, Bolivia is certainly not a chronic-inflation country. Annual inflation averaged only 5.5 percent during the 1960s, and was below 10 per cent in all but 4 years during 1961-77. By the end of the 1970s, however, political instability led to high inflation. In 1982 inflation jumped to 123.5 per cent, as the debt crisis cut short the inflow of foreign credit and forced the government to resort to monetary financing. High inflation skyrocketed into hyperinflation, reaching 62.7 per cent a month in April 1984. Hyperinflation thus started less than two years after annual inflation reached three-digit levels. It lasted 18 months and was stopped by the September 1985 stabilization.

From 1987-91 annual inflation averaged 16.9 per cent.[8]

The explosive nature of the inflationary process in hyperinflation is also clear from other historical episodes. In Germany, for instance, annual inflation averaged only 1.8 per cent between 1900 and 1913. In July 1914, one month before the outbreak of World War I, note convertibility was suspended to prevent further losses of gold reserves. During the war (1914-18), annual inflation averaged 25.2 per cent. In 1919 inflation jumped to 226.4 per cent and, after slowing down to 79.3 per cent in 1920 and 142.4 per cent in 1921, climbed to a monthly rate of 89 per cent a month in August 1922. The hyperinflation lasted 17 months and came to an abrupt end in January 1924. Annual inflation averaged 3.8 per cent during 1925-29.[9,10]

2.2 Stopping Hyperinflation: Stylized Facts

Hyperinflations offer a fascinating laboratory for the study of monetary phenomena.[11] Astronomical rates of inflation serve to isolate many aspects of reality, which, under normal conditions, are likely to be obscured by other considerations. For further reference, it is useful to list the hyperinflations (and subsequent stabilizations) that will be referred to in this chapter.

- The post-World War I European hyperinflation: Austria (October 1921-August 1922), Germany (August 1922-November 1923), Hungary (March 1923-February 1924), Poland (January 1923-January 1924) and Russia (December 1921-January 1924).[12] The common theme in these episodes is how hyperinflation was successfully brought under control by the introduction of drastic fiscal reforms, giving central banks greater independence and restoring (or virtually restoring) convertibility of the domestic currency in terms of the dollar or gold, as emphasized by Sargent (1982) in his paper on the hyperinflations in Austria, Germany, Poland, and Hungary.
- The post-World War II European hyperinflations: Hungary (August 1945-July 1946) and Greece (November 1943-December 1945).[13] The Hungarian stabilization fits the pattern identified by Sargent (1982) of drastic reforms that achieve immediate price stability. In contrast, the Greek stabilization was a more diffused process, since it took the government over a year and three attempts to finally put the required measures in place.
- The Taiwanese hyperinflation (1945-49).[14] The interesting feature of this episode, which has not achieved the fame of its European counterparts, is that, according to Makinen and Woodward (1989),

stabilization apparently took place not only without any fiscal adjustment, but, more important, with no prospects of any future fiscal adjustment. It was only in mid-1952 that massive aid from the United States helped in balancing the budget.

• The Bolivian hyperinflation (April 1984-September 1985).[15] The key components of the stabilization programme were a drastic fiscal correction, unification of exchange rates, and a return to full convertibility — capital controls had been in place since late 1982. Unlike other hyperinflations referred to above, which were based on a fixed exchange rate, the exchange rate system in Bolivia during the stabilization plan is best characterized as a dirty float.[16] However, when the exchange rate markets were unified, the official exchange rate depreciated by 1,600 per cent in one day, thus eliminating the parallel market premium practically overnight. The exchange rate stabilized immediately after this initial adjustment, providing a de facto anchor to the system.

For the purposes here, two main stylized facts regarding hyperinflation stabilization need to be emphasized:[17] (1) inflation is stopped immediately; and (2) output costs are relatively small.

(1) Inflation stops abruptly. In most instances, price stability was achieved virtually overnight following exchange rate stabilization.[18] To illustrate this point, Table 2.2 shows monthly averages for the rates of devaluation and inflation 12 months before and 12 months after the exchange rate was stabilized in eight hyperinflations (Austria, Poland, Germany, Greece, Hungary after each World War, Bolivia and Taiwan).[19] The figures clearly show how anchoring the exchange rate can ensure a swift return to price stability. The most dramatic examples are Hungary 1946 and Germany, where the monthly inflation rate in the 12 months before stabilization averaged 19,800 per cent and 455.1 per cent, respectively. After stabilization, the monthly average dropped to 1.3 per cent and 0.3 per cent, respectively. In more moderate hyperinflations, such as Hungary after World War I where monthly inflation averaged 33.3 per cent before stabilization, the same phenomenon of overnight price stability took place. Even when price stability was not fully achieved, as in Bolivia and Taiwan, the drop in inflation was substantial. Not surprisingly, in Bolivia and Taiwan, the exchange rate did not stabilize completely.[20]

In summary, the evidence clearly suggests that, in hyperinflation- ary situations, price stability can be the immediate result of using the exchange rate as the nominal anchor. As discussed in section 4, during

Table 2.2 Devaluation, Inflation and Money Growth in Hyperinflations (in per cent per month)

Country	Devaluation Rate	Inflation Rate	Money Growth
Austria (October 1922)			
October 1921-September 1922	32.6	46.0	35.7
October 1922-September 1923	-0.4	0.4	8.7
Poland (February 1924)			
February 1923-January 1924	63.7	66.2	62.7
February 1924-November 1924	0.8	1.2	11.1
Greece (February 1946)	—		
February 1945-January 1946	—	27.0	31.6
February 1946-December 1946	—	-0.8	13.4
Taiwan (June 1949)			
January 1948-May 1949	—	30.7	23.7
June 1949-December 1950	—	6.7	11.4
Germany (January 1924)			
January 1923-December 1923	409.8	455.1	419.7
January 1924-December 1924	-3.9	0.3	12.0
Hungary (April 1924)			
April 1923-March 1924	28.0	33.3	28.1
April 1924-March 1925	0.0	0.2	8.5
Hungary (August 1946)			
August 1945-July 1946	—	19,800.0	12,200.0
August 1946-July 1947	—	1.3	14.2
Bolivia (October 1985)			
October 1984-September 1985	44.0	57.6	48.5
October 1985-September 1986	4.9	5.7	8.3

Note: The date in parentheses following the country name indicates the month in which the exchange rate stabilized. Money refers to notes in circulation, except in Bolivia and Taiwan where it indicates M1.

Sources: Austria, Germany, and Hungary 1924: Sargent (1982); Poland: Sargent (1982) and Llach (1990); Greece: Makinen (1984); Hungary 1946: Cagan (1956) and Bomberger and Makinen (1983); Taiwan: Makinen and Woodward (1989); and Bolivia: IMF, *International Financial Statistics* (various issues), and Morales (1988).

hyperinflation virtually all prices are indexed to the dollar or, which amounts to the same thing, quoted in dollars; hence, stabilizing the exchange rate is tantamount to achieving price stability.[21]

2) Output costs are relatively small. Although this second stylized fact is certainly more controversial than the first one, a review of the evidence suggests that hyperinflations have been stopped with small output costs compared to those that would have resulted from stopping inflation in low-inflation countries.[22] There are two key difficulties in assessing the output effects of stopping hyperinflation. First, available data are usually sparse and unclear. Second, the real effects of stabilization *per se* are difficult to disentangle from the real dislocations that characterize the transition from hyperinflation to price stability. Moreover, in the European hyperinflations following the two World Wars, the effects of the war itself and the burden of heavy reparations payments have also tended to blur the picture.

Of the nine hyperinflations listed above (Tables 2.3a-2.3g present data for seven episodes), economic activity appears to have increased following stabilization in three cases — Germany, Greece and Russia. In *Germany*, the per capita index of industrial production rose substantially in 1924 — the year following stabilization — from the depressed level of 1923 that had resulted mainly from the French occupation of the Ruhr and the policy of passive resistance. The rate of unemployment also decreased substantially from its peak of 23.6 per cent in the fourth quarter of 1923, to 3.8 per cent in the second quarter of 1925. In the summer of 1925, a recession set in. Garber (1982) attributes this recession not to the monetary stabilization per se, but rather to a reallocation of industry, as the capital goods sector had been heavily subsidized during the hyperinflation.

In *Greece*, the sparse available evidence seems to suggest that there were no output costs. In fact, as Table 2.3b shows, national income increased after the stabilization, and unemployment apparently decreased.[23] In *Russia*, Rostowski (1992) reports that the economy continued to grow strongly after stabilization: industrial output increased by about 30 per cent in 1923-24, with higher growth concentrated after stabilization (the reforms took place in February and March 1924), and by about 45 per cent in 1924-25.

In two cases — Taiwan and Bolivia — there appear to be no costs associated with stabilization. In *Taiwan*, Makinen and Woodward (1989) report small, if any, costs after stabilization. The unemployment rate increased only slightly even though Taiwan was forced to absorb nearly half a million mainlanders early in the stabilization. National income kept growing at positive rates, albeit less rapidly than during hyperinflation.[24]

Table 2.3a Real Effects of Stopping Hyperinflations: Germany
       (January 1924)

Year/Quarter	Unemployment Rate	Index of Per Capita Industrial Production[a] (1913 = 100)
1920:1	—	
2	—	
3	—	
4	—	61
1921:1	—	
2	—	
3	—	
4	—	77
1922:1	—	
2	—	
3	—	
4	—	86
1923:1	5.0	
2	5.8	
3	6.6	
4	23.6	54
1924:1	22.7	
2	9.8	
3	11.8	
4	7.9	77
1925:1	7.1	
2	3.8	
3	4.2	
4	12.0	90
1926:1	22.0	
2	18.3	
3	16.5	
4	15.0	86
1927:1	14.5	
2	7.4	
3	5.0	
4	8.3	111

Note: In Tables 2.3a-2.3g, the date in parentheses following the country name indicates the month in which the exchange rate stabilized.
[a]Annual data.
Source: Garber (1982).

Table 2.3b Real Effects of Stopping Hyperinflations: Greece
        (February 1946)

Year	Number of Unemployed	Real National Income (Per cent change)
1945	—	5.5
1946	197.000[a]	62.1
1947	122.000[b]	33.9

Notes:
[a]Summer 1946.
[b]31 December, 1947.
Source: Makinen (1984).

Table 2.3c Real Effects of Stopping Hyperinflations: Bolivia
        (October 1985)

Year	Unemployment Rate	Real GDP (Per cent change)
1980	5.8	0.6
1981	9.7	1.0
1982	10.9	-4.4
1983	13.0	-4.5
1984	15.5	-0.6
1985	18.0	-1.0
1986	20.0	-2.5
1987	20.5	2.6
1988	18.0	3.0
1989	25.0	2.8

Source: IMF, *International Financial Statistics* (various issues), and Ministry of Labour.

In *Bolivia* the stabilization plan in and of itself does not seem to have had much impact on the real sector. As shown in Table 2.3c, real gross domestic product (GDP) had been falling and unemployment rising since the early 1980s, as a result of internal political chaos and the onset of the debt crisis. There is no apparent reason why this negative trend should have ended in 1985-86. Moreover, the Bolivian economy suffered severe external shocks in late 1985 and 1986: the terms of trade deteriorated substantially as international prices of tin and hydrocarbons collapsed; sales of natural gas to Argentina fell significantly; and large disruptions resulted from a campaign to curtail the illegal drug trade. According to Sachs (1986), a conservative estimate would put the export revenue loss at 10-15 per cent of gross national product (GNP) in one year. In 1987 real GDP began to increase again, even if at a slow rate.

In two other cases — Austria and Hungary in 1946 — there appears to be conflicting evidence. In *Austria*, the number of unemployed increased following the stabilization of September 1922, peaking in February 1923, although it had started to increase even before stabilization. According to estimates provided by Wicker (1986), the unemployment rate peaked in 1926 at 7 per cent (Table 2.3d). Assuming unemployment to be 3 per cent in 1921, he concluded that the rise in unemployment of 4 percentage points could be attributed to the stabilization. In contrast, the behaviour of real GNP tells a somewhat different story. After increasing by 9 per cent in 1922 (the stabilization took place in September), real GNP fell by 1.1 per cent in 1923, but rose by 11.7 and 6.8 per cent in 1924 and 1925, respectively.[25]

Table 2.3d Real Effects of Stopping Hyperinflations: Austria (October 1922)

Year	Unemployment Rate	Real GNP (Per cent change)
1921	—	10.7
1922	—	9.0
1923	—	-1.1
1924	5.6	11.7
1925	6.3	6.8
1926	7.0	1.6
1927	6.2	3.1

Source: Wicker (1986).

In *Hungary* 1946 the unemployment rate began to increase in the first quarter of 1947 (the stabilization took place in August 1946), and reached 11.5 per cent in December 1947 (Table 2.3e).[26] In contrast, national income rose by 20 per cent in the 12 months following stabilization. Industrial production increased by 9.8 per cent in the six months following stabilization. After falling somewhat in the first quarter of 1947, it increased again and, in October 1947, was 35 per cent above the prestabilization level. Reinforcing the evidence in favour of very small output costs, studies reported in Siklos (1989) by the Hungarian Institute of Economic Research concluded that in 1946-47, GDP was only 0.1 per cent lower relative to the business cycle peak of 1928-29 and 50 per cent higher relative to the business cycle trough year of 1932-33.

Table 2.3e Real Effects of Stopping Hyperinflations: Hungary (August 1946)

Year/Month		Index of Production (1946:1 = 100)	Unemployment Rate[a]
1946	January	100.0	
	February	103.0	
	March	104.7	
	April	111.2	
	May	134.8	
	June	115.1	
	July	128.7	
	August	136.5	5.0
	September	136.5	
	October	154.2	
	November	157.2	
	December	141.5	5.0
1947	January	141.3	
	February	—	
	March	—	7.9
	April	114.7	
	May	122.3	
	June	125.8	
	July	125.7	
	August	130.8	8.6
	September	151.5	
	October	173.8	
	November	—	
	December	—	11.5

Note: [a] Data not available on a regular monthly basis.
Source: Siklos (1989).

In the last two cases — Poland and Hungary in 1924 — according to estimates reported by Wicker (1986), the unemployment rate rose substantially, reaching a peak of 12.7 per cent in *Poland* during 1925 (Table 2.3f) and 14.5 per cent in the first quarter of 1925 in *Hungary* (Table 2.3g). In Poland, however, even though the number of unemployed increased after the January 1924 stabilization, the level reached in December (159,060) was no worse than before the stabilization (the number of unemployed peaked in January 1922 at 221,444).

In summary, of the nine episodes, available evidence suggests that there were no output costs resulting from monetary stabilization *per se* in five (Germany, Greece, Russia, Taiwan and Bolivia); there is conflicting evidence for two (Austria and Hungary in 1946), since both unemployment and economic activity increased; and unemployment increased in two (Poland and Hungary in 1924; output data are not available in either case).

In sharp contrast, the real costs of disinflation in industrial countries are estimated to be substantial.[27] For instance, according to Gordon (1982, p. 39) in the United States (in the period after 1922), there is 'abundant evidence that only 10 to 40 per cent of nominal demand changes are absorbed by the inflation rate in the first year after such changes'. This implies that a deceleration in nominal spending growth from 10 to zero per cent would result in a fall in inflation of only 1-4 per cent and a corresponding drop in real output from 9 per cent to 6 per cent. Gordon (1982) argued that this basic message holds true for other industrialized countries.

An alternative way of looking at the costs of disinflation is to estimate the 'sacrifice ratio', or cumulative per cent output loss per per centage point reduction in inflation. Estimates for the United States lie anywhere from 3 to 18 (Sachs 1985). The evidence, therefore, seems to warrant the conclusion that hyperinflations have been stopped at relatively small cost compared to low-inflation countries.[28] As discussed in section 4, the fact that in hyperinflations backward-looking contracts (so prevalent in industrial and chronic-inflation countries) disappear is probably at the heart of the difference in output costs.

2.3 Stopping Chronic Inflations: Stylized Facts

The ten episodes of stabilization in chronic inflation countries that serve as background for the theoretical discussion can be divided as follows.[29]

Table 2.3f Real Effects of Stopping Hyperinflations: Poland
(February 1924)

Year	Unemployment Rate
1922	1.2
1923	1.0
1924	5.6
1925	12.7
1926	8.5
1927	6.7

Source: Wicker (1986).

Table 2.3g Real Effects of Stopping Hyperinflations: Hungary
(April 1924)

Year/Quarter	Unemployment Rate
1924:1	7.7
2	8.8
3	10.1
4	12.6
1925:1	14.5
2	13.3
3	9.5
4	10.8
1926:1	11.3
2	9.7
3	7.3
4	7.9

Source: Wicker (1986).

- Latin American heterodox programmes of the 1960s. This group comprises stabilization plans in Argentina (March 1967) Brazil (March 1964), and Uruguay (June 1968) (see Tables 2A.2-2A.4 in the Appendix).[30] The common elements of these plans were, first, a fixed exchange rate (with periodic devaluations in Brazil) as the main nominal anchor; and second, the use of incomes policies in varying degrees. Whereas price controls were mainly voluntary in Argentina and Brazil, in Uruguay there was a comprehensive freeze similar to that of the heterodox programmes of the mid-1980s. All three programmes achieved an initial decline in inflation. However, the reduction in inflation was sustained only in Brazil, lasting well into the 1970s, and reaching 12.7 per cent in 1973 (Table 2.1). In Argentina and Uruguay, loss of fiscal discipline led to a resumption in inflation.
- Southern cone stabilization programmes of the late 1970s. This group comprises stabilizations programmes in Argentina (December 1978), Chile (February 1978), and Uruguay (October 1978; see Tables 2A.5-2A.7 in the Appendix).[31,32] These programmes shared two key characteristics in their design. First, all were orthodox programmes (that is, there were no price or wage controls). Second, in all three cases the exchange rate policy consisted in announcing a devaluation schedule (the 'tablita', or 'little table') against the dollar, with a decreasing rate of devaluation. Chile eventually fixed the exchange rate in June 1979. In spite of fiscal balance in both Chile and Uruguay, the slow convergence of inflation and the corresponding real appreciation of the domestic currency proved fatal. All three programmes ended in dramatic fashion with large exchange rate and financial crises.
- Heterodox programmes of the mid-1980s. This group comprises the Austral Plan in Argentina (June 1985), the Cruzado Plan in Brazil (February 1986), the Israeli plan (July 1985), and the Mexican plan (December 1987).[33] A key common element of the four plans was the use of wage and price controls to counter the inertial component of inflation. The Israeli and Mexican plans were successful in bringing down inflation to about 20 per cent. In Argentina and Brazil, however, inflation quickly resumed and soon reached higher levels than before the programmes.

The key stylized facts shared by most of these programmes are (1) inflation converges only slowly to the rate of devaluation; (2) there is a sustained real appreciation of the domestic currency; (3) the current account and the trade balance deteriorate; and (4) real activity increases at the beginning of the programme and later contracts.[34]

(1) Slow convergence of inflation. To illustrate the slow convergence
of the inflation rate to the devaluation rate, Figure 2.1 shows four-
quarter changes (that is, changes over same quarter of previous
year) of devaluation and inflation for the ten programmes just
described.[35,36] The evidence clearly suggests that inflation takes
a long time to converge, if at all, to the rate of devaluation. This
lack of convergence is particularly striking in the Southern cone
tablitas. These programmes were based on the belief that the
inflation rate would quickly converge to the world inflation plus the
preset rate of devaluation. However, to the surprise of policy
makers, such convergence was remarkably slow. In fact, as Figure
2.1 shows, inflation convergence was never achieved. To judge
from the three heterodox programmes of the 1960s, this slow
adjustment was nothing new.

Given the nonconvergence of inflation in the tablitas, it is hardly
surprising that some analysts concluded (for instance, Dornbusch
1982) that wage and price controls should be part of a stabilization
package. Fiscal adjustment was viewed as a necessary, but not
sufficient, condition for a successful stabilization attempt due to the
inertial components of inflation. As a result, all four major
programmes of the 1980s resorted to price and wage controls.[37] As
Figure 2.1 illustrates, convergence continued to be a problem,
although not as severe as before. Even in successful programmes
such as Israel's and Mexico's, inflation has yet to converge to the
policy-determined devaluation rate.

(2) Sustained real appreciation of the domestic currency. Given the
slow convergence of inflation, it is hardly surprising that the real
exchange rate, defined as the relative price of traded goods in terms
of nontraded goods, fell during most plans (see Figure 2.2).[38]
Sustained real appreciation proved to be fatal for most programmes,
because it led to unsustainable trade and current account deficits.
Failed programmes are thus characterized by U-shaped curves for
the real exchange rate. The largest appreciations occurred in the
tablitas. In both Argentina and Uruguay, the real exchange rate (set
to 100 in the quarter before the programme was implemented) had
halved by the time the programmes ended (see Tables 2A.5 and
2A.7 in the Appendix).

(3) The current account and the trade balance deteriorate. As a result
of the real appreciation, the current account deteriorated as shown
in Figure 2.3.[39] In Chile the current account deficit reached 14.5

Figure 2.1 Inflation and Devaluation (Percentage Change Over Same Quarter of Previous Year, Monthly Rate)

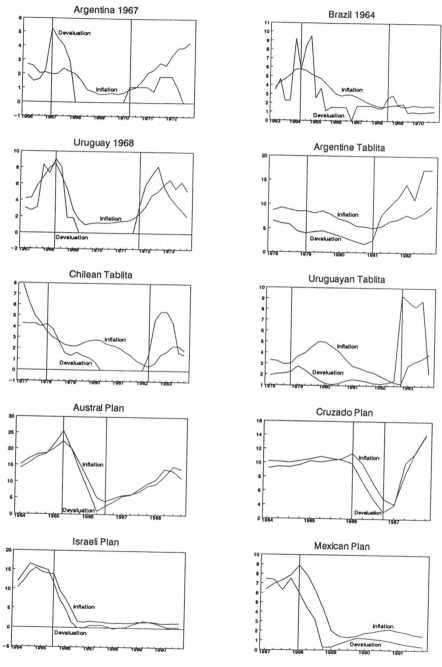

Source: IMF, <u>International Financial Statistics</u> (various issues).

Figure 2.2 Real Effective Exchange Rates

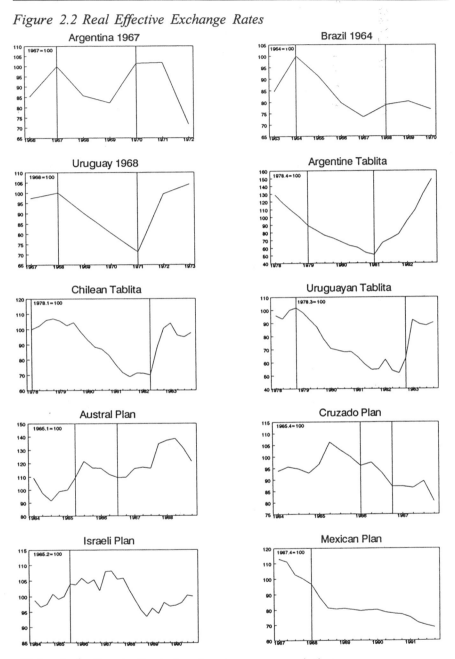

Note: A decline in the index denotes an appreciation.
Source: Tables 2A.2-2A.11, appendix.

Figure 2.3 Current Account (Millions of U.S. Dollars)

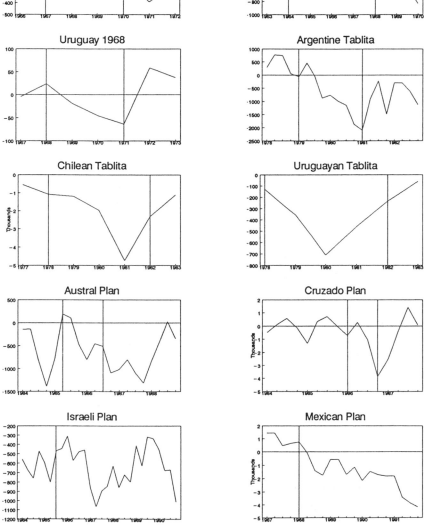

Source: IMF, Internationnal Financial Statistics (various issues).

*Note: Data are quarterly, except for Argentina 1967, Brazil 1964, Uruguay 1968, Chilean tablita, and Uruguayan tablita, where annual data are used.

For Israel, the figures correspond to the trade balance. A minus number indicates a deficit.

of GDP in 1981, and in the Uruguayan tablita, it reached 7 per cent of GDP in 1980. Current account deficits were financed by large capital inflows. This is particularly evident in the southern cone tablitas (see Tables 2A.5-2A.7 in the Appendix). In Chile, for instance, capital inflows reached a peak of US$4,800 million (15 per cent of GDP) in 1981. The trade balance also deteriorated substantially (see Tables 2A.2-2A.11). Large increases in imports of durable goods played a key role in the deterioration of the trade balance (see the evidence reported in Drazen 1990).

(4) Real activity increases at the beginning of the programme and later contracts. The peculiar phenomenon of an initial expansion in an inflation stabilization programme — traditionally viewed as generating initial output losses — was brought to the forefront by the southern cone tablitas of the late 1970s. As illustrated in Figure 2.4, real private consumption (real GDP for Uruguay) increased sharply in the first stages of the tablita programmes.[40] Later — and in the cases of Chile and Uruguay even *before* the programmes ended — a sharp contraction in consumption (and output) occurred. With the heterodox programmes of the mid-1980s, this issue came alive once again. The case of Israel was particularly striking because the same boom-recession cycle was observed in spite of the success of the programme.[41] The same pattern characterized the heterodox programmes of the 1960s, with the exception of Brazil. Kiguel and Liviatan (1992a) analysed 12 stabilization plans (which include the 10 depicted in Figure 2.4) and concluded that the boom-recession cycle in real output remains even when considered relative to the trend.

3.   THE MODEL

This section presents an analytical framework, based on Calvo and Végh (1993), which will prove useful in interpreting the evidence presented in the previous section. Since the model is described in detail elsewhere, most formal derivations will be bypassed and emphasis will be placed on the results and their intuition.

Consider a small open economy with predetermined exchange rates. There are two (nonstorable) goods: a tradeable good, c^*, and a nontradeable (or home) good, c. The representative consumer maximizes

Figure 2.4 Real Private Consumption (Percentage Change Over Same Quarter of Previous Year)

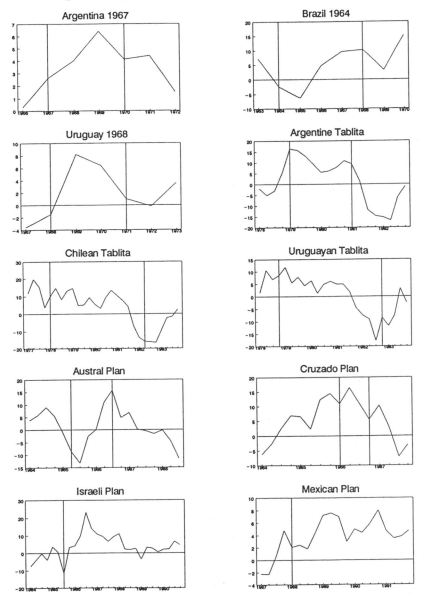

Note: For Argentina 1967, Brazil 1964, and Uruguay 1968, annual percentage changes.
Source: Tables 2.5-2.14, appendix.

$$\int_0^\infty [\log(c_t) + \log(c_t^*)]\exp(-\beta t)dt, \tag{2.1}$$

where β denotes the constant and positive subjective discount rate.

The consumer is required to use money to carry out purchases. The cash-in-advance constraint is thus

$$\alpha(c_t/e_t + c_t^*) = m_t, \tag{2.2}$$

where α is a positive constant, and e, the real exchange rate, is defined as the relative price of traded goods in terms of home goods; that is $e \equiv EP^*/P$, where E is the nominal exchange rate (in units of domestic currency per unit of foreign currency), P^* is the (constant) price of the traded good in foreign currency, and P is the domestic price of the home good.[42] Real money balances in terms of traded goods are denoted by m; that is, $m \equiv M/EP^*$, where M stands for nominal domestic money balances.

The consumer holds an internationally traded bond, b, which bears a constant real interest rate (in terms of traded goods) equal to r. Real financial wealth, a, is thus $a_t = m_t + b_t$. The lifetime constraint faced by the consumer is

$$a_0 + \int_0^\infty (y_t/e_t + y_t^* + \tau_t)\exp(-rt)dt \ =$$

$$\int_0^\infty (c_t/e_t + c_t^* + i_t m_t)\exp(-rt)dt, \tag{2.3}$$

where a_0 denotes initial real financial wealth; y and y^* stand for output of home and traded goods, respectively; τ denotes real transfers from the government; and i stands for the domestic nominal interest rate. Equation (2.3) equates the consumer's lifetime expenditure to his or her lifetime resources. The consumer's expenditure includes the 'rental' cost of real money balances, *im*.

The consumer's optimization problem consists in choosing optimal paths of c_t, c_t^*, and m_t to maximize his or her lifetime utility (equation (2.1)) subject to the cash-in-advance constraint (equation (2.2)), and the intertemporal budget constraint (equation (2.3)), given his or her initial real financial wealth, a_0, and the paths of y_t, y_t^*, τ_t, and e_t. The first-order conditions are (in addition to equations (2.2) and (2.3)).

$$1/c_t^* = \lambda(1 + \alpha i_t),$$ (2.4)

and

$$c_t = e_t c_t^*,$$ (2.5)

where λ is the (time-invariant) Lagrange multiplier associated with constraint (2.3), which can be interpreted as the marginal utility of wealth.[43] Equation (2.4) is the familiar condition whereby the consumer equates the marginal utility of consumption of traded goods to the marginal utility of wealth times the 'price' of traded goods. In the present context, the relevant price of the traded good — which will be referred to as the *effective* price — consists of the market price (unity) plus the opportunity cost of holding the α units of real money balances that are necessary to purchase the good, αi. Equation (2.5) indicates that the consumer equates the marginal rate of substitution between traded and home goods to the relative price of traded goods in terms of home goods (that is, the real exchange rate).

Perfect capital mobility implies that

$$i_t = r + \varepsilon_t,$$ (2.6)

so that the nominal rate interest falls, one-to-one, with the rate of devaluation.

Consider now the supply side of the economy. It will be assumed that the economy is endowed with a constant flow endowment of the tradeable good, y^*. The supply of the home good is demand determined and follows the staggered-prices model of Calvo (1983).[44] Calvo (1983) showed that the *rate of change* of the inflation rate is *negatively* related to excess demand. Formally

$$\dot{\pi}_t = -\theta D_t,$$ (2.7)

where $\pi(\equiv \dot{P}/P)$ is the rate of inflation of home goods; and D, a measure of excess demand in the home goods market, is defined as $D_t = y_t - \bar{y}$, where $\bar{y}$ can be interpreted as the full-employment level of output. Equation (2.7) can be derived in a framework in which firms set prices in a non-synchronous manner, taking into account the expected future path of excess demand and of the average price prevailing in the economy. Since only a small number of firms may change their individual prices at any point in time, the price level is a predetermined variable; but inflation is free to jump, because it reflects changes in individual prices charged by firms. When higher demand emerges, some firms increase their individual prices, and thus, inflation rises. Over time, the proportion of firms that have yet to respond to excess demand declines, so that inflation falls over time. Hence, the change in inflation is a negative function of aggregate demand, as equation (2.7) indicates.

Imposing equilibrium in the home goods market (that is, $c_t = y_t$) and using equation (2.5) and the definition of excess aggregate demand, equation (2.7) can be rewritten as

$$\dot{\pi}_t = \theta(\bar{y} - e_t c_t^*). \tag{2.8}$$

Differentiating $e = EP^*/P$ with respect to time yields (recalling that P^* is assumed constant)

$$\dot{e}_t = (\varepsilon_t - \pi_t)e_t. \tag{2.9}$$

For given paths of c^* and the policy variable ε, equations (2.8) and (2.9) form a dynamic system for π and e.[45]

To close the model, aggregate resource constraints need to be considered. Assuming that the government transfers back to the public interest income on net foreign assets and revenues from money creation, it can be shown (see Calvo and Végh 1993) that the economy's resource constraint is

$$k_0 + y^*/r = \int_0^\infty c_t^* \exp(-rt)dt, \tag{2.10}$$

where k_0 denotes the economy's initial stock of foreign bonds. Equation (2.10) states that the present value of tradeable resources must equal the present value of consumption of traded goods. Under the assumption that domestic credit just compensates the consumer for the depreciation of nominal money balances, the current account is given by

$$\dot{k}_t = y^* + rk_t - c_t^*, \tag{2.11}$$

which indicates that the current account balance is the difference between traded goods income and consumption of traded goods.

3.1 Permanent Reduction in Devaluation Rate

Consider now a permanent reduction in the rate of devaluation. Specifically, suppose that at time 0 (the present), policymakers announce that the rate of devaluation will be reduced immediately from ε^h to ε^l. Moreover, the announcement is *fully credible*; that is, the public expects the rate of devaluation to remain at the lower level, ε^l, forever.

At time 0, the nominal interest falls by the same amount as the rate of devaluation, as indicated by equation (2.6). Since the policy is fully credible, the nominal interest rate is expected to remain at the lower level, $r + \varepsilon^l$, forever. This implies that the consumption of traded goods does not change. The reason is that a constant nominal interest rate, no matter what the level is, implies, by first-order condition (2.4), that consumption of traded goods is constant over time. Even if the effective price of consumption is reduced, the fact that it remains constant over time implies that there are no incentives to engage in intertemporal consumption substitution. Since tradeable resources do not change, consumption of traded goods must remain at the same level.

From the system (2.8) and (2.9), it follows that, given that c^* is not affected by permanent changes in the rate of devaluation, a fall in π that exactly matches the fall in ε immediately moves the system to a new steady state. Naturally, the (average) inflation rate of the economy, which is a weighted average of the inflation rate of home goods, π, and that of traded goods ε, also falls instantaneously to its new level, ε^l. Therefore, *an exchange rate-based stabilization programme that is fully credible reduces the inflation rate instantaneously at no real costs.*

It is worth emphasizing that, even though the price level is sticky and individual prices are set in a staggered manner, no real effects result from a reduction in the devaluation rate that is perceived as being permanent. This shows, as emphasized by Calvo and Végh (1993), that price level rigidity does not, by itself, imply stickiness in the inflation rate. The reason is that in this framework, firms act in a forward-looking manner.[46]

4. STOPPING HYPERINFLATION

Despite its simplicity, the exercise just undertaken analysing the effects of a permanent reduction in the rate of devaluation provides a useful conceptual framework for discussing the end of hyperinflations. The reason, as this section argues, is that the model captures two distinguishing characteristics of hyperinflations: the absence of backward-looking behaviour, and the presence of a high degree of credibility. Hence, it seems reasonable to identify, if only as a first approximation, the above analytical exercise with experiences of stopping hyperinflation.

4.1 Absence of Backward-Looking Behaviour

The disappearance of long-term nominal contracts in hyperinflation episodes is a recurrent theme in the literature (see, for instance, Cagan 1989). Furthermore, a key characteristic of hyperinflations is that at some point all prices become indexed to the nominal exchange rate. Wage contracts, for instance, are renegotiated more frequently as inflation accelerates. At first, wage readjustments are based on a cost of living index. As the interval between readjustments becomes shorter, however, the cost of living index must be replaced by another index that is available on a weekly or even daily basis. The quotation of a foreign currency — usually the US dollar — provides such an index; the dollar quotation is available on a continuous basis and is widely circulated.

The de facto indexation of all prices in the economy to the foreign exchange implies that nominal contracts virtually cease to exist. Thus, all backward-looking behaviour is eradicated from the economy. Since one of the key features of the model presented in section 3 is the absence of backward-looking behaviour, the model can be taken to apply to hyperinflation episodes.

4.2 High Credibility

It has been argued (see, for instance, Kiguel and Liviatan 1988) that two characteristics of hyperinflationary processes make a stabilization attempt more credible than attempts to stop chronic inflation.

First, the need for seigniorage (that is, revenues from money creation) as the cause of high inflation comes across more clearly in hyperinflations than in chronic inflations. Since the fiscal nature of the inflationary process is more obvious, the public may become more easily convinced that closing the budget deficit is enough to ensure price stability. In contrast, in chronic-inflation countries, the relationship between inflation and revenues from money creation is much less clear, which may raise doubts in people's minds as to whether a fiscal reform — even if successfully implemented — may be enough to halt inflation. Thus, given that in hyperinflations the source of the inflationary process is easily identified and widely agreed upon, the announcement of a stabilization programme that includes a fiscal reform should command a high degree of credibility.

The second factor that may increase the credibility of a stabilizatíon programme is that hyperinflation creates such a chaotic social and economic environment that the public becomes convinced that the situation is untenable. This sense of urgency in tackling the problem is likely to lend more credibility to a stabilization programme. In contrast, chronic-inflation countries learn how to live with high inflation by adopting various indexation mechanisms. An example of this ability to adapt to chronic inflation can be observed in the behaviour of real revenues from taxation. In hyperinflations, the Olivera-Tanzi effect drastically reduces real revenues from taxation; this is not the case in chronic inflations (see Kiguel and Liviatan 1988).

There is also more direct evidence on the presence of high credibility in hyperinflation stabilizations. As emphasized by Sargent (1982), the real monetization of the economies in which hyperinflation was successfully stopped is dramatic.[47] In the aftermath of stabilization, monthly growth rates of notes in circulation above 10 per cent alongside a basically stable price level have been observed in many episodes (Germany, Hungary 1946, Greece and Poland), as shown in Table 2.2. In Hungary 1946, for instance, notes in circulation increased by a factor of 4.9 in the 12 months following stabilization.[48] Such enormous increases in real money balances can only be attributed to a drastic reduction in inflationary expectations, as a result of the high credibility of the programme.

4.3 Matching Theory with Evidence

It has been argued that backward-looking behaviour all but disappears during hyperinflations and that attempts to stop hyperinflations enjoy high credibility. Therefore, the analytical experiment undertaken in section 3, which assumes full credibility in the context of a model in which there is no backward-looking behaviour, may be considered a reasonable first approximation to understanding hyperinflation stabilization.

The next step is to match theory with evidence. If full credibility is assumed, the model predicts that stabilizing the nominal exchange rate should lead to an immediate halt in inflation at no real cost. This prediction is in accordance with the evidence provided in section 2: price stability has been achieved overnight with relatively small output costs. The costs that did emerge are more attributable to real dislocations — sometimes policy induced, such as Germany's policy of subsidizing the capital goods industry with the inflation tax — than to the monetary stabilization itself.

Admittedly, the model is a highly stylized version of the real world and ignores many important aspects, in particular supply-side and structural considerations that have played an important role in past hyperinflations. But its usefulness lies precisely in its simplicity, because it isolates what is regarded as key aspects in actual episodes. Furthermore, by enriching the formulation of the supply side, the same model could be used to tackle real sector considerations.

5. STOPPING CHRONIC INFLATION

This section will interpret the evidence presented in section 1 on stopping chronic inflation in terms of the analytical model developed in section 3.[49] The key assumption behind the analytical exercise developed in this section is that there is lack of credibility. Unlike programmes designed to stop hyperinflation, stabilization attempts in chronic-inflation countries are likely to suffer from lack of credibility. Chronic-inflation countries have learned to live with high inflation and, as a result, the incentives to eradicate inflation are much lower than in hyperinflations. Furthermore, given past failures, policymakers will have a hard time convincing a sceptical public that the current stabilization plan will be sustained over time.

The spreads between domestic and devaluation-adjusted foreign interest rates provide at least a crude measure of credibility. Large positive spreads suggest lack of credibility, since they indicate that the public expected a devaluation (under a fixed exchange rate) or a larger devaluation than the one preannounced (in a tablita programme). Tables 2A.5-2A.11 in the Appendix show the presence of large spreads throughout the programmes, except, as one would expect, in the quarters preceding a nonscheduled devaluation.[50] In the Argentine tablita (Table 2A.5 in the Appendix), for instance, the spread reaches its maximum of 45.7 per cent (in annual terms) in the third quarter of 1980. In the following quarter the spread becomes negative, reflecting the devaluation that finally ended the programme. In Mexico (Table 2A.11 in the Appendix), the spread has been positive since the beginning of the programme. It declined, however, during 1989 as the authorities switched from a fixed exchange rate to a constant (in absolute terms) daily devaluation.

Lack of credibility will be modelled as temporary policy. Suppose that at time 0 policymakers announce a permanent reduction in the devaluation rate, but the public believes that the stabilization will be abandoned at some time T in the future. Under this scenario, the public acts as though the reduction in the devaluation rate were temporary. Hence, the effects of temporary policy may be reinterpreted as arising from noncredible policy. Formally, then, consider a temporary reduction in the rate of devaluation. Suppose that initially (that is, prior to time 0), the rate of devaluation is ε^h. At time 0, the expected path becomes

$$\varepsilon_t = \varepsilon^l, \qquad \text{for } 0 \le t < T, \qquad\qquad (2.12a)$$

$$\varepsilon_t = \varepsilon^h, \qquad \text{for } t \ge T, \qquad\qquad (2.12b)$$

where $T > 0$ and $\varepsilon^h > \varepsilon^l$. The rate of devaluation falls at time 0 but is expected to increase back to its original level at time T.

The lower rate of devaluation during the period $[0,t)$ — hereafter referred to as the 'transition' — implies, by the assumption of perfect capital mobility (equation (2.6), that the path of the nominal interest rate is given by $i_t = r+\varepsilon^l$, for $0 \le t < T$, and $i_t = r+\varepsilon^h$, for $t \ge T$. Since the nominal interest rate is time invariant (that is, its time derivative is zero), the first-order condition (equation (2.4)) indicates that consumption of traded goods is time invariant, even though its level may change. Because the nominal interest rate is lower during the transition than it is after T, equation (2.4) shows that consumption of traded goods is higher during the transition than afterwards (recall that λ does not change at T). The reason is that the effective price of consumption is lower during the transition. Since the resource constraint (equation (2.10)) must be satisfied for any equilibrium path, consumption of traded goods during the transition will be above initial permanent income of traded goods, while consumption of traded goods after T will be below initial permanent income of traded goods (see Figure 2.5, panel A).[51] Otherwise, the resource constraint would be violated.

The current account path, which follows from the consumption path just described and equation (2.11), is illustrated in Figure 2.5, panel B. At time 0, the current account jumps into deficit because of the sudden increase in consumption of traded goods. During the transition (that is, for $0 \le t < T$), the trade deficit remains constant but the current account deteriorates because interest income on net foreign assets declines. At time T, the current account jumps into balance. As discussed in section 2, the current account has deteriorated substantially throughout the different programmes (see Figure 2.3). The current account deficit usually reflects sizeable trade deficits (see Tables 2A.2-2A.11 in the Appendix).

Figure 2.5, panel C, illustrates the time path of inflation of home goods.[52] On impact, there are two effects on the inflation rate of home goods that go in opposite direction. On the one hand, the lower rate of devaluation exerts a dampening effect on inflation of home goods. On the other hand, aggregate demand increases (see below), which tends to push

Figure 2.5 Temporary Reduction in Devaluation Rate

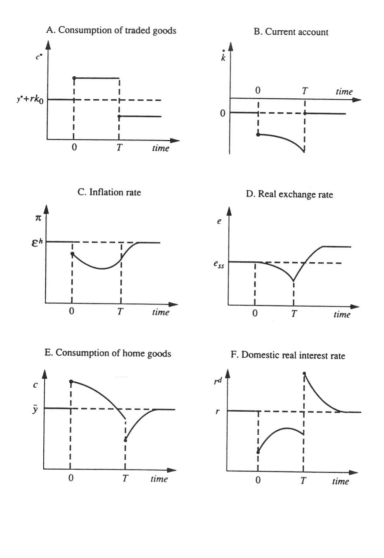

inflation up. In the absence of the aggregate demand effect, inflation of home goods would fall, one-to-one, with the rate of devaluation (which is what happens under full credibility). However, because of the aggregate demand effect, the rate of inflation of home goods falls by less than the rate of devaluation, and could even increase. Inflation falls over time at the beginning of the programme but later begins to rise in anticipation of the expected resumption of the higher devaluation rate.[53] When time T is reached, the authorities face the choice of abandoning the programme (thus validating the public's expectations) or sticking to the lower rate of devaluation. If the authorities abandon the programme, inflation continues to increase toward its initial level, as in Figure 2.5, panel C. If the authorities stick to the stabilization plan, then inflation jumps downwards at time T and converges from below to the lower devaluation rate.

The (average) inflation rate of the economy is a weighted average of the inflation rate of traded goods, ε, and the rate of inflation of home goods, π, with the weights depending on the weight of traded and home goods in the utility function. Since the devaluation rate is constant, the inflation rate exhibits the same qualitative behaviour during the transition as inflation of home goods. The model thus predicts that, due to lack of credibility, the inflation rate exhibits inertia. The U-shaped time profile of inflation predicted by the model is typical of that observed in failed programmes (which include all the programmes depicted in Figure 2.1, except Israel and Mexico).[54] The behaviour of inflation in successful plans, such as Israel and Mexico, is consistent with the assumption that policymakers stuck to the stabilization plan.

Panel D in Figure 2.5 illustrates the behaviour of the real exchange rate.[55] The real exchange rate falls during the transition (that is, there is a real appreciation of the domestic currency), because the inflation rate of home goods is always above the rate of devaluation. At time T, whether or not the plan is abandoned, the real exchange rate begins to increase (that is, there is a real depreciation).[56] If the plan is not abandoned, inflation falls below the devaluation rate to generate the real depreciation.

This U-shaped time profile of the real exchange rate predicted by the model is the one that has generally been observed in practice (see Figure 2.2).

Consider now the time path of consumption of home goods illustrated in Figure 2.5, panel E. On impact, as already noted, consumption of home goods increases as follows from equation (2.5) and the increase in c^*. Intuitively, since the relative price of home goods in terms of traded goods has not changed, there are no incentives to change consumption of home goods relative to consumption of traded goods. During the transition, consumption of home goods falls as the real exchange rate decreases (that is, the relative price of home goods increases). If T is large enough, the economy enters into recession (that is, output falls below its full-employment level) before the plan is expected to be discontinued. For a small T, output will remain above its full-employment level during all of the transition. At time T, consumption of home goods jumps downwards, accompanying the fall in consumption of traded goods. After T, the real exchange rate increases, and therefore consumption of home goods rises.

The evidence depicted in Figure 2.4 for private consumption is consistent with the predictions of the model, in that there is an early consumption boom followed by a contraction. Moreover, in two of the longest programmes (Uruguay, 17 quarters; and Chile, 18 quarters), consumption fell *before* the end of the programmes. In Uruguay, as Table 2A.7 in the Appendix indicates, the annual rate of change of consumption was negative in 1980 and the four-quarter change in real GDP turned negative in the last quarter of 1981, one year before the end of the programme. In Chile, the four-quarter change in both private consumption and real GDP turned negative in the fourth quarter of 1981, two quarters before the end of the programme. If one identifies the actual duration of the programme with T, this fact is consistent with the prediction that the higher is T, the more likely it is that the contractions will take place before the programme ends. Even if the programme is not abandoned at T, the behaviour of real variables remains the same, as argued above. Hence, the model is also capable of rationalizing consumption patterns such as Israel's, where the recession took place in spite of the success of the programme.

Consider now the time path of the domestic real interest rate (that is, $r^d = i\text{-}\pi$), which is illustrated in Figure 2.5, panel F. The inflation rate of home goods falls by less on impact than the nominal interest rate does; therefore, the domestic real interest rate falls on impact. During the transition, the domestic real interest rate stays below its initial level. At time T, the domestic real interest rate jumps upwards, owing to the sudden increase in the nominal interest rate. The domestic real interest rate falls afterwards towards its unchanged steady-state value, given that inflation increases.

The predictions of the model with respect to the behaviour of the real interest rate seem to hold for the Southern cone programmes but not for the rest of the programmes.[57] The Uruguayan tablita (Table 2A.7 in the Appendix) is the best example: the (*ex post*) real lending rate fell substantially when the programme was implemented and was negative during the first three quarters of 1979. In 1980 it became positive and reached a peak of 48.2 per cent (in annual terms) in the fourth quarter of 1981, undoubtedly contributing to the contraction in economic activity. In the Argentine tablita (Table 2A.5 in the Appendix), the real lending rate was also negative in the first two quarters of the programme (even if it increased with respect to the fourth quarter of 1978). In the Chilean tablita (Table 2A.6 in the Appendix), the real lending rate fell from very high levels, reaching 5.8 per cent, six quarters into the programme.

In the rest of the programmes for which data are available (the four heterodox programmes of the mid-1980s), real interest rates increased (see Tables 2A.8-2A.11 in the Appendix). A possible explanation for this phenomenon lies in the use of additional nominal anchors. The Israeli 1985 plan, for instance, had an explicit target for bank credit, which was to be achieved by a combination of higher reserve requirements and a higher discount rate (see Barkai 1990). The idea was to offset the expansionary effects of a large increase in credit to the private sector. In fact, credit to the private sector declined in real terms at the beginning of the programme, which may explain the initial (although brief) downturn in the last two quarters of 1985. In contrast, in the southern cone tablitas, real credit grew strongly. Analytically, high interest rates can be rationalized by modelling the use of additional monetary anchors (see Calvo and Végh 1991).

In summary, a noncredible, exchange rate-based stabilization yields predictions that are generally consistent with the stylized facts. In particular, the model generates a boom-recession cycle and U-shaped curves for both inflation and the real exchange rate, as has been observed in most programmes. The key missing ingredient in explaining high real interest rates at the beginning of the programme seems to be the presence of additional nominal anchors.

6. FINAL REMARKS

This last section discusses the quantitative importance of lack of credibility (or the 'temporariness' hypothesis) in explaining the observed consumption booms and the role of backward indexation, and then offers some concluding remarks.[58]

6.1 Quantitative Relevance of the Temporariness Hypothesis

A crucial, and relatively unexplored, question is the quantitative relevance of the temporariness hypothesis. Given that intertemporal elasticities of substitution are generally low, it is not clear whether models that rely on intertemporal substitution effects can explain the magnitude of observed rises in consumption. Since what triggers all effects in the model is the temporary (as perceived by the public) fall in the nominal interest rate relevant for consumption decisions, a first question is whether nominal deposit interest rates (that is, the interest rate relevant for consumption decisions) have fallen in different programmes. Figure 2.6 shows that in the four heterodox programmes of the mid-1980s (Austral, Cruzado, Israeli and Mexican), deposit rates did indeed fall dramatically. [59] In the southern cone tablitas, however, the fall was considerably less, particularly in Uruguay where the deposit rate soon reached its initial level.

The empirical question is therefore: can the observed fall in nominal interest rates account for a sizeable fraction of the rise in private consumption in a temporariness model? A first attempt to answer this question can be found in Reinhart and Végh (1992). Using estimates of the intertemporal elasticities of their own and other available estimates, they concluded, based on a very simple simulation exercise, that the temporariness hypothesis accounted for an important fraction (over 60 per cent) of the actual increase in consumption in the four heterodox programmes of the 1980s. [60] In contrast, it only accounts for less than 15 per cent in the tablitas. The key difference, as discussed above, is that in the four heterodox programmes, nominal interest rates dropped sharply, whereas in the southern cone tablitas, the fall was considerably less. An important caveat is that durable goods, which are likely to play a crucial role in any empirical application, are not modelled. Elasticities of substitution are bound to be higher if a distinction is made between durable and nondurable goods as found by Fauvel and Samson (1991) for Canada. [61]

Therefore, although further work is warranted, Reinhart and Végh's (1992) results suggest that some other factors (for instance, negative or falling real interest rates) may have played an important role in the tablitas.

6.2 Backward Indexation

In the model presented in section 2, inflation 'stickiness' results from lack of credibility. Alternatively, inflation inertia could result from backward-looking behaviour. [62] In this spirit, Rodriguez (1982) assumed adaptive expectations and showed how, due to an initial fall in real interest rates, there would be a consumption boom. In a setting of rational expectations, Calvo and Végh (1994a) incorporated backward-looking contracts in a model similar to that of section 2 and, in contrast to Rodriguez (1982), concluded that a fully credible, exchange rate-based stabilization will lead to a recession if the intertemporal elasticity of substitution is smaller than the elasticity of substitution between traded and home goods (which seems

Figure 2.6 Nominal Deposit Interest Rates (Per cent per Year)

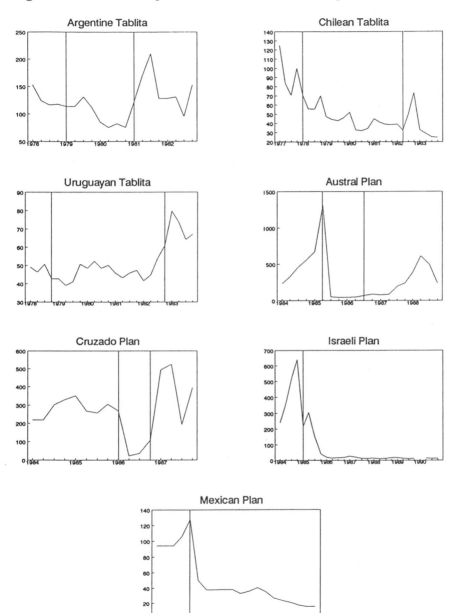

Source: Tables 2A.2-2A.11, appendix.

to be the relevant case in practice; see Ostry and Reinhart 1992).

Intuitively, the real appreciation of the domestic real interest rate has both expansionary effects — since it reduces the domestic real interest rate — and recessionary effects — since it increases the relative price of home goods. Hence, backward-looking contracts, *per se*, may not be capable of explaining the observed expansion. If, in addition, there is lack of credibility, then the net effect on consumption will still depend on the configuration parameter, but an increase in consumption becomes more likely since the temporariness effect is always expansionary. Hence, the key ingredient in explaining a consumption boom appears to be lack of credibility and not backward indexation.

6.3 Conclusions

A unified theoretical framework has been used to interpret the main stylized facts associated with stopping both hyperinflation and chronic inflation. The model predicts that, in the absence of backward indexation, a credible stabilization programme stops inflation in its tracks with no real effects. This experiment was taken as a reasonable first approximation to a hyperinflationary situation. Although the evidence regarding the output costs of stopping hyperinflation is spotty and subject to debate, a good case can be made that hyperinflation has, in fact, been stopped suddenly with no major costs. The contractionary forces that have come into play seem to result from real distortions brought about by hyperinflation rather than by monetary stabilization itself.

A noncredible reduction in the rate of devaluation has been used to interpret stabilization in chronic-inflation countries. The model predicts a slow convergence of the inflation rate, a boom-recession cycle in the home goods sector, a current account deficit and real appreciation of the domestic currency. This is consistent with the key stylized facts observed in these episodes. The model also predicts a fall in domestic real interest rates on implementation of the programme. This prediction is consistent with the experience of the southern cone tablitas, but not with that of the major heterodox plans of the mid-1980s.

The model used in this chapter, based on Calvo and Végh (1993), appears to offer a reasonably good description of reality and should prove useful as a benchmark for interpreting the outcome of stabilization programmes in high-inflation countries. Naturally, many issues remain to be further analyzed, but three seem to stand out.

First, the behaviour of real interest rates in the aftermath of stabilization programmes deserves further attention, from an analytical point of view. Contrary to common perceptions, lack of credibility does not necessarily generate high real interest rates. As mentioned above, additional nominal anchors are likely to be a key ingredient. In this respect, the issue of tight credit policy during stabilization policy, an issue raised by Barkai (1990) for the case of Israel, seems crucial.

Second, the role of credibility needs to be endogenized. The model analysed in the chapter takes the existence of credibility, or the lack thereof, as exogenous to the model. As long as credibility has an exogenous component — given, for instance, by past experiences — the essence of the model should not change. Common sense suggests, however, that credibility is gained or lost as a programme unfolds, since the evolution of the different variables (for instance, the real exchange rate) provides valuable information regarding the sustainability of the programme.[63] Casual evidence suggests that credibility often follows an inverted U-shaped pattern, rising at first and decreasing later. This credibility pattern has been found in the Cruzado Plan (Agénor and Taylor 1992). Guidotti and Végh (1991) developed a model of endogenous credibility in which this pattern arises.

Finally, it would be important to model supply-side considerations that may come into play in periods of high inflation, and study the interaction between real factors and monetary stabilization. This is bound to be particularly useful in understanding stabilization programmes in Eastern Europe and the former Soviet Union where high inflation and structural changes are likely to coexist in the foreseeable future.

ENDNOTES

* The author is grateful to Pierre-Richard Agénor, Saúl Lizondo, Peter Montiel, and, especially, Mohsin Khan, Carmen Reinhart and Ratna Sahay for helpful comments and suggestions. This paper has greatly benefited from the author's joint work with Guillermo Calvo on inflation stabilization. Reprinted with permission from *International Monetary Fund Staff Papers*, Vol. 39 (September 1992), pp. 626-95.

1. As discussed below, the 1985 Bolivian stabilization, characterized by a 'dirty' floating, is an exception to this rule. The exchange rate, however, stabilized immediately and acted as a de facto nominal anchor.

2. It is worth emphasizing that, in the model, inflation 'inertia' results from the lack of credibility and not from backward-looking indexation.

3. Cagan (1956, p. 25) defines hyperinflation 'as beginning in the month the rise in prices exceeds 50 percent and as ending in the month before the monthly rise in prices drops below that amount and stays below for at least a year'.

4. Pazos (1972, p. 19), commenting on the inflation rate during the German hyperinflation, points out that 'oscillations were so large and so erratic that the chart [of the inflation rate] seems to register the movements of an object that has been let loose in a frictionless environment and is reacting, without offering resistance, to the external forces being applied to it'.

5. In Argentina, for instance, inflation rates of close to 30 per cent in the mid-1960s were viewed as intolerable, prompting the 1967 stabilization plan, which brought inflation down to 7.6 per cent in 1969. By today's standards, such rates would still provoke uneasiness but would certainly not be looked upon as unacceptable. Changes in public perception about inflation are not merely confined to developing countries. In the United States, for instance, inflation rates of around 5 per cent, which are viewed with complacency today, prompted the Nixon administration to impose price controls in August 1971.

6. In particular, note that in these three countries, with one exception (Argentina in 1969, as a result of the 1967 stabilisation plan), inflation has never been in the single digits in the last three decades. In contrast, in the United States inflation has been below 10 per cent in all but four years since 1961.

7. Long periods of chronic inflation may eventually lead to hyperinflation: the monthly inflation rate reached 76.5 per cent in Argentina in May 1989, and 51.5 per cent in Brazil in December 1989. However, these hyperinflationary outbursts, which represent an explosive stage of a long period of chronic inflation, have different characteristics from the traditional hyperinflations studied below (see Kiguel and Liviatan 1992b).

8. In all four successful stabilizations (Chile, Bolivia, Israel and Mexico), annual inflation has remained around 20 per cent, still well above inflation in the United States, which averaged 4.7 per cent during the 1980s. The reasons why inflation has failed to come down to international levels remain unclear.

9. Annual data from 1900 to 1913 (for a cost of living index) are from Mitchell (1975). Annual data from 1914 onwards (for wholesale prices) are from Bresciani-Turroni (1937).

10. As suggested above, Pazos (1972) associates high oscillations of the inflation rate with hyperinflationary periods. In effect, the evidence suggests that there is a positive correlation between the mean and the standard deviation of monthly inflation, so that the standard deviation is highest during hyperinflations (see Végh 1991).

11. The world's record inflation, according to Cagan (1989), occurred in Hungary after World War II, when prices rose by an average monthly rate of 19,800 per cent between August 1945 and July 1946 and 4.2×10^{16} per cent in the peak month of July.

12. Dates in parentheses indicate the hyperinflationary period. These episodes have been studied by, among many others, Cagan (1959), Dornbusch and Fischer (1986), Rostowski (1992), Sargent (1982) Wicker (1986), and Yeager (1981). See also Végh (1991) and the references therein.

13. On Hungary, see Bomberger and Makinen (1983) and Siklos (1989); on Greece, see Makinen (1984). The end of the Greek hyperinflation, December 1945, differs from Cagan's (1956) date of November 1944, because inflation fell below 50 per cent per month only until August 1945.

14. All references to Taiwan for the period 1945-52 are to Taiwan Province of China. This hyperinflation was separate from the one taking place in mainland China, since Taiwan constituted a separate currency area.

15. See Sachs (1986) and Morales (1988). Table 2A.1 in the Appendix contains the main macroeconomic variables.

16. Private agents were allowed to buy and sell foreign exchange freely, but the central bank would sell foreign exchange rate to the public in a daily auction and buy foreign exchange at the average price fixed in the last auction. For each auction, the central bank would fix both a base price at which it would sell foreign exchange and the amount that it would offer; bidders would not have access to this information beforehand.

17. The discussion focuses on those aspects that are the most relevant for the discussion of the theoretical model in the next section.

18. With the exception of Bolivia (see the above discussion), the exchange rate was generally stabilized by fixing the value of the domestic currency in terms of gold or a foreign currency.

19. For the Polish, Greek and Taiwanese stabilizations, slightly different periods had to be considered because of insufficient data.
20. In the Taiwanese stabilization, the black market rate stood 60 per cent above the official rate six months after stabilization (see Makinen and Woodward 1989).
21. Naturally, this assertion should not be taken to mean that stabilizing the exchange rate is sufficient to ensure lasting price stability. If permanent fiscal measures are not taken, inflation may resume shortly. In the Greek stabilization, for instance, the successful stabilization of 24 January, 1946, was preceded by two failed attempts to stabilize (in November 1944 and June 1945). Inflation fell drastically immediately after the first two attempts (for two to four months), but came back with a vengeance shortly thereafter (see Makinen 1984). In Poland, there were also two failed stabilizations before the successful January 1924 plan (see Yeager 1981).
22. Sargent (1982) has been the chief proponent of this idea. The most influential dissenters are probably Garber (1982) and Wicker (1986).
23. It is not clear whether the figures on unemployed reported in Table 2.3b are comparable; see Makinen (1984).
24. Makinen and Woodward (1989) argue that growth before stabilization was artificially high due to the large-scale reconstruction after World War II and the use of the inflation tax to expand state enterprises and give subsidized loans.
25. Layton and Rist (1925) suggested that the explanation for the conflicting behaviour of output and unemployment in Austria during the winter of 1924-25 lay in the incentives to achieve greater efficiency provided by price stability. Specifically, firms could not pass on increases in costs in the form of higher prices and thus had an incentive to shed labour to become more efficient. Layton and Rist (1925, pp. 16-17) concluded that 'reorganization in the factories is thus the chief explanation of the apparent anomaly that unemployment has increased side by side with a steady improvement in economic activity'.
26. Beginning in March 1947, Hungary began to move to a centrally-planned system (in October 1948, the first three-year plan was introduced). Hence, figures for 1948 and beyond are not comparable.
27. As discussed below, inflation stabilization in chronic-inflation countries also leads to sizeable real effects.
28. Of course, in making this comparison one would like to take into account the fact that unlike inflationary periods in industrialized countries, output during hyperinflations is likely to have been well below potential.
29. Tables 2A.2 to 2A.11 in the Appendix contain the main macroeconomic indicators for each episode. Subject to data availability, the same variables are reported in all episodes to facilitate comparisons.
30. Dates refer to month of implementation of the programmes. On the Uruguayan 1968 stabilization plan, see Finch (1979) and Viana (1990). The Brazilian 1964 plan is discussed by Kakfa (1967), Pazos (1972) and Foxley (1980). The Argentine stabilization of 1967 is discussed by De Pablo (1974). Another heterodox programme of interest in Argentina is the Peronist stabilization of 1973-75 (see Di Tella 1989).
31. The Chilean stabilization consisted of two stages. From July 1976 to January 1978, the exchange rate began to be used explicitly for stabilization. Beginning in February 1978, a lasting preannounced schedule was introduced (see Corbo 1985).
32. These episodes are discussed, among many others, by Corbo (1985), Hanson and Melo (1985), Ramos (1986), Kiguel and Liviatan (1988) and Edwards (1991). Another orthodox stabilization programme of interest is the Argentine stabilization of 1959-62 (see Petrecolla 1989).
33. Discussions of these programmes can be found in, for instance, Dornbusch and Simonsen (1987), Kiguel and Liviatan (1989), Bruno et al. (1988), and Bruno et al. (1991).
34. Only those stylized facts relevant for the analytical discussion of the next sections are emphasized. See Kiguel and Liviatan (1992a) for a more complete discussion.

35. With the exception of the southern cone tablitas and the Cruzado Plan, there were initial maxidevaluations in all other programmes, which explains initial spikes in the four-quarter devaluation rate.
36. Vertical bars indicate the quarters in which the programmes were implemented and abandoned. When the programmes were implemented late in a given quarter (in particular, the Argentine tablita on 20 December 1978, and the Mexican Plan on 15 December 1987), the beginning of the programme was taken to be the following quarter.
37. The fiscal adjustment was all but absent, however, in Brazil and soon deteriorated in Argentina.
38. In Israel the depreciation of the dollar in international markets that began in 1985 explains the initial behaviour of the real exchange rate. To facilitate comparisons across different episodes, the initial real exchange rate (that is, the real exchange rate in the quarter before the plan was implemented) has been set equal to 100. When only annual data were available, the real exchange rate was set to 100 in the year in which the programme was implemented.
39. Current account figures for Israel are somewhat misleading due to the presence of grants, which explains why Figure 2.3 reports trade balance figures for Israel.
40. In Chile the boom in consumption had already begun during the first stage of the stabilization programme (July 1976-January 1978). Specifically, after falling by 11.4 per cent in 1975, consumption remained basically unchanged in 1976, and increased 16.0 per cent in 1977 (data from Central Bank of Chile). For Uruguay, consumption figures, available only on an annual basis, show the same pattern as real GDP (Table 2A.7 in the Appendix).
41. Note, however, that four years into the programme, Mexico is still enjoying a consumption boom.
42. Equation (2.2) already incorporates the fact that, given a positive nominal interest rate, the cash-in advance constraint will hold with equality at an optimum.
43. To ensure the existence of a steady state, it has been assumed that $\beta = r$.
44. For simplicity, it is assumed that only the price of the home good is sticky. For an alternative specification, see Calvo and Végh (1991b).
45. The determinant of the matrix associated with the linear approximation of the system (2.8) and (2.9) is negative, which indicates the existence of saddle-path stability.
46. This need not be the case in other models of staggered contracts. For instance, in Fischer's (1986) model, a permanent reduction in the rate of devaluation causes real effects, because the price established in the contract does not remain fixed during the life of the contract.
47. The cash-in-advance specification of the model implies that real money demand does not increase as a result of the fall in the nominal interest rate. The remonetization usually observed in actual episodes could be captured by introducing money as an argument in the utility function. In that case, a permanent reduction in the rate of devaluation would increase real money balances, while still leaving the consumption of either good unchanged.
48. In this respect, the Bolivian hyperinflation is more of an exception, in that remonetization has been slow. By 1991, the ratio of M1 to GDP was 6.7 per cent, up from 2.6 per cent in 1985 but still lower than prehyperinflationary levels (7.4 per cent in 1982; data from Morales (1988) and IMF, *International Financial Statistics*, various issues).
49. As argued in section 2, backward-looking behaviour is one of the main characteristics of chronic inflation. For analytical simplicity, this feature is ignored in the model (see the discussion in section 6).
50. Spreads are computed using the LIBOR rate and the one-quarter-ahead devaluation rate.
51. Initial permanent income is given by $y^* + rk_0$.
52. For a formal derivation, see Calvo and Végh (1991a).
53. This presumes that T is large. If T is small, π always falls during the transition (see Calvo and Végh 1991a).

54. It can also be shown that the less credible the programme, the lower the initial fall (or the larger the initial increase) in the inflation rate. Hence, as intuition would suggest, the initial behaviour of inflation is very much dependent on the credibility of the programme.
55. The steady-state real exchange rate increases because steady-state consumption of traded goods decreases while steady-state consumption of home goods remains constant at its full-employment level.
56. Calvo and Végh (1991a) show that all real effects remain the same no matter what the authorities do at time T (assuming, of course, that if the authorities stick to the plan, the public now sees it as permanent). Formally, once-and-for-all changes in the rate of devaluation are everywhere superneutral; that is, only nominal variables are affected.
57. Since *ex ante* real interest rates cannot be observed, the model's predictions are compared with *ex post* real interest rates. However, the comparison should be viewed as suggestive only, because, especially at the beginning of a stabilization programme, *ex post* real interest rates might differ substantially from *ex ante* real interest rates.
58. Policy conclusions that would follow from this framework are discussed in an earlier version of this paper (Végh 1991).
59. Considering the deposit rate in the quarter before the plan was implemented and its minimum value during the duration of the plan, deposit rates (in annual terms) fell from 671 per cent to 44.3 percent in the Austral Plan; from 305 per cent to 22.6 per cent in the Cruzado Plan; from 305.8 per cent to 11.9 per cent in the Israeli Plan; and from 106.1 per cent to 15.1 per cent in the Mexican Plan (see Tables 2A.8-2A.11 in the Appendix). The behaviour just described holds for lending rates or other nominal rates (see Tables 2A.8-2A.11 in the Appendix).
60. Bufman and Leiderman (1992) also emphasized the important role, from a quantitative point of view, that temporariness plays in explaining the consumption boom in Israel.
61. Needless to say, data availability is a formidable challenge when it comes to durable goods consumption in developing countries.
62. Pazos (1972) and Dornbusch and Simonsen (1987) discussed the notion of inflation inertia arising from backward indexation. Wage indexation based on past inflation was particularly important in the Chilean tablita (see Corbo 1985 and Edwards 1990). Since inflation was decreasing, backward-looking indexation resulted in a substantial increase in real wages (see Table 2A.7 in the Appendix).
63. Végh (1991) differentiates between *ex ante* credibility (how the public perceives the plan when it is implemented), and *ex post* credibility (credibility that is gained as the programme evolves).

REFERENCES

Agénor, P.-R. and Taylor, M. (1992), 'Testing for Credibility Effects', *Staff Papers*, International Monetary Fund, September, pp. 545-71.

Arrau, P. and De Gregorio, J. (1991), 'Financial Innovation and Money Demand: Theory and Empirical Implementation', Policy Research and External Affairs Working Paper No. 585, The World Bank, Washington, DC.

Baliño, T.J.T. (1991), 'The Argentine Banking Crisis of 1980', in *Banking Crises: Cases and Issues*, ed. by V. Sundararajan and T.J.T. Baliño, The International Monetary Fund, Washington, DC.

Barkai, H. (1990), 'The Role of Monetary Policy in Israel's 1985 Stabilization Effort', Working Paper 90/29, International Monetary Fund.

Bomberger, W.A. and Makinen, G.E. (1983), 'The Hungarian Hyperinflation and Stabilization of 1945-1946', *Journal of Political Economy*, Vol. 91, pp. 801-24.

Bresciani-Turroni, C. (1937), *The Economics of Inflation: A Study of Currency Depreciation in Post-War Germany*, G. Allen & Unwin, Ltd., London.

Bruno, M., Fischer, S., Helpman, E., and Liviatan, N. (eds.) (1991), *Lessons of Economic Stabilization and Its Aftermath*, MIT Press, Cambridge, Massachusetts.

Bruno, M., Di Tella, G., Dornbusch R., and Fischer S. (eds.) (1988), *Inflation Stabilization: The Experience of Israel, Argentina, Brazil, Bolivia, and Mexico*, MIT Press, Cambridge, Massachusetts.

Bufman, G. and Leiderman, L. (1992), 'Simulating an Optimizing Model of Currency Substitution', *Revista de Análisis Económico*, Vol. 7, pp. 109-124.

Cagan, P. (1956), 'The Monetary Dynamics of Hyperinflation', in M. Friedman (ed.), *Studies in the Quantity Theory of Money*, University of Chicago Press, Chicago.

————, (1989), 'Hyperinflation', in J. Eatwell, M. Milgate & P. Newman (eds.), *Money*, The Macmillan Press Limited, New York.

Calvo, G.A., (1983), 'Staggered Prices in a Utility-Maximizing Framework', *Journal of Monetary Economics*, Vol. 12, September, pp. 383-98.

————, (1986), 'Temporary Stabilization: Predetermined Exchange Rates', *Journal of Political Economy*, Vol. 94, December, pp. 1319-29.

———— and Végh, C.A. (1990), 'Credibility and the Dynamics of Stabilization Policy: A Basic Framework', IMF Working Paper 90/110, International Monetary Fund, Washington, DC; forthcoming in the *Proceedings of the VI World Congress of the Econometric Society*, Cambridge University Press, Cambridge.

———— (1991a), 'Exchange Rate-Based Stabilization Under Imperfect Credibility', Working Paper 91/77, August, International Monetary Fund, Washington, DC.

———— (1991b), ' Exchange Rate-Based Stabilization: The Dynamics of Non-credible Policy', unpublished, International Monetary Fund, Washington, DC.

————, (1992), 'Stabilization Dynamics and Backward-Looking Contracts', unpublished, International Monetary Fund, Washington, DC.

Capie, F. (1986), 'Conditions in Which Very Rapid Inflation Has Appeared', in K. Brunner & A.H. Meltzer (eds.), *The National Bureau Method, International Capital Mobility and Other Essays*, Carnegie-Rochester Conference Series on Public Policy, Vol. 24, pp. 115-69.

Corbo, V. (1985), 'Reforms and Macroeconomic Adjustments in Chile During 1974-84', *World Development*, Vol. 13, August, pp. 893-916.

————, de Melo, J. and Tybout, J. (1986), 'What Went Wrong with the Recent Reforms in the Southern Cone', *Economic Development and Cultural Change*, Vol. 34, April, pp. 607-40.

De Pablo, J.C., (1974), 'Relative Prices, Income Distribution, and Stabilization Plans: The Argentine Experience, 1967-1970', *Journal of Development Economics*, Vol. 1, December, pp. 167-89.

Di Tella, G. (1983), *Argentina Under Perón, 1973-76*, St. Martin's Press, New York.

————, (1989), 'Argentina's Economy Under a Labour-Based Government, 1973-76', in G. Di Tella & R. Dornbusch (eds.), *The Political Economy of Argentina, 1946-83*, Macmillan Press, London.

———— and Dornbusch, R. (eds.) (1989), *The Political Economy of Argentina, 1946-83*, Macmillan Press, London.

Dornbusch, R. (1982), 'Stabilization Policies in Developing Countries: What Have We Learned', *World Development*, Vol. 10, September, pp. 701-8.
—————— and Fischer, S. (1986), 'Stopping Hyperinflation Past and Present', *Weltwirtschaftliches Archiv*, Band 122, March, pp. 1-47.
Dornbusch, R. and Simonsen, M.H. (1987), 'Inflation Stabilization with Incomes Policy Support: A Review of the Recent Experience in Argentina, Brazil, and Israel', Group of Thirty, New York.
Drazen, A. (1990), 'Can Exchange Rate Freezes Induce Business Cycles?', unpublished, University of Maryland, College Park, Maryland.
Edwards, S. (1990), 'Stabilization and Liberalization Policies in Eastern Europe: Lessons from Latin America', unpublished, University of California, Los Angeles.
—————— and Edwards, A.C. (1991), *Monetarism and Liberalization: The Chilean Experiment*, University of Chicago Press, Chicago (reprint, 1991).
Fauvel, Y. and Samson, L. (1991), 'Intertemporal Substitution and Durable Goods: An Empirical Analysis', *Canadian Journal of Economics*, Vol.24, February, pp. 192-205.
Finch, M.H.J., 'Stabilization Policy in Uruguay since the 1950s', in R. Thorp & L. Whitehead (eds.), *Inflation and Stabilization in Latin America*, Holmes & Meier, New York.
Fischer, S. (1986), 'Exchange Rate Versus Money Targets in Disinflation', Chp. 8 in *Indexing, Inflation, and Economic Policy*, MIT Press, Cambridge, Massachusetts.
Foxley, A. (1980), 'Stabilization Policies and Stagflation: The Cases of Brazil and Chile', *World Development*, Vol. 8, September, pp. 887-912.
Garber, P.M. (1982), 'Transition from Inflation to Price Stability', in K. Brunner & A.H. Meltzer (eds.), *Monetary Regimes and Protectionism*, Carnegie-Rochester Conference Series on Public Policy, Vol. 16, Spring, pp. 887-912.
Gordon, R.J. (1982), 'Why Stopping Inflation May Be Costly: Evidence from Fourteen Historical Episodes', in R.E. Hall (ed.), *Inflation: Causes and Effects*, University of Chicago Press, Chicago.
Guidotti, P.E. and Végh, C.A. (1991), 'Losing Credibility: The Stabilization Blues', unpublished, International Monetary Fund, Washington, DC.
Hanson, J. and de Melo, J. (1985), 'External Shocks, Financial Reforms, and Stabilization Attempts in Uruguay During 1974-83', *World Development*, Vol. 13, August, pp. 917-39.
Heymann, D. (1991), 'From Sharp Disinflation to Hyperinflation, Twice: The Argentine Experience', in M. Bruno, S. Fischer, E. Helpman & N. Liviatan (eds.), *Lessons of Economic Stabilization and Its Aftermath*, MIT Press, Cambridge, Massachusetts.
International Monetary Fund, *Government Finance Statistics*, International Monetary Fund, Washington, DC, various issues.
——————, International Financial Statistics, International Monetary Fund, Washington, DC, various issues.
Kafka, A. (1967), 'The Brazilian Stabilization Program, 1964-66', *Journal of Political Economy*, Vol. 75, August Supplement, pp. 596-634.
Keynes, J.M. (1920), *The Economic Consequences of Peace*, Macmillan Press, London.
Kiguel, M. and Liviatan, N. (1988), 'Inflationary Rigidities and Orthodox Stabilization Policies: Lessons from Latin America', *The World Bank Economic Review*, Vol. 2, September, pp. 273-298.
——————, (1989), 'The Old and the New in Heterodox Stabilization Programs: Lessons from the 1960s and the 1980s', Policy Planning, and Research Department Working

Paper Series No. 323, World Bank, Washington, DC.

————— (1992a), 'The Business Cycle Associated with Exchange Rate-Based Stabilizations', *The World Bank Economic Review*, Vol. 6, May, pp. 279-305.

—————(1992b), 'Stopping Three Big Inflations', unpublished, World Bank, Washington, DC.

Layton, W.T. and Rist, C. (1925), *The Economic Situation of Austria*, League of Nations, Geneva.

Lemgruber, A.C., (1977), 'Inflation in Brazil', in L.B. Krause & W.S. Salant (eds.), *Worldwide Inflation: Theory and Recent Experience*, The Brookings Institution, Washington, DC.

Llach, J.J. (1990), 'Las Hiperestabilizaciones sin Mitos', unpublished, Instituto Torcuato Di Tella, Buenos Aires.

Makinen, G.E. (1984), 'The Greek Stabilization of 1944-46', *American Economic Review*, Vol. 74, December, pp. 1067-74.

————— and Woodward, G.T. (1989), 'The Taiwanese Hyperinflation and Stabilization of 1945-52', *Journal of Money, Credit and Banking*, Vol. 21, February, pp. 90-105.

Mitchell, B.R. (1975), *European Historical Statistics: 1750-1970*, Columbia University Press, New York.

Morales, J.A. (1988), 'Inflation Stabilization in Bolivia', in M. Bruno, G.Di Tella, R. Dornbusch & S. Fischer (eds.), *Inflation Stabilization: The Experience of Israel, Argentina, Brazil, Bolivia, and Mexico*, MIT Press, Cambridge, Massachusetts, pp. 307-46.

Ostry, J.D. and Reinhart, C.M. (1992), 'Private Saving and Terms of Trade Shocks: Evidence from Developing Countries', *Staff Papers*, International Monetary Fund, Vol. 39, September, pp. 495-517.

Pazos, F. (1972), *Chronic Inflation in Latin America*, Praeger Publishers, New York.

Peréz-Campanero, J., and Leone, A.M. (1991), 'Liberalization and Financial Crisis in Uruguay (1974-87)', in V. Sundararajan and T.J.T. Baliño (eds.), *Banking Crisis: Cases and Issues*, International Monetary Fund, Washington, DC.

Petrecolla, A. (1989), 'Unbalanced Development, 1958-1962', in G. Di Tella & R. Dornbusch (eds.), *The Political Economy of Argentina, 1946-83*, Macmillan Press, London.

Ramos, J. (1986), *Neoconservative Economics in the Southern Cone of Latin America, 1973-1983*, The Johns Hopkins University Press, Baltimore.

Reinhart, C.M. and Végh, C.A. (1992), 'Nominal Interest Rates, Consumption Booms, and Lack of Credibility: A Quantitative Examination', unpublished, International Monetary Fund, Washington, DC.

Rodriguez, C.A. (1982), 'The Argentine Stabilization Plan of December 20th', *World Development*, Vol. 10, September, pp. 801-11.

Rostowski, J. (1992), 'The Benefits of Currency Substitution During High Inflation and Stabilization', *Revista de Análisis Económico*, Vol. 7, pp. 91-107.

Sachs, J. (1985), 'The Dollar and the Policy Mix: 1985', *Brookings Papers on Economic Activity: 1*, The Brookings Institution, Washington, DC, pp. 117-97.

————— (1986), 'The Bolivian Hyperinflation and Stabilization', NBER Working Paper No. 2073, National Bureau of Economic Research, Cambridge, Massachusetts.

Sargent, T.J. (1982), 'The Ends of Four Big Inflations', in R.E. Hall (ed.), *Inflation: Causes and Effects*, University of Chicago Press, Chicago.

Siklos, P.L. (1989), 'The End of the Hungarian Hyperinflation of 1945-46', *Journal of Money, Credit and Banking*, Vol. 21, May, pp. 135-47.

Végh, C.A. (1991), 'Stopping High Inflation: An Analytical Overview', IMF Working Paper 91/107, International Monetary Fund, Washington, DC, November.

Viana, L. (1990), 'Uruguay's Stabilization Plan of 1968', unpublished, CERES, Uruguay.

Wicker, E. (1986), 'Terminating Hyperinflation in the Dismembered Habsburg Monarchy', *American Economic Review*, Vol. 76, June, pp. 350-64.

Yeager, L.B. et al. (1981), *Experiences with Stopping Inflation*, American Enterprise Institute, Washington, DC.

APPENDIX

Statistical Appendix

The Appendix contains tables with selected macroeconomic indicators for eleven stabilization programmes in high-inflation countries: Bolivia 1985 (Table 2A.1); Argentina 1967 (Table 2A.2); Brazil 1964 (Table 2A.3); Uruguay 1968 (Table 2A.4); Argentina 1978 (Table 2A.5); Chile 1978 (Table 2A.6); Uruguay 1978 (Table 2A.7); Argentina 1985, Austral Plan, (Table 2A.8); Brazil 1986, Cruzado Plan (Table 2A.9); Israel 1985 (Table 2A.10); and Mexico 1987 (Table 2A.11).

Subject to data availability, the same variables are reported for each episode to facilitate comparisons across different episodes. Four-quarter changes indicate percentage change over same quarter of the previous year.

Table 2A.1 Bolivian 1985 Stabilization

Year/ Quarter	Devaluation Rate Official (1)	Devaluation Rate Parallel (2)	Inflation Rate (3)	Inflation Rate (4Q change) (4)	Nominal Deposit Rate (5)	Nominal Lending Rate (6)	Real Lending Rate (7)	Spread (8)	M1 (4Q change) (9)	Credit to Private Sector (4Q change) (10)	Real Private Consumption (Annual change) (11)	Real GDP (Annual change) (12)	Real Wage (1985=100) (13)	Real Effective Exchange Rate (1985:2=100) (14)	Trade Balance (millions of U.S. dollars) (15)	Capital Account Balance (millions of U.S. dollars) (16)	Fiscal Balance (in percent of GDP) (17)
1984 1	0.0	496.0	682.5	426.8	45.0	62.0	-96.5	-99.5	253.2	122.7				213.1			
2	27,050.0	196.3	4,518.3	957.0	108.3	120.7	-56.5	-95.2	426.1	374.9				252.1			
3	3,772.1	29,110.8	407.0	999.6	140.0	150.0	-96.9	-75.4	777.7	627.4				164.5			
4	771.0	308.7	7,860.6	1,854.3	140.0	150.0	-99.8	-99.7	1,788.6	978.9	-3.5	-0.6	125.1	106.5	312	49	-29.4
1985 1	83,837.2	171,003.4	123,729.9	6,831.4	20.0	34.0	-96.9	-78.0	3,935.3	3,914.1				118.2			
2	399.2	14,631.5	4,217.8	6,715.8	25.0	44.0	-99.6	-100.0	6,364.1	3,968.7				100.0			
3	5,355,597.6		38,803.3	20,072.4	120.0	379.5	-21.2	-66.9	11,417.1	20,112.3				50.0			
4	513.7	1,076.0	508.6	10,507.3	110.0	231.1	-44.7	22.1	5,769.6	18,939.2	17.0	-1.0	100.0	345.1	161	-42	-10.1
1986 1	59.0	1,071.4	498.8	2,697.2	249.8	756.6	519.1	219.4	1,848.5	5,160.9				350.7			
2	1.5	66.0	38.4	1,083.5	86.3	219.0	70.4	70.4	747.2	2,790.9				328.0			
3	2.1	9.9	27.3	183.0	49.7	123.0	102.3	39.1	160.0	336.7				319.2			
4	1.3	-3.7	10.3	84.6	40.0	89.5	62.4	12.6	86.1	152.0	-7.9	-2.5	76.9	316.8	-51	90	-3.4
1987 1	17.1		16.7	22.7	35.8	70.1	53.3	11.4	94.2	159.2				323.6			
2	14.6		11.0	16.1	31.3	60.4	55.6	13.5	60.7	116.1				340.3			
3	8.0		3.1	10.2	31.1	54.2	37.6	1.6	61.0	70.7				343.1			
4	20.3		12.1	10.6	34.5	42.8	34.1	8.1	39.9	48.4	4.5	2.6	81.0	356.2	-128	33	-7.7
1988 1	15.3		6.4	8.1	28.8	41.4	5.0	1.5	27.5	21.3				373.8	-17	-14	
2	16.6		34.7	13.5	28.1	40.4	5.3	17.2	28.9	23.3				366.8	10	25	
3	1.7		33.3	21.0	27.4	38.5	23.3	4.7	21.1	32.3				344.0	-39	67	
4	12.2		12.3	21.0	26.7	38.9	28.5	3.9	35.3	42.0	2.0	3.0	97.0	352.6	-2	-56	-6.5
1989 1	11.8		8.1	21.5	24.2	36.9	30.4	-3.1	35.9	44.7				360.9	-29	-110	
2	16.7		4.9	14.2	22.9	36.7	17.1	-19.8	26.1	42.8				357.5	4	-91	
3	39.7		16.7	10.4	24.8	36.9	2.3	-1.4	16.6	39.7				383.9	7	8	
4	16.2		33.8	15.4	22.7	38.6	23.3	-2.3	2.4	49.8	2.5	2.8	99.3	395.0	12	57	-5.1
1990 1	15.6		12.5	16.5	20.6	40.0	31.5	3.0	3.6	52.2				425.0	-1	40	
2	8.0		6.4	16.9	28.0	43.7	20.5	1.6	18.3	52.5				439.6	16	-65	
3	16.1		19.2	17.6	22.8	42.0	6.7	-2.9	34.4	57.9				455.4	24	104	
4	16.9		33.1	17.4	23.9	41.6	1.1	1.4	39.5	43.7	1.6	2.6	109.8	457.9	16	3	-3.3

Sources: IMF, International Financial Statistics (various issues); except columns (2) and (13), from Central Bank of Bolivia, and column (17), from Central Bank of Bolivia, SAFCO, and Fund estimates.
Note: All rates of change and interest rates are expressed in percent per year. Horizontal line indicates the beginning of the program. The spread between the parallel and the official rate has been negligible since 1987. Columns (11), (12), (13), (15),(16), and (17) report annual figures; column (7) is computed using the one-quarter-ahead inflation rate; column (8) is defined as the ratio of (1 plus) the deposit rate to (1 plus) the three-month LIBOR rate times (1 plus) the one-quarter-ahead devaluation rate; column (16) includes errors and omissions (a positive sign indicates a capital inflow); and column (17) refers to the balance of the nonfinancial public sector (a minus sign denotes a deficit).

Table 2A.2 Argentine 1967 Stabilization

Year/ Quarter	Deval-uation Rate (1)	Inflation Rate (2)	Inflation Rate (4Q change) (3)	M1 (Annual change) (4)	Credit to Private Sector (Annual change) (5)	Real Private Con-sumption (Annual change) (6)	Real GDP (Annual change) (7)	Real Wage (1967=100) (8)	Real Exchange Rate (1967=100) (9)	Trade Balance (millions of U.S. dollars) (10)	Capital Account Balance (millions of U.S. dollars) (11)	Fiscal Balance (in percent of GDP) (12)
1966 1	0.0	29.2	37.7									
2	39.3	22.6	35.4									
3	27.2	16.0	27.6									
4	67.1	48.4	28.5	35.0	36.0	0.3	0.6	100.6	85.1	600	-236	-4.6
1967 1	301.2	21.8	26.6									
2	0.0	24.3	27.0									
3	0.0	39.2	33.0									
4	0.0	34.7	29.8	62.7	31.1	2.6	2.7	100.0	100.0	495	414	-1.9
1968 1	0.0	10.8	26.8									
2	0.0	-1.4	19.6									
3	0.0	3.4	11.1									
4	0.0	27.4	9.5	24.9	46.5	4.0	4.3	96.9	85.7	333	86	-2.1
1969 1	0.0	1.8	7.2									
2	0.0	-0.9	7.4									
3	0.0	6.7	8.2									
4	0.0	23.8	7.5	21.3	27.0	6.4	8.6	101.5	82.2	217	8	-1.6
1970 1	0.0	6.0	8.5									
2	70.6	11.7	11.8									
3	0.0	14.4	13.8									
4	0.0	51.6	19.7	6.5	19.4	4.1	5.4	105.3	101.4	274	239	-1.7
1971 1	0.0	42.8	29.0									
2	46.4	23.7	32.3									
3	66.8	43.7	40.1									
4	0.0	38.5	36.9	13.5	70.1	4.4	3.6	108.8	101.8	698	-55	-4.3
1972 1	0.0	98.1	48.6									
2	0.0	58.6	58.1									
3	0.0	47.0	59.0									
4	0.0	64.4	66.0	65.0	58.6	1.5	1.6	98.7	71.6	256	162	-5.2

Sources: IMF, International Financial Statistics (various issues); except columns (6) and (8), from Fundacion Mediterranea; column (7), from Dornbusch and Di Tella (1989); column (9), from Kiguel and Liviatan (1989); and column (12), from Di Tella (1983).
Note: All rates of change and interest rates are expressed in percent per year. Horizontal lines indicate the beginning and end of the program. All columns except (1), (2), and (3) report annual figures; column (11) includes errors and omissions (a positive sign indicates a capital inflow); and column (12) refers to the nonfinancial public sector (a minus sign denotes a deficit).

Table 2A.3 Brazilian 1964 Stabilization

Year/Quarter	Devaluation Rate (1)	Inflation Rate (2)	Inflation Rate (4Q change) (3)	M1 (4Q change) (4)	Credit to Private Sector (4Q change) (5)	Real Private Consumption (Annual change) (6)	Real GDP (Annual change) (7)	Real Wage (1964=100) (8)	Real Effective Exchange Rate (1964=100) (9)	Trade Balance (millions of U.S. dollars) (10)	Capital Account Balance (millions of U.S. dollars) (11)	Fiscal Balance (in percent of GDP) (12)
1963 1	0.1	73.4	54.6	58.5	50.7							
2	190.0	85.5	66.6	57.6	53.3							
3	0.0	78.7	72.3	56.4	49.2							
4	0.0	92.4	82.4	64.1	55.0	7.2	3.2	103.9	84.5	112	127	-4.2
1964 1	2,273.6	128.5	95.4	79.1	66.2							
2	-40.9	89.2	96.4	90.8	79.8							
3	233.3	67.3	93.2	93.7	92.2							
4	69.4	62.8	85.3	85.1	80.2	-2.5	3.1	100.0	100.0	344	-53	-3.2
1965 1	0.0	99.0	79.0	84.5	68.3							
2	0.0	67.9	73.7	82.8	64.9							
3	0.0	30.6	63.3	84.2	59.9							
4	107.4	25.0	52.8	77.6	57.5	-6.3	4.2	95.2	91.2	655	-75	-1.6
1966 1	0.0	51.8	42.8	58.5	50.7							
2	0.0	53.0	39.5	42.0	48.9	4.7	4.9	89.3	79.6	438	34	-1.1
3	0.0	38.6	41.6	26.7	39.9							
4	0.0	24.1	41.4	16.7	33.8							
1967 1	123.7	34.8	37.2	24.9	36.4							
2	0.0	34.1	32.8	34.6	42.6							
3	0.0	20.1	28.1	42.2	49.4							
4	0.0	13.6	25.3	43.6	58.3	9.6	11.4	86.4	73.4	213	54	-1.7
1968 1	97.9	20.9	22.0	50.2	75.3	10.2	9.7	89.3	78.8	26	636	-1.2
2	0.0	28.7	20.7	40.4	68.8							
3	74.3	25.0	21.9	38.8	70.2							
4	14.8	19.0	23.4	43.3	65.4							
1969 1	19.0	22.0	23.6	34.5	53.7	3.2	8.9	91.2	80.3	318	817	-0.6
2	5.1	20.1	21.5	32.5	51.0							
3	10.2	25.3	21.6	30.0	43.9							
4	20.7	28.5	23.9	29.0	42.3							
1970 1	13.5	16.8	22.6	27.4	42.5	15.2	11.3	92.3	76.8	232	1,331	-0.4
2	6.4	18.4	22.1	31.2	43.4							
3	14.8	28.6	22.9	27.5	35.7							
4	21.0	23.9	21.8	26.6	34.7							

Sources: IMF, International Financial Statistics (various issues); except columns (8) and (9), from Kiguel and Liviatan (1989); and column (12), from Lemgruber (1977).

Note: All rates of change are expressed in percent per year. Horizontal lines indicate the beginning and end of the program. Columns (6) through (12) report annual figures; column (11) includes errors and omissions (a positive sign indicates a capital inflow); and column (12) refers to the operational balance of the nonfinancial public sector (a minus sign denotes a deficit).

Table 2A.4 Uruguayan 1968 Stabilization

Year/ Quarter	Deval-uation Rate (1)	Inflation Rate (2)	Inflation Rate (4Q change) (3)	M1 (4Q change) (4)	Credit to Private Sector (4Q change) (5)	Real Private Con-sumption (Annual change) (6)	Real GDP (Annual change) (7)	Real Wage (1968=100) (8)	Real Exchange Rate (1968=100) (9)	Trade Balance (millions of U.S. dollars) (10)	Capital Account Balance (millions of U.S. dollars) (11)	Fiscal Balance (in percent of GDP) (12)
1967 1	61.5	119.3	63.2	26.4	7.9					7.0		
2	11.7	61.8	65.6	34.5	5.0					3.6		
3	58.0	191.1	97.3	48.9	1.2					-2.6		
4	1,565.6	130.9	121.0	111.8	61.5			112.1	97.4	5.7	-13.0	-3.0
1968 1	0.0	268.5	151.6	107.8	61.6	-3.6	-4.1			18.9		
2	144.1	105.7	167.2	104.6	95.5					-3.4		
3	0.0	46.8	125.2	89.2	83.0					9.6		
4	0.0	5.3	85.0	54.3	57.1	-1.5	1.6	100.0	100.0	18.3	-31.0	-1.7
1969 1	0.0	16.6	38.7	70.5	52.2					19.4		
2	0.0	19.6	21.2	61.6	22.4					12.5		
3	0.0	10.9	12.9	79.2	17.7					-5.8		
4	0.0	14.8	15.4	62.2	23.4	8.2	6.1	111.5	90.0	7.7	46.0	-2.5
1970 1	0.0	19.7	16.2	40.3	26.3					-3.6		
2	0.0	18.1	15.8	39.4	42.8					35.1		
3	0.0	11.5	16.0	19.6	56.8					-6.2		
4	0.0	19.9	17.2	15.2	46.1	6.4	4.7	110.0	80.6	9.0	6.0	-1.3
1971 1	0.0	27.4	19.1	18.5	53.2					19.1		
2	0.0	19.0	19.3	28.9	46.4					29.7		
3	0.0	28.3	23.6	40.9	41.1					-12.1		
4	379.8	60.6	33.0	54.9	48.1	1.0	-1.1	115.7	71.4	-21.2	26.0	-5.8
1972 1	233.5	90.1	46.9	60.8	74.1					-4.9		
2	71.3	124.4	72.2	47.0	91.1					19.0		
3	63.7	59.4	81.8	40.8	88.9					-2.0		
1973 1	63.8	130.6	99.0	47.2	104.6	-0.2	-3.5	95.9	99.4	8.5	-61.0	-2.6
2	77.6	160.3	115.2	50.5	92.1					23.0		
3	16.0	33.4	89.0	67.3	84.8					39.3		
4	16.4	134.0	108.1	74.3	75.3					-10.9		
	11.9	38.0	83.0	80.0	63.8	3.6	3.3	94.3	104.2	4.0	-64.0	-1.4

Sources: IMF, International Financial Statistics (various issues); except columns (6), (7), and (12), from Viana (1990); and columns (8) and (9), from Kiguel and Liviatan (1989).

Note: All rates of change are expressed in percent per year. Horizontal lines indicate the beginning and end of the program. Columns (6) through (9), (11) and (12) report annual figures; column (11) includes errors and omissions (a positive sign indicates a capital inflow); and column (12) reports figures for the nonfinancial public sector (a minus sign denotes a deficit).

86

Table 2A.5 Argentine 1978 Stabilization (Tablita Programme)

Year/ Quarter	Deval- uation Rate (1)	Inflation Rate (2)	Inflation Rate (4Q change) (3)	Interest Rates Nominal Deposit Rate (4)	Nominal Lending Rate (5)	Real Lending Rate (6)	Spread (7)	M1 (4Q change) (8)	Credit to Private Sector (4Q change) (9)	Real Private Con- sumption (4Q change) (10)	Real GDP (4Q change) (11)	Real Wage (1978 =100) (12)	Real Effective Exchange Rate (1978:4 =100) (13)	Trade Balance (millions of U.S. dollars) (14)	Capital Account Balance (millions of U.S. dollars) (15)	Fiscal Balance (in percent of GDP) (16)
1978 1	112.0	196.3	171.4	152.7	260.6	26.5	64.5	131.4	253.3	-1.9	-2.0		128.8	549	913.7	
2	43.0	185.1	188.9	123.6	159.3	14.6	42.0	165.0	203.7	-5.1	-5.5		118.0	1,011	128.5	
3	45.8	126.3	178.6	116.2	144.1	-8.5	10.5	159.9	172.2	-3.0	-5.4		108.7	1,010	-498.0	
4	79.9	166.9	167.3	117.8	141.0	-20.8	11.0	159.7	181.0	5.3	0.0	100.0	100.0	343	-606.1	-3.2
1979 1	76.4	204.3	169.0	113.8	131.1	-3.0	14.7	131.4	184.0	16.4	7.2		89.4	457	936.0	
2	67.9	138.4	157.3	113.7	128.9	-15.1	23.3	121.9	204.3	15.7	8.2		83.1	1,137	1,132.3	
3	56.5	169.5	168.7	131.2	148.1	26.1	41.7	129.2	216.3	13.0	5.4		76.7	447	1,023.0	
4	46.0	96.7	149.0	111.7	131.1	17.3	35.7	137.8	228.6	9.4	8.3	114.8	72.9	-259	1,394.4	-2.7
1980 1	35.9	97.1	123.4	85.3	117.9	10.0	25.6	141.2	224.0	5.6	1.9		68.2	12	1,198.7	
2	26.8	98.2	113.3	75.0	93.2	11.5	31.1	121.4	188.7	6.2	-2.0		63.3	-113	-877.1	
3	18.2	73.2	91.0	82.2	104.6	9.1	45.7	115.0	153.3	7.8	2.6		60.4	-442	1,643.3	
4	12.8	87.6	88.7	75.1	92.6	12.2	-24.8	96.7	108.5	10.8	3.6	128.4	53.7	-830	-74.7	-3.6
1981 1	99.5	71.6	82.3	120.7	170.1	17.6	-85.8	39.4	107.3	9.4	-0.8		50.9	-324	-1,598.1	
2	1,233.4	129.8	89.2	170.3	234.1	20.5	-15.3	42.4	133.5	1.4	-1.8		66.9	515	827.0	
3	171.2	177.2	112.8	210.0	275.5	66.9	7.8	48.6	142.1	-11.9	-11.5		71.9	751	348.9	
4	142.7	125.0	122.7	127.8	164.3	0.9	-69.4	70.1	166.0	-14.7	-12.0	114.8	77.8	-230	1,493.8	-8.1
1982 1	550.4	161.8	147.5	127.8	157.7	50.4	-42.2	105.5	154.6	-15.4	-7.5		95.2	824	619.5	
2	240.6	71.3	130.0	130.7	171.0	-36.2	-94.7	145.0	132.4	-16.8	-10.5		108.8	1,131	-2,430.4	
3	3,673.8	324.5	155.8	95.5	115.1	-51.4	-27.9	245.4	203.6	-6.1	-2.9		130.5	512	147.6	
4	140.7	342.6	203.0	152.5	165.1	-39.5	-37.8	247.5	210.5	-1.0	1.3	102.5	148.7	297	-671.7	-7.2

Sources: IMF, International Financial Statistics (various issues); except column (5), from Balino (1991); columns (10) and (11), from Central Bank of Argentina: column (12), from Ramos (1986); and column (13), from Fund staff estimates.

Note: All rates of change and interest rates are expressed in percent per year. Horizontal lines indicate the beginning and end of the program. Column (6) is computed using the one-quarter-ahead inflation rate; column (7) is defined as the ratio of (1 plus) the deposit rate to (1 plus) the three-month LIBOR rate times (1 plus) the one-quarter-ahead devaluation rate; columns (12) and (16) report annual figures; column (15) includes errors and omissions (a positive sign indicates a capital inflow); and column (16) reports figures for the central government (a minus sign denotes a deficit).

Table 2A.6 Chilean 1978 Stabilization (Tablita Programme)

Year/Quarter	Devaluation Rate (1)	Inflation Rate (2)	Inflation Rate (4Q change) (3)	Nominal Deposit Rate (4)	Nominal Lending Rate (5)	Real Lending Rate (6)	Spread (7)	M1 (4Q change) (8)	Credit to Private Sector (4Q change) (9)	Real Private Consumption (4Q change) (10)	Real GDP (4Q change) (11)	Real Wage (1978=100) (12)	Real Effective Exchange Rate (1978:1=100) (13)	Trade Balance (millions of U.S. dollars) (14)	Capital Account Balance (millions of U.S. dollars) (15)	Fiscal Balance (in percent of GDP) (16)
1977 1	24.5	90.4	149.7	124.6	265.0	108.9	36.3	204.7		11.7	11.9		⋮	152		
2	56.8	74.7	106.4	83.6	148.0	61.5	-9.7	201.0		19.8	9.6		⋮	39		
3	92.4	53.5	78.6	70.8	107.5	38.4	-9.1	154.7		15.4	6.1		⋮	-135		
4	76.7	49.9	66.3	99.8	132.1	74.6	36.7	113.0	178.0	3.6	7.8	101.8		29	677	-1.1
1978 1	36.5	33.0	52.1	70.9	101.3	49.4	25.6	101.3		9.8	3.6		100.0	141		
2	26.7	34.7	42.5	55.6	79.8	34.7	25.2	92.4		14.7	6.4		102.1	-154		
3	15.1	33.4	37.6	55.5	73.9	36.8	30.8	79.1		8.1	8.9		106.0	-103		
4	9.2	27.2	32.0	70.0	89.6	51.2	27.8	83.8	145.0	13.0	7.3	100.0	107.0	-122	1,818	-0.2
1979 1	19.6	25.4	30.1	47.4	67.6	24.5	-8.9	48.9		14.6	10.4		105.4	129		
2	45.7	34.6	30.1	44.1	60.5	5.8	30.1	56.9		4.8	8.2		102.4	6		
3	0.0	51.8	34.4	42.7	59.6	13.1	27.7	56.6		5.1	8.8		104.4	1		
4	0.0	41.1	37.9	46.1	60.8	24.2	27.2	60.3	87.0	9.3	6.4	108.3	98.4	-72	2,141	4.9
1980 1	0.0	29.5	39.0	52.0	61.9	21.4	30.7	70.5	71.1	5.6	6.7		92.9	217		
2	0.0	33.3	38.7	32.7	43.6	12.1	17.5	58.0	74.9	3.0	5.7		88.2	70		
3	0.0	28.1	32.9	31.8	41.0	5.0	18.9	57.9	65.7	9.4	3.6		87.0	-243		
4	0.0	34.4	31.3	34.2	42.0	20.0	15.1	58.3	76.8	13.3	7.7	118.1	83.0	-348	3,216	5.5
1981 1	0.0	18.4	28.4	45.0	52.3	36.4	24.1	52.6	73.7	10.5	8.5		76.9	-242		
2	0.0	11.7	22.8	40.9	50.7	37.8	19.7	35.3	75.9	7.7	8.9		71.7	-437		
3	0.0	9.3	18.0	38.8	51.0	41.5	17.1	21.8	69.8	4.2	7.4		68.9	-556		
4	0.0	6.7	11.4	38.5	54.1	49.7	21.0	15.6	39.4	-7.1	-2.8	128.8	71.4	-383	4,800	2.4
1982 1	0.0	2.9	7.6	38.9	55.2	56.4	-40.4	2.6	51.8	-13.7	-9.5		71.2	19		
2	101.4	-0.8	4.5	32.4	47.7	17.1	-74.1	-3.9	53.0	-16.0	-1.5		70.0	181		
3	343.2	26.1	8.3	50.1	64.2	5.4	-5.4	-6.0	44.0	-16.1	-4.7		87.6	247		
4	40.8	55.8	19.0	73.2	88.4	58.6	58.9	-14.0	57.1	-16.7	-14.3	128.3	100.5	254	946	-2.3
1983 1	-0.5	18.7	23.3	33.1	50.3	19.9	-3.5	17.3	41.4	-9.4	-7.7		103.8	364		
2	26.1	25.4	30.8	29.0	44.1	13.6	-6.3	18.0	26.4	-2.4	-2.8		96.0	448		
3	25.9	26.8	30.9	25.0	39.2	10.0	-11.3	23.5	24.4	-1.7	-11.8		94.7	337		
4	27.9	26.5	24.3	24.9	37.7	28.8	10.2	30.5	13.0	2.4	6.1	114.7	97.6	228	-3,168	-2.6

Sources: IMF, International Financial Statistics (various issues); except columns (10) and (11), from Arrau and De Gregorio (1991); column (12), from Ramos (1986); and column (16), from IMF, Government Finance Statistics (various issues).

Note: All rates of change and interest rates are expressed in percent per year. Horizontal lines indicate the beginning and end of the program. Column (6) is computed using the one-quarter-ahead inflation rate; column (7) is defined as the ratio of (1 plus) the deposit rate to (1 plus) the three-month LIBOR rate times (1 plus) the one-quarter-ahead devaluation rate; column (9) for 1977 through 1979 and columns (12), (15) and (16) report annual figures; column (15) includes errors and omissions (a positive sign indicates a capital inflow); and column (16) reports figures for the general government (a minus sign denotes a deficit).

Table 2A.7 Uruguayan 1978 Stabilization (Tablita Programme)

Year/ Quarter	Devaluation Rate (1)	Inflation Rate (2)	Inflation Rate (4Q change) (3)	Nominal Deposit Rate (4)	Nominal Lending Rate (5)	Real Lending Rate (6)	Spread (7)	M1 (4Q change) (8)	Credit to Private Sector (4Q change) (9)	Real Private Consumption (4Q change) (10)	Real GDP (4Q change) (11)	Real Wage (1978 =100) (12)	Real Effective Exchange Rate (1978:3 =100) (13)	Trade Balance (millions of U.S. dollars) (14)	Capital Account Balance (millions of U.S. dollars) (15)	Fiscal Balance (in percent of GDP) (16)
1978 1	0.0	23.7	48.1	49.1	76.7	15.9	-17.8	36.5	73.9		1.5		95.9	26.7		
2	44.4	52.5	46.6	46.4	73.1	17.2	-20.5	62.3	80.9		10.6		93.4	16.4		
3	49.3	47.6	41.9	50.7	74.9	17.1	-10.1	52.8	79.5		6.9		100.0	-34.1		
4	34.1	49.4	42.8	42.7	71.3	1.4	-5.2	85.1	76.4	5.6	8.5	100.0	101.9	-30.0	265.3	-0.8
1979 1	28.2	68.9	54.4	42.7	69.5	-2.2	-2.0	97.3	92.8		11.9		98.2	-15.3		
2	23.8	73.2	59.4	39.1	61.9	-14.8	2.6	103.5	105.8		5.5		92.4	-37.8		
3	17.2	90.0	69.8	41.2	62.5	-13.1	9.4	118.7	110.5		7.9		87.3	-103.9		
4	11.4	86.9	79.5	50.7	68.3	0.9	16.1	71.7	120.2	13.6	4.3	96.9	78.0	-157.9	430.9	0.2
1980 1	9.5	66.7	79.0	48.6	67.1	17.8	9.9	57.0	115.1		6.3		70.8	-198.5		
2	16.9	41.8	70.2	52.4	68.3	6.9	1.1	23.6	93.6		1.3		69.3	-139.4		
3	24.2	57.4	62.4	48.6	65.4	22.9	-1.1	23.1	89.9		4.9		68.1	-79.8		
4	23.8	34.6	49.6	50.2	65.4	32.2	9.9	47.4	79.7	-1.6	6.1	97.3	68.3	-13.9	827.3	0.2
1981 1	17.4	25.1	39.2	45.9	63.6	26.2	14.9	37.8	67.2		4.9		64.4	-98.5		
2	11.8	29.7	36.2	43.2	57.4	12.0	8.7	44.6	59.4		5.0		58.9	-57.4		
3	18.5	40.4	32.3	45.9	58.5	26.6	13.2	25.0	52.4		1.8		54.5	-77.4		
4	15.0	25.2	29.9	47.5	59.6	48.2	9.7	8.3	40.4	-2.7	-4.4	104.5	54.9	-45.2	495.3	-1.4
1982 1	15.0	7.7	25.2	41.7	49.1	33.8	7.4	-2.5	30.6		-7.5		62.2	-64.9		
2	17.5	11.4	20.5	44.8	54.6	26.0	-0.2	-5.0	24.7		-9.0		53.7	-50.7		
3	26.6	22.7	16.5	54.0	66.0	39.7	-97.0	-5.3	18.5		-17.9		51.8	20.1		
4	4,098.1	18.8	15.0	60.8	76.1	-26.5	39.2	39.2	90.9	-13.3	-8.5	104.2	63.3	85.8	-181.4	-9.0
1983 1	-11.3	139.6	40.4	79.8	105.3	56.0	33.9	55.2	76.6		-11.8		92.4	77.2		
2	-5.4	31.6	46.4	73.7	101.9	48.4	-23.8	63.6	45.6		-7.6		89.4	105.0		
3	64.9	36.0	50.2	64.2	84.8	25.6	-36.0	69.2	47.7		3.2		88.1	29.0		
4	95.0	47.2	58.5	67.1	84.8	18.4	-53.1	9.0	10.5	-13.6	-2.6	82.7	90.5	93.6	-5.9	-3.9

Sources: IMF, International Financial Statistics (various issues); except columns (4) and (5), from Perez-Canpanero and Leone (1991); column (12), from Ramos (1986); and column (16) from IMF, Government Finance Statistics (various issues).

Note: All rates of change and interest rates are expressed in percent per year. Horizontal lines indicate the beginning and end of the program; column (6) is computed using the one-quarter-ahead inflation rate; column (7) is defined as the ratio of (1 plus) the deposit rate to (1 plus) the three-month LIBOR rate times (1 plus) the one-quarter-ahead devaluation rate; columns (10), (12), (15) and (16) report annual figures; column (15) includes errors and omissions (a positive sign indicates a capital inflow); and column (16) reports figures for the general government (a minus sign denotes a deficit).

Table 2A.8 Argentine 1985 Stabilization (Austral Programme)

Year/ Quarter	Devaluation Rate Official	Parallel	Inflation Rate	Inflation Rate (4Q change)	Nominal Deposit Rate	Interest Rates Nominal Lending Rate	Real Lending Rate	Spread	M1 (4Q change)	Credit to Private Sector (4Q change)	Real Private Consumption (4Q change)	Real GDP (4Q change)	Real Wage (1980 =100)	Real Effective Exchange Rate (1985:1 =100)	Trade Balance (millions of U.S. dollars)	Capital Account Balance (millions of U.S. dollars)	Fiscal Balance (in percent of GDP)
	(1)	(2)	(3)	(4)	(5)	(6)	(7)	(8)	(9)	(10)	(11)	(12)	(13)	(14)	(15)	(16)	(17)
1984 1	291.7	156.9	508.6	446.6	232.3	339.6	-41.4	-49.9	502.9	366.7	3.7	1.9		109.3	1,379	-268	-11.0
2	501.2	54.0	650.7	559.1	333.5	618.1	-22.6	-62.2	545.5	429.8	5.8	4.1		97.7	1,462	-16	-9.3
3	929.8	92.6	827.4	655.3	463.6	708.0	-11.2	-65.0	550.0	497.2	8.9	1.1		91.7	886	-306	-6.9
4	1,337.4	86.7	810.0	688.0	558.0	1,808.0	72.7	-55.8	501.6	554.1	5.5	2.7	129.1	98.8	255	598	-9.3
1985 1	1,252.1	190.7	1,004.4	814.6	671.0	1,267.5	-23.5	-76.2	486.3	684.8	-1.1	-1.1		100.0	900	-103	-10.1
2	2,875.7	148.9	1,687.8	1,036.2	1,315.0	3,141.0	804.0	1,207.0	728.6	1,030.6	-8.7	-4.6		109.8	1,712	111	-6.5
3	0.0	24.4	258.5	795.9	51.1	139.5	82.1	39.7	761.6	676.6	-13.2	-8.8		121.5	1,411	-264	-3.0
4	0.0	-11.8	31.6	452.4	44.3	93.2	37.6	33.4	571.5	372.1	-2.6	-3.1	100.0	116.7	855	581	-2.0
1986 1	0.0	8.2	40.4	229.9	44.3	83.6	12.0	-12.7	372.9	177.4	0.1	0.7		116.4	649	-293	-4.7
2	53.1	-2.0	63.9	81.5	46.6	68.9	-20.7	-34.0	153.8	46.4	10.9	6.2		111.6	888	918	-2.2
3	107.3	51.3	113.0	59.4	67.5	110.1	1.4	-17.7	85.2	62.4	15.7	11.6		109.3	632	-84	-1.5
4	91.5	39.1	107.2	78.5	86.6	167.6	25.1	-21.6	84.8	83.7	4.8	4.4	109.3	109.5	277	179	-8.7
1987 1	124.1	27.7	113.9	98.3	78.0	135.7	24.7	-10.5	95.6	110.6	6.9	3.5		116.0	343	595	-5.1
2	87.0	14.3	88.9	105.5	83.4	162.6	-16.8	-62.6	84.2	119.5	0.2	3.5		117.0	470	-494	-5.7
3	357.5	97.2	215.7	126.7	195.0	365.9	6.8	-33.4	86.7	149.3	-0.5	1.3		116.2	123	-443	-8.1
4	313.2	43.8	336.1	173.1	239.1	306.6	45.2	....	124.7	196.0	-1.6	1.8	102.2	134.6	81	204	-5.9
1988 1	291.5	57.9	179.9	192.1	386.6	391.6	-15.3	-38.4	121.1	239.2	-0.2	2.9		137.2	641	-95	-9.3
2	638.2	90.0	480.0	286.7	610.8	607.7	-32.9	84.8	191.0	343.6	-4.4	-0.4		138.6	1,013	-176	-5.1
3	258.0	56.8	954.8	422.8	497.1	520.1	93.6	252.6	340.4	398.1	-11.6	-5.5		131.2	1,335	614	-3.5
4	56.2	13.4	220.2	383.9	236.5	201.8	4.4	57.5	337.9	355.7	-7.1	-6.7	97.3	121.1	1,253	-77	-6.1

Sources: IMF, International Financial Statistics (various issues); except columns(2) and (17), from Heymann (1991); columns (11) and (12); from Central Bank of Argentina; column (13), from Kiguel and Liviatan (1989); and column (14), from Fund staff estimates.

Note: All rates of change and interest rates are expressed in percent per year. Horizontal lines indicate the beginning and end of the program. Column (13) reports annual figures; column (7) is computed using the one-quarter-ahead inflation rate; column (8) is defined as the ratio of (1 plus) the deposit rate to (1 plus) the three-month LIBOR rate times (1 plus) the one-quarter-ahead devaluation rate; column (16) includes errors and omissions (a positive sign indicates a capital inflow); and column (17) refers to the operational balance of the nonfinancial public sector (a minus sign denotes a deficit).

Table 2A.9 Brazilian 1986 Stabilization (Cruzado Programme)

Year/ Quarter	Devaluation Rate Official (1)	Devaluation Rate Parallel (2)	Inflation Rate (3)	Inflation Rate (4Q change) (4)	Nominal Deposit Rate (5)	Interest Rates Nominal Savings Rate (6)	Interest Rates Real Savings Rate (7)	Spread (8)	M1 (4Q change) (9)	Credit to Private Sector (4Q change) (10)	Real Private Consumption (4Q change) (11)	Real GDP (4Q change) (12)	Real Wage (1985 =100) (13)	Real Effective Exchange Rate (1985.4 =100) (14)	Trade Balance (millions of U.S. dollars) (15)	Capital Account Balance (millions of U.S. dollars) (16)	Fiscal Balance (in percent of GDP) (17)
1984 1	238.8	55.0	195.3	187.6	219.7	...	...	3.3	109.0	131.7	-6.2	3.9		93.8	2,386	-1,472	
2	180.7	83.4	190.2	195.4	219.1	...	...	-13.3	119.5	156.2	-2.8	4.0		95.7	3,600	-1,065	
3	230.0	318.4	216.9	193.6	302.2	...	...	2.9	148.7	175.0	2.5	5.7		94.8	3,623	-1,282	-5.8
4	249.3	272.1	214.8	204.1	329.5	...	...	2.3	204.1	205.3	6.9	10.1	94.1	93.0	3,477	-1,780	
1985 1	281.5	259.7	273.6	222.5	350.0	309.0	51.0	26.6	208.9	221.4	6.6	12.2		96.8	2,021	-196	
2	226.1	274.0	170.8	217.0	268.3	248.4	-2.7	16.1	243.5	241.6	2.3	3.6		106.3	3,484	-2,077	
3	193.2	380.1	258.0	226.8	258.3	176.9	-20.0	2.6	304.5	262.9	12.3	9.2		102.9	3,627	-3,053	
4	223.0	225.3	246.4	234.7	305.0	284.4	-26.0	23.6	335.1	262.4	14.4	10.9	100.0	100.0	3,334	-3,496	-13.0
1986 1	203.0	254.5	419.6	263.5	269.9	327.1	213.0	242.8	641.0	345.4	10.9	4.2	104.2	96.1	2,460	-1,832	
2	0.0	102.7	36.4	206.2	22.6	21.7	11.7	14.5	729.5	298.9	16.4	14.1	110.9	97.6	3,700	-3,286	
3	0.0	74.4	9.0	127.5	36.7	27.4	1.1	-4.1	491.9	262.0	11.1	12.3	112.9	93.1	2,484	-1,860	
4	34.2	101.3	26.1	76.7	108.7	78.8	-51.4	-59.7	330.8	214.2	5.5	7.5	116.5	87.2	-340	-1,540	-14.5
1987 1	388.5	24.6	288.1	62.1	491.9	612.0	-26.0	-62.2	146.3	150.1	10.2	11.0	103.2	87.2	585	-1,505	
2	1,372.2	197.0	862.5	164.2	524.4	948.5	134.3	198.3	99.3	196.9	2.8	6.6	105.1	86.5	2,887	-3,299	
3	95.4	473.7	347.6	276.0	193.4	161.4	-27.8	-30.6	146.1	204.9	-7.1	-2.2	97.2	89.5	4,380	-2,475	
4	294.0	163.3	262.3	389.6	394.4	325.3	-44.0	-27.5	212.2	231.6	-3.1	-2.0	104.3	80.5	3,306	-3,805	-14.4

Sources: IMF, International Financial Statistics (various issues); except column (2), from Centro de Estudios Economicos; columns (11) and (12), from Conjuntura Economica; column (13), from IBGE; column (14), from Fund staff estimates; and column (17), from IMF, Government Finance Statistics (various issues).

Note: All rates of change and interest rates are expressed in percent per year. Horizontal lines indicate the beginning and the end of the program. Column (7) is computed using the one-quarter-ahead inflation rate; column (8) is defined as the ratio of (1 plus) the deposit rate to (1 plus) the three-month Libor rate times (1 plus) the one-quarter-ahead devaluation rate; column (13) reports annual figures for 1984 and 1985; Column (16) includes errors and omissions (a positive sign indicates a capital inflow); and column (17) reports annual figures for the central government (a minus sign denotes a deficit).

Table 2A.10 Israeli 1985 Stabilization

Year/ Quarter	Deval- uation Rate (1)	Inflation Rate (2)	Inflation Rate (4Q change) (3)	Nominal Deposit Rate (4)	Nominal Lending Rate (5)	Real Lending Rate (6)	Spread (7)	M1 (4Q change) (8)	Credit to Private Sector (4Q change) (9)	Real Private Con- sumption (4Q change) (10)	Real GDP (4Q change) (11)	Real Wage (1985:2 =100) (12)	Real Effective Exchange Rate (1985:2 =100) (13)	Trade Balance (millions of U.S. dollars) (14)	Capital Account Balance (millions of U.S. dollars) (15)	Fiscal Balance (in percent of GDP) (16)
1984 1	309.0	334.2	225.1	239.5	452.4	0.8	-45.6	128.0	230.0	-7.6	-0.1	96.1	98.7	-560	458	
2	466.1	447.8	296.0	357.8	710.7	54.0	-50.6	195.0	305.5	-4.0	0.3	105.9	96.7	-672	873	
3	730.7	426.5	401.9	516.2	1,062.0	43.3	-14.2	264.6	419.3	-0.4	4.7	110.8	97.5	-761	-256	
4	541.5	710.9	464.5	639.9	1,067.1	315.8	106.1	351.2	468.6	-3.9	4.4	101.0	100.8	-473	-344	-13.0
1985 1	226.4	180.7	406.2	215.4	499.8	28.8	-38.1	405.8	426.0	3.7	2.8	105.9	99.1	-599	-229	
2	367.5	365.8	386.1	305.8	715.3	71.5	95.7	354.1	407.6	0.5	8.0	100.0	100.0	-803	224	
3	91.6	375.4	373.8	150.9	612.2	406.4	123.3	385.0	327.5	-11.5	5.2	85.3	103.9	-472	-299	
4	3.9	40.7	205.8	43.0	186.3	172.2	32.4	244.8	173.4	3.2	-0.6	84.3	103.6	-448	-466	-2.8
1986 1	-0.2	5.2	139.2	21.6	78.9	38.4	12.7	248.3	118.0	4.2	4.7	97.1	105.8	-312	-349	
2	0.1	29.2	73.6	14.5	51.7	34.8	9.2	190.8	63.8	9.9	0.5	102.0	104.1	-575	-141	
3	-2.1	12.6	21.1	17.7	53.4	18.9	12.2	126.6	32.2	23.2	4.4	102.0	105.2	-479	301	
4	-1.2	29.0	18.5	20.5	57.0	28.1	-16.8	112.9	36.4	14.1	5.1	104.9	101.8	-459	-486	0.7
1987 1	36.5	22.5	23.2	28.4	67.8	42.2	20.0	51.2	42.0	10.9	3.8	102.0	107.9	-857	665	
2	0.6	18.0	20.4	21.7	65.8	51.7	13.4	64.3	40.9	9.6	7.8	112.7	108.1	-1,068	573	
3	0.1	9.3	19.5	13.3	57.5	34.0	26.4	56.7	39.3	6.5	6.1	106.9	105.5	-895	436	
4	-16.4	17.5	16.8	14.2	54.7	31.5	0.2	49.5	36.2	9.3	5.8	113.7	105.8	-846	-196	-3.3
1988 1	5.6	17.7	15.6	14.4	46.3	20.2	-8.8	52.6	29.1	11.1	8.0	112.7	102.0	-631	-23	
2	17.2	21.8	16.5	12.0	42.3	32.7	-0.9	33.7	29.1	2.1	0.2	117.6	98.7	-860	589	
3	5.1	7.3	15.9	13.2	40.0	14.8	-5.5	27.9	26.7	1.9	1.0	115.7	95.6	-722	62	
4	10.6	22.0	17.0	18.6	38.0	5.6	-20.0	11.3	28.5	2.5	1.7	118.6	93.6	-800	-1,284	-8.1
1989 1	36.0	30.7	20.1	17.7	39.5	17.1	-28.2	10.6	26.9	-3.5	-1.7	110.8	96.3	-416	1,456	
2	49.3	19.2	19.5	13.6	32.4	17.4	9.4	26.3	25.9	3.1	4.4	117.6	94.5	-632	-185	
3	-5.5	12.8	21.0	11.9	27.7	7.0	6.9	33.4	26.9	2.7	1.8	117.6	98.0	-321	-347	
4	-4.0	19.4	20.4	13.3	26.9	12.7	-2.0	44.3	21.5	0.5	2.1	113.7	96.8	-338	-737	-3.9
1990 1	6.5	12.6	15.9	...	...	...	...	32.4	22.3	2.0	5.5	111.8	97.2	-454	-371	
2	17.9	21.1	16.4	14.4	27.2	6.9	9.8	25.9	20.1	2.0	3.5	116.7	98.0	-677	134	
3	-4.0	19.0	18.0	13.9	25.8	4.8	7.2	20.1	19.1	6.6	5.6	113.7	100.4	-671	-64	
4	-1.7	20.0	18.2	13.9	25.3	12.0	-29.1	30.7	23.2	4.4	5.6	112.7	100.0	-1,014	241	-4.4

Sources: IMF, International Financial Statistics (various issues); except column (12), from Bank of Israel; column (13), from Fund staff estimates; and column (16), from Government Finance Statistics (various issues).

Note: All rates of change and interest rates are expressed in percent per year. Horizontal lines indicate the beginning and the end of the program. Column (6) is computed using the one-quarter-ahead inflation rate; column (7) is defined as the ratio of (1 plus) the deposit rate to (1 plus) the three-month LIBOR rate times (1 plus) the one-quarter-ahead devaluation rate; column (15) includes errors and omissions (a positive sign indicates a capital inflow); and column (16) reports figures for the central government (a minus sign denotes a deficit).

Table 2A.11 Mexican 1987 Stabilization

Year/ Quarter	Devaluation Rate	Inflation Rate	Inflation Rate (4Q change)	Nominal Deposit Rate	Interest Rates Nominal Treasury Bill Rate	Real Treasury Bill Rate	Spread	M1 (4Q change)	Credit to Private Sector (4Q change)	Real Private Consumption (4Q change)	Real GDP (4Q change)	Real Wage (1987:4 =100)	Real Effective Exchange Rate (1987:4 =100)	Trade Balance (millions of U.S. dollars)	Capital Account Balance (millions of U.S. dollars)	Fiscal Balance (in percent of GDP)
	(1)	(2)	(3)	(4)	(5)	(6)	(7)	(8)	(9)	(10)	(11)	(12)	(13)	(14)	(15)	(16)
1987 1	121.0	139.1	109.4	94.3	103.8	-16.0	-12.6	77.9	78.4	-2.2	-0.6		113.0	2,315	430	
2	108.9	142.7	124.3	94.3	98.8	-18.3	0.0	92.5	92.5	-2.3	-0.3		111.2	2,445	2,632	
3	81.3	143.3	134.2	94.3	96.3	-27.2	-53.7	122.9	118.0	0.8	4.7		102.7	1,903	-155	
4	291.6	169.5	148.4	106.1	113.4	-42.7	68.1	118.8	158.1	4.8	6.3	100.0	100.0	1,770	-2,756	1.8
1988 1	13.5	272.3	177.4	127.7	134.5	51.9	112.8	132.0	127.8	2.1	3.1		96.5	1,537	-2,751	
2	0.0	54.3	147.7	50.4	52.1	27.4	40.0	146.1	125.6	2.4	1.3		88.0	854	-1,300	
3	0.0	19.4	107.3	38.3	41.1	25.0	27.5	101.5	87.8	1.8	0.8		81.4	-267	-2,777	
4	0.0	12.9	66.8	38.3	48.9	19.5	9.0	68.6	82.9	4.5	1.0	98.1	80.7	-456	-1,881	-3.6
1989 1	16.3	24.6	26.9	38.3	49.2	27.4	8.3	39.8	98.6	7.2	2.6		81.0	237	206	
2	16.3	17.2	18.4	38.3	52.9	34.5	8.9	17.6	100.4	7.6	4.9		80.3	61	-573	
3	15.6	13.7	17.0	32.9	38.7	16.0	6.2	25.2	109.9	7.0	4.1		79.6	-293	3,735	
4	14.9	19.6	18.7	35.8	39.2	-4.7	9.0	37.6	97.6	3.0	2.4	96.8	80.0	-650	379	-1.7
1990 1	14.7	46.0	23.5	40.4	44.4	16.8	14.7	38.0	94.4	5.0	3.3		80.2	215	-1,121	
2	13.0	23.6	25.2	34.7	38.0	11.0	12.2	49.4	84.0	4.4	2.6		78.6	-1,288	2,927	
3	10.7	24.3	28.0	26.3	30.2	3.5	8.4	42.7	82.8	5.9	4.7		77.8	-1,021	3,861	
4	7.8	25.8	29.6	23.5	26.5	-4.6	8.7	63.4	73.5	8.0	5.9	105.5	77.2	-932	4,355	2.3
1991 1	4.9	32.7	26.5	20.8	22.9	6.7	7.6	70.1	75.7	4.7	4.1		75.3	-1,635	2,158	
2	5.1	15.3	24.3	17.2	19.5	7.3	5.0	63.6	73.0	3.5	5.6		71.6	-2,413	4,571	
3	5.1	11.4	21.0	15.1	17.6	-1.7	6.6	100.0	66.5	3.8	3.6		69.9	...	...	
4	2.0	19.6	19.5	15.3	17.0	-5.2	7.9	122.5	62.1	4.7	3.0	115.5	68.6	...	...	3.3

Sources: IMF, International Financial Statistics (various issues); except columns (10), (11), (12), and (16) from Banco Central de Mexico; and column (13), from Fund staff estimates.

Note: All rates of change and interest rates are expressed in percent per year. Horizontal line indicates the beginning of the program. Column (6) is computed using the one-quarter-ahead inflation rate; column (7) is defined as the ratio of (1 plus) the deposit rate to (1 plus) the three-month LIBOR rate times (1 plus) the one-quarter-ahead devaluation rate; columns (12) and (16) report annual figures; column (15) includes errors and omissions (a positive sign indicates a capital inflow); and column (16) reports figures for the operational balance of the public sector (a minus sign denotes a deficit).

93

PART II

Conditions Conducive to High Inflation

3. Currency Competition, Inflation, Gresham's Law and Exchange Rate*

Peter Bernholz

1. INTRODUCTION

> Thus in advanced inflation, 'Gresham's Law' was reversed: good money tended to drive out bad, and not the other way round; the reason being the irreducible need for a serviceable medium of exchange in any modern economy
>
> League of Nations (1946, p. 48).[1]

Whereas Gresham's law that bad money drives out good[2] has found widespread recognition and application in empirical historical research, this is not true for the reverse law quoted above as valid for advanced inflations. As will be shown below, the phenomena described by it are quite general. It is thus surprising that it has not been stated as a theorem in economic theory. Moreover, if both Gresham's law and its reverse should be true, then they must hold under different conditions. But these conditions have, to my knowledge, never been formulated, though it is well known that Gresham's law holds only for fixed exchange rates, so that it may be suspected that the reverse law is true under flexible rates.

In this chapter both laws will be considered together in a model explaining a complete cycle of inflation from its very beginning to the demise of the inflating money in advanced or hyperinflation. Four relevant stylized periods of inflation will be described in this simple model which is related to the 'monetary approach', to the balance of payments and the exchange rate (see, e.g., Frenkel and Johnson 1976), to the theory of currency substitution (see, e.g., Connolly 1978 and Girton and Roper 1981) and of competing moneys (Starbatty 1982). In doing so it will be assumed that domestic agents hold both a stable and an inflating kind of money and that only the former is also demanded in the rest of the world. This rest of the world is supposed to be large compared to the inflating small country. The increase of the money supply in this country will be supposed to arise from the financing of a constant real budget deficit, which is exogenous to the model.[3] The paper is organized as follows. In section 2 historical evidence will be presented to show that the reverse law has been present in many advanced inflations. This refers to period four of the model. Section 3 formulates the model and derives results for the four periods of inflation. In section 4 empirical evidence concerning the other periods will be presented. Section 5 offers some concluding comments.

2. EMPIRICAL EVIDENCE FOR THIERS' LAW, THE REVERSE OF GRESHAM'S LAW

In all the markets nothing was to be seen but gold and silver, and the wages of the lower classes were paid in no other medium. One would have imagined that there was no paper in France. The mandats were in the hands of speculators only

(Louis A. Thiers, 1840, p. 111)

Many contemporaries, historians and economists have observed that, in advanced inflations, good money drives out bad. Let us call the phenomenon Thiers' law, since this French historian not only noted 'that specie, which was supposed to be hoarded or carried abroad, found its way into circulation. That which had been hidden came forth; that which had quitted France returned. The southern provinces were full of piasters, which came from Spain' during the advanced state of the inflation of the great French Revolution. But he goes on to stress that they 'were introduced among us from necessity. Gold and silver came, whithersoever the demand calls them; only their price is higher and keeps up till the quantity is sufficient and the want is supplied' (1840, p. 111). The latter hypothesis strongly recalls David Hume's 'Of the Balance of Trade' (1955), but Hume did not connect it with inflating paper money and a flexible exchange rate.

Now, Thiers' law has been observed in many other historical cases of advanced hyperinflation. Especially interesting are those in which, like in the French inflation of 1789-96, governments were not able to substitute a stable money for the inflating one. For in these cases stable money returned not only without, but against the determined efforts of governments to keep it out of circulation to preserve the base of the inflation tax. But in the end the returning stable money absolutely drove out the bad money, so that one can speak of a 'naturally emerging' or an unplanned currency reform. The government finally only legalized the stable money, since it was forced to decree that its taxes must be paid in stable money after the inflation tax had been eroded.

In Table 3.1 several of these cases have been put together, which G. Subercaseaux (1912) in his highly interesting 'El Papel Moneda' calls the 'abnormal way of reestablishing the metallic money the demonetization of paper money'. This is in contrast to the normal way of instituting a stable currency by changing the monetary regime. Now, if Thiers' law holds for countries getting rid of advanced inflation by a natural return to stable and the repudiation of unstable money, we should also expect a gradual substitution of bad by good money in cases in which advanced inflation is later ended by a currency reform, i.e., by a change of the monetary regime. This can, indeed, be documented for several advanced inflations, like the Polish and German in the 1920s (League of Nations 1946, p. 48; Holtfrerich 1980, pp. 301ff.) and the Greek and Chinese in the 1940s (Delivanis and Cleveland 1950, pp. 96-101; Chou 1963, p. 27).

The amount of stable money circulating is usually not known to statistical bureaus. Moreover, the government may even not want to publish this information as far as it is available. Thus no time series exist for these data, so that an econometric estimation of the relative real amounts of bad and good money in the hands of the public as a function, e.g. of the rate of inflation, is not possible.[4] There exist, however, some estimates for the real amount of stable money in Germany in 1923, i.e. shortly before the monetary reform of 15 November 1923. Young (1925, vol. 1, p. 402) mentions that 'According to the 1924 report of the second committee of experts the value of foreign bank notes held in Germany at the end of 1923 amounted to about 1,200,000,000 gold marks'. Beusch (1928, p. 8) reports that 'the substitution of the domestic currency by foreign media of payment progressed everywhere. ... In August 1923 this sum was estimated to amount to 2-3 million gold marks. If this is correct, then the value of foreign currencies in German economic transactions was nearly ten times as large as that of the circulating paper mark notes' (my translation). In addition to this amount, 1.1 billion gold marks of value-

Table 3.1: Advanced Inflations Ending in Total Natural Substitutions of Bad Through Good Money

Country	Period	Earlier Currency Reforms that Failed[1]	Kind of Good Money	Source
Ming China	1375-1448		silver bullion, copper coins (limited)	Bernholz (1993)
USA	1776-81	March 1780: new dollar bills 1:20	specie and state paper money	Phillipps (1972, 170ff.) Bezanson (1951, 325ff.)
France	1789-96	February 1796: mandats territoriaux 1:30	gold and silver specie	Thiers (1840)
Peru	1875-87	September 1880:[2] incas 1:8	silver coins	Garland (1908, 58ff.)
Mexico	1913-17	June 1916: infalsificable currency 10:1	gold and silver specie	Banyai (1976, 73ff.) Kemmerer (1940, 114-15)

Notes:

[1] By a currency reform, we understand a change of the monetary regime with the intention of establishing a new stable money. The mere removal of zeros or introduction of newly denominated paper notes is not considered to be a currency reform.

[2] From the report given by Garland it is doubtful whether a currency reform was seriously intended.

stable 'emergency money' was circulating together with value-stable issues denominated in rye, coal and other units. All this adds up to more than 4 billion gold marks in value-stable money, compared to 6 billion in 1914 and to a real value of 80-800 million gold marks of the inflating paper marks circulating after June 1923 (Lansburgh 1929, pp. 43ff.; Holtfrerich 1980, pp. 209ff.).

It follows that Thiers' law was fully at work in Germany in the early 1920s like in other advanced inflations. It is thus not surprising that Holtfrerich (1980, p. 310) concludes 'that the stabilization of currency was rather necessary in Germany because of a crisis of the state than of the economy. The economy had widely changed to a foreign currency standard, with which it could have lived. ... The crisis originated since the Reich would not and could not tolerate the use of foreign currency for domestic transactions wanted by the economy because of reasons of national self-preservation and especially as long as the inflation was needed as a source of revenue' (my translation).

3. A MODEL OF THE INFLATIONARY PROCESS AND OF CURRENCY SUBSTITUTION

In this section a simple model will be set up from which some general characteristics of inflation from its beginnings to its end can be derived. Four periods of the inflationary process will be distinguished, though periods three and four especially are usually interwoven in reality. These characteristics correspond to stylized facts which have been observed in historical cases of inflation.

In the first period a new kind of money is introduced at a fixed parity with the old to finance a budget deficit. Since this kind of money is superior in some, but inferior in other respects to the old, it is readily accepted by the public and replaces part of the old money. In period two, after an optimal composition of the two moneys has been reached by the public, the government goes on issuing the new, now bad money to finance the same constant real budget deficit. With a fixed parity or exchange rate between the two types of money, the additional new money flows to the monetary authorities who exchange it against the old one, and thus lose official reserves. In both of these periods the balance of payments shows a deficit.

In period three, after official reserves have been exhausted whereas the budget deficit remains, the government tries to maintain the parity (fixed exchange rate) between old and new money by making it legal tender and by trying to enforce its use with penalties. As a consequence the bad money drives the good money out of the portfolios of the public. Gresham's law works and the balance of payments is in deficit.

In period four, after the good money has left the country and with an ongoing budget deficit still financed by money creation, even the severest penalties cannot maintain a fixed exchange rate. The price level and the exchange rate begin to rise at an increasing rate. The balance of payments turns to a surplus; Thiers' law holds, the good drives out the bad money.

In specific historical cases one or the other period of this stylized description may be wholly or partly absent. There may have been just one kind of paper money circulating domestically in the beginning, with a fixed exchange rate to foreign money, and it is this paper money which is then inflated. Thus period one is missing in subsequent developments. Or the budget deficit is brought under control before period four can occur. Or the new type of money (e.g. banknotes or state-issued paper money) is not made legal tender and no penalties for not using it are introduced, so that period three is absent. But the historical evidence shows that all periods have been observed, and that there are historical cases, e.g. those in Table 3.1, in which all periods have been experienced.

Subsequently, the old money will be called gold and the new money paper money. This is, however, just a way to simplify matters. The money which is 'value stable' over all periods can also be, e.g., banknotes. And the inflating money can even consist of metal with a lower intrinsic value (given the parity) than the 'value-stable' money. In the latter case, however, the highest possible rate of inflation is technically more limited than with paper money.

3.1 The Model

We consider a small country and the rest of the world, which both use gold (coins) as money. The total constant stock of money is called $\bar{G}$, the variable stocks held by the rest of the world G^*, by the monetary authorities of the small (domestic) country G^B, and by its public G. Thus

$$G^B + G + G^* = \bar{G} \tag{3.1}$$

Beginning in $t = 0$, the small country has to finance a constant real budget deficit of amount A, so that with price level P we get for the nominal deficit D^5 in terms of paper money (see (3.10)

$$D = PA \tag{3.2}$$

The deficit is financed by issuing paper money. The change in the nominal amount of this money is given by the balance sheet identity of the monetary authorities (e.g. the central bank):

$$\dot{M} = w\dot{G}^B + D \tag{3.3}$$

where w denotes the exchange rate (or the parity) between the two kinds of money. Equation (3.3) implies that no money is issued by buying from the public assets other than gold.

Let us turn now to the domestic real demand for money. Here we differentiate between the real demand for both types of money and the real demand for each of them. It is assumed that total real demand depends positively on real national income Y, and negatively on the foreign nominal interest rate, r^*. The latter corresponds to the real rate of interest, since no inflation or deflation occurs abroad, where only gold money is used. In addition to these usual assumptions it is postulated that total real money demand depends negatively on a parameter s, which symbolizes certain advantages of holding paper money compared to gold (e.g., smaller weight) and also transfer and penalty costs which may be imposed by the government on holding gold money. Taken together the total real money demand of the domestic public may be assumed to be:

$$L = aY^b(1 + r^*)^{-c}(1+s)^{-d}, \tag{3.4}$$

where a,b,c and d are positive constants. Subsequently, Y, r^* and, except for period three, s are assumed constant.

The real demand for paper money, L^M, is supposed to be a constant fraction of total real money demand if s, r^* and r, the domestic nominal interest rate are given. It decreases, however, with $r-r^*$ and increases with s. The real demand function for paper money thus looks as follows:

$$L^M = gL(1 + r-r^*)^{-h}(1 + s)^k, \tag{3.5}$$

with g, h and k being positive constants.

The interpretation of (3.5) is straightforward. With given advantages of holding paper money, s = const., and $r = r^*$, i.e., without paper money inflation (see (3.10)-(3.13)), the public want to hold a fixed share, $g(1+s)^k$, of total real money holdings in paper money, and the complementary share, $1-g(1+s)^k$, in gold money. This can be called the optimal portfolio of the two kinds of money *given* monetary stability. Note that the composition of the optimal portfolio depends on the size of s. On the other hand, if r rises, then it becomes relatively more costly to hold paper money, so that the composition of the optimal portfolio changes in favor of gold money. Note also that because of assumption (3.11) below, $r-r^*$ corresponds to the expected rate of change of the exchange rate.

From this discussion, it follows that the coefficient of L in (3.5), which we may call C, cannot be greater than one. For not more than the total real money demand can be demanded in terms of paper money. Consequently,

$$C \equiv g\,(1 + r\text{-}r^*)\text{-}h(1 + s)^k \leq 1 \qquad (3.5a)$$

We also postulate that $0 \leq d < k$, for the influence of a change of s on total real money demand should be smaller than on the real demand for paper money. Finally, we assume that the real demand of the domestic public for gold money is equal to total real money demand minus the real stock of paper money, M/P, owned by the public:

$$L^G = L - \frac{M}{P} \qquad (3.6)$$

for $s = s_0$, i.e., for the initial value of s at time $t = 0$, we assume the strict inequality in 5a. to hold. This implies that there exists an optimal ratio of L^M to L^G, with $L^M < L$ for $s = s_0$. This follows immediately, if we add the equilibrium conditions for the two moneys

$$M \leq PL^M, \qquad (3.7)$$

$$wG = PL^G. \qquad (3.8)$$

Note that (3.8) has been expressed in terms of the paper money (see (3.10)). In (3.7), we have taken into account that not enough paper money may be supplied to correspond to demand, since period one begins without any stock of paper money. Since, for $s = $ constant, the total real demand for both moneys is constant according to (3.4), the real demand for gold money is greater than the optimal demand for it (for $s = s_0$) according to (3.6), if the optimal demand for paper money is greater than its supply. For then $L^G > L - L^M$. If, on the other hand, the equality holds in (3.7) then $L^G = L - L^M$, and the optimal composition of paper and gold money has been realized.

Finally we have to take into account that the small country is an open economy. For its balance of payments B we get in terms of the paper money

$$(3.9)$$

$$B = w(\dot{G} + \dot{G}^B)$$

The surplus (deficit) is equal to the increase (decrease) of the gold stock in terms of paper money held by the public and as official reserves. This definition is somewhat different from the usual one since it takes into account changes in 'reserves' held by the public. Further, the validity of the purchasing power parity and the open interest rate parity are postulated:

$$P = wP^*, \tag{3.10}$$

$$r = r^* + \frac{\dot{w}}{w} \tag{3.11}$$

Note that $\dot{w} = \dot{w}^E$, i.e. the equality of actual and expected change of the exchange rate, has been assumed. The foreign price level P^* and the interest rate r^* are taken to be constant. Finally

$$w = q, \ if \ wG^B > fM \quad (0 \le f < 1) \tag{3.12}$$

$$\pi \equiv \frac{\dot{P}}{P} \tag{3.13}$$

$$G_0 \ge 0, \ G_0^B > 0, \ M_0 \ge 0. \tag{3.14}$$

q and f are constants. According to (3.12), the exchange rate and thus the parity among the two moneys is fixed so long as official reserves cover a certain percentage of the paper money in circulation.

3.2 First Period: Introduction of Paper Money

We start in $t = 0$ with a situation in which $M_0 = 0$, $wG_0^B > fM_0$ and $B_0 = 0$. Now the government begins with the help of the monetary authorities to issue paper money to finance the budget deficit. Since $M_0 < P_0 L_0^M$ the public is ready to take up this paper money until equality holds in (3.7). Assume that this happens in $t = T_1$ and that $G_{T_1}^B \ge fM_{T_1}$. (If the latter condition were not fulfilled, the system would move directly to the third period before T_1). Since L is constant and the same is true for P because of (3.10) and (3.12), it follows from (3.8) and (3.6) that

$$wG = PL^G = PL - M \tag{3.15}$$

But then, because of (3.9), (3.3) and (3.2)

$$B = -\dot{M} + w\dot{G}^{B} = -w\dot{G}^{B} - D + w\dot{G}^{B},$$ (3.16)

$$B = -D = -PA.$$

Finally, the newly created money corresponds to the budget deficit, $\dot{M} = D$, and thus from (3.3)

$$\dot{G}^{B} = 0.$$ (3.17)

In the first period all the newly issued paper money is taken up by the public who get rid of a corresponding amount of gold. This amount flows out of the country and gives rise to an equal balance of payments deficit, which is again equal to the budget deficit. This process comes to an end when in time T_1 the public has acquired an optimal amount of paper money (see Figure 3.1), so that for $r = r^*$, $w = q$ and $\pi = 0$, equality holds in (3.7).

It should be noted that up to this time the issue of paper money cannot be considered to be an issue of bad money, quite the contrary. The public prefers the new paper money to gold and this is used to buy more goods and services abroad, so that the issue of paper money increases welfare in two respects.

3.3 Second Period: Fixed Exchange Rate and Loss of Official Reserves

In this period the government goes on to finance the budget deficit by issuing paper money. Official reserves $wG^{B} > fM$, so that $w = q$ according to (3.12) and thus $P =$ constant and $r = r^*$ because of (3.10) and (3.11). But now equation (3.7) holds and L and L^{M} are constant according to (3.4) and (3.5). It thus follows from (3.6) and equations (3.7) and (3.8):

$$wG = PL^{G} = PL - PL^{M},$$ (3.18)

so that wG is also constant. As a consequence $-\dot{M} = w\dot{G} = 0$ from (3.7) and (3.18). Taking (3.2), (3.3) and (3.9) we thus get:

$$0 = w\dot{G}^B + D = w\dot{G}^B + PA,$$

$$D = -w\dot{G}^B = PA,$$

$$B = w\dot{G}^B = -D = -PA$$

In this period the public adhere to their optimal portfolio of the two moneys. The additional amount of paper money issued is converted at the monetary authorities into gold, which flows out of the country. The budget deficit is equal to the balance of payments deficit and to the loss of official reserves. The stock of money in the hands of the public remains unchanged. Since these are well-known results of the monetary approach to the balance of payments, no further comment is necessary. Finally, denote as T_2 the time at which $wG^B = fM$, so that period two extends from T_1 to T_2.

3.4 Third Period: Gresham's Law at Work

Since official reserves have now reached their minimum, the fixed exchange rate can no longer be maintained by official interventions in the exchange market but only by government regulations. Foreign credit to monetary authorities is excluded in our model, and anyway would merely postpone the date at which official interventions must be ended, given that more paper money is continually being issued.

Suppose then that the government makes the paper money legal tender and introduces and increases, if necessary, penalties against a discount of the paper money or a premium on gold or, what is the same, a change of the exchange rate between gold and paper money. In our model this means changing s in equations (3.5) and (3.4) in such a way that w and thus r and P remain unchanged (equations (3.10) and (3.11)). It implies, moreover, that the real demand for paper money grows, whereas the demand for gold money decreases (see also (3.5a) and (3.6)).

Note first that now $\dot{G}^B = 0$, i.e., interventions in the exchange market have ended. Then, from (3.2), (3.3) and (3.9):

$$\dot{M} = D = PA, \tag{3.19}$$

$$B = w\dot{G} \tag{3.20}$$

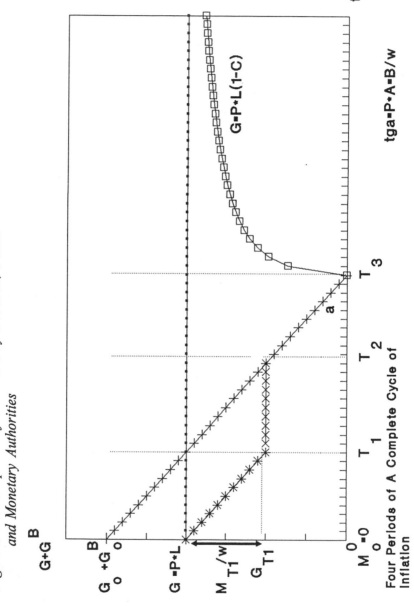

Figure 3.1: Development of Gold Held by Domestic, Public and Monetary Authorities

108

From equations (3.7), (3.5) and (3.5a) we get, since $\pi = r - r^* = 0$ according to (3.10)-(3.13),

$$\frac{M}{P} = CL$$

$$\dot{M} = (\dot{C}L + C\dot{L})P$$

$$\frac{\dot{M}}{M} = \frac{\dot{C}}{C} = \frac{\dot{L}}{L}$$

Thus because of (3.4) and (3.5a):

$$\frac{\dot{M}}{M} = (k - d)(1 + s)^{-1} \dot{s} > 0.$$

The absolute increase in transfer costs and (or) penalties must be proportional to the relative growth of the minimal stock of paper money to force the public to hold the paper money. Note that $\dot{s} > 0$ because of (3.19) and of $k - d > 0$.

Let us look at the development of wG. From equations (3.5)-(3.8) it follows

$$wG = PL^G = PL - PL^M = P(L - CL),$$

$$w\dot{G} = P(\dot{L} - \dot{L}^M) = P(\dot{L} - \dot{C}L - C\dot{L}),$$

$$\frac{w\dot{G}}{PCL} = \frac{1\dot{L}}{CL} - \frac{\dot{C}}{C} - \frac{\dot{L}}{L} = \left[\frac{1}{C} - 1\right]\frac{\dot{L}}{L} - \frac{\dot{C}}{C}$$

so that because of (3.5), (3.5a) and (3.4)

$$\frac{w\dot{G}}{PCL} = -\left[k - d + \frac{d}{C}\right](1 + s)^{-1}\dot{s}$$

By using (3.10) this can be written as

$$\dot{G} = -P * L^M\left[k - d + \frac{d}{C}\right](1 + s)^{-1}\dot{s} < 0.$$

This implies, because of (3.20), a negative balance of payments.

Summing up, the bad paper money drives out the good money, because the government issues more paper money to finance the budget deficit and takes measures to force it on the public at a fixed parity with gold. The public reduces its gold stock, the gold leaves the country and the balance of payments is negative. This process goes on until the gold has completely vanished at time T_3 (see Figure 3.1).

In reality, of course, the government may not be able to increase the penalties adequately or to find out whether its rules are being violated. In this case transactions with gold may be undertaken secretively, at an increased exchange rate (agio), or part of the gold holdings may be hidden. But even then the higher transaction costs for using gold as a medium of exchange should lower the real demand for it and lead to an outflow.

If s is not increased sufficiently, the exchange rate, price level and interest rate begin to rise. In this case periods three and four are interwoven. But there is still first an outflow of gold because the exchange rate is held below its equilibrium level.

We note that there is good reason for the government to make the paper money legal tender and to force its use on the public at a fixed parity with gold. For by doing so it increases the base for the later inflation tax. Moreover, in the third period it can prevent or at least lower — outside the model — the inflation tax and get the resources corresponding to the budget deficit from abroad without seeming to burden the public.

Let us stress finally that the developments of period three are parameter-driven in our model. They depend fully on an adequate increase of s. This corresponds, however, to reality since regulations and penalties are legal measures of the government. An incorporation of such policies into our model would require a political-economic model not presently available.

3.5 Fourth Period: The Return of Good Money

...the paper money quickly disappeared from circulation (in Mexico) in November 1916, and gold and silver came back into general circulation almost as if by magic.

Banyai (1976, p. 76)

If government policy in raising s is successful, G decreases until all gold formerly held by the public has left the country. Thus in T_3 $G = 0$ and $wG^B < fM$ so that, with additional paper money still issued to finance the budget deficit, it is impossible to keep w fixed. Let us consider the consequences.

Recall that $\dot{G}^B = 0$, so that because of (3.2) and (3.3)

$$\dot{M} = PA. \tag{3.21}$$

From equations (3.7), (3.4), (3.5) and (3.5a)

$$\frac{M}{P} = L^M = CL. \tag{3.22}$$

s is assumed again to be constant,[6] whereas w is now variable. It follows then from (3.10)-(3.13) that

$$\ln P = \ln w + \ln P *,$$

$$\pi = \frac{\dot{P}}{P} = \frac{\dot{w}}{w}, \tag{3.23}$$

$$r = r * + \pi,$$

$$\dot{r} = \dot{\pi}. \tag{3.24}$$

Differentiating (3.22) with respect to t and using (3.23) and (3.24) we derive

$$\frac{\dot{M}P - M\dot{P}}{P^2} = \dot{L}^M = \dot{C}L + C\dot{L}$$

Multiplying by $P/M = 1/L^M = 1/CL$ it follows that

$$\frac{\dot{M}}{M} - \pi = \frac{\dot{C}}{C} + \frac{\dot{L}}{L}$$

Thus because of (3.4) and (3.5a)

$$\frac{\dot{M}}{M} - \pi - h(1+\pi)^{-1}\dot{\pi},$$ (3.25)

so that

$$\frac{\dot{M}}{M} < \pi$$ (3.26)

if $\dot{\pi} > 0$, and $\pi > -1$ which should be true to be in accord with the empirical evidence. Equation (3.26) has been well confirmed for all advanced inflations (Bernholz, Gaertner and Heri, 1985; for Austria, Germany, Hungary, Poland and Russia in the early 1920s and France in the 1790s see Bresciani-Turroni 1937, pp. 160-65). It means that the real stock of paper money M/P, approaches zero with $t \to \infty$. The base of the inflation tax shrinks towards zero, thus implying an ever increasing inflation tax rate π to finance the constant real budget deficit.

We will discuss the meaning of the condition $\dot{\pi} > 0$ in the setting of the model in a moment. Before doing so, let us complete our derivations.

Inserting (3.21) and (3.22) into (3.25) we get

$$\frac{A}{CL} = \pi - h(1+\pi)^{-1}\dot{\pi},$$

Using (3.5a) it follows that

$$\frac{A}{g(1+s)^k L}(1+\pi)^h = \pi - h(1+\pi)^{-1}\dot{\pi},$$

$$(1+\pi)[\pi - B(1+\pi)^h] = h\dot{\pi}$$ (3.27)

with

$$B \equiv \frac{A}{g(1+s)^k L} \text{ , a constant.}$$

The differential equation (3.27) determines $\pi(t)$. It is obviously critically dependent on $A/gL,s,k$ and h, i.e., especially on the real budget deficit in relation to the optimal real demand for paper money and on the interest elasticity of the demand for money.

It has already been mentioned that the stylized facts of advanced inflations and of hyperinflations require that $\dot{\pi} > 0$. To see what this means within the model, let us analyze (3.27) and first set $\dot{\pi} > 0$. Obviously this is true if either

$$1 + \pi_1 = 0$$

$$\pi_1 = -1,$$

or if $\quad \pi = B(1 + \pi)^k.$

The first result is useless for our purpose, since it does not correspond to any empirical facts for inflation. The second equation can be analysed by considering function $x = \pi$ and $y = B(1 + \pi)^h$ in Figure 3.2.

For $0 < h < 1$, which is a reasonable assumption considering available econometric estimations, there exists one inflation equilibrium, i.e., $\dot{\pi} = 0$, for a positive rate of inflation, namely π_2. For all $\pi > \pi_2$, $\dot{\pi}$ increases with π, which implies a π growing beyond all bounds. $\dot{\pi} < 0$, however, for $\pi < \pi_2$. This means that the rate of inflation decreases and finally becomes negative, ending up at $\pi = \pi^1 = -1$.

The latter result makes no sense empirically. The conclusion must therefore be that in the present model, to explain growing inflation caused by a constant real budget deficit, the rate of inflation $\pi = \dot{w}/w$ has to jump at time T_3 to a value greater than π_2. This implies, of course, a corresponding jump in the exchange rate and the price level, a trait of models of the type postulating rational expectations, as has been noted by several economists (Sargent and Wallace, 1973; Black, 1974).

If the real budget deficit financed by issuing paper money is not too high, the jump of the rate of inflation required in the beginning may not appear unreasonable. Still, looking at the empirical evidence for some advanced inflations and hyperinflations, this characteristic of the model is inadequate.[7] In spite of this we stick to the model for simplicity and do not introduce adaptive expectations or some form of learning implying changes in the expectation formation mechanism, especially since we have already done so in an earlier paper (Bernholz, Gaertner and Heri 1985).

We conclude that if π and $\dot{w}/w$ jump to a value greater than π_2 at time T_3, $\dot{\pi}$ is positive, and π grows beyond all bounds. But then from (3.5) $L^M \to 0$ as $t \to \infty$.

Let us now look at the development of the gold stock held by the public. From (3.8), (3.6), (3.7) and (3.10)

$$G + P^* L^G = P^* (L - L^M),$$

so that because of (3.5) and (3.5a)

$$G = P^* (1 - C)L, \tag{3.28}$$

$$\dot{G} = P^* (\dot{L} - \dot{C}L - C\dot{L}) = -P^* \dot{C}L, \tag{3.29}$$

since $\dot{L} = 0$ according to (3.4). Using (3.5) and (3.5a) it follows that

$$\dot{G} = ghP^* (1 + s)^k L(1 + \pi)^{-(1+h)} \dot{\pi}.$$

Since $\dot{G}^B = 0$, we derive from (3.9)

$$B = w\dot{G} > 0.$$

In period four, therefore, the balance of payments turns into surplus, gold flows into the country and the public substitutes gold for paper money. What is the intuitive explanation of this process reversing the balance of payments deficit of the earlier periods? Obviously, in a monetized economy the public is adapted to the advantages of using money compared to barter. But with the rate of inflation of the paper money increasing beyond all bounds, the real demand for paper money decreases and approaches asymptotically zero, since the cost of holding paper money is rising with inflation. But the public still prefer to use money for their purchases and sales. Thus the real demand for gold money increases. But to this excess demand there must correspond an excess supply of goods, services and financial assets of the same value. Since this relates to the whole domestic economy, the excess supply necessarily corresponds to the balance of payments surplus. The outside world pays with their stable money for its deficit which is equal to the domestic surplus.

As a consequence, the excess demand of the public for stable money is satisfied. Thiers' law is at work, with $M/P = L^M$ approaching asymptotically zero with $t \to \infty$. G/P^* approaches L, the total real demand for money (see Figure 3.1).

Figure 3.2: Alternative Inflation Paths

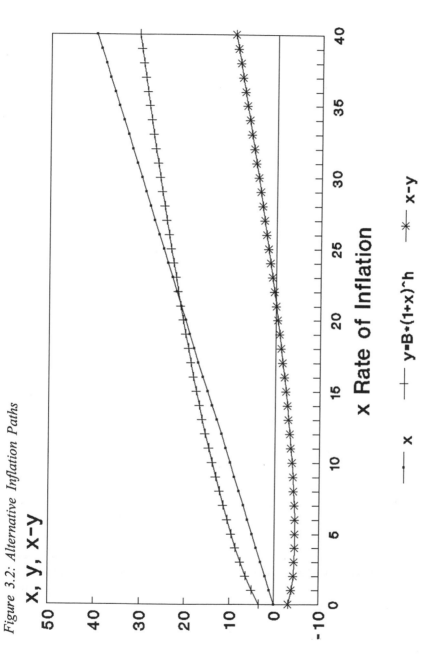

x, y, x−y

x Rate of Inflation

— x   —|— y=B*(1+x)^h   —*— x−y

In the model inflation can go on indefinitely with an increasing rate sufficient to finance the budget deficit at an always decreasing base (i.e., of the real stock of paper money) for the inflation tax. This is certainly not true in reality, in which paper money will be totally repudiated at some time T_4, depending on several factors like the technical sophistication of the payments system, the patience of the public, the damages wrought by the inflation etc. It seems in fact, that the highest possible rate of inflation has risen substantially from the French *assignats* inflation, to the German inflation in the 1920s and the Hungarian inflation in the 1940s.

Finally let us look at the rate of growth of G. It follows from (3.28) and (3.29) that

$$\frac{\dot{G}}{G} = \frac{-\dot{C}L}{(1-C)L}.$$

Using equations (3.5) and (3.7) we get

$$\frac{\dot{G}}{G} = \frac{-\dfrac{d}{dt}\left[\dfrac{M}{P}\right]}{L - \dfrac{M}{P}} > 0.$$

As had to be expected, the growth of the gold stock held by the public corresponds exactly to the decrease of its real stock of paper money.

4. SOME EMPIRICAL EVIDENCE CONCERNING PERIODS ONE TO THREE

Let us consider some empirical evidence for period one, which cannot usually be observed today, and for periods two and three. We turn first to Austria which was on a silver standard when paper money, the 'Bankozettel', was brought into circulation in 1771. At first, the issue of this money was moderate and it remained convertible at 1:1 parity until 1797. It was highly estimated by the public and commanded at times a premium of 1-2 per cent (Wagner 1861, pp. 582-3). In 1788, 1794 and 1796 new amounts of paper money were issued, which drove the metallic money out of circulation and led to an abolishment of convertibility in

Figure 3.3: Alternative Paths for Inflation

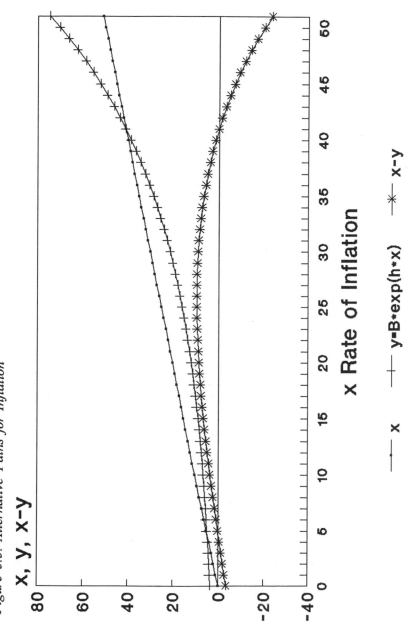

x, y, x-y

x Rate of Inflation

—●— x   —+— y=B*exp(h*x)   —*— x-y

1797 and enforced circulation of the Bankozettel (Wagner 1861, pp. 588-91). Thus the events of periods two and three took place.

An early experiment in paper money was undertaken by John Law in 1716-20. In the beginning the banknotes were convertible at a fixed parity and did not cause inflation until March 1719 (Hamilton 1936/37; Lüthy 1959). According to Storch (1823, vol. 3, p. 401) the banknotes even gained 'one per cent or more against the metallic money in which they were payable'. Things changed rapidly when Law began, from June 1719, to issue more and more banknotes to float the securities of the newly created Company of the Indies and, from September 1719, to buy back the interest-bearing public debt, which he had contracted to refund (Hamilton 1936/37, pp. 54-5; Lüthy 1959, p. 318). Convertibility was suspended, inflation began, specie left the country and the use of gold and silver was forbidden. In January 1720, it was forbidden to keep more than 500 livres in specie or in any form of gold and silver. Violation of this order led to confiscation and an additional fine of 10,000 livres. Deposits with banks, notaires and governmental agencies had to be changed into banknotes. Moreover, already in 1719 and also in 1720, Law tampered several times with the nominal value of gold and silver money, presumably also to discourage its use (Hamilton 1936/7, pp. 60 and 64; Luethy 1959, pp. 320-23).

It seems obvious from the latter part of this story that in reality periods two and three of our development of the model cannot be fully separated. But this would even be predicted by the model, if *s* were not raised sufficiently to fully prevent an increase in the exchange rate. The good money would, under such conditions, still be undervalued compared to the bad money, and leave the country. But inflation would now begin with the rise of the exchange rate though, until specie had been fully driven out of circulation, at a lower rate than the growth of the paper money.

The events described above can be found in many other historical episodes. Let us just mention three of them. In the early 1700s Sweden was on a copper standard. But copper was costly to handle and to transport. As a consequence, so-called transfer notes were introduced, which soon began to circulate as money and replaced copper. In the 1730s, the notes carried up to 2 per cent premium compared to the copper plates. From the beginning of the 1740s more notes were issued, the paper money began to show a discount and the metal holdings of the Riksbank were gradually exhausted (Joerberg 1972, vol. 1, pp. 78-9). Thus we can observe not only the events of period one but also of period two of our model. In 1745 convertibility was suspended and paper money made legal tender (Eagley 1971; Bernholz 1982).

We need refer only briefly to the experience of the United States during the Civil War. The issue of the new paper money, the greenbacks, did not initially endanger convertibility. But in 1862 the parity could no longer be maintained, because of excessive issues. Gold went to a premium, paper money was made legal tender and the free gold market suppressed for some time (Mitchell 1908).

Finally we turn to Peru in the 1870s. Before 1875 notes had been issued by several banks which were convertible into silver. In this year, however, the treasury showed a large deficit since the revenues stemming from guano sales were just sufficient to pay the interest on the foreign debt incurred a few years before for the construction of railways. The deficit was covered by credits from the banks which issued additional notes of about the same amount. As a consequence they lost a great part of their gold reserves which left the country. In December the government allowed the banks to suspend convertibility for four months. But further issues of paper money to finance budget deficits prevented a return to convertibility and led to an increase of the exchange rate and to inflation (Garland 1908, pp. 35-42).

The penalties introduced during period three have sometimes been much harsher than even those imposed by Law. During the French Revolution the Convent National decreed in a law of August 1793, that 'Each Frenchman convicted of refusing to pay assignat money, or of taking or giving it at a discount, will be fined 3000 livres and be imprisoned for 6 months the first time. In case of reversion the fine will be doubled and he will be condemned to 20 years in prison in chains' (Jastrow 1923, p. 67, my translation).

In May 1794 harsh penalties were decreed 'against all those who are found guilty of buying or selling specie, of paying, fixing or proposing different prices for payment in specie and assignats, or of asking which money payment should be received before concluding or finishing a transaction' (Jastrow 1923, p. 70, my translation).

Measures against limiting the use of good money are by no means confined to early times. Austria centralized the buying and selling of foreign exchange at the Devisenzentrale in July 1922. Any violation of the rigid exchange controls was punished with severe penalties and informers were rewarded (Bordes, 1924). Germany, too, introduced tougher and tougher exchange controls during the great inflation (see Beusch 1928, pp. 89-101, for a list of many laws and executive orders from 1922).[8] For example, from December 1922 foreign exchange could be purchased only with the permission of the Internal Revenue, though there were exceptions for firms having a confirmation from their (public) chambers of commerce.

In the great Chinese inflation during and after World War II, selling and buying of gold and silver were prohibited and severe penalties imposed from 1939-43 and in 1947/48 (Chou 1963, pp. 224-7).

5. CONCLUSIONS

The model used in this article to explain widespread historical events is a simple one. For example, purchasing power parity and open interest parity certainly do not always hold. The same is true for the implied Fisher relation stating that the real rate of interest (in our case r^*) equals the nominal interest rate minus the rate of inflation.

In fact, there seems to be a systematic undervaluation of the inflating currency with flexible exchange rates, until either a stabilization or hyperinflation removes it (Bernholz 1982; Bernholz, Gaertner and Heri 1985). Also, the expected rate of inflation is usually not equal to the actual rate. Often, moreover, foreign countries experience inflation themselves, so that the relative increase of their money supplies together with growing (not constant, as in the model) real national incomes have to be taken into account. Finally, real deficits are usually not constant, inflation usually even increases them if it is high enough. And certainly not all countries are small.

We have seen, however, that the simplicity of the model has great advantages. It allows us to find the causes responsible for certain general events which can all be observed in a few, and of which some are present in all inflations studied. This is satisfying, for it is with this aim that general theories are developed.

Let us summarize some of the results. First, a continuous flow of new money into the economy leads to inflation only after a more or less extended time, if the old money is also used abroad, which has historically been the case with gold and silver, but can also be true not only for different commodity moneys but also for moneys based on substantial foreign reserves.

Second, a real budget deficit cannot be maintained permanently. The government must either reduce it or the inflating bad money will be substituted in time by the good money and the base of the inflation tax be eroded. There, of course, we neglect the asymptotical developments predicted by the model.

Third, because of the latter relationships, governments which see themselves unable or unwilling to control the real budget deficit, are strongly motivated to try to preserve the basis of the inflation tax by making the bad money legal tender, forcing its use on the public, prohibiting the use of the old money and introducing exchange controls. All these measures will, however, in the end be inadequate to deal with the situation.

Fourth, Gresham's law works at an earlier period of the inflationary process, when the government tries to maintain the fixed parity between the two moneys, i.e., a double standard of currency (like the old bimetallism). Thiers' law will operate only later when the increase of the now flexible exchange rate and of the rate of inflation lower the real demand for the inflating money.

It should be obvious how these results must be modified if real national income grows, if the old money is also inflating, but at a lower rate, and if the country considered is large.

ENDNOTES

*	Reprinted from *Journal of Institutional and Theoretical Economics (JITE)*, 145(3), Sept. 1989, pp. 465-88, with minor corrections. Endnote 4 and the reference to Ming China in Table 3.1 have been added. I am grateful to Hans-Jürgen Jaksch, Malte Faber, Martin Hellwig, Hans Gersbach, Wilfried Reiss and the participants of a Basel University seminar for helpful suggestions, and to Juliane Heinritz-Deichmann for helping to find the figures for the German hyperinflation.
1.	'In August 1923 the value of the paper money in circulation in Germany amounted, on some days, to scarcely 80 million gold marks. ... The explanation is given precisely by the fact, that alongside the paper mark, there circulated a large quantity of foreign exchange and of "emergency money" (Notgeld). ... The history of the assignats also showed that the phase characterized by a depreciation of the assignats, more rapid than the increase of the quantities issued, coincided with the reappearance and growing diffusion of metallic money in the circulation. Hence ... the principle of Gresham is reversed, and good money drives out the bad' (Bresciani-Turroni (1937, p. 174).
2.	It seems that Sir Thomas Gresham did not formulate clearly 'Gresham's law' and that it already had been known before him. The term 'Gresham's Law' was probably coined by MacLeod (1863, p. 464). For evidence see Jastrow (1923, pp. 45-50).
3.	The idea of an exogenous real budget deficit has been successfully applied by Jaksch (1986) to the German hyperinflation of the 1920s and to the recent advanced inflation in Argentina.
4.	An exception is the Soviet hyperinflation of the 1920s, since the government itself introduced a competing, more stable money at the end of 1922. See Bernholz (1995), who also gives an econometric estimation.
5.	Strictly speaking, A, D are rates of change of the real and nominal budget deficits, respectively. These concepts are usually defined per period (not to be confused with the periods used in the expositions), e.g., per year.
6.	Note that the events in the model in period four are thus *not* parameter driven, as they were in period three. In reality, of course, the government may try to increase s further to force the paper money on to the public. Empirically this policy has never been finally successful. It thus seems to be warranted to keep s constant at some level.

7.   There are some other problems connected with models combining rational expectations with the usual types of demand for money functions. This is the case if they are used to explain inflationary processes in which the money supply is itself dependent on the price level or rate of inflation. First, these models are very sensitive in their qualitative results to changes in parameter values. E.g., in our model we get two inflation equilibria ($\dot{\pi} = 0$) instead of π_2, if $h > 1$. Note that the equilibrium with the lower rate of inflation is now unstable, whereas that with the higher rate is stable. The same result is true, as has been noted by Bruno and Fischer (1986), if the (paper) money demand function $L^M = gL\exp(-h\pi)$ is used (Figure 3.3). In both cases no advanced or hyperinflation can be explained with the model if the upper inflation equilibrium implies too low a rate of inflation. Moreover, in both models no positive inflation equilibrium exists if A/L and/or h are sufficiently great. To my knowledge the literature rather neglects these empirical problems. Concerning the nonexistence of an inflation equilibrium, Dornbusch and Fischer (1986, p. 4) remark cryptically that 'Hyperinflation would be a strong possibility'. But $\dot{\pi}$ is negative in this case, so that π should fall (see Figure 3.3).

         Finally, Black (1974) and Sargent and Wallace (1973) have pointed out that with rational expectations there typically exists an infinity of solutions for the price path depending on the initial jump in the price level. In our model it is obvious that the initial jump of π in $t = T_3$, determines $\dot{\pi}$ and thus the time paths of π and P. This is another problem connected with the assumption of rational expectations, which we do not want to discuss in the present paper. We simply assume that π jumps at $t = T_3$ to a value greater than π_2 (Figure 3.2). This assures that a hyperinflationary process, like those observed, gets started.

8.   Austria and Germany suspended gold convertibility at the outbreak of World War I. Periods three and four were intertwined from that time onwards, with the events of period four getting more and more weight after the war. From 1914-16 especially, the Reichsbank succeeded in inducing the public to exchange substantial amounts of gold into banknotes.

REFERENCES

Banyai, R.A. (1976), *Money and Finance in Mexico During the Constitutionalist Revolution 1913-1917*, Tai Wan Enterprises, Taipei.

Bernholz, P. (1982), 'Flexible Exchange Rates in Historical Perspective' *Princeton Studies in International Finance*, 49, International Finance Section, Department of Economics, Princeton University.

Bernholz, P. (1993), 'Paper Money Inflation, Prices, Gresham's Law and Exchange Rates in Ming China'. Unpublished Paper, WWZ, Universität Basel, 4003 Basel, Switzerland.

Bernholz, P. (1995), 'Currency Substitution During Hyperinflation in the Soviet Union, 1922-24', *The Journal of European Economic History*.

Bernholz, P., Gaertner, M. and Heri, E.(1985), 'Historical Experiences with Flexible Exchange Rates', *Journal of International Economics* 19, pp. 21-45.

Beusch, P. (1928), *Währungszerfall und Währungsstabilisierung*, Springer, Berlin.

Bezanson, A. (1951), *Prices and Inflation During the American Revolution, Pennsylvania, 1770-1790*, University of Pennsylvania Press, Philadelphia.

Black, F. (1974), 'Uniqueness of the Price Level in Monetary Growth with Rational Expectation', *Journal of Economic Theory*, 7, pp. 53-65.

Bordes, J. van W. (1924), *The Austrian Crown*, King, London.

Bresciani-Turroni, C. (1937), *The Economics of Inflation*, Allen & Unwin, London, 1st edition, in Italian, 1931.

Bruno, M. and Fischer, S. (1986), 'The Inflationary Process: Shocks and Accommodation', in Ben-Porath, Y. (ed.), *The Israeli Economy. Maturing Through Crisis*, Harvard University Press, Cambridge, Mass., pp. 347-69.

Chou, S.-H. (1963), *The Chinese Inflation, 1937-1949*, Columbia University Press, New York and London.

Connolly, M. (1978), 'The Monetary Approach to an Open Economy: The Fundamental Theory', in Putnam, B.H. and Wilford, O.S. (eds.), *The Monetary Approach to International Adjustment*, Praeger, New York.

Delivanis, D. and Cleveland, W. (1950), *Greek Monetary Development 1939-1948*, Indiana University, Bloomington, Indiana.

Dornbusch, R. and Fischer, S. (1986), 'Stopping Hyperinflations Past and Present', *Weltwirtschaftliches Archiv* 122, pp. 1-47.

Eagley, R.V. (ed. and transl.) (1971), 'The Swedish Bullionist Controversy: P.N. Christiernin's *Lectures on the High Price of Foreign Exchange in Sweden*', American Philosophical Society, Philadelphia.

Frenkel, J.A. and Johnson, H.G. (eds.) (1976), *The Monetary Approach to the Balance of Payments*, Allen & Unwin, London.

Garland, A. (1908), *Estudio sobre los Medios Circulantes Usados en el Peru*, Imprenta la Industria, Lima.

Girton, L. and Roper, D. (1981), 'Theory and Implications of Currency Substitution', *Journal of Money, Credit and Banking*, 13(1), pp. 12-30.

Hamilton, E.J. (1936/37), 'Prices and Wages at Paris Under John Law's System', *The Quarterly Journal of Economics*, LI, pp. 42-70.

Holtfrerich, C.-L. (1980), *Die deutsche Inflation*, de Gruyter, Berlin and New York.

Hume, D. (1955), 'Of the Balance of Trade', in Rotwein, E. (ed.), *David Hume. Writings on Economics*, Thomas Nelson & Sons, Edinburgh, pp. 60-77.

Jaksch, H.-J. (1986), 'Kleine ökonometrische Modelle für sich rasch entwertende Währungen', *Ifo-Studien*, 32, pp. 241-7, Ifo-Institut, München.

Jastrow, J. (1923), *Textbuch 4, Geld und Kredit*, 5th edition, Berlin.

Joerberg, L. (1972), *A History of Prices in Sweden*, 2 vols., C.W.K. Cleerup, Lund, Sweden.

Kemmerer, E.W. (1940), *Inflation and Revolution*, Princeton University Press, Princeton, N.J.

Lansburgh, A. (1929), 'Banken (Notenbanken)', in Elster L. and Weber, A. (eds.), *Handwörterbuch der Staatswissenschaften*, Ergänzungsband, Gustav Fischer, Jena, pp. 35ff.

League of Nations (1946), *The Course and Control of Inflation. A Review of Monetary Experience in Europe after World War I*, Economic, Financial and Transit Department, League of Nations, Geneva.

Luethy, H. (1959), *La Banque Protestante en France*, vol. 1, SEVPEN, Paris.

MacLeod, H.D. (1863), *Dictionary of Political Economy*, London.

Mitchell, W.C. (1908), *Gold, Prices and Wages under the Greenback Standard*, University of California Press, Berkeley.

Phillipps, H. Jr. (1972), *Continental Paper Money*, Augustus M. Kelley, Clifton, 1st Edition 1865.

Sargent, T.J. and Wallace, N. (1973), 'The Stability of Models of Money and Growth with Perfect Foresight', *Econometrica* 41(4), pp. 1043-8.

Starbatty, J. (1982), 'Zur Umkehrung des Gresham'schen Gesetzes bei Entnationalisierung des Geldes', *Kredit und Kapital*, 15(3), pp. 387-409.

Storch, H. (1823), *Cours d'Economie Politique*, edited by Say, J.-B., Aillaud, J.P. and Bossnage, P., Rey & Gravier, Paris.

Subercaseaux, G. (1912), *El Papel Moneda,* Santiago de Chile.

Thiers, L.A. (1840), *History of the French Revolution*, Translated by F. Shoberl, 3 vols., Carey & Hart, Philadelphia, 1st edition, in French 1825.

Wagner, A. (1861), 'Zur Geschichte und Kritik der österreichischen Bankozettel-periode', *Tübinger Zeitschrift für die gesamte Staatswissenschaft*, 17, pp. 577-631.

Young, J.P (1925), *European Currency and Exchange Investigation,* Commission of Gold and Silver Inquiry, United States Senate, Serial 9, vol. 1, Government Printing Office, Washington.

4. Rapid Inflation: Deliberate Policy or Miscalculation?

Alex S. Cukierman[*]

1. INTRODUCTION

High inflations, particularly when they reach the hyperinflation stage, seem like bizarre events. Inflation imposes costs on society and existing evidence suggests that in most, if not all hyperinflations, steady state real revenues from monetary expansion could have been increased by decreasing the rate of inflation. This raises doubts about the rationality of governments that inflate at high rates or, at the very least, about their understanding of the way the economy operates. A basic question is why these governments inflate at high and accelerating rates only ultimately to stabilize by changing the monetary regime. Answering this and related questions requires better understanding of the motives and constraints facing the inflating governments.

Allan Meltzer has long been committed to a line of investigation that tries to bridge the gap between economics and politics in order to produce a better understanding of how economic policy is actually made. This chapter follows this tradition by trying to uncover some of the motives, institutional constraints, and historical conditions that may induce government to follow policies whose ultimate consequence is very rapid or even hyperinflation. The central theme is that, although policy errors may be part of the story, a substantial part of hyperinflationary policies can be understood in terms of deliberate choices made by rational governments.

The recent macro-policy-oriented literature has identified several motives that tempt governments to inflate. Among the most prominent are the employment and the revenue motives. This chapter focuses exclusively on the latter motive which probably was the major driving force during the

classic post-World War I hyperinflations as well as during the recent
Bolivian hyperinflation.[1]

Section 2 opens the chapter by presenting evidence on the behaviour
of revenues from seigniorage in Germany during the well-known post-
World War I hyperinflation. A puzzling feature is that those revenues
tended to increase, on average, as the rate of inflation increased contrary
to what is implied by available estimates of the demand for money in
Germany during the hyperinflation. This result is robust to alternative
ways of evaluating seigniorage. A related regularity is that actual real
money balances move substantially more smoothly than those that are
predicted by making use of any of the available estimates of money
demand under perfect foresight.[2]

Section 3 presents indicators for the behaviour of inflationary
expectations during the German hyperinflation. These indicators are drawn
from the forward exchange market and from the domestic credit market.
Both indicators suggest that expectations seriously underestimated actual
developments particularly in 1923 when the already high rate of monetary
expansion climbed to unprecedented heights.[3]

Section 4 presents a framework in which a government's willingness
to trade higher inflation for seigniorage revenues undergoes stochastic
changes over time and in which a government has more accurate
information about the persistence of those changes than the public.
Because of this information structure the public learns gradually but
optimally about changes in a government's inflationary intentions. A
government cares about both the present and the future but may have a
positive time preference. Due to the slow adjustment of expectations
current seigniorage revenues can be increased by raising monetary growth
even if such policy eventually decreases seigniorage. Governments that
become more desirous of immediate seigniorage revenues may find it
rational to follow such a policy. This result provides a resolution of the
seeming paradox that most high-inflation governments ultimately operated
their economies in a range of expected inflation in which a decrease in
inflation would have increased steady-state revenues from seigniorage.[4]
It also resolves the puzzle raised by the positive correlation between
monetary expansion and seigniorage revenues during much of the German
hyperinflation and provides an explanation for the large and somewhat
persistent downward biases in expectations within an optimal forecasting
framework. Last but not least the discussion in section 4 is consistent with
the view that even during hyperinflationary episodes the governments in
charge were following deliberate but rational (given their objectives and
constraints) inflationary policies. The tremendous inflationary acceleration
which occurred in Germany in 1923 is rationalized in terms of an increase

in the government's need for immediate seigniorage revenues following the Ruhr's invasion.

Section 5 provides an explanation for the fact that hyperinflations are allowed to accelerate for a while only to be finally stabilized. The main idea is that due to expectational and other lags, an acceleration in the rate of monetary expansion can temporarily increase seigniorage even if it ultimately decreases it. Policymakers with strong time preference for seigniorage may find it profitable to engage in such a policy as long as expectations have not adjusted. But once this adjustment takes place and seigniorage revenues drop below a certain threshold, the old regime is no longer useful to the policymaker who then finds it advantageous to introduce a monetary reform. This provides a qualitative analysis of the factors that determine the timing of stabilization.[5]

Europe in the immediate post-World War I period was the nursing ground for some of the classic hyperinflations. Against this background sections 6 and 7 provide answers to two questions. First, why was deficit financing used? Second, given the size of deficits, why was the fraction financed by money creation so large in some of the countries? The answer given to the first question is that many individuals in all of the countries that emerged from the war (expecting to have substantially higher future incomes) wanted to borrow resources against their future higher labour incomes but could not do so because of financial constraints. Being unable to borrow through private capital markets, they managed partially to fulfil this desire via the political system by inducing governments to create deficits.[6] This factor also provides a partial answer to the second question.

But for the countries that lost the war, and in particular for Germany, the large foreign exchange-denominated reparations provided an additional powerful incentive to resort to inflationary finance. In the German case a large fraction of reparations was conditional on Germany's ability to pay. A smoothly functioning fiscal system would have been taken as a signal that Germany was able to pay more and would have triggered an increase in reparation demands on the part of the allies. By contrast heavy reliance on inflationary finance, by creating the opposite impression, would have contained the demands of the allies, as was actually the case at the end of the hyperinflation. In addition, because of the stipulation that reparations had to be paid in foreign exchange, it was more likely that the fraction expropriated for reparations out of conventional taxes would be larger than the same fraction from seigniorage revenues. Under those circumstances most German voters preferred the inflation tax to regular current or future taxes, independently of the size of their wealth. Those ideas are described verbally in section 6 and demonstrated within the framework of a decisive voter model of the type pioneered by Meltzer and Richard (1981) in section 7. Concluding remarks follow.

2. THE PUZZLING BEHAVIOUR OF REVENUES FROM SEIGNIORAGE DURING THE GERMAN HYPERINFLATION

The post-World War I German hyperinflation is one of the best-known and relatively well-documented hyperinflations. As opposed to some recent high inflations in Argentina, Brazil and Israel, the German government financed well over 50 per cent of its expenditures by means of seigniorage during the hyperinflation years.[7] It is therefore well accepted that the revenue motive was the major force behind the inflationary policies followed by the German authorities.[8] But given this premise and estimates of the elasticity of money demand with respect to expected inflation, most of the rates of inflation prevailing in Germany, at least since mid-1922, imply irrational behaviour on the part of the government. The reason is that, to the extent that the public did not systematically underestimate actual inflation, estimates of money demand imply that inflation was in a range in which a decrease in it would have increased the government's revenue from seigniorage.

Under perfect foresight Cagan's (1956) original estimate of the semi-elasticity of money demand (α) which is 5.46 implies that steady-state revenues from seigniorage decrease as inflation goes up beyond 18.3 per cent per month.[9] Sargent (1977) points out some econometric problems in Cagan's estimate and reestimates α, using both Cagan's as well as Barro's (1970) data under the assumption of rational expectations. The lowest point estimate obtained by Sargent is 2.344. This would imply that at any rate of inflation above 42.7 per cent per month, further inflationary acceleration decreases government's steady state revenues from seigniorage. However, Sargent is not able to pinpoint α very precisely. Christiano (1987) points out that the estimation procedure is sensitive to the shock restrictions imposed on the money-supply process and manages to obtain more precise estimates of α by imposing several alternative money-supply rules. The lowest significantly different than zero estimate of α he obtains is 1.76. This estimate implies that the critical point beyond which steady state seigniorage decreases with inflation is 56.8 per cent. A quick look at column (1) of Table 4.1 establishes that inflation was most of the time above even this large rate from July 1922 until the stabilization at the end of 1923.[10]

Does this mean that the German government was acting irrationally in terms of its own objectives? A natural point of departure for an investigation of the rationality of a government that persistently speeds up the rate of nominal growth in order to get more seigniorage is to examine whether seigniorage increased or decreased as inflation accelerated. In general, seigniorage in month t can be calculated as

$$\frac{M_{t+1} - M_t}{\bar{P}_t} \qquad (4.1)$$

where M_t are nominal money balances at the beginning of month t and $\bar{P}_t$ is the average price level over the month. Such seigniorage figures (in percentages of November 1920 real money balances) are reported in column (3) of Table 4.1. It is apparent that in general, as the magnitude of inflation increased, seigniorage increased. Particularly striking is the large increase in seigniorage during the last several months of the hyperinflation when the monthly rate of inflation was well above one thousand per cent.[11]

Since this finding is so blatantly in conflict with conventional wisdom about the relationship between inflation and seigniorage, it is advisable to examine the possibility that it is due to a measurement problem. In particular it should be noted that the expression in equation (4.1) is a discrete approximation of the precise expression for monthly seigniorage which is the integral over the month of momentary rates of seigniorage. While the difference between those two measures is usually small at low or moderate rates of inflation, it may become quite important at high rates. In order to evaluate the correct measure of seigniorage, rates of money growth and of inflation at each instant are required. Such data is unavailable. But it is possible to approximate this ideal measure by computing it analytically and by assuming that, within each month, the instantaneous rates of inflation and of monetary expansion are distributed uniformly. More precisely let μ_t^i and π_t^i be the instantaneous rates of monetary growth and of inflation in month t. Then

$$M_{t+\tau} = M_t e^{\mu_t^i \tau} \; ; \; P_{t+\tau} = P_t e^{\pi_t^i \tau} \quad 0 \le \tau \le 1 \qquad (4.2)$$

where M_t and P_t are nominal money balances and the price level at the beginning of month t. Instantaneous seigniorage revenues are

Table 4.1 *Inflation, Money Growth, Seigniorage and Real Money Balances, Germany 1921-1923 (Monthly)*

Period	(1) (2) Monthly Rates of Change		(3) (4) Seigniorage		(5) (6) (7) Real Money Balances in (Percentages of 11/20 balances)		
	Prices	Money	Calculated Discretely	Calculated Continuously	Actual	Predicted	(6)/(5)
1920-12	-0.024	0.071	7.33	7.86	109.66	119.88	1.09
1921- 1	-0.011	-0.032	-3.45	-3.46	107.34	117.27	1.09
2	-0.036	0.012	1.33	1.37	112.62	122.44	1.09
3	-0.019	0.030	3.37	3.58	118.20	118.85	1.01
4	-0.012	0.021	2.43	2.58	122.09	117.37	0.96
5	0.015	0.014	1.73	1.70	121.97	112.02	0.92
6	0.045	0.049	5.78	5.86	122.43	106.26	0.87
7	0.184	0.028	3.29	2.73	106.29	83.19	0.78
8	0.203	0.035	3.17	2.92	91.43	80.44	0.88
9	0.132	0.079	6.93	6.47	87.17	91.22	1.05
10	0.285	0.060	4.75	3.81	71.91	69.65	0.96
11	0.191	0.103	6.26	6.26	66.58	82.14	1.23
12	0.036	0.126	8.27	8.95	72.33	107.88	1.49
1922- 1	0.024	0.015	1.07	0.98	67.72	99.21	1.47
2	0.216	0.040	2.58	2.10	57.92	78.63	1.36
3	0.245	0.089	4.45	4.04	50.66	74.71	1.47
4	0.091	0.075	3.48	3.58	49.93	98.03	1.96
5	0.052	0.082	4.06	4.11	51.38	105.07	2.05
6	0.254	0.114	5.58	4.65	45.65	73.57	1.61
7	0.653	0.122	4.60	2.96	30.99	36.47	1.18
8	0.681	0.255	5.72	4.56	23.14	34.70	1.50
9	0.717	0.331	6.23	4.53	17.94	32.56	1.81
10	1.003	0.482	6.13	4.51	13.28	19.69	1.48
11	0.614	0.606	5.62	6.24	13.21	39.02	2.95
12	0.555	0.700	8.10	8.01	14.44	43.29	3.00
1923- 1	0.997	0.550	5.75	4.34	11.21	19.88	1.77
2	0.325	0.770	5.90	9.91	14.97	64.91	4.35
3	-0.059	0.571	16.33	14.74	24.99	127.56	5.10
4	0.292	0.186	4.48	3.75	22.93	68.75	3.00
5	0.928	0.308	5.61	3.46	15.55	22.45	1.44
6	2.026	1.019	10.23	6.00	10.38	3.25	0.31
7	5.979	1.521	7.99	2.18	3.75	0.00	0
8	16.895	14.213	14.91	8.01	3.19	0.00	0
9	85.692	41.565	26.15	4.22	1.57	0.00	0
10	173.075	87.449	7.91	2.61	0.80	0.00	0
11	12.337	159.311	12.45	216.58	9.62	0.00	0
12	0.272	0.240	1.73	2.00	9.38	71.30	7.60

Notes: Inflation and money growth are rates of change from the beginning to the end of each month in decimal points. They have been calculated using data on the mid-month Wholesale Price Index and on end-of-the-month quantity of notes in circulation from pp. 526-530 of Young (1983). Monthly mid-month to mid-month rates of inflation were converted to rates of inflation over each month by taking (geometric) averages of adjacent mid-month to mid-month inflation rates.

Monthly real revenues from inflation are expressed in percentages of end-of-November 1920 real money balances. The inflation tax in column (3) is calculated by dividing the change in notes in circulation over the month by the average level of the Wholesale Price Index during the month. The inflation tax in column (4) is obtained by expressing the monthly inflation tax as the integral, over the month, of momentary inflation taxes under the assumption that monetary expansion and inflation are uniformly distributed over the month. Further details appear in the text.

Actual and predicted real money balances refer to the end of each month and are expressed in percentages of end-of-November 1920 real money balances. Real money balances at the end of each month are obtained from those at the end of the previous month by using the rates of money growth and of inflation over the month. Predicted real balances (in terms of 11/20 balances) are calculated by using Christiano's (1987) recent estimate of the semi-elasticity of money demand (α) which is 1.76 and the assumption of perfect foresight.

$$\frac{\dot{M}_{t+\tau}}{P_{t+\tau}} = m_t \mu_t^i e^{(u_t^i - \pi_t^i)\tau} \quad 0 \leq \tau \leq 1 \tag{4.3}$$

where $m_t \equiv M_t/P_t$. Integrating equation (4.3) over the month,

$$\int_0^1 \frac{\dot{M}_{t+\tau}}{P_{t+\tau}} d\tau = m_t \mu_t^i \frac{e^{\mu_t^i - \pi_t^i} - 1}{\mu_t^i - \pi_t^i}. \tag{4.4}$$

The relationships between monthly and instantaneous rates of change are given by

$$\mu_t^i = \ln(1 + \mu_t) \tag{4.5}$$

$$\pi_t^i = \ln(1 + \pi_t) \tag{4.6}$$

where μ_t and π_t are the rate of monetary expansion and the rate of inflation from the beginning to the end of month t. By using equations (4.4), (4.5) and data on μ_t and π_t, it is possible to obtain estimates of seigniorage that are not subject to biases caused by the use of an average monthly price level. Such estimates, again in percentages of real balances at the end of November 1920, are presented in column (4) of Table 4.1.[12] Seigniorage still goes up as the rate of inflation accelerates from negative rates in early 1921 to over ten thousand per cent per month at the end of 1923. The total amount of yearly seigniorage from column (4) of Table 4.1 is presented along with the yearly rates of inflation and of monetary expansion in Table 4.2. The increase in seigniorage is particularly large in 1923. Since most of this increase is due to a tremendous increase in the last month of the hyperinflation, total seigniorage in 1923 is also presented only for the first ten months of 1923 at a yearly rate. For this alternative calculation seigniorage in 1923 is still larger than seigniorage in 1922 which in turn is larger than total seigniorage in 1921.

Table 4.2 Yearly Seigniorage and Inflation, Germany 1921-1923 [a]

		(Per cent Per Year)	
Year	Seigniorage	Inflation	Monetary Expansion
1921	42.77	142	66
1922	50.27	4226	1030
1923	277.80	85.54×10^9	38.75×10^7
1923[b]	71.06		

Notes:
[a] Seigniorage is in percentages of November 1920 real money balances. It is calculated from column (4) of Table 4.1.
[b] Seigniorage during the first ten months of 1923 at a yearly rate.

I conclude that contrary to what is implied by most empirical estimates of money demand functions during the German hyperinflation, seigniorage did not decrease as high inflation penetrated the hyperinflation range and continued to accelerate.[13] A related regularity is that monetary expansion and seigniorage are positively correlated on a month-by-month basis during most of the hyperinflation (compare columns (2) and (4) of Table 4.1).

In order to obtain more information about the cause of the divergence between actual seigniorage and the amount predicted by theory and available estimates of α, it is instructive to compare actual real money balances at the end of each period with those predicted under perfect foresight by conventional estimates of money demand for Germany during the hyperinflation. Since the tax rate (which is the rate of monetary expansion) is the same for both actual and predicted seigniorage, any differences between those two magnitudes must originate from differences between the actual and predicted behaviour of real money balances. Actual and predicted real money balances, measured in terms of end-of-November 1920 real balances are presented in columns (5) and (6) of Table 4.1. Predicted balances are computed using the low estimate of 1.76 for α from Christiano (1987). The ratio between predicted and actual real money balances is presented in column (7). A striking regularity that emerges from comparison of this ratio with inflation is that it tends to go down when inflation accelerates and to go up when inflation decelerates. This feature holds practically throughout the entire three years but is particularly striking in 1921 and in 1923. From the beginning to the second half of 1921 inflation goes from negative to positive values. Concurrently the ratio between predicted and actual balances goes down. In 1923 this negative correlation is even more strongly in evidence. As inflation plunges into the negative range in March 1923, the ratio between predicted and actual balances shoots up. Then as inflation rapidly moves up into the high cliffs of the second half of 1923, the ratio goes down abruptly and becomes zero from July 1923 until the end of the hyperinflation.

The upshot is that actual real balances adjust to changes in the rate of inflation more slowly than predicted balances do. This feature becomes even stronger if higher estimates of α are used instead of the low 1.76 estimate. Actual balances generally move in the same direction as predicted balances, but more slowly. This phenomenon is consistent with each of the following two distinct but not necessarily mutually exclusive hypotheses. One is that the long-run adjustment of money demand to a change in expected inflation is larger than the short-run adjustment because the institutions of monetary exchange adjust slowly. The other is that, due to an inability to separate persistent from transitory inflationary developments, inflationary expectations lag behind actual inflationary developments even if the public uses all the information at its disposal in an optimal manner. The following section presents evidence from the foreign exchange and from the capital markets on the behaviour of inflationary expectations during the German hyperinflation.

3. EVIDENCE ON THE BEHAVIOUR OF INFLATIONARY EXPECTATIONS DURING THE GERMAN HYPERINFLATION

There is no direct model free measure of inflationary expectations during the German hyperinflation.[14] But it is possible to get an idea about the behaviour of those expectations by examining data on the one month forward rate of exchange between the mark and the pound sterling during the hyperinflation. The advantage of this data, besides being model free, is that it is based on market data which reflects the beliefs of market participants about the future course of the exchange rate.[15] Although exchange rate expectations need not perfectly coincide with inflationary expectations, the correlation between them is likely to be very high. Frenkel (1977, p. 656) reports that the correlation among various price indices and the exchange rate exceeded 0.99 during the hyperinflation and concludes that 'it seems reasonable to identify the expectations on the exchange rate with the expectations on the price level'. Even if we do not subscribe to such a strong relation between those expectations, it is highly likely that one can learn about the qualitative features of the relationship between actual and expected inflation from the parallel relationship between the actual and the previously expected rate of depreciation of the exchange rate. In particular, lags in the adjustment of expected depreciation behind actual depreciation will be taken as being indicative of similar lags in the adjustment of expected inflation to actual inflationary developments.

The first two columns of Table 4.3 present data on the expected and the actual rates of depreciation of the mark with respect to the pound sterling. At each moment the one month forward percentage discount is taken as a measure of the rate of depreciation expected to occur over the next month. The corresponding actual depreciation over the same forecast span is displayed in column (2). Thus, according to the table, a 0.8 per cent appreciation of the mark was expected to occur at the beginning of January 1921 until the beginning of February 1921. The actual appreciation was 6.9 per cent. An examination of the relationship between actual and expected depreciation in Table 4.3 reveals that, generally, the fluctuations in the actual rate of change in the exchange rate were substantially larger than the fluctuations in its expected counterpart. Individuals underpredicted large depreciations as well as large appreciations. Particularly striking is the fact that as the rate of depreciation accelerated from 1921 to 1923, expected depreciation lagged behind quite substantially. Until May of 1922 the one month forward mark consistently sold at a small premium with respect to the pound sterling in spite of the fact that between May of 1921 and May of 1922, the actual average rate of depreciation was 18.7 per cent per month. As the rate of depreciation accelerated through the rest of 1922 and 1923, expected depreciation also increased gradually but, at least for as long as there is data on forward rates,[16] it trailed far behind actual developments. The lag in the adjustment of exchange rate expectations became particularly dramatic during July-September 1923 when the mark price of sterling rose by leaps and bounds. The data are therefore consistent with the view that there were substantial lags in the adjustment of exchange rate expectations. Since movements in the exchange rate and in local price indices were highly correlated, it is likely that inflationary expectations similarly lagged behind inflationary developments.

This conclusion is confirmed by data on the daily money rate. This rate is consistently below the actual rate of inflation as can be seen from a comparison of columns (3) and (4) in Table 4.3. The daily rate fluctuates in a relatively narrow range (between 0.3 and 0.4 of a per cent per month) until mid-1922 and starts an almost steady climb thereafter, reaching a maximum of 128 per cent per month in October 1923. However, the gap between actual inflation and the daily rate tends to widen as inflation accelerates in 1923, indicating that the extent of inflation underestimation rose with inflation. These data too are therefore consistent with the view that there were substantial lags in the adjustment of inflationary expectations and that the degree of underestimation became particularly high during the last phases of hyperinflation, when the rate of inflation reached unprecedented heights.

Casual historical evidence lends further support to the view that the extent of inflation had been seriously underestimated at the time. Holtfrerich (1986, p. 191) notes that foreigners continued to buy paper marks in the form of bank notes and mark deposits into the year 1922. This behaviour reflected the belief, held roughly until the beginning of 1922, that the prewar parity of the mark was going to be reestablished by the Reichsbank. Economic policy debates at the time left the impression that such a course of action was a real possibility. The publication in June 1922 of the recommendation by the J.P. Morgan Committee to postpone long-term lending to Germany and the murder of Rathenau shattered this belief (Holtfrerich 1986). The forward premium became a discount and the nominal daily market rate started to increase, too. But the actual depreciation of the mark and actual inflation increased much more as can be seen in Table 4.3.

Table 4.3 Market Indicators of Expected Inflation During the German Hyperinflation (Decimals)

		(1)	(2)	(3)	(4)
		Monthly Depreciation of the Mark		Daily Money Rate (Monthly)	Actual Monthly Rate of Inflation
		Expected	Actual		
1921-	1	-0.008	-0.069	0.003	-0.011
	2	-0.005	0.000	0.003	-0.036
	3	-0.008	0.019	0.003	-0.019
	4	-0.008	0.049	0.003	-0.012
	5	-0.006	-0.046	0.003	0.015
	6	-0.005	0.116	0.003	0.045
	7	-0.005	0.042	0.003	0.184
	8	-0.005	0.112	0.003	0.203
	9	-0.005	0.352	0.004	0.132
	10	-0.003	0.960	0.003	0.285
	11	-0.003	-0.069	0.003	0.191
	12	-0.002	-0.109	0.003	0.036
1922-	1	-0.004	0.109	0.004	0.024
	2	-0.002	0.245	0.003	0.216
	3	-0.001	0.197	0.004	0.245
	4	0.000	-0.034	0.004	0.091
	5	0.000	0.731	0.003	0.052
	6	0.000	0.725	0.004	0.254
	7	0.001	0.798	0.004	0.653
	8	0.005	0.720	0.005	0.681
	9	0.026	0.561	0.006	0.717
	10	0.052	2.164	0.006	1.003
	11	0.154	0.353	0.007	0.614
	12	0.111	0.089	0.007	0.555
1923-	1	0.076	2.097	0.009	0.997
	2	0.182	-0.358	0.019	0.325
	3	0.160	-0.071	0.009	-0.059
	4	0.062	0.804	0.010	0.292
	5	0.106	1.202	0.015	0.928
	6	0.128	1.357	0.015	2.026
	7	0.391	10.413	0.056	5.979
	8	0.962	22.313	1.118	16.895
	9	0.444	24.847	1.267	85.692
	10			1.280	173.075

Notes: Expected and actual rates of depreciation of the mark are calculated using data
on one month forward rates and spot rates, respectively. The raw data are from
Einzig (1937) pp. 450-5 and refer to the exchange rate of the mark to the
pound sterling. The expected rate of depreciation over the next month is
proxied by the relative forward discount of the mark, and actual depreciation
is calculated over a matching time span. The dates for which forward and spot
quotations are used are located at the beginning of each month, the precise
date varies between the first and the eighth of each month. Until November
1921 one month forward contracts terminate at the end of each calendar
month. Hence, the time span covered by the contract may be somewhat shorter
than one month if the quotation is taken after the first of the month. From
December 1921 forward contracts are for a full one month forward period.
The figures for the daily money rate are from Table 23 of Holtfrerich (1986).
They have been converted into decimals per month to allow quick comparison
with the actual inflation figures.
The rates of inflation figures are from column (1) of Table 4.1.

In conclusion the evidence that is available from both the foreign
exchange market and the capital market supports the view that inflationary
expectations lagged behind actual inflationary developments, particularly
when inflation accelerated abruptly. The next section presents a framework
in which such lags are compatible with rational expectations and uses their
presence to resolve the puzzle raised by the behaviour of seigniorage
during the hyperinflation.

4. A RESOLUTION OF THE PUZZLE

The evidence of the previous sections raises several issues. First, it calls
for a reconciliation of the fact that seigniorage generally increased as
inflation and monetary expansion rose during the German hyperinflation,
with the commonly expressed view that lowering inflation would have
increased seigniorage. Second, it raises the possibility that German
policymakers were not necessarily acting irrationally. Finally, it raises a
question about the extent to which the systematic underprediction of
inflation and devaluation (particularly in 1923) reported in section 3 is
consistent with a rational formation of expectation.

This section presents a framework that is consistent with the view that,
even in 1923 when inflation accelerated to unprecedented heights,
policymakers were acting rationally given their objectives and constraints.
This framework is also consistent with the evidence in section 2,
according to which seigniorage generally increased with inflation.

Furthermore, it implies that the large and sustained downward biases in the public's prediction of inflation, particularly in 1923, were not inconsistent with the view that expectations were being formed optimally.

The two main elements of the framework are first that a government cares about the entire future profile of seigniorage revenues and inflation with, possibly, strict preference for nearer outcomes. Second, a government's preference for seigniorage versus inflation avoidance shifts stochastically through time and the government or the central bank *has more timely* information about those shifts than the public.[17] In particular a government has better information about the degree of persistence of changes in the relative importance it attributes to price stability and seigniorage revenues. The public learns about those shifts in objectives by observing past policies chosen by the government. But since those objectives are affected both by persistent and by transitory shocks, optimal learning implies that persistent changes in relative objectives are detected by the public only gradually. This enables policymakers temporarily to increase seigniorage revenues by increasing the rate of monetary expansion even if this policy eventually drives expected inflation above the point at which the elasticity of money demand is larger than unity. Governments that become more desirous of seigniorage revenues use this temporary trade-off to increase seigniorage in the short run at the expense of higher inflation and even lower seigniorage in the long run. Since the trade-off is temporary, policymakers with strong time preference are more likely to follow policies that will eventually increase inflation and decrease seigniorage.

The German experience, particularly in 1923, conformed to this pattern. In particular the analytical framework that follows implies that: (a) monetary expansion and seigniorage revenues may be positively related even at very high rates of inflation as is the case in Table 4.1; (b) a government with a strong desire for immediate seigniorage does not necessarily act irrationally when it increases current seigniorage at the cost of higher inflation and lower future seigniorage; (c) when large persistent increases occur in a government's desire for seigniorage, expectations may be systematically biased downward for a while as is the case in Table 4.3. This is due to the process of gradual but optimal learning.

Before plunging into the specifics of the model used to illustrate those ideas, it is important to remark that sluggish adjustments of the institutions that are designed to reduce the need for holding money can also create a temporary trade-off between current and future seigniorage. In particular it may be rational for a government with a sufficiently strong time preference to inflate beyond the unit elasticity point of the long-run demand for money even when the public has perfect foresight. Part of the events in Germany, particularly during the early phases of the hyper-inflation, were probably due to this delayed adjustment of institutions. I have chosen to ignore possible differences between the long and the short-run demand for money because of this element and to focus instead on lags in the adjustment of expectations.[18] This choice was dictated first by the evidence of section 3 which suggests that lags in expectations were quite important during the German hyperinflation and second in order to maintain the analytical framework within manageable proportions.

4.1 A Model of Seigniorage, Governmental Objectives and the Public's Beliefs

Let M_t be nominal money balances in period t. Seigniorage obtained by government because of monetary expansion between period t and period $t + 1$ is

$$g_t \equiv \frac{M_{t+1} - M_t}{P_t} = \frac{M_{t+1} - M_t}{M_t} \frac{M_t}{P_t} \equiv \mu_{t+1} \, m_t \qquad (4.7)$$

where μ_{t+1} is the rate of monetary expansion between period t and period $t - 1$ and m_t are real money balances in period t. The decision-making process of government is such that the decision about μ_{t+1} is made in period t. The specification in (4.7) embodies the assumption that government spends the addition to money balances between period t and period $t + 1$ at period t's prices.[19]

Demand for real money balances in period t assumes the familiar form due to Cagan

$$De^{-\alpha \pi^*_{t+1}} \qquad (4.8)$$

where

$$\pi^*_{t+1} \equiv E[\pi_{t+1} \,|\, I_t] \qquad (4.9)$$

is the rate of inflation expected by the public, as of t, to occur between t and $t + 1$. I_t denotes the information set available to the public in period t and De and α are positive constants. In order to focus on the effects of the policymaker's informational advantage, I abstract from possible lags in the adjustment of money-economizing institutions by assuming that there is no difference between the long- and the short-run demand for money as implied by equation (4.8). The price level in each period is determined from the money-market equilibrium condition

$$m_t \equiv \frac{M_t}{P_t} = De^{-\alpha \pi_{t+1}^*}. \tag{4.10}$$

Equation (4.10) and its lagged counterpart imply

$$1 + \pi_t = (1 + \mu_t)e^{\alpha(\pi_{t+1}^* - \pi_t^*)}. \tag{4.11}$$

Taking natural logarithms of (4.11) and using the approximation $\ln(1+x) = x^{20}$

$$\pi_t = \mu_t + \alpha(\pi_{t+1}^* - \pi_t^*). \tag{4.12}$$

No policymaker, including the one who presided over the post-World War I German hyperinflation, likes inflation *per se*. But governments are willing to tolerate some monetary expansion in order to obtain seigniorage. An essential feature of hyperinflation is that the desire for seigniorage in comparison to inflation aversion fluctuates in a not totally predictable manner over time and that policymakers become informed of such shifts more quickly than the public at large. The policymaker may not be fully informed about his future objectives, but he is in a better position than the public to evaluate those objectives. Furthermore, in choosing current monetary expansion government takes account of the future as well as of the present. But different governments may discount the future to a different degree. Those characteristics are modelled by postulating that the policymaker's decision strategy is

$$\{\mu_i, \ i=1,2,...\} \overset{Max}{} E_{G0} \sum_{i=0}^{\infty} \beta^i \left[x_i g_i - \frac{\mu_{i+1}^2}{2}\right] \tag{4.13}$$

$$x_i = A + p_i + \varepsilon_i, \quad A>0, \tag{4.14}$$

$$p_i = \rho \, p_{i-1} + v_i, \quad 0<\rho<1, \tag{4.15}$$

where v and ε are serially and mutually uncorrelated normal variates with zero means and variances σ_v^2 and σ_ε^2, respectively. β is the government's subjective discount factor and x_i measures government's desire for seigniorage in comparison to its aversion to inflation.[21] E_{G0} is a conditional expected value operator that is conditioned on the information available to government in period 0.

The higher is x_i the more willing are policymakers to trade higher monetary expansion for more seigniorage. Equations (4.14) and (4.15) state that, in addition to the nonstochastic term, A, the shift parameter x_i is affected by a persistent stochastic component p_i, (whose degree of persistence is measured by ρ) and by a transitory shock ε_i.

The policymaker knows the current and past values of ρ_i and ε_i and therefore also of x_i. The public does not have direct knowledge about the realizations of those variables, but it can make inferences about them from its knowledge of past rates of monetary expansion. Hence the policymaker has better information than the public not only about the state of its current preferences but about their persistence as well. This information advantage can be used, by him, temporarily to increase current seigniorage at the expense of future seigniorage when this is advantageous.

The information set, I_t, of the public includes, in addition to the deterministic and stochastic structure of the model, observations about rates of monetary expansion up to and including period t. Using this information, the public forms expectations about future monetary growth which are used in turn to form rational forecasts of inflation as in equation (4.9). Linearity of a government's decision rule is essential for the calculation of those expectations. Such linearity obtains if seigniorage, g_i, is linear in its arguments. It is shown in part 1 of the Appendix that a linear approximation of seigniorage is

$$g_i = G_0 + G_1 \mu_{i+1} - G_2 \pi_{i+1}^* \qquad (4.16)$$

where

$$G_1 \equiv De^{-\alpha\mu_m}, \ G_2 \equiv \alpha\mu_m G_1, G_0 \equiv \mu_m G_2 \qquad (4.17)$$

and μ_m is some mean steady-state rate of inflation. This approximation neglects the nonlinearities in the seigniorage function g_i. But it has the virtue of making it possible to investigate explicitly the effects of the policymaker's informational advantage on monetary expansion and seigniorage in a world of rational expectations.[22]

Using (4.16) in (4.13) the policymaker's decision problem may be rewritten as

$$\underset{\{\mu_i, \ i=1,2,...\}}{\overset{Max}{}} E_{G0} \sum_{i=0}^{\infty} \beta^i \ [x_i(G_0 + G_1\mu_{i+1} - G_2\pi^*_{i+1}) \ - \ \frac{\mu^2_{i+1}}{2}] \ (4.13a)$$

where, due to the rationality of expectations and the persistence in governmental objectives, π^*_{i+1} depends on actual rates of monetary expansion prior to period $i + 1$.

The policymaker knows the process by which the public forms the expectation π^*_{i+1}. This process must be consistent with the actual strategy followed by government. The government's strategy is derived, in turn, by solving the maximization problem in equation (4.13a), taking the process for the formation of π^*_{i+1} as given. In other words, π^*_{i+1} is a rational expectation of next period's inflation formed by using the public's knowledge about the policymaker's strategy in conjunction with all the relevant information available.

In order to derive the equilibrium solution of the model, I proceed in two steps. First I postulate the public's beliefs about the behaviour of money growth in the economy. Then I show that when a government maximizes (4.13a), given those beliefs, the strategy that emerges validates the public's beliefs.

The public believes that the rate of monetary expansion is given by

$$\mu_{i+1} = B_0 A + Bp_i + \psi_i \qquad (4.18)$$

where ψ_i is a normal variate with zero mean and variance σ^2_ψ, and B_0 and B are known constants which depend on the underlying parameters of government's objective function. It is shown in part 2 of the Appendix that those beliefs about μ in conjunction with the public's knowledge of equation (4.12) imply

$$\pi^*_{i+1} = B_0 A + \theta \sum_{s=0}^{\infty} \lambda^s \ (\mu_{i-s} - B_0 A) \qquad (4.19)$$

$$\theta \equiv \frac{\rho - \lambda}{1 + \alpha(1 - \rho)}, \qquad (4.20)$$

$$\lambda \equiv \tfrac{1}{2} \ [\frac{1+r}{\rho} + \rho] - \sqrt{\tfrac{1}{4}(\frac{1+r}{\rho} + \rho)^2 - 1}, \qquad (4.21a)$$

$$r \equiv B^2 \frac{\sigma_\nu^2}{\sigma_\psi^2}, \qquad (4.21b)$$

where λ is a number between 0 and ρ. Using (4.17) and (4.19) in (4.13a), the policymaker's decision problem may be rewritten

$$\{\mu_i, \; i=1,2,...\} \; \underset{E_{G0}}{\overset{Max}{}} \sum_{i=0}^{\infty} \beta^i [x_i \{G_0 + G_1 \; \mu_{i+1} - G_1 \alpha \mu_m (1 - \frac{\theta}{1-\lambda}) B_0 A$$

$$- G_1 \alpha \mu_m \; \theta \sum_{s=0}^{\infty} \lambda^s \; \mu_{i-s}\} - \frac{\mu_{i+1}^2}{2}]. \qquad (4.22)$$

The policymaker chooses the actual value of μ_1 and a contingency plan for μ_i, $i \geq 2$. Recognizing that in each period in the future the policymaker faces a problem that has the same structure as period zero's problem, the stochastic Euler equations necessary for an internal maximum of (4.22) are[23]

$$G_1 [x_i - \alpha \mu_m \theta \beta E_{Gi}(x_{i+1} + \beta \lambda x_{i+2} + ...)] - \mu_{i+1} = 0 \; \; i = ,1,2,... \; . \; (4.23)$$

Although the policymaker knows x_i in period i (and the public does not), he is uncertain about values of x beyond period i. Based on the information available to him in period i, he computes a conditional expected value for x_{i+j}, $j \geq 1$. In view of (4.14) and (4.15).

$$E_{Gi} x_{i+j} = \rho^j x_i + (1-\rho^j)A. \qquad (4.24)$$

Substituting (4.24) into (4.23), summing up the resulting infinite geometric progressions and rearranging

$$\mu_{i+1} = D \; [(1 - \frac{\beta \alpha \mu_m (\rho - \lambda)}{(1 - \beta \lambda)(1 + \alpha(1 - \rho))} A$$

$$+ (1 - \frac{\rho \beta \alpha \mu_m (\rho - \lambda)}{(1 - \rho \beta \lambda)(1 + \alpha(1 - \rho))} (p_i + \varepsilon_i)]. \qquad (4.25)$$

Rationality of expectations implies that the coefficients of A and of p_i should be the same across equations (4.18) and (4.25), respectively, so

$$B_0 = (1 - \frac{\beta \alpha \mu_m (\rho - \lambda(B))}{(1 - \beta \lambda(B))(1 + \alpha(1 - \rho))})D \qquad (4.26a)$$

$$B = (1 - \frac{\rho \beta \alpha \mu_m (\rho - \lambda(B))}{(1 - \rho \beta \lambda(B))(1 + \alpha(1 - \rho))})D. \qquad (4.26b)$$

The dependence of λ on B through equation (4.21) is stressed by writing λ as a function of B. It is shown in part 3 of the Appendix that subject to plausible restrictions

$$1 \geq B_0, \quad B > 0 \qquad (4.27)$$

and that equations (4.26) imply a unique solution for B_0 and B. Rationality of expectations also implies (by comparing (4.18) and (4.25) that

$$\psi_i = B\varepsilon_i, \quad \sigma_\psi^2 = B^2 \sigma_\varepsilon^2. \qquad (4.28)$$

This completes the demonstration of the fact that the public's beliefs are rational and that equation (4.25) (or (4.18)) describes the behaviour of money growth chosen by a government. In view of (4.18) and (4.28), equation (4.19) may be rewritten

$$\pi_{i+1}^* = B_0 A + \theta B \sum_{s=0}^{\infty} \lambda^s (p_i = \varepsilon_i) \qquad (4.29)$$

which implies that there are persistent effects of past values of a government's relative desire for seigniorage and the inflation tax on current inflationary expectations as is the case, for example, with adaptive expectations. This sluggishness is caused by the public's inability to separate persistent from transitory changes in a government's desire to use seigniorage as a source of revenue for financing the budget. It induces temporary but persistent deviations between actual and expected inflation. This enables a government in turn, to increase current seigniorage even when inflation is in the range of money demand in which the elasticity of this demand is larger than unity.

4.2 Resolution of the Seigniorage Puzzle in Terms of the Model

A striking feature of seigniorage during all phases of the German hyperinflation is that it usually increases when the rate of monetary growth increases (columns (2), (3), and (4) of Table 4.1). This is puzzling when (as was the case during the second part of the hyperinflation) the rate of inflation is in the range of money demand in which the elasticity of this demand is larger than one. The puzzle disappears when the informational advantage of policymakers is recognized explicitly as in the model of the previous subsection. As can be seen from equation (4.16), seigniorage increases from one period to the next if the rate of monetary expansion increases by enough in comparison to the increase in expectations. Since the change in expectations depends on a weighted average of differences between *past* rates of monetary expansion (equation (4.19)), seigniorage always increases when current monetary growth is sufficiently larger than past rates of monetary expansion.

Essentially, the policymaker always possesses the ability to increase current seigniorage because inflationary expectations, being based on information up to the previous period, are temporarily given. This ability is independent of the elasticity of money demand since expectations are fixed for the period. It is related to Calvo's (1978) result that under perfect foresight optimal monetary policy is bound to be time inconsistent. However, unlike in Calvo's model, the fact that the currently chosen policy affects future expectations checks the temptation of the policymaker to inflate without bounds.[24]

The factors that determine the correlation between current seigniorage and current monetary expansion can be seen more clearly by substituting (4.17) and (4.18) into (4.16) and by rewriting period i's seigniorage as[25]

$$g_i = K + G_1 [\mu_{i+1} - \frac{\alpha \mu_m (\rho - \lambda)}{1 + \alpha (1 - \rho)} \sum_{s=0}^{\infty} \lambda^s \mu_{i-s}]. \qquad (4.30)$$

Equation (4.30) implies that seigniorage increases over time when the rate of monetary expansion increases in comparison to past rates of monetary expansion and decreases when the current rate decreases in comparison to past rates. This implication is qualitatively consistent with the behaviour of money growth and seigniorage during the German hyperinflation and therefore with the view (from equation (4.25) that the urge of the German government to obtain seigniorage progressed over time and reached an acute dimension in 1923.[26]

An additional, not exclusive interpretation of the German government's policy, particularly during the last phases of the hyperinflation, is in terms of an increase in the rate of time preference. It is useful, before fully developing this point, to step back and to relate the formal analysis below to the last stages of the German hyperinflation in 1922 and 1923. In January of 1923 French and Belgian troops occupied the Ruhr in an attempt to make Germany pay the high reparations that were decided upon in May 1921. The German government reacted by decreeing a state of passive resistance that required higher governmental expenditures and therefore larger amounts of seigniorage. In terms of the model this can be thought of as a situation in which, due to the conflict, the rate of time preference for current seigniorage increased (β went down). Accordingly I turn next to an investigation of the effect of a change in β on the rate of monetary expansion.

Inspection of equations (4.26) reveals that both B_0 and B are decreasing functions of β. Equation (4.25) implies, therefore, that the lower is β, the larger is the average monetary expansion DB_0A. Moreover, for positive realizations of $p_i + \varepsilon_i$, lower values of β reinforce this average effect by increasing the effect of $p_i + \varepsilon_i$ on the rate of monetary expansion chosen by the policymaker. Hence the acceleration of inflation in 1923 is consistent with the view that, following the Ruhr's invasion, the urge of the German government for seigniorage intensified dramatically and so did the urgency of this urge. In terms of the model, 1923 can be characterized by particularly large realizations of x_i as well as by a downward shift in the structural parameter β.

It is also interesting to note that, other things the same, the larger is the short-run instability in the policymaker's objectives as measured by σ_ε^2, the larger the average rate of monetary expansion picked by him.[27] The intuitive reason is that in the presence of larger short-run instability in a government's desire for seigniorage, it takes longer for the public to detect changes in governmental objectives. As a consequence the negative effect of a current monetary acceleration on the policymaker's ability to collect seigniorage in the future occurs later, making it more profitable for him to obtain more current seigniorage by picking a higher rate of monetary expansion.[28]

4.3 A Rational Expectations Explanation for the Lagging Forward Premium and for the Relative Sluggishness of Real Balances

The consistent underestimation of the mark's depreciation implied by the behaviour of the forward premium in 1923 can be understood within the above framework, as the natural consequence of a large persistent increase in x_i. The model implies that such an increase will cause money growth to rise. But due to the public's inability to perfectly separate persistent from transitory changes in the policymaker's relative preference for seigniorage, the consequent rise in μ and in inflation may be underestimated for a while. This can be illustrated by using equations (4.12), (4.19), and (4.25) to calculate unexpected inflation.

$$\pi_i - \pi_i^* = B \frac{1 + \alpha(1 - \lambda)}{1 + \alpha(1 - \rho)} [p_{i-1} + \varepsilon_{i-1} - (\rho - \lambda)$$

$$\sum_{s=0}^{\infty} \lambda^s (p_{i-2-s} + \varepsilon_{1-2-s})].$$

(4.31)

Equation (4.31) suggests that when a large persistent shock occurs in government's preferences, it induces a systematic divergence between actual and expected inflation for several periods.[29] In particular when there is a large positive innovation, v, to the persistent component of the policymaker's preferences in period $i - 1$, p_{i-1} is large in comparison to previous values of p. As a result $\pi_i - \pi_i^*$ becomes positive implying an underestimation of inflation. The higher value of p raises subsequent inflationary expectations but only gradually. Formally this is reflected in equation 31. through the fact that in the expressions for $\pi_{i+j} - \pi_{i+j}^*$, $j \geq 1$, the larger values of p from period $i - 1$ on are weighted along with the lower, preperiod $i - 1$ values of p pulling π_{i+j}^* down and creating a downward bias in expectations for a while after the occurrence of the large persistent shock. Those implications are fully consistent with the evidence of Table 4.3 according to which during 1923 the forward premium systematically underpredicted the subsequent devaluation of the mark.[30] They also provide an explanation for the sluggish adjustment of interest rates.

Equations (4.12) and (4.25) suggest that when the value of p in period $i - 1$ rises, so does the rate of inflation in period i. Equation (4.31) implies that a rise in p_{i-1} also causes an increase in the size of unexpected inflation. The upshot is that the model implies a positive correlation between inflation and unexpected inflation, providing an explanation for the fact (Table 4.3) that the gap between inflation and interest rates widened as inflation increased.

4.4 The Model and the Facts - A Final Overview

In conclusion the data on seigniorage, money growth and expectations during the German hyperinflation in conjunction with the analysis of this section provide a possible explanation for the inflationary acceleration of 1923 as the consequence of a desperate but deliberate attempt on the part of a policymaker with an extremely strong and rising desire for immediate seigniorage to satisfy this urge. The positive correlation between monetary growth and seigniorage suggests that German policymakers were able *temporarily* to satisfy this urge. The substantial lags in the adjustment of inflationary expectations explain why they were able to achieve this aim even at rates of inflation for which the elasticity of money demand was substantially above unity.[31] Finally, the model suggests that they chose to use their short-run information advantage in spite of its obvious ultimate inflationary consequences because of their strong preference for current seigniorage.

The lag in the adjustment of expectations also provides an explanation for the sluggish behaviour of actual real balances in comparison to those that are predicted, under perfect foresight, by Christiano's (1987) estimate of α. But as pointed out at the beginning of this section, part of the sluggishness in real balances, particularly during the final phases of the hyperinflation, may additionally be due to slow adjustment of money-saving institutions. Both types of lags induce policymakers with strong time preference to inflate at high rates.

Obviously part of the gigantic acceleration of inflation in 1923 might have been due to miscalculations as well. For example, it is likely that German policymakers underestimated the extent to which conventional tax revenues would fall as a result of the inflationary acceleration of 1923. Since some of the increased desire for seigniorage in 1923 was a consequence of this inflation-induced decrease in ordinary tax receipts,[32] part of the inflation in this year may be due to a prior underestimation of this effect. But there is little doubt that a substantial part of the tremendous inflationary acceleration of 1923 was a direct result of the increased hunger of the German government for immediate seigniorage triggered by the policy of passive resistance to the Ruhr's occupation.

The framework of this section also sheds a different light on the apparent irrationality of the Israeli government that inflated at more than 100 per cent per year during the early eighties in spite of the fact that *total* revenues from inflation were negative (Fischer (1984)). This was due to the fact that the Israeli government had large balances of low interest, unindexed loans, when inflation accelerated at the end of the seventies (Sokoler (1987)). Due to the existence of those balances, inflation decreased the future real redemption value of government loans but did not affect current cash flows since most of those loans were long term. The negativity of the total inflation tax was due to the fact that this loss on capital account was larger than the amount of current resources obtained through current expansion of the base. The discussion in this section suggests that such behaviour is compatible with maximization of the present value of seigniorage revenues when a government has strong time preference.[33]

5. WHY IS HYPERINFLATION ALLOWED TO DEVELOP ONLY TO BE STABILIZED LATER ON?

The framework of the previous section also sheds light on why inflation is allowed to accelerate for a while during hyperinflation and is finally stabilized. Such behaviour can be understood as the consequence of a string of persistent increases in x_i in equation (4.13a) during the accelerating phases of the hyperinflation. Those increases induce government to increase monetary expansion and therefore inflation (equations (4.25) and (4.12)) in order temporarily to increase seigniorage. This effect induces a higher inflation the larger the time preference of the policymaker (the lower B). After a while expectations adjust upwards and reach the high inflation range, too. Provided x_i rises sufficiently or if β is small enough or both, inflation rises above the point of unit elasticity. Due to the persistent-transitory confusion, expectations do not necessarily follow actual inflation into this range for a while. During this period, higher monetary expansion serves the policymaker's purposes since it increases his revenues from seigniorage.

But once expectations rise into the range in which the elasticity of real money demand with respect to expectations is larger than unity, the higher rate of monetary expansion unambiguously decreases the value of the policymaker's objectives. The reason is that, in comparison to the period just prior to the string of increases in x_i, monetary expansion is higher and revenues from seigniorage are lower. Moreover, this situation is expected (by government) to persist under the old regime, making the maximized value of the objective function in (4.13a) rather low. If this value decreases below a certain threshold that is determined by the cost of monetary reform, there is a switch in regime. More precisely, when the expected difference between the value of a government's objectives with and without a monetary reform becomes larger than the cost of such a reform, the policymaker decides to stabilize inflation. From the point of view of the policymaker the main target of a stabilization is to decrease inflationary expectation swiftly. After those expectations have adjusted to a highly inflationary environment, the policymaker may experience difficulties even if he becomes more conservative in his attitude to seigniorage (x went down) in the meantime. The reason is that inflationary expectations are now slow to adjust downwards, maintaining the maximized value of his objectives in (4.13a) at a low level. Under such circumstances a credible stabilization improves the policymaker's objectives by bringing expectations down swiftly.

Paradoxically the likelihood that high inflation will be terminated by a change in regime is larger the higher is the range of inflation attained. With higher inflation, inflationary expectations reach a higher range more quickly, making the maximized value of a government's objective function under the old regime lower. This may help explain why hyperinflations usually end with very credible stabilizations, whereas South American-type inflations, in which yearly inflation fluctuates between one hundred and one thousand per cent, are not always stabilized with the same level of determination.

6. WHY DO GOVERNMENTS RESORT TO INFLATIONARY FINANCE?

To this point the analysis has taken the fact that a government requires as much revenue as possible from the inflation tax as given exogenously. This section provides an answer to the obvious underlying positive question: why or under what circumstances is inflationary finance used? This question can be divided into two subquestions: the first asks under what circumstances a government is likely to resort to deficit financing, and the second asks why this deficit is financed by money rather than by bonds. Analysis of these questions requires some positive hypotheses about government behaviour. Here I take the view that, in a democracy, governmental decisions reflect to a large extent the wishes of the decisive voter.[34] The question then becomes: why do the majority of voters prefer the costs associated with a large inflation tax to those resulting from direct taxation, bond financing or a smaller total government budget?

A notable feature of most classical hyperinflations is that they occurred following wars after a part of the infrastructure of those countries was destroyed. As a consequence the social rates of return to rebuilding of the infrastructure and to public outlays for this purpose were high. The average individual emerged from the war with little wealth and with an expectation that as the process of reconstruction proceeds at a fast pace, his income is going to rise substantially.[35] He therefore wanted to borrow resources from his future high income in order to finance current consumption. Individuals at the top of the wealth distribution could satisfy this desire by running down some of their wealth. However, the bulk of the population who had little or no wealth desired to borrow against its future labour income. But markets in which individuals could borrow against their future (expected) higher labour incomes were largely unavailable. As a consequence a large part of the population in countries like Germany, Hungary, Austria, and even France found itself constrained to hold current consumption below the level they would have chosen, had more perfect capital markets been available. Clearly, given the level of government expenditures, those individuals had a preference for bond rather than for tax financing of the budget because such financing enabled them to achieve a superior intertemporal allocation of consumption. Some of them might even have desired a lower government budget in order to alleviate their current tax burden even more. But this preference was probably checked for many individuals by the high private return expected from governmental expenditures used to rebuild the physical and social infrastructure of the country.

It seems, therefore, that a majority of individuals in many post-World War I European countries wanted to maintain a substantial investment in public goods as well as levels of private consumption that were high in relation to the wealth they privately owned at the time. The governments of those countries responded by maintaining reasonably high budgets (by the standards of the time) and by financing a sizeable part of those budgets through deficits. Those policies were particularly in evidence in Germany, Austria, and Hungary, countries that lost the war. But they appeared, although to a lesser extent, in France as well.[36]

The argument up to now explains why there was a preference towards deficit finance in many of the war-ravaged European countries following World War I. It does not explain why some of those countries, like Germany, chose to finance those deficits almost exclusively by money creation while others, like France, used some combination of bond and of inflationary finance. In general, given the level of the deficit, individual attitudes towards bond- versus money-financing of the deficit are determined by the general equilibrium effects of bond-financing on the stock of capital and by the loss in utility due to the inflation tax. Given the deficit, a shift towards more bond-financing and less inflationary finance affects individual welfare through several channels. First, if the decrease in the portion of the deficit that is financed by money creation is associated with a decrease in inflation, there is an increase in individual welfare because the cost of holding the medium of exchange is lower. Second, the increase in bond-financing induces some crowding out of private capital since the consumption of wealth-constrained individuals increases. To the extent that labour and capital are complements, this causes an increase in the return to capital and a decrease in real wages. Individuals whose major source of income is from wages dislike this change, whereas those who derive their income mostly from capital like it.[37] If the first type of individual comprisess the majority, some combination of bond and of inflationary finance is to be expected, particularly if the costs of crowding out and of inflationary finance in terms of individual welfare increase at the margin as bond-financing and the rate of inflation increase, respectively. Hence, when the decisive voter relies mostly on wage income, some inflationary finance is to be expected given that there is a budgetary deficit.[38]

The above discussion seems to provide an appropriate vehicle for understanding the motivation for mild or intermediate inflations of the type experienced in France prior to Poincaré.[39] But it is hard to believe that the above forces alone were sufficient to unleash the heavy reliance on money creation and the consequent fury of hyperinflation experienced by the countries whose monetary dynamics are analysed in Cagan's (1956) seminal study. I believe that at least for the countries which lost the war in 1918 there was an additional powerful motive for such heavy reliance on inflationary finance triggered by the burden of reparations imposed. Although the arguments supporting this hypothesis are developed using the specific experience of Germany as an illustration, its qualitative features probably apply to other countries that had to pay reparations, like Austria and Hungary, as well.

After several years of uncertainty about their magnitudes the reparations to be paid by Germany were fixed in May of 1921, at a level that was equal to almost three times that year's national income.[40] But only 39.4 per cent of this obligation represented a definitely set schedule of payments. The rest — 61.6 per cent of the total, known as 'C bonds' — was made contingent on Germany's ability to pay. The Reparations Commission was empowered to demand interest payments on this tranche when it considered Germany capable of paying more (Holtfrerich 1986, p. 143). Both tranches of reparations were to be paid in foreign exchange. The allies, and in particular the French and Belgians, were quite insistent on prompt payment and were dead serious about using force to implement those demands as the January 1923 invasion of the Ruhr later demonstrated. The 'C bonds' stipulation meant that 'a financial "Sword of Damocles" was suspended over the German economy' (Holtfrerich

1986). Under those circumstances most Germans expected, quite realistically, that fiscal responsibility would be taken as a signal of an increase in Germany's ability to pay and would trigger total or partial activation of payments against the 'C bonds'. On the other hand a large dose of inflationary finance was expected to decrease the likelihood of such an event, since it would have been taken as a sign of Germany's inability to pay.[41] Holtfrerich (1986, p. 167) cites Reichsbank reports to the government according to which 'not until reparation obligations had been reduced to a level consonant with the taxable capacity of the population would the Reich be in a position to renounce this "extremely injurious mode of financing"'.[42] He concludes later (p. 171) that until the fixing of reparations in May 1921 the central bank had regarded the costs of stabilizing inflation as acceptable, since it had assumed lower reparation figures. However, once the May 1921 high and contingent figures were announced the Reichsbank changed its view and no longer regarded 'the cost of its stabilizing the currency by fiscal deflation as lower than the benefits of achieving it'.

Although they do not identify the mechanism creating the negative-link between reparations to be paid and the extent of inflationary finance explicitly, those statements make it clear that policymakers at the time perceived the existence of such a link. I believe several mechanisms contributed to the creation of this negative relation. The first and most important one was the belief that fiscal and monetary stability would trigger payments on the 'C bonds'. The second is related to the fact that reparations payments had to be made in foreign exchange. Since the allies would not accept paper marks, seigniorage was less likely to be expropriated for payment of reparations than receipts from taxes or issuance of debt.[43]

Due to the unreasonably high total amount of reparations requested in May 1921, it is unlikely that Germany would have paid everything that was demanded no matter the domestic method of taxation used. However, it is likely that, owing to the reasons sketched above, the Allies would have demanded and obtained more resources with a smoothly functioning German fiscal system than under the system of inflationary finance actually used between 1921 and 1923.

Hence, Germans from all levels of income and wealth had a *ceteris paribus* preference for inflationary finance. In addition to the usual conflicts about the domestic distribution of tax burdens,[44] German voters were highly concerned about the international distribution of resources between Germany and the Allies. With respect to this second conflict all German voters, whether capitalists or workers, had an obvious common interest. They all were willing to accept a high tax rate on real money balances, since the effective cost of financing the German public good by other means was even higher. This interpretation is consistent with the high fraction of the total German government's budget financed by money creation and the relatively small fraction of reparations paid during the hyperinflation period (Table 4.4).

The ideas of this section are illustrated more rigorously in the next section.

Table 4.4: The Inflation Tax and Reparations Payments in Percentages of Total Government Outlays - Germany 1921-1923

Fiscal Years[a]	Percentage of Budget Financed by Money Creation[b]	Percentage of Budget Used to Pay Reparations
1921	56	31.5
1922	64	18.2
1923	89	7.7

Notes: [a] April 1 to March 31. The figures for 1923 cover the period from April to December.
[b] Calculated under the assumption that all deficits were financed by the creation of notes.
Source: Calculated from Table 2 of Alesina (1987).

7. FINANCIAL WEALTH CONSTRAINTS AND REPARATIONS AVOIDANCE AS FACTORS THAT INDUCED INFLATIONARY FINANCE — A FORMAL ANALYSIS

The ideas of the previous section are demonstrated in this one by means of a two-period model in which the size of the government's budget as well as the composition of its financing between money, bonds and lump-sum taxes is determined by the preferences of the decisive voter.

7.1 Individual Behaviour

The economy is inhabited by L individuals who live for two periods. All individuals have the same time separable utility function that depends on consumption and real money balances in each of the two periods. This function is

$$u(c_1) + \tilde{\ell}(m_1) + \beta [v(c_2) + \ell(m_2)] \tag{4.32}$$

where c_1 and c_2 are consumption in the first and second periods and m_1 and m_2 are real money balances in the two periods. The component functions $u(\cdot)$, $v(\cdot)$, $\tilde{\ell}(\cdot)$ all have positive and decreasing first partial derivatives which become very large as the respective arguments go to zero. Each individual inelastically supplies one unit of labour in each of the two periods and obtains real wages w_1 and w_2 in the first and in the second period, respectively. There are three assets in the economy: money, government bonds, and productive capital. Each individual enters period 1 with a (possibly) different amount and a different composition of wealth. There is no uncertainty so that government bonds and productive capital are perfect substitutes in portfolios. Let M_1 and B_1 be the nominal amounts of money with which a representative individual starts the first period, and let k_1 be the amount of physical capital in his possession at that time.[45] The government imposes real lump-sum taxes T_1 and T_2 in the two periods respectively. In the first period the individual collects his wage, pays taxes and can use the remainder, as well as his total first period wealth, to buy consumption, bonds, money, or capital to be transferred to the second period. The first period nominal budget constraint is therefore[46]

$$P_1 c_1 + M_2 + B_2 + P_1 k_2 = P_1(w_1 - T_1) + M_1 + B_1 + P_1 k_1. \tag{4.33}$$

where P_i, $i = 1,2$, is period i's price level. Dividing by P_1 and rearranging

$$c_1 = A_1 - (1 + \pi_2)(m_2 + b_2) - k_2 \tag{4.33a}$$

where

$$A_1 \equiv w_1 - T_1 + b_1 + k_1 + m_1 \tag{4.34}$$

and

$$b_i \equiv \frac{B_i}{P_i}, \quad i = 1,2; \quad 1 + \pi_2 \equiv \frac{P_2}{P_1}.$$

Here b_i is the real value of the individual's bond portfolio in period i and π_2 is the rate of inflation between the first and the second period.

In the second period the individual collects a real rate of interest, r_2, on the capital and the bonds that he has decided to transfer from the first to the second period. Since this is the last period, he consumes all the resources at his disposal in this period. Hence, the second period's budget constraint is[47]

$$c_2 = w_2 - T_2 + m_2 + (1 + r_2)k_2 + (1 + r_2)(1 + \pi_2)b_2. \qquad (4.35)$$

Individuals cannot increase their consumption beyond the resources available to them in the first period because there are no markets in which they can borrow against their future labour income. Formally this constraint implies

$$m_2 \geq 0; \quad k_2 \geq 0; \quad b_2 \geq 0. \qquad (4.36)$$

Substituting (4.33a) and (4.35) into (4.32) the typical individual problem can be formulated as[48]

$$\begin{aligned}
\underset{\{m_2, k_2, b_2\}}{Max} \quad & \{u[A_1 - (1 + \pi_2)(m_2 + b_2) - k_2] \\
& + \beta v[w_2 - T_2 + m_2 + (1 + r_2)k_2 + (1 + r_2)(1 + \pi_2)b_2] + \beta \ell(m_2)\}
\end{aligned} \qquad (4.37)$$

subject to the constraints in (4.36). Forming the Lagrangean and differentiating with respect to the three choice variables m_2, k_2, and b_2 we obtain the first order conditions

$$u'[\cdot](1 + \pi_2) + \beta(v'[\cdot] + \ell'[\cdot]) + \lambda_1 = 0 \qquad (4.38a)$$

$$-u'[\cdot] + \beta(1 + 1r_2)v'[\cdot] + \lambda_2 = 0 \qquad (4.38b)$$

$$-u'[\cdot](1 + \pi_2) + \beta(1 + n_2)v'[\cdot] + \lambda_3 = 0 \qquad (4.38c)$$

where $u'(\cdot)$, $v'(\cdot)$ and $\ell'(\cdot)$ denote first order partial derivatives and

$$n_2 \equiv (1+r_2)(1+\pi_2) - 1 \tag{4.39}$$

is the nominal rate of interest on bonds held from the first to the second period. λ_1, λ_2, and λ_3 are the Lagrange multipliers associated with the constraints $m_2 \geq 0$, $k_2 \geq 0$ and $b_2 \geq 0$, respectively. Since $\ell'(m_2)$ goes to infinity as m_2 approaches zero the constraint $m_2 \geq 0$ is not binding and $\lambda_1 = 0$. Using (4.39) in (4.38c) the last two first-order conditions may be rewritten

$$(1 + \pi_2)[-u' + \beta(1 + r_2)v'] = -\lambda_3$$

which implies $\lambda_3 = (1 + \pi_2)\lambda_2$ so that (4.38b) and (4.38c) collapse to one condition only. This is simply a reflection of the fact that since k_2 and b_2 are perfect substitutes, the individual is indifferent to the composition of his portfolio between capital and bonds as long as the total of those two assets is held fixed. Hence, we can relabel this total as

$$a_2 \equiv k_2 + b_2 \tag{4.40}$$

and try to rewrite the maximization problem in (4.37) as a function of this aggregate asset instead of its two constituents. It would seem that since b_2 is multiplied by π_2 while k_2 is not, this is not feasible. The reason for this divergence is that bonds are denominated in nominal terms and depreciate in value because of inflation while capital does not. For any dollar invested in bonds in period 1 the individual obtains a real bond portfolio that is worth only $1/1+\pi_2$ units of consumption in the second period. But since he gets the nominal interest rate in (4.39), his final (gross) real return is

$$(1 + n_2) \, \frac{1}{1 + \pi_2} = 1 + r_2$$

which is the market real rate of return. The component $\pi_2(1+r_2)$ fully compensates the individual for inflation on both the principal and the interest. For the problem as written in (4.37), this compensation is paid in the second period. If instead it had been paid in the first period while holding its present value constant, neither the utility of the individual nor his choices would be affected since he can always undo this change by buying less bonds. But the present value of the compensation for inflation is $\pi_2 b_2$, so that shifting of the compensation from the second to the first period amounts to adding $\pi_2 b_2$ to the individual's resources in the first period and subtracting $(1+r_2)\pi_2 b_2$ from his resources in the second period. The upshot of this discussion is that the maximization problem in (4.37) is equivalent to the following simpler problem

$$\text{Max}_{\{m_2,\, a_2\}} \quad u[A_1 - (1+\pi_2)m_2 - a_2] + \beta v[w_2 - T_2$$

$$+ m_2 + (1+r_2)a_2] + \beta \ell (m_2)\} \tag{4.41}$$

subject to the wealth constraint

$$a_2 \geq 0. \tag{4.42}$$

The first-order conditions for this equivalent problem are

$$-(1+\pi_2)u'[\cdot] + \beta (v'[\cdot] + \ell'[\cdot]) = 0 \tag{4.43a}$$

$$-u'[\cdot] + \beta(1+r_2)v'[\cdot] + \lambda = 0 \tag{4.43b}$$

where $\lambda \geq 0$ is the Lagrange multiplier associated with the constraint in (4.42). For a financially constrained individual, $\lambda > 0$ and $a_2 = 0$. For an unconstrained individual, $a_2 > 0$ and $\lambda = 0$.

7.4 Production and the Public Sector

I turn now to a description of the production opportunities of the economy and of a government's budget constraints. The first and second periods' aggregate production functions are, respectively

$$Y_1 = f(K_1, L) \tag{4.44a}$$

$$Y_2 = H(G_1)\, f(K_2, L) \tag{4.44b}$$

where

$$K_1 \equiv \sum_{i=1}^{L} k_{1i}; \quad K_2 \equiv \sum_{i=1}^{L} k_{2i}. \tag{4.45}$$

$f(\cdot)$ is homogeneous of degree one in its arguments and it satisfies the usual properties: positive and decreasing marginal productivities. Labour and capital are complements, so $f_{KL} > 0$. G_1 is the total amount of public expenditures in the first period. It can be thought of as a productive investment designed to rebuild the economy's infrastructure. Its essential feature is that it augments the economy's productive capacity in the second period. Formally

$$H'(G_1) > 0, \quad H(0) = 1. \tag{4.46}$$

If a government does not invest in rebuilding the infrastructure, the production function in period two remains the same as in period one. Positive amounts of public outlays augment the productive capacity of the economy in period two as shown by equations (4.44b) and (4.46).

Public expenditure in the first period can be financed by either lump--sum taxes, issuance of bonds that are repaid in the second period, or by printing money. There is no public investment in infrastructure in the second period. In this period lump-sum taxes are imposed only in order to repay the national debt issued in the first period. The government budget constraints in periods one and two are given, respectively, by

$$G_1 = \left[LT_1 + (1 + \pi_2) \sum_{i=1}^{L} b_{2i} \right] (1 - R) + \sum_{i=1}^{L} [(1 + \pi_2) m_{2i} - m_{1i}] - \sum_{i=1}^{L} b_{1i} \tag{4.47a}$$

$$LT_2 = (1 + n_2) \sum_{i=1}^{L} b_{2i} \tag{4.47b}$$

where R is a reparations factor between zero and one which reflects the fact that part or all of the receipts from lump-sum taxes and issuance of bonds are confiscated for payment of war reparations. Seigniorage revenues are free from this confiscatory payment.[49]

Assuming competitive factor markets, the real wage rate and the return to capital in the second period are given by

$$w_2 = H(G_1) f_L(K_2, L) \tag{4.48a}$$

$$r_2 = H(G_1) f_K(K_2, L) \tag{4.48b}$$

where f_L and f_K are the partial derivatives of $f(\cdot)$ with respect to labour input and capital, respectively. Inserting (4.47b) and (4.48b) into (4.47a) and rearranging we obtain

$$G_1 = L[(T_1 + \frac{T_2}{1 + H(G_1)f_K(K_2,L)}) + (1 + \pi_2)\bar{m}_2 - (\bar{m}_1 + \bar{b}_1)] \quad (4.49)$$

where bars over variables denote per capita values of those variables. Equation (4.49) incorporates the first and second periods' budget constraints from (4.47) as well as the effect of a change in government expenditures on the return to capital. It implies that given $\bar{m}_1$ and $\bar{b}_1$ which are inherited from the past only three out of the four fiscal variables T_1, T_2, π_2 and G_1 are independent. Once the political system produces a decision about T_1, T_2 and π_2, G_1 is determined by (4.49).

7.3 General Characterization of Individuals' Preferences Towards the Size of the Public Sector and the Structure of Taxation

In order to determine what the fiscal policy of a government that satisfies the desires of the majority of voters is likely to be, it is necessary to evaluate the effect of this policy on the welfare of voters. Since G_1 is fully determined once a choice of the vector $\{T_1, T_2, \pi_2\}$ has been made, it suffices to evaluate the effect of each of the components in this vector on individual welfare, subject to the constraint in (4.49). Let $V(G_1,T_1,T_2,\pi_2)$ be the maximum value of utility that an individual who solves the maximization problem in (4.41) achieves for given values of G_1, T_1, T_2, and π_2. $V(\cdot)$ is the indirect utility of the individual as a function of the four fiscal policy variables chosen by a government. In order to evaluate the effect of changes in the components of the vector (T_1,T_2,π_2) on this indirect utility, differentiate $V(\cdot)$ totally with respect to each of these components. Using the envelope theorem this yields[50]

$$\frac{dV}{dT_1} = -\lambda + \beta v'[H'(f_L + a_2 f_K)\frac{dG_1}{dT_1} + H(f_{LK} + a_2 f_{KK})\frac{dK_2}{dT_1} - (1 + r_2)] \quad (4.50a)$$

$$\frac{dV}{dT_2} = \beta v'[H'(f_L + a_2 f_K)\frac{dG_1}{dT_2} + H(f_{LK} + a_2 f_{KK})\frac{dK_2}{dT_2} - 1 \quad (4.50b)$$

$$\frac{dV}{d\pi_2} = -m_2 u' + \beta v'[H'(f_L + a_2 f_K)\frac{dG_1}{d\pi_2} + H(f_{LK} + a_2 f_{KK})\frac{dK_2}{d\pi_2}] (4.50c)$$

here dG_1/dI and dK_2/dI $(I = T_1,T_2,\pi_2)$ are the total general equilibrium changes in G_1 and in K_2 as a result of a change in I. dG_1/dI summarizes the total change in G_1 as a result of a change in I because of three types of effects. First, because any change in I $(I = T_1,T_2,\pi_2)$ affects G_1 directly through the government budget constraint in (4.49). Second, because the changes in I and in G_1 trigger general equilibrium effects that are due to capital stock, K_2, changes. As a consequence the returns to capital and labour change as can be seen from (4.48). Hence, G_1 changes not only because of the direct change in either of T_1,T_2, or π_2 but also because of the induced change in r_2. Finally, the changes in returns to factors as well as in the parameters of governmental financial policy induce adjustments in real money balances, $\bar{m}_2$, which (as can be seen from (4.49)) also affect G_1.

Similarly dK_2/dI summarizes the total effect on K_2 of two distinct changes induced by the change in I. First, K_2 changes because of the direct effects that a change in either of T_1,T_2 or π_2 has on the demand for capital by individuals. Second, the change in K_2 as well as the change in G_1 trigger changes in returns to factors of production, as can be seen from (4.48). This causes an additional simultaneous realignment of the capital stock desired by individuals. This discussion also suggests that dG_1/dI and dK_2/dI are determined simultaneously. It is shown in part 4 of the Appendix that

$$\frac{dG_1}{dT_1} = \frac{1}{D}\{A[(1+\pi_2)\frac{\partial\bar{m}_2}{\partial T_1} + 1 - R] + B\frac{\partial K_2}{\partial T_1}\} \quad (4.51a)$$

$$\frac{dG_1}{dT_2} = \frac{1}{D}\{A[(1+\pi_2)\frac{\partial\bar{m}_2}{\partial T_2} + \frac{1-R}{1+r_2}] + B\frac{\partial K_2}{\partial T_2}\} \quad (4.51b)$$

$$\frac{dG_1}{d\pi_1} = \frac{1}{D}\{A[(1+\delta)\bar{m}_2 + B\frac{\partial K_2}{\partial\pi_2}\} \quad (4.51c)$$

and

$$\frac{dK_2}{dI} = \frac{1}{A}[\frac{\partial K_2}{\partial I} + H'(f_L\frac{\partial K_2}{\partial w_2} + f_K\frac{\partial k_2}{dr_2})\frac{dG_1}{dI}].\qquad(4.52)$$

Here δ is the short-run elasticity of $\bar{m}_2$ with respect to $1+\pi_2$, $\partial \bar{m}_2/\partial I$ ($I=T_1,T_2$) are the direct effects of changes in current and future taxes on average money balances in the second period, $\partial K_2/\partial I$ ($I = T_1,T_2,\pi_2$) are the direct effects of changes in current and future taxes and inflation on the capital stock in the second period, and[51]

$$A \equiv L(1+r_2)^2[1-H(f_{LK}\frac{\partial K_2}{\partial w_2} + f_{KK}\frac{\partial K_2}{\partial r_2})]\qquad(4.53a)$$

$$B \equiv LH(1+r_2)^2(1+\pi_2)[f_{LK}\frac{\partial \bar{m}_2}{\partial r_2} + f_{KK} + \frac{\partial \bar{m}_2}{\partial r_2}]-(1-R)T_2\ f_{KK}].\qquad(4.53b)$$

The crucial ultimate expressions for evaluating individual attitudes to different types of taxes and to public expenditures are in equations (4.50). Each of those expressions is composed of at least three qualitatively similar (across equations) terms. First are the direct negative effects of increased taxes on welfare. Those terms are $\beta v'(1+r_2)$ for an increase in T_1, - $\beta v'$ for an increase in T_2, and $m_2 u'$ for an increase in π_2. Second are the contributions of the changes in governmental expenditures on welfare through the consequent changes in productivity. This element is represented by the terms in dG_1/dI, $I = T_1$, T_2, π_2. Third, there are induced general equilibrium effects on capital which affect individual welfare by changing returns to capital and labour. This is captured by the terms $dK_2|dI$, $I = T_1$, T_2, π_2. Finally, an increase in current taxes, T_1, forces financially constrained individuals to reduce their current consumption even further, decreasing their welfare. This is represented by $-\lambda$. Obviously, for financially unconstrained individuals $\lambda = 0$.

It is shown in part 5 of the Appendix that $\partial K_2/\partial w_2$ is negative.[52] Since $f_{LK} > 0$ this implies $f_{LK}(\partial K_2/\partial w_2) < 0$. The sign of $\partial K_2/\partial r_2$ depends on whether the substitution effect of an increase in r_2 dominates the income effect. Assuming that the substitution effect dominates, $\partial K_2/\partial r_2$ is positive and $f_{KK}(\partial K_2/\partial r_2) < 0$. It follows that A is positive. It is shown in part 5 of the Appendix that, if the behaviour of aggregate money balances is dominated by unconstrained individuals, $\partial \bar{m}_2/\partial w_2$ is positive.[53] Assuming that when the real rate goes up people decrease their holdings of money balances, $\partial \bar{m}_2 / \partial r_2$ is negative. Since $f_{LK} > 0$ and $f_{KK} < 0$ this implies that B is positive. It is also shown in part 4 of the Appendix that under a weak sufficient condition D is positive as well. The rest of the discussion is conducted, therefore, under the presumption that A, B, and D are all positive.

Consider next the sign of dK_2/dI in equation (4.52). Since $\partial K_2 / \partial w_2$ and $\partial K_2 / \partial r_2$ have opposite signs, the sign of $f_L(\partial K_2 / \partial r_2) + f_K(\partial K_2 / \partial r_2)$ is ambiguous. I assume that whatever the sign of this expression, it does not dominate the sign of the entire expression in brackets on the right-hand side of (4.52). Since $A > 0$ this implies that the sign of dK_2/dI is dominated by the direct effects of changes in the tax rates T_1, T_2 and π_2 on the capital stock.[54] If consumption smoothing is the major force determining the demand for assets, the direct effect of an increase in T_1 on K_2 is negative since unconstrained individuals decrease their capital stock in order to maintain first-period consumption. Since the direct effect dominates and $A > 0$, this implies $dK_2/dT_1 < 0$. It is shown in part 5 of the Appendix that $\partial K_2 / \partial T_2 > 0$. Since this effect dominates and $A > 0$, this implies $dK_2/dT_2 > 0$. Finally, if substitution effects dominate portfolio behaviour $\partial K_2 / \partial \pi_2$ is positive implying, since $A > 0$ and since direct effects dominate, that $dK_2/d\pi_2$ is positive as well. The upshot is that if direct effects dominate

$$\frac{dK_2}{dT_1} < 0; \quad \frac{dK_2}{dT_2} > 0; \quad \frac{dK_2}{d\pi_2} > 0. \tag{4.54}$$

4.4 The Effect of Reparations on Current Taxes

Consider a *ceteris paribus* increase in current taxes that is meant to increase future productivity by increasing G_1. Since $\partial K_2 / \partial T_1$ and $\partial \bar{m}_2 / \partial T_1$ are both negative,[55] the expression for dG_1/dT_1 in equation (5.51a) is negative unless R is sufficiently smaller than one. If R is sufficiently large to make dG_1/dT_1 negative an increase in current taxes, taking all the readjustments in the economy into consideration, actually *decreases* government investments in infrastructure.[56] This effect obviously decreases the welfare of *all* individuals. This is confirmed formally by the fact that the coefficient of dG_1/dT_1 in (4.50a) is always positive so that a negative overall response of G_1 to an increase in T_1 contributes a negative term to dV/dT_1.

If in addition the individual is financially constrained, $\lambda > 0$ and an increase in T_1 decreases the individual's welfare also by forcing him to decrease his first-period consumption. Since from (4.54) $dK_2/dT_1 < 0$, the only term that contributes a positive quantity to dV/dT_1 is $\beta v' H f_{KK}$ $(dK_2/dT_1)a_2$. It reflects the fact that the welfare of wealthy individuals goes up due to the increase in the rate of return on wealth triggered by the decrease in the capital stock. For financially constrained individuals this effect is obviously zero (since $a_2 = 0$), so they are always unambiguously worse off when current taxes are increased if $dG_1/dT_1 < 0$. Actually, it is likely that for most individuals in the economy, except perhaps the very wealthy, the positive effect of an increase in T_1 on welfare through a higher return will be dominated by the decrease in G_1 as well as by the other negative terms in (4.50a).

In conclusion when (as was the case in Germany after May 1921) the expected reparations factor, R, is relatively high *all* individuals in the economy, except perhaps the very wealthy, strictly prefer no current taxes at all. I believe this result goes a long way in explaining the low proportion of taxes in Germany during the hyperinflation. Moreover, it can be used to rationalize the further decrease in this proportion in 1922 and 1923 (Table 4.4) as the consequence of an increase in the anticipated value of R following the announcement, in May 1921, of a reparations sum that was several times the size of GNP. A lot has been made of the fact that right-wing parties in Germany at the time managed to block taxes on capital while left-wing parties managed to block taxes on labour.[57] The analysis of this subsection is consistent with the view that blocking was so easy because of the underlying *common interest of both parties* to minimize current noninflationary tax payments.

Even in the absence of reparations it is likely that some deficit-financing would have been created because of the relatively large number of financially constrained individuals after the war. But the reparations transformed this tendency from a stream into a torrent of deficits.

4.5 The Effect of Reparations on Bond Financing of the Deficit

Consider a ceteris paribus increase in current bond issues designed to increase future productivity by increasing G_1. Since this is equivalent to an increase in future taxes, T_2, the effect of such a change on individual welfare can be analysed by focusing on dV/dT_2 in equation (4.50b). Since $\partial K_2/\partial T_2$ is positive and $\partial \bar{m}_2/\partial T_2$ is negative,[58] the sign of the expression for dG_1/dT_2 in (4.51b) is ambiguous in general. But the larger is R, the smaller $1-R$ and the more likely it is that dG_1/dT_2 is negative or positive but small. Hence, a high reparations factor makes it more likely that dV/dT_2 is either positive but small or negative. Individuals with small wealth are likely to have, *ceteris paribus*, a preference for future taxes since such taxes increase the real wage by increasing the capital stock. On the other hand individuals with large amounts of wealth are likely to dislike future taxes since the increase that such taxes induce in the capital stock lowers the return to their wealth. Hence, it is likely that individuals in the economy will be opposed or in favour of bond-financing of public investments depending on whether they are wealthy or not. The larger is R the more likely it is that the majority will be opposed to bond-floating as a method for financing the deficit. This conclusion is consistent with the observation that in 1922 and 1923 Germany financed only negligible parts of its deficit by borrowing from the public.

4.6 Voters Preferences for Inflationary Finance in the Presence of Reparations

If δ, the short-run elasticity of money demand with respect to inflation, is smaller than one in absolute value,[59] the effect of an increase in π on governmental investment in infrastructure and therefore on productivity is unambiguously positive (equation (4.51c). Hence, the term involving $dG_1/d\pi_2$ contributes a positive element to the expression for $dV/d\pi_2$ in equation (4.50c). On the other hand the tax on real money balances taken alone decreases V. The magnitude of this decrease is larger for individuals with higher real money balances as can be seen from the term $-m_2 u'$. Finally, as before, the increase in the capital stock triggered by substitution away from money is liked or disliked by the individual depending on whether he has a small or a large amount of wealth. Thus, in general, more wealthy individuals who also have higher real balances are more likely to be against inflationary finance and less wealthy individuals are likely to be for it. But even the more wealthy may be in favour of inflationary finance if the overall effect of an increase in such finance on the rate of return to wealth is positive. This total effect is given by

$$H' f_K \frac{dG_1}{d\pi_2} + f_{KK} \frac{dK_2}{d\pi_2}$$

and is positive if the marginal productivity of governmental investments in infrastructure, $H'f_K$, is large. Due to social and other disruptions caused by the war, this marginal productivity is likely to have been large after the war in most European countries and in Germany in particular.

8. CONCLUDING REMARKS

The evidence presented in this chapter is consistent with the surprising conclusion that during most of the German hyperinflation, the government possessed the ability to increase seigniorage temporarily by stepping up the rate of monetary growth. Moreover, expectations seem to have lagged quite substantially behind actual development particularly when inflation and depreciation shifted from one range to another. This is consistent with the view that the public had difficulties in separating persistent from transitory shifts in the government's objectives. This informational limitation as well as lags in the adjustment of money-saving institutions enabled the Reichsbank to maintain and even increase seigniorage in spite of the fact that real balances were on an almost continuously downward course during the hyperinflation.[60] It is therefore reasonable to expect that under lower inflationary circumstances there are similar, and most likely longer, lags in the full adjustment of real balances and of expected inflation. Those lags make it possible and rational for governments with strong time preference to increase the rate of inflation in order temporarily to increase seigniorage revenues. As expectations and institutions adjust, money demand gradually decreases further, making it necessary for such the governments to speed up the rate of inflation in order to prevent seigniorage from decreasing.

This process is self-limiting since after a while real money balances have decreased so much that the present value of inflation tax revenues becomes sufficiently small, in comparison to the present value of the costs of inflation, to make a change in monetary regime worthwhile. At this point hyperinflation is stabilized. Thus, the entire process of accelerating inflation followed by an ultimate stabilization can be viewed as the consequence of an attempt by a government with a strong desire for seigniorage revenues to extract them for as long as the lags in the adjustment of expectations and of institutions make the present value of such taxes net of the costs of inflation, sufficiently large. This observation also suggests that substantial amounts of revenues from seigniorage can be obtained only temporarily. The evolution of hyperinflation in Germany and its stabilization at the end of 1923 conformed to this pattern. In the German case, an additional incentive for stabilizing at that particular time was the creation of the Dawes plan and the not unrelated decrease in the government's financing of passive resistance.[61] The plan reduced the immediate menace of reparations on receipts from ordinary taxes, making it politically feasible to return to conventional methods of financing the budget.

The German central bank was also very slow in adjusting its discount rate in the face of rising inflation. As a consequence it shared the revenue from seigniorage with those parties in the private economy, like industrialists, who had access to the discount window. The discount rate (measured per year) was 5 per cent until July 1922 and rose to 10 per cent at the end of that year. It then gradually rose from 10 per cent at the beginning of 1923 to 90 per cent at its end.[62] The smallness of those rates by comparison to inflation and to market rates in 1923 is rather surprising. It is noteworthy that since the end of May 1922 the Reichsbank became legally independent of the central government[63] and was responsible to a board of directors, many of whom were private bankers and industrialists. Contrary to the Allies' expectation the Reichsbank did not use its newly acquired power to curb the rate of monetary expansion. Instead, from June 1922, it discounted private commercial bills along with Treasury bills, thus giving the business sector a share of seigniorage revenues. This raises the possibility that the very slow adjustment of the discount rate was the consequence of a deliberate policy designed to transfer resources to sectors that were heavily represented in the directorate of the Reichsbank.

Inflation also generated a substantial international redistribution of resources in favor of Germany through paper mark assets that were held by foreigners. Holtfrerich (1986, p. 296) estimates this redistribution to be of the same order of magnitude as total reparations payments made by Germany between 1919 and 1923. This provided an additional incentive to inflate over and above the desire to reduce reparations payments or to finance domestic public expenditure. However, it is unlikely that this incentive had any serious effect on the desire to inflate after 1922, since the real value of monetary assets held by foreigners was reduced to an already negligible quantity by the end of that year.

Finally, this chapter has focused almost exclusively on the revenue motive for inflation, abstracting from other possible motives like employment.[64] This seems appropriate for the hyperinflations of the twenties, in which all other motives were dominated by revenue considerations, but not for some recent high inflations in Argentina, Brazil and Israel. In those countries inflation was high but it did not reach the proportions of the classic hyperinflations. This would seem to suggest that governments that inflate exclusively or mainly because of revenue considerations are more likely to let high inflation develop into hyperinflation than the governments which have different concerns like employment in mind. The recent Bolivian inflation confirms this pattern. The inflationary outburst in Bolivia was triggered by a large and sudden decrease in government's tax revenues underlying the important role of revenues from seigniorage. The Bolivian inflation is also the only one of the recent high inflations that reached hyperinflationary dimensions before being stabilized.[65]

ENDNOTES

*   Originally published in *Carnegie-Rochester Conference Series on Public Policy* 29 (1988), 11-76 and reprinted with permission from North-Holland Elsevier, Tel-Aviv University. I benefited from useful discussions with Alberto Alesina, Karl Brunner, Zvi Eckstein, Robert Flood, Jacob Frenkel, Peter Garber, Zvi Hercowitz, Carl Holtfrerich, Finn Kydeland, Allan Meltzer, Manfred Neumann, Pierre Siklos, Guido Tabellini and Juergen Von Hagen. The usual disclaimer applies. The Horowitz Institute project on Central Banking provided partial financial assistance.

1.   However, during the recent high (but not hyper) inflations in Argentina, Brazil and Israel the employment motive was relatively more important although the revenue motive played a role as well. An analysis of the interaction between those two motives during the recent Israeli inflation appears in Cukierman (1988). The Argentinian and Brazilian experiences are described in Dornbusch and Fischer (1986) and Helpman and Leiderman (1988), and the recent Bolivian experience in Sachs (1987) and Morales (1988). A third motive for inflationary policies from which I abstract is reduction of deficits in the balance of payments (Cukierman and Liviatan 1987). A general historical survey of conditions under which high inflations have appeared is in Capie (1986).

2.   Such estimates have been provided by Cagan (1956), Sargent (1977) and Christiano (1987).

3.   This statement is based on data until September 1923 since data on forward rates and interest rates are not available thereafter.

4.   Sargent (1977), for example, expresses the widely held view that this observation reflects an apparently irrational behaviour by the creators of money (pg. 60).

5.   As far as I know all existing literature on stabilization takes its timing as exogenous. Examples are Flood and Garber (1980a, 1980b), Sargent (1986), Drazen and Helpman (1986) and Bental and Eckstein (1987).

6.   This is analogous to the role of bequest constraints in creating deficits through the political system (Cukierman and Meltzer 1987).

7.   Graham (1967), pp. 40-41. By contrast during the high Israeli inflation seigniorage usually was less than 3 per cent of total government expenditures (Cukierman 1988).

8.   A brief discussion of other motives for inflationary policies appears in the concluding section.

9.   This statement is based on the well-known result (Bailey 1956 and Cagan 1956) that in the absence of growth, with perfect foresight, and a Cagan-type money demand function of the form $\exp[-\alpha\pi]$ (where π is inflation), steady-state seigniorage is maximized when π is equal to $1/\alpha$.

10.   Studies of money demand in Israel summarized by Offenbacher (1985) also imply that during the last two years preceding the 1985 stabilization, inflation was in the elastic range of the money demand function.

11.   Bental and Eckstein (1987) report a similar trend.

12.   Note that for low rates of change the two measures of seigniorage are similar. But they are sometimes quite different at high rates of inflation (compare columns (3) and (4)).

13.   Evidence presented in Graham (1967), pp. 40-41 is consistent with the view that seigniorage was substantially higher in 1923 than in 1922.

14.   Most empirical studies of the demand for money during the hyperinflation, like those of Cagan (1956), Sargent (1977) and Christiano (1987), test a joint hypothesis that includes both the form of money demand and the process of expectations formation. An exception is Frenkel (1977).

15.   These data pass simple tests of market efficiency (Frenkel 1977).

16.   These data terminate in September 1923 and are available again only from November 1924 and on.

17.   Such shifts may reflect the changing evaluation of policymakers about their ability to raise funds via conventional taxes, as well as changes in the urgency with which they require those funds to carry out the activities of government. It is very likely that with the policy of passive resistance declared after the Ruhr's invasion in January 1923, the German government's desire for immediate seigniorage went up substantially.

        The first element of the framework is identical to Grossman and Van Huyck's (1986) formulation. The main difference between their model and the present one is that reputation here is due to learning rather than to a strategic interaction between the public and government.

18.   A previous version of the paper investigates the polar case in which there is perfect foresight but there are differences between the short- and the long-run adjustments of money demand to changes in expected inflation. (Evidence that such differences may be non-negligible at least for mild inflations is provided by Cukierman, Lennan and Papadia (1985) for major EC countries and by Piterman (1985) for Argentina and Israel.) This framework, too, implies that governments with high time preference may choose to inflate at rates above the rate at which the elasticity of long-run money demand is unity.

        Differences between the short- and the long-run demand for money arise because a sustained increase in expected inflation triggers institutional adjustments designed to further reduce the need to hold and to use the costly money (Brunner and Meltzer 1971). Use of alternative means of payments, limited barter arrangements, changes in the frequency of wage payments and more efficient banking are costly institutional changes. Hence they are introduced gradually only after the public has become convinced that the higher inflation is a persistent phenomenon.

19.   It implies that the increment to nominal money balances raises prices only after it has been spent on the market.

20.   This approximation is reasonably accurate even for the German hyperinflation provided the interval between consecutive periods is sufficiently small.

21.   For simplicity the rate of monetary expansion is used as a proxy for the costs of inflation to government.

22.   Since the approximation is used only in the solution of a government's decision problem, it can be interpreted as describing the behaviour of a government that, due to computational constraints, operates subject to bounded rationality.

23.   Sargent (1979, Ch. 14). The problem in (4.22) is formally equivalent to that on page 1107 of Cukierman and Meltzer (1986b). An argument similar to that in footnote 14 of that article implies that the transversality condition is satisfied for any $\beta < 1$. This condition is sufficient for an internal maximum.

24.   Another important difference is that the decision rule of the policymaker here is time consistent.

25.   The explicit form of K is

$$K \equiv G_1 \, \alpha \, \mu_m [\mu_m - \frac{(1-\rho)(1+\alpha(1-\lambda))}{(1-\lambda)(1+\alpha(1-\rho))} \ B_0 \ A]$$

26.   In terms of the model this implies large positive realizations of p_i and perhaps also of ε_i in 1923.

27.   This can be seen by nothing that DB_0A is an increasing function of λ, since the sign of the partial derivative of B_0 with respect to λ is the same as that of $1-\rho$ which is positive and by noting that λ is an increasing function σ_ε^2. The last fact is demonstrated in Cukierman and Meltzer (1986b).

28.   In terms of Grossman and Van Huyck (1986) terminology, the 'punishment' for high current monetary expansion comes later and is therefore discounted more heavily. But unlike in Grossman and Van Huyck the loss in the policymaker's 'reputation' due to a higher current monetary expansion is a byproduct of the public's attempt to learn optimally about the changing pattern of the policymaker's objectives rather than to exogenous deterrence mechanisms.

29.   This divergence cannot be used, at the time, by individuals to improve their forecasts since expectations are rational. Further details about why this is the case appear in section 5 of Brunner, Cukierman and Meltzer (1980) and in Cukierman and Meltzer (1982).

30.   This statement implicitly relies on a weak version of purchasing power parity (PPP). Frenkel (1977) presents evidence that PPP held during the German hyperinflation and that exchange rate expectations are therefore a good proxy for price level expectations.

31.   Under perfect foresight the unit elasticity point would have been crossed around mid-1922. But the data on expectations from the forward market suggests that it was crossed only about a year later.

32.   This is the so-called 'Olivera-Tanzi' effect familiarized by the more recent South American and Israeli inflations.

33.   This is not meant to imply that the Israeli governments of the time did not miscalculate, nor that they inflated only, or even mainly, because of revenue considerations. See also Parkin (1984).

34.   This paradigm has been used previously to explain intratemporal redistribution (Meltzer and Richard 1981), progressive taxation (Cukierman and Meltzer 1986a), and the existence of deficits in a neo-Ricardian world (Cukierman and Meltzer 1987).

35.   This expectation actually turned out to be correct for Germany and several other European countries following World War I (Alesina 1987, Table 6).

36.   Alesina (1988).

37.   A detailed analysis of this mechanism in the context of a neo-Ricardian economy appears in Cukierman and Meltzer (1987).

38.   In the presence of distortionary taxes this is likely to be the outcome even in the absence of a deficit because of optimal taxation considerations (Helpman and Sadka 1979).

39.   For a description of the facts see Eichengreen and Wyplosz (1988).

40.   In May 1921 reparations were fixed at 132 billion gold marks (Graham 1967, p. 8). Official estimates of German GNP for the hyperinflation years are not available. However Graham (footnote 79, p. 320) estimates that 1921 income was 46 billion gold marks, which implies that reparations were 2.87 times larger than yearly income. This is probably a lower bound since alternative estimates of income yield substantially higher ratios.

41.   This assumption actually turned out to be correct as demonstrated by the Dawes plan at the end of the hyperinflation. Webb (1985) also expressed the view that inflationary finance was selected in order to produce economic conditions that would result in the lowering of reparations payments.

42.   Meaning inflationary finance.

43.   Obviously, seigniorage revenues too could have been used to buy foreign exchange in order to hand it over to the Allies. Although such a policy was feasible in principle, it would have meant that the Reichsbank would have dumped large quantities of freshly printed paper marks on international foreign exchange markets. Any attempt to discharge a nonnegligible fraction of reparations via this method would have caused

a sharp and continued process of depreciation of the mark, thereby eliminating the Reichsbank's ability to raise a sufficient amount of foreign exchange through this method. As a matter of fact in an ideal world of rational expectations the mere knowledge that this method was being used on a grand scale to pay reparations would probably have immediately driven the foreign exchange value of the mark to zero or close to it. In any case the Allies did not like the depreciation of the mark because of the competitive edge it gave to German goods in their markets and actually tried to slow it down. This was one of the reasons for the Allies' (and the US in particular) interest in stabilizing the German hyperinflation. Ordinary taxes are not afflicted by the same problems, at least not to the same extent, for several reasons. First, the additional demand for foreign exchange in this case is naturally limited by the amount of taxes collected. Second ordinary taxes crowd out domestic demand, releasing more resources for exports net of imports. This effect works to maintain the value of the Mark without simultaneously exerting downward pressures on it because of monetary expansion.

Another potential way to use seigniorage for reparations would have been for the Reichsbank to acquire goods and services in Germany by printing money and handing them over to the Allies in kind. But this way of using seigniorage for reparations was naturally limited by the fact that the Allies wanted to spend most of the reparations outside Germany.

44.   This conflict was well publicized as a consequence of parliamentary debates about the distribution of tax burdens between labour and capital (Maier 1975).

45. B_1 includes any interest that might have accumulated. The individual's index is deleted for simplicity. k_1 is measured in units of the single good available in the economy.

46.   Note that he buys the capital to be transferred into the next period (k_2) at period one's prices.

47.   Money in the second period yields utility directly and also because it is eventually used to buy second-period consumption.

48.   The first-period utility from money has been deleted since it is not affected by the choice of m_2, b_2, and k_2.

49.   For simplicity the reparations factor for seigniorage revenues is assumed to be zero. The main qualitative results of this section would be unaffected if it had been positive but smaller than the fraction of reparations extracted from ordinary taxes.

50.   In deriving (4.50a) use has been made of the fact that either $\lambda = 0$ or $da_2/dT_1 = 0$ and of the first order condition in (4.43b). Here f_{LK} and f_{KK} denote the second partial derivatives of $f(\cdot)$ with respect to its arguments.

51.   In general I follow the convention of using partial derivative symbols to denote direct effects. The explicit expression for D is given in part 4 of the Appendix.

52.   The intuition is that when current resources are larger, unconstrained individuals want to transfer more resources to the future.

53.   This just confirms that money is a normal good.

54.   The effects which are dominated are the changes in the capital stock that are due to changes in factor returns because of the change in G_1.

55.   The negativity of $\partial \bar{m}_2/\partial T_1$ is demonstrated in part 5 of the Appendix.

56.   Since $\partial K_2/\partial T_1$ and $\partial \bar{m}_2/\partial T_1$ are both negative, this obviously occurs for R smaller than one.

57.   Examples are Bresciani-Turroni (1937), pp. 57-60, Maier (1975) and Alesina (1988).

58.   This is demonstrated in part 5 of the Appendix which confirms the usual presumption that money is a normal good.

59.   The evidence on the behaviour of seigniorage during the German hyperinflation is consistent with the view that it is smaller than one. See section 2.

60.   Seigniorage did not systematically decrease as inflation accelerated and sometimes increased during the Austrian, Hungarian and Polish hyperinflations in the twenties (Bental and Eckstein 1987). This finding supports the view that in other

hyperinflations, too, there were lags either in the adjustment of expectations or in the adjustment of money demand or in both.

61.   Bresciani-Turroni (1937), p. 355.

62.   The average monthly discount rates in 1923 (in percentages per year) were:

January	February	March	April	May	June	July	August	September
11	12	12	15	18	18	18	30	75

October	November	December
90	90	90

During 1924 it was 10 per cent. Source: *Die Reichsbank 1901-1925*, Berlin/Drunderei der Reichsbank, pp. 34-95.

63.   Holtfrerich (1986), p. 168.
64.   The employment motive for inflation has been stressed by Kydland and Prescott (1977).
65.   Other recent high inflations occurred in Argentina, Brazil, Israel and Mexico. A detailed discussion of the Bolivian experience appears in Morales (1988) and Sachs (1987). The fact that during the 1985 stabilization the Bolivian government tolerated substantial unemployment backs up the view that the employment motive was weak in comparison to the revenue motive in Bolivia.

REFERENCES

Alesina, A. (1988), 'The End of Large Public Debts', F. Giavazzi and L. Spaventa (eds.), *High Public Debt: The Italian Experience*, Cambridge University Press, Cambridge.

Bailey, M.J. (1956), 'The Welfare Cost of Inflationary Finance', *Journal of Political Economy*, 64, pp. 93-110.

Barro, R.J. (1970), 'Inflation, the Payments Period, and the Demand for Money', *Journal of Political Economy*, 78, pp. 1228-63.

Barro, R.J. and Gordon, D.B. (1983), 'A Positive Theory of Monetary Policy in a Natural Rate Model', *Journal of Political Economy*, 91, pp. 589-610.

Bental, B. and Eckstein, Z. (1987), 'The Dynamics of Inflation with Constant Deficit Under Expected Regime Change', unpublished manuscript, Technion, Israel Institute of Technology and University of California, San Diego.

Bresciani-Turroni, C. (1937), *The Economics of Inflation — A Study of Currency Depreciation in Post War Germany*, George Allen & Unwin Ltd., London.

Brunner, K., Cukierman, A. and Meltzer, A.H. (1980), 'Stagflation, Persistent Unemployment and the Permanence of Economic Shocks', *Journal of Monetary Economics*, 6, pp. 467-92.

Brunner, K. and Meltzer, A.H. (1971), 'The Uses of Money: Money in the Theory of an Exchange Economy', *American Economic Review*, 61, pp. 784-805.

Cagan, P. (1956), 'The Monetary Dynamics of Hyperinflation', in M. Friedman (ed.), *Studies in the Quantity Theory of Money*, University of Chicago Press, Chicago.

Calvo, G.A. (1978), 'On the Time Consistency of Optimal Policy in a Monetary Economy', *Econometrica*, 46, pp. 1411-28.

Capie, F. (1986), 'Conditions in Which Very Rapid Inflation Has Appeared', in K. Brunner & A.H. Meltzer (eds.), *Carnegie-Rochester Conference Series on Public Policy*, 24, pp. 115-68.

Christiano, L.J. (1987), 'Cagan's Model of Hyperinflation Under Rational Expectations', *International Economic Review*, 28, pp. 33-49.

Cukierman, A. (1988), 'The End of the High Israeli Inflation - An Experiment in Heterodox Stabilization', in M. Bruno, G. Di-Tella, R. Dornbusch & S. Fischer (eds.), *Inflation Stabilization: The Experience of Israel, Argentina, Brazil, Bolivia and Mexico*. MIT Press, Cambridge, Mass.

Cukierman, A., Lennan, K. and Papadia, F. (1985), *Inflation Induced Redistributions via Monetary Assets in Five European Countries: 1974-1980, — Studies in Banking and Finance*, Vol. 2, North Holland Publishing Company and the EC Publication Office, Amsterdam, pp. 295-352.

Cukierman, A. and Liviatan, N. (1987), 'Rules, Discretion, Credibility and Reputation', unpublished manuscript, Tel-Aviv University (Hebrew).

Cukierman, A. and Meltzer. A.H. (1982), 'What Do Tests of Market Efficiency Show in the Presence of the Permanent-Transitory Confusion?', unpublished Manuscript, December, Carnegie Mellon University.

Cukierman, A. and Meltzer, A.H. (1986a), 'A Positive Theory of Progressive Income Taxation', unpublished manuscript, Carnegie-Mellon University.

Cukierman, A. and Meltzer, A.H. (1986b), 'A Theory of Ambiguity, Credibility and Inflation Under Discretion and Asymmetric Information', *Econometrica*, 54, pp. 1099-128.

Cukierman, A. and Meltzer, A.H. (1987), 'A Political Theory of Government Debt and Deficits in a Neo Ricardian Framework', paper presented at the 4th Pinhas Sapir Conference on Economic Effects of the Government Budget, Tel-Aviv University, December 1986.

Dornbusch, R. and Fischer, S. (1986), *Stopping Hyperinflation: Past and Present*, Weltwirtschaftliches Archiv.

Drazen, A. and Helpman, E. (1986), 'Inflationary Consequences of Anticipated Macroeconomic Policies', working paper No. 2006, NBER.

Eichengreen, B. and Wyplosz, C. (1988), 'The Economic Consequences of Franc Poincaré', in Helpman, Sadka and Razin (eds.). *The Economic Effects of the Government Budget*, MIT Press, Cambridge, Mass.

Einzig, P. (1937), *The Theory of Forward Exchange*, MacMillan and Company Ltd., London.

Fischer, S. (1984), 'The Economy of Israel', K. Brunner and A.H. Meltzer (eds.). *Carnegie-Rochester Conference Series on Public Policy*, 20, pp. 7-52.

Flood, R.P. and Garber, P. (1980a), 'An Economic Theory of Monetary Reform', *Journal of Political Economy*, 88, pp. 24-58.

Flood, R.P. and Garber, P. (1980b), 'Market Fundamentals Versus Price Level Bubbles: The First Tests', *Journal of Political Economy*, 88, pp. 745-70.

Frenkel, J.A. (1977), 'The Forward Exchange Rate, Expectations and the Demand for Money: The German Hyperinflation', *American Economic Review*, 67, pp. 653-70.

Graham, F.D. (1967), *Exchange, Prices and Production in Hyper-inflation Germany, 1920-1923*, Russell & Russell, New York. Originally published by Princeton University Press in 1930.

Grossman, H.I. and Van Huyck, J.B. (1986), 'Seigniorage, Inflation and Reputation, *Journal of Monetary Economics*, 18, pp. 21-32.

Helpman, E. and Leiderman, L. (1988), 'Stabilization in High Inflation Countries; Analytical Foundations and Recent Experience', in K. Brunner & A.H. Meltzer (eds.), *Carnegie-Rochester Conference Series on Public Policy*, 28.

Helpman, E. and Sadka, E. (1979), 'Optimal Financing of the Government's Budget: Taxes, Bonds, or Money?', *American Economic Review*, 69, pp. 152-60.

Holtfrerich, C.L. (1986), *The German Inflation 1914-1923*, Walter de Gruyter, Berlin and New York.

Kydland, F.E. and Prescott, E. (1977), 'Rules Rather than Discretion: The Inconsistency of Optimal Plans', *Journal of Political Economy*, 85, pp. 473-92.

Maier, C. (1975), *Recasting Bourgeois Europe; Stabilization in France, Germany and Italy in the Decade after World War I*, Princeton University Press, Princeton, NJ.

Meltzer, A.H. and Richard, S. (1981), 'A Rational Theory of the Size of Government', *Journal of Political Economy*, 89, pp. 914-27.

Morales, J.A. (1988), 'Inflation Stabilization in Bolivia', in R. Dornbusch & S. Fischer (eds.), *Inflation Stabilization: The Experience of Israel, Argentina, Brazil, Bolivia and Mexico*, MIT Press, Cambridge, Mass.

Offenbacher, A. (1985), 'Introduction: Empirical Studies of Money Demand in Israel', *Bank of Israel Economic Review*, No. 60, pp. 3-16 (Hebrew).

Parkin, M. (1984), 'A Comment on Fischer', in K. Brunner & A.H. Meltzer (eds.). *Carnegie-Rochester Conference Series on Public Policy*, 20, pp. 53-6.

Piterman, S. (1985), 'The Irreversibility of the Relationships Between Inflation and Real Money Balances', *Bank of Israel Economic Review*, No. 60, pp. 71-81 (Hebrew).

Sachs, J. (1987), 'The Bolivian Hyperinflation and Stabilization', *American Economic Review Papers and Proceedings*, 77, pp. 279-83.

Sargent, T.J. (1977), 'The Demand for Money During Hyperinflations Under Rational Expectations: I', *International Economic Review*, 18, pp. 59-82.

Sargent, T.J. (1979), *Macroeconomic Theory*, Academic Press, New York.

Sargent, T.J. (1986), *The Ends of Four Big Inflations, Rational Expectations and Inflation*, Harper and Row, New York.

Sokoler, M. (1987), 'The Inflation Tax on Real Balances, the Inflation Subsidy on Credit and the Inflationary Process in Israel', *Economic Review*, 59: Bank of Israel Research Department, pp. 1-26.

Webb, S.B. (1985), 'Fiscal News and Inflationary Expectations in Germany After World War I', *Journal of Economic History*, 46, pp. 769-94.

Young, J.P (1983), *European Currency and Finance*, Garland Publishing Company Inc., New York and London. Reissue of Commission of Gold and Silver Inquiry — US Senate — Foreign Currency and Exchange Investigation, Serial 9 (Volume I), 1925.

APPENDIX

1. Derivation of a Linear Approximation for g_j;

Inserting (4.10) in (4.7).

$$g_i = \mu_{i+1} \, De^{-\alpha\pi^*_{i+1}} \equiv \psi(\mu_{i+1}, \pi^*_{i+1}). \qquad (4A.1)$$

Equations (4.16) and (4.17) in the text are obtained by expanding $\psi(\cdot)$ linearly around the point $\mu_{i+1} = \pi^*_{i+1} = \mu_m$. Note that this point corresponds to a deterministic nonstochastic steady state with no real growth in which the money supply grows at the constant rate μ_m.

2. Derivation of Equation (4.19)

Taking expected values, conditional on I_t, of both sides of (4.12) and rearranging

$$\pi^*_{t+1} \equiv E[\pi_{t+1} \mid I_t] = \frac{1}{1+\alpha} \left[{}_t\mu^*_{t+1} + \alpha E[\pi_{t+2} \mid I_t] \right]$$

where

$${}_t\mu^*_{t+j} \equiv E[\mu_{t+j} \mid I_t], \; j \geq 1. \qquad (4A.2)$$

Leading (4.12) by j periods, taking expected values as of period t (conditional on I_t) we, similarly, obtain

$$E[\pi_{t+j} \mid I_t] = \frac{1}{1+\alpha} \left[{}_t\mu^*_{t+1} = \alpha E[\pi_{t+j} \mid I_t] \right], \; j \geq 1. \qquad (4A.3)$$

Using (4A.3) recursively in (4A.1) add infinitum

$$\pi^*_{t+1} = \frac{t}{1+\alpha} \sum_{j=1}^{\infty} \left(\frac{\alpha}{1+\alpha} \right)^{j-1} {}_t\mu^*_{t+j}. \qquad (4A.4)$$

Since the public knows that the behaviour of money growth is given by
(4.18) and since $E[\psi_{t+j}|I_t] = 0$ for all $j \geq 1$

$$_t\mu^*_{t+j} = B_0A + BE[p_{t+j}|I_t], \, j \geq 1. \tag{4A.5}$$

Cukierman and Meltzer (1986b, p. 1105) show that given (4.14), (4.15),
(4.18), and the distributions of v and ε

$$E[p_{t+1}|I_t] = \frac{\rho - \lambda}{B} \sum_{s=0}^{\infty} \lambda^j [\mu_{t-s} - B_0A] \tag{4A.6}$$

where λ is given by (4.21a). Due to (4.15)

$$E[p_{t+j}|I_t] = \rho^{j-1} E[p_{t+1}|I_t], \, j \geq 1. \tag{4A.7}$$

Substituting (4A.6) into (4A.7), substituting the resulting expression into
(4A.5). and using the resulting expression in (4A.4)

$$\pi^*_{t+1} = \frac{1}{1+\alpha} [(1+\alpha)B_0A + (\rho - \lambda) \sum_{j=1}^{\infty} \frac{\rho\alpha}{1+\alpha})^{j-1}$$
$$\sum_{s=0}^{\infty} \lambda^s [\mu_{t-s} - B_0A]]. \tag{4A.8}$$

Equation (4.19) in the text is obtained by summing up one of the infinite
geometric progressions in (4A.8) and by rearranging.

3. Derivation of Equation (4.27) and Demonstration of the
   Uniqueness of the Solution for B_0 and B

Since $0 < \rho < 1$ and $0 \leq \beta \leq 1$,

$$\beta\rho^2 < 1. \tag{4A.9}$$

Footnote 11 of Cukierman. and Meltzer (1986b) implies $1 \geq \rho - \lambda \geq 0$. In
view of this, and (4A.9)

$$0 \leq \frac{\rho\beta(\rho-\lambda)}{1-\rho\beta\lambda} < 1 \tag{4A.10}$$

which implies in turn that

$$0 \leq \frac{\rho\beta(\rho-\lambda)}{(1-\rho\beta\lambda)(1+\alpha(1-\rho))} < 1. \tag{4A.11}$$

If, on average, a government operates in the range in which the elasticity of money demand is not larger than unity, it makes sense to approximate seigniorage around a value of μ_m that is no larger than $1/\alpha$. Assuming this is the case, $\alpha\,\mu_m \leq 1$ which together with (4A.11) implies

$$0 \leq \alpha\,\mu_m \frac{\rho\beta(\rho-\lambda)}{(1-\rho\beta\lambda)(1+\alpha(1-\rho))} < 1. \tag{4A.12}$$

Equation (4A.12) implies that the right-hand side of (4.26b) is always positive. The discussion on page 1108 of Cukierman and Meltzer (1986b) implies that λ is monotonically decreasing in B. Since the right-hand side of (4.26b) is increasing in λ, it follows that it is also monotonically decreasing in B. Since the right-hand side of (4.26b) is always positive and monotonically decreasing in B, there is a unique value of B that satisfies this equation. Given this solution equation (4.26a) implies a unique solution for B_0.

Equations (4A.12) and (4.26b) also imply that $1 \geq B > 0$.

Since $\rho < 1$ and $\beta\lambda \leq \lambda$

$$0 \leq \frac{\beta(\rho-\lambda)}{(1-\beta\lambda)(1+\alpha(1-\rho))} < 1 \tag{4A.13}$$

which implies together with the condition $\alpha\mu_m \leq 1$ that $1 \geq B_0 > 0$.

4. Derivation of the Expressions for dG_1/d_1 $(I{=}T_1,T_2,\pi_2)$
   in Equations (4.51a,b,c)

Differentiating (4.41) totally with respect to T_1, T_2 and π_2 we obtain, respectively

$$\frac{dG_1}{dT_1} = L[(1-R) - \frac{(1-R)T_2}{(1+r_2)^2}J_{T_1} + (1+\pi_2)\frac{d\bar{m}_2}{dT_1}] \qquad (4A.14a)$$

$$\frac{dG_1}{dT_2} = L[\frac{1-R}{1+r_2} - \frac{(1-R)T_2}{(1+r_2)^2}J_{T_2} + (1+\pi_2)\frac{d\bar{m}_2}{dT_2}] \qquad (4A.14b)$$

$$\frac{dG_1}{dT_3} = L[\bar{m}_2 - \frac{(1-R)T_2}{(1+r_2)^2}J_{\pi_2} + (1+\pi_2)\frac{d\bar{m}_2}{d\pi_2}] \qquad (4A.14c)$$

where

$$J_I \equiv H'f_K\frac{dG_1}{dI} + Hf_{KK}\frac{dK_2}{dI}, \quad I = T_1, T_2, \pi_2. \qquad (4A.15)$$

Differentiating equations (4.48a,b) totally with respect to the dummy variable I

$$\frac{dw_2}{dI} = H'f_2\frac{dG_2}{dI} + Hf_{KL}\frac{dK_2}{dI}$$

$$\qquad (4A.16)$$

$$\frac{dr_2}{dI} = H'f_K\frac{dG_2}{dI} + Hf_{KK}\frac{dK_2}{dI}$$

Differentiating K_2 and $\bar{m}_2$ totally with respect to I

$$\frac{dK_2}{dI} = \frac{\partial K_2}{\partial I} + \frac{\partial K_2}{\partial w_2}\frac{dw_2}{dI} + \frac{\partial K_2}{\partial r_2}\frac{dr_2}{dI}$$

$$\qquad (4A.17)$$

$$\frac{d\bar{m}_2}{dI} = \frac{\partial \bar{m}_2}{dI} + \frac{\partial \bar{m}_2}{\partial w_2}\frac{dw_2}{dI} + \frac{\partial \bar{m}_2}{\partial r_2}\frac{dr_2}{dI}$$

Substituting (4A.16) into (4A.17a) and rearranging

$$\frac{dK_2}{dI} = \frac{1}{L} \left[\frac{\partial K_2}{\partial I} + H'(f_L \frac{\partial K_2}{\partial w_2} + f_K \frac{\partial K_2}{\partial r_2}) \frac{dG_1}{dI} \right] \quad (4A.18)$$

where

$$Q = 1 - H(f_{LK} \frac{\partial K_2}{\partial w_2} + f_{KK} \frac{\partial K_2}{\partial r_2}).$$

Substituting (4A.16) and (4A.18) into (4A.17b) and rearranging

$$\frac{d\bar{m}_2}{dI} = \frac{1}{Q} [Q\{ \frac{\partial \bar{m}_2}{\partial I} + H'[f_L \frac{\partial \bar{m}_2}{\partial w_2} + f_K \frac{\partial \bar{m}_2}{\partial r_2}] \frac{dG_1}{dI} \} \quad (4A.20)$$

$$+ H\{f_{LK} \frac{\partial \bar{m}_2}{\partial w_2} + f_{KK} \frac{\partial \bar{m}_2}{\partial r_2}\} \{ \frac{\partial K_2}{\partial I} + H'[f_L \frac{\partial K_2}{\partial w_2} + f_K \frac{\partial K_2}{\partial r_2}] \frac{dG_1}{dI} \}].$$

Equations (4.51) in the text follow by inserting (4A.18) and (4A.20) into equations (4A.14) where

$$D \equiv Q[(1 + r_2)^2 \{1 - L(1 + \pi_2)H'[f_L \frac{\partial \bar{m}_2}{\partial w_2} + f_K \frac{\partial \bar{m}_2}{\partial r_2}]\} + L(1 - R)T_2H'f_K]$$

$$(4A.21)$$

$$+ LH' (f_L \frac{\partial K_2}{\partial w_2} + f_K \frac{\partial K_2}{\partial r_2})[(1 - R)T_2Hf_{KK} - (1 + n_2)(1 + r_2)H(f_{LK} \frac{\partial \bar{m}_2}{\partial w_2}$$

$$+ f_{KK} \frac{\partial \bar{m}_2}{\partial r_2})].$$

Since $H' > 0$, $f_K > 0$, $f_{LK} > 0$, $f_{KK} < 0$, and $1 - R \geq 0$ jointly sufficient (but not necessary) conditions for D to be positive are;

$$f_{LK} \frac{\partial K_2}{\partial w_2} + f_{KK} \frac{\partial K_2}{\partial r_2} < 0. \tag{4A.22a}$$

$$f_L \frac{\partial K_2}{\partial w_2} + f_K \frac{\partial K_2}{\partial r_2} < 0. \tag{4A.22b}$$

$$f_L \frac{\partial \overline{m}_2}{\partial w_2} + f_K \frac{\partial \overline{m}_2}{\partial r_2} < 0. \tag{4A.22c}$$

It is shown in part 5 of the Appendix that $\partial K_2/\partial w_2 < 0$ and that $\partial \overline{m}_2/\partial w_2 > 0$. The sign of $\partial K_2/\partial r_2$ depends on whether the income or the substitution effect dominates. If those two effects make $\partial K_2/\partial r_2$ small in absolute value relatively to the absolute value of $\partial K_2/\partial w_2$, (4A.22a) and (4A.22b) are dominated by their first terms and are therefore negative as required. It is shown in part 5 of the Appendix that $\partial \overline{m}_2/\partial w_2 > 0$. The sign of $\partial \overline{m}_2/\partial r_2$ depends on whether the substitution or the wealth effect of an increase in r_2 dominates. If those two conflicting effects make $\partial \overline{m}_2/\partial r_2$ relatively small in absolute value, (4A.22c) is dominated by its first term and is therefore negative.

Speaking loosely, the above discussion implies that a sufficient condition for $D > 0$ is that the signs of the expressions in (4A.22) be dominated by the terms whose signs are unambiguous.

5. Comparative Statics with Respect to w_2 and T_1

a. Proof that $\partial K_2/\partial w_2 < 0$.

Since $K_2 \equiv \sum_{i=1}^{L} k_{2i}$ it is enough to show that $\partial k_{2i}/\partial w_2 \le 0$ for all i and that it is strictly negative for some i. For an individual who is not constrained, $\lambda = 0$ in equation (4.43b). Totally differentiating equations (4.39) with respect to w_2 and solving for $\partial a_2/\partial w_2$

$$\frac{\partial a_2}{\partial w_1} = -\frac{\beta}{|S|} v''(n_2(1+\pi_2)u'' + \beta(1+r_2)\delta^2 \ell) \tag{4A.23}$$

where $|S|$ is the determinant of the second-order partial derivatives of the maximum problem in (4.41) and is positive by the second-order condition for a maximum. The individual's index, i, has been deleted for simplicity. If the nominal rate of interest, n_2, is positive, (4A.23) is negative since the second partial derivatives of utility, v'', u'', and ∂'', are all negative. But $a_2 \equiv k_2 + b_2$. If the total quantity of bonds is constant, the decrease in a_2 takes the form of an equal size decrease in k_2. Hence, $\partial k_2/\partial w_2 < 0$ for an unconstrained individual.

For a strictly constrained individual $a_2 = 0$, and an increase in w_2 does not affect a_2 since the individual desires to decrease a_2 even further but is unable to because of the constraint $a_2 \geq 0$. Hence, $\partial k_2/\partial w_2 = 0$. Assuming not all individuals are constrained

$$\frac{\partial K_2}{\partial w_2} < 0. \qquad \text{QED}$$

b. Proof that $\partial \bar{m}_2/\partial w_2 > 0$ when unconstrained individuals dominate

Since $\bar{m}_2 \equiv \sum_{i=1}^{L} m_{2i}/L$ and since unconstrained individuals dominate, it is enough to show that $\partial m_{2i}/\partial w_2 > 0$ for such individuals. For unconstrained individuals $\lambda = 0$ and $a_2 > 0$. Inserting this constraint into (4.43), totally differentiating with respect to w_2 and solving for $\partial m_2/\partial w_2$

$$\frac{\partial m_2}{\partial w_2} = \frac{\beta}{|S|} u'' v'' \qquad \text{QED}$$

which is positive. Again the individual's index is deleted for simplicity.

c. Proof that $\partial \bar{m}_2/\partial T_1 < 0$ if $n_2 > 0$

Differentiating (4.43) totally with respect to T_1 for an unconstrained individual ($\lambda = 0$, $a_2 > 0$) and solving for $\partial m_2/\partial T_1$

$$\frac{\partial m_2}{\partial T_1} = -\frac{\beta}{|S|} (1 + r_2) u'' v'' n_2$$

which is negative for $n_2 > 0$.

For a constrained individual $a_2 = 0$ and equation (4.43a) alone determines m_2. Differentiating it with respect to T_1

$$\frac{\partial m_2}{\partial T_1} = -\frac{(1+\pi_2)u''}{S_{mm}}$$

where S_{mm} is the second partial of (4.41) with respect to m_2 and is negative by the second order condition for a maximum. Since $u'' < 0$, $\partial m_2/\partial T_1$ is negative for a constrained individual as well. Hence,

$$\frac{\partial \bar{m}_2}{\partial T_1} < 0.$$ QED

PART III

Empirical Studies of the Money-Prices Nexus

5. Money, Credit and Wages in Hyperinflation: Post-World War I Germany

Richard C.K. Burdekin and Paul Burkett*

1. INTRODUCTION

The nature of the money-supply process remains a crucial issue in econometric analyses of the German hyperinflation. Its importance stems not only from the direct link between the money supply and the price level but also from the role of increased inflationary expectations — which gave rise to an acceleration of velocity — in explaining why the rate of inflation exceeded the rate of money growth during the hyperinflationary period, as demonstrated by Cagan (1956). Following the classic historical study by Bresciani-Turroni (1937), most quantitative analyses have focused on the combination of large government deficits and rising expected inflation as the underlying cause of the apparent endogeneity of the money supply with respect to the price level.[1]

Sargent and Wallace (1973), in particular, argue that the negative effect of price inflation on real money holdings — in conjunction with the failure to raise government tax receipts — necessitated increasingly rapid growth of the nominal money supply in order to finance real government expenditures.[2] This emphasis on fiscal pressures is mirrored in much of the literature on the more recent post-World War II inflations, in which considerable attention has been paid to the role of government budget deficits in inducing monetary accommodation to finance these deficits, thereby fuelling the inflation process.[3]

By contrast, the role of *private sector* pressure in stimulating monetary expansion in Weimar Germany and in more recent — and less extreme —

inflations has been the object of relatively little quantitative scrutiny. This is surprising given that, in those analyses of post-World War II inflations that have allowed for both private sector pressure (as channelled, for example, through a wage-price spiral) and public sector pressure, strong effects of the private sector pressure are often indicated. Willett and Laney (1978), for example, find both wage push and budget deficits to be important in explaining rates of monetary expansion in Italy and the United Kingdom, together with some evidence that the wage variables may have been of dominant importance over the 1956-76 period studied.[4]

Certainly, exclusive focus on the role of the budget deficit may be misplaced — as suggested also in Willett et al. (1988) and in other contributions to the Willett (1988) volume. From this perspective, an examination of the importance of 'wage push' in supplementing government fiscal pressures during the German hyperinflation seems long overdue. As one of the most explosive inflations on record, the German experience would appear to be an ideal testing ground for evaluating the relative importance of these two potential explanations of the enormous rates of monetary expansion observed at that time.

The present chapter extends Webb's (1985) fiscalist explanation of money supply growth during the German hyperinflation to allow for wage push effects. As discussed in section 2 below, Webb's 'debt-expectations' analysis is a useful starting point because it recognizes that monetization of *private* debt played an important role in the money supply process — without, however, incorporating the potential impact of wage pressures on private credit demands. Section 3 develops our extension of Webb's (1985) estimation framework to include wage-push pressures on the money supply. This extension utilizes a real wage target model of workers' money wage demands, in which the responses of money wages to changes in the observed real wage and expected inflation are affected by labor market conditions, as proxied by the current unemployment rate. The analysis also incorporates some additional modifications of Webb's model — involving differencing of the variables — in the light of the stationarity tests presented in section 4.

Section 5 gives regression results for the modified debt-expectations model, with and without wage-push effects. In addition, the empirical work reconsiders the impact of two dummy variables — representing possible structural changes in Reichsbank policy — which were previously found to be insignificant by Webb (1985). To anticipate, the estimation results provide striking support for the role of wage pressures in augmenting fiscal influences on the money supply during the German hyperinflation. Furthermore, we find evidence of significant changes in

Reichsbank policy associated with both the resumption of commercial bill discounts in mid-1922 and the foreign exchange market intervention of the Reichsbank in early 1923.

2. MONEY SUPPLY ENDOGENEITY DURING THE GERMAN HYPERINFLATION

It is well known that during the latter stages of the German hyper-inflation, discounts of *private* commercial bills, along with other private-sector loans by the Reichsbank and its Loan Bureaus, accounted for a significant portion of money supply growth.[5] In fact, at the time *The Manchester Guardian Commercial* (3 August 1922, p. 126) reported that 'the considerable increases in note circulation in recent weekly reports are attributable less to increased demands made by the Government than to fresh credits required by private persons, who, on the one hand, return their Treasury bills, and, on the other, have succeeded in procuring credits through negotiating commercial bills'. Nonetheless, this phenomenon has received virtually no attention in the econometric literature on the German hyperinflation, with the notable exception of Webb's (1985) 'debt-expectations' model of the money-supply process.

Webb (1985; 1986) attributes the accelerated monetization of private and government debt to increased inflation expectations driven by adverse 'fiscal news', i.e., by specific events such as breakdowns in reparations negotiations which indicated a reduced ability of the government to bring future expenditures and tax revenues into balance.[6] This perspective is echoed in Webb's (1984, p. 507) conclusion that government 'spending, taxes, and announcements about them' — rather than private sector wage push effects — were 'the fundamental exogenous variables' determining the monetization of private *and* government debt during the German hyperinflation.

However, an alternative explanation for the acceleration of the Reichsbank's private sector lending operations is that firms' credit demands increased in response to rising wage costs associated with a more rapid adjustment of money wages to inflation. This view is adopted by Laursen and Pedersen (1964) and is also reflected in Robinson's (1938, pp. 510-11) earlier determination

> that either exchange depreciation or a budget deficit may initiate inflation, and ... the German history provides examples of both cases. But the essence of inflation is a rapid and continuous rise of money

wages. Without rising money wages, inflation cannot occur, and whatever starts a violent rise in money wages starts inflation.

The intensified efforts of workers and their trade unions to index wages more effectively as the inflation proceeded are discussed by Graham (1930, pp. 72-3), who notes that '[a]fter a prolonged struggle' wages began to be quoted 'in foreign currencies or in conventional gold units'. The increasing trend towards shorter contract periods and schemes for indexing wages to *expected* changes in the cost of living which emerged after the collapse of the mark in 1921 are detailed by Schippel (1922, p. 563), Graham (1930, pp. 90-3), Bry (1960, pp. 223ff.) and Horsman (1988, pp. 12-3). A contemporary source, Colles (1922, p. 464), further observed that

> the wild vagaries in the value of the mark have led to constantly recurring and, for the most part, ephemeral strikes, with the result that wages have locally, in many industries, been advanced in hot haste as the mark fell in accordance, not with the 'cost-of-living' index ... but in sympathy with the *external* depreciation of the currency. In November last, *e.g.*, the workers at Krupp's asked for 2,000 marks a month as a 'living cost bonus' but later demands have not been so moderate (emphasis in original).

The potential importance of wage-push pressures during the German hyperinflation is also supported by the tremendous increases in trade union membership and strike activity which took place after World War I, along with the successful conclusion of the trade unions' campaign for the 8-hour workday in 1918 discussed by Maier (1975, p. 59).[7] In this connection, Franco (1990, p. 185) suggests that 'a very strong pressure exercised by workers to recover 1914 real wages' created 'a wage push of very significant proportions' in the post-World War I inflations in Germany and other European countries.

While Bresciani-Turroni (1937, p. 47) generally argues that 'the fundamental cause of the depreciation of the mark was the budget deficit, which provoked continued issues of paper money', the same author (1937, p. 366) nonetheless provides a suggestive account of the interaction between wage pressures, private credit demand, and Reichsbank policy during the German hyperinflation:

> So long as the workers adapted themselves to the fall in real wages, which was a result of the inflation, entrepreneurs experienced no 'shortage of capital'. ... So long as there is great unemployment, the

workers generally accept the fall in the rate of real wages; but when unemployment ceases the position of the workers is strengthened and they demand higher wages. ... The German financial papers agree that the symptoms of a shortage of capital were apparent from the second half of 1922. It was then that the resistance of the workers to the reduction in real wages (which was a result of the depreciation of the currency) became more and more insistent. The working classes sought to re-establish the earlier level of real wages and to keep it stable. The profits which entrepreneurs derived from the inflation decreased. They began to experience difficulties in financing their businesses. It is well known that from the beginning of the second half of 1922 there was an increasing demand for bank advances for entrepreneurs; a demand which the commercial credit banks, whose deposits were continually falling, were incapable of satisfying. ... It was then that the Reichsbank intervened by extending enormously its short-term loans. Thanks to these loans the shortage of capital was temporarily evaded. Employers were able to pay higher money wages; but the prices of all kinds of consumption goods increased immediately, and the attempt of the working classes to increase real wages came to nothing. They then obtained a fresh rise in money wages; there followed a new expansion of credit and a further rise of prices and of money wages. The consequence was a formidable increase in the volume of Reichsbank loans.

The analysis in this quotation can be referred to as the 'wage-push model' of money-supply determination, since the basic causal linkages run from changes in real wages, unemployment and expected inflation to nominal wages, and from nominal wages to private credit demand which is accommodated by the Reichsbank. What the wage-push model adds to Webb's (1985) debt-expectations approach is the linkage between wage costs and private credit demand, and the hypothesis that the unemployment rate exerted a significant influence on wage growth. The wage-push approach posits that as money wage growth accelerated, the output-supply functions of more and more firms became *temporarily* credit constrained, in the sense that they had to 'pay their factors of production *before* they receive[d] revenues from sales, and [had to] borrow in order to do so' (Blinder, 1987, p. 329).[8]

In this view, the Reichsbank's accommodation of private and government credit demands itself tended further to increase the price level, hence counteracting — or *even more* reversing — the momentary rise in real wages achieved by workers, thus instigating additional money wage demands. In short, the wage-push approach need not imply that workers were able to achieve permanent increases in their real wages, since the Reichsbank's credit policy operated counter to this goal. As such, this approach is quite consistent with a situation in which 'real wages would periodically lag behind rising prices and then catch up with new settlements' (Maier, 1975, p. 363).[9]

3. EXTENDING THE DEBT-EXPECTATIONS MODEL TO INCORPORATE WAGE PRESSURES

The starting point for Webb's (1985) debt-expectations model is a simple version of the government budget constraint:

$$DEBT_t = DEBTPUB_t + MB_t = (1 - \lambda_t)DEBT_t$$

$$+ \lambda_t DEBT_t \quad (0 \le \lambda_t \le 1) \tag{5.1}$$

where DEBT is the stock of government debt outstanding, DEBTPUB is the amount of government debt held by the public, and MB (the monetary base) is assumed for simplicity to be backed solely by the central bank's government debt holdings amounting to the fraction λ of DEBT. Solving equation (5.1) for MB and taking logs gives:

$$\ln MB_t = \ln \lambda_t + \ln DEBT_t \tag{5.2}$$

Webb (1985) then posits that the fraction of government debt which the public is not willing to hold is determined by expected inflation (EXP), and the interest rate charged on Treasury bill discounts (BR):

$$\ln \lambda_t = a_1 EXP_t + a_2 BR_t \tag{5.3}$$

where the hypothesized signs of the parameters are $a_1 > 0$ and $a_2 < 0$.

Increases in expected inflation or a lower Reichsbank rate cause the public to discount a larger fraction of government debt at the Reichsbank — with the money balances so obtained then used to purchase commodities and/or foreign exchange. Webb (1986, p. 786) further argues that increases in expected inflation placed upward pressure on monetization of debt not only from the demand side (due to a lower expected real discount rate), but also by contracting private-sector deposits and hence the supply of private bank credit.

Substituting (5.3) into (5.2) gives Webb's (1985) estimating equation for the monetary base:

$$\ln MB_t = a_0 + a_1 EXP_t + a_2 BR_t + a_3 \ln DEBT_t + \varepsilon_t \qquad (5.4)$$

where the expected signs of the coefficients are $a_1 > 0$, $a_2 < 0$, and $a_3 > 0$; and ε_t is an error term.

Equation (5.4) can also explain additions to MB due to increased Reichsbank holdings of *private* debt, to the extent that such private debt monetization is itself determined by changes in EXP and BR. This analysis implies that the money supply was determined by the level of government debt outstanding in conjunction with the fractions of private *and* government debt monetized by the Reichsbank. Given that the Reichsbank discount rate showed little response to inflation, it seems reasonable to assume that the rates at which private and government debt were discounted at the Reichsbank were primarily determined by expected inflation.[10] Webb's (1986) additional argument that increases in EXP were mostly a function of 'fiscal news' yields the conclusion that the money supply was fiscally driven during the German hyperinflation.

While Webb's (1985) estimates of equation (5.4) appear to support the debt-expectations view, this evidence may be problematic for two reasons. First, results of unit root tests (see section 4 below) indicate that all the variables in equation (5.4) are non-stationary in the non-differenced form utilized by Webb. Second, as noted above, equation (5.4) assumes that increases in the Reichsbank's holdings of *private* debt reflected only upward pressures on the <u>fraction</u> of private debt monetized, as determined by expected inflation and the Reichsbank discount rate. Hence, equation (5.4) is underspecified if the acceleration of private-sector lending by the Reichsbank occurred partly in response to increases in *total* private credit demand — due, for example, to the wage-push pressures discussed in section 2.[11]

In order to deal with these problems, we first re-express the monetary base (MB) as the portion of *total* (private *plus* government) debt held by the Reichsbank (TDEBT):

$$MB_t = \theta_t TDEBT_t \qquad (0 \le \theta_t \le 1) \qquad (5.5)$$

Taking log second differences gives:

$$\Delta^2 \ln MB_t = \Delta^2 \ln \theta_t + \Delta^2 \ln TDEBT_t \qquad (5.6)$$

where the Δ^2's denote second differencing, and the determination of the right-hand-side variables in equation (5.6) is specified as follows:

$$\Delta^2 \ln \theta_t = b_1 \Delta^2 EXP_t + b_2 \Delta^2 BR_t \qquad (5.7)$$

$$\Delta^2 \ln TDEBT_t = b_3 \Delta^2 \ln DEBT_t + b_4 \Delta^2 \ln W_t \qquad (5.8)$$

As in Webb's (1985) analysis, we assume that changes in the fraction of TDEBT monetized at the Reichsbank respond positively to increases in expected inflation or reductions of the discount rate. Equation (5.8) specifies changes in total debt as a positive function of changes in government debt and of private debt — with the latter assumed to be a linear-positive function of the log second difference of nominal wages (W). Such a reduced-form treatment is necessitated by the lack of data on private debt outstanding. [12]

Substitution of (5.7) and (5.8) into (5.6) gives our modified estimating equation for changes in the monetary base:

$$\Delta^2 \ln MB_t = b_0 + b_1 \Delta^2 EXP_t + b_2 \Delta^2 BR_t$$

$$+ b_3 \Delta^2 \ln DEBT_t + b_4 \Delta^2 \ln W_t + \varepsilon_t \qquad (5.9)$$

where the predicted coefficient signs are $b_1 > 0$, $b_2 < 0$, $b_3 > 0$ and $b_4 > 0$, with any exogenous changes in the growth of private debt outstanding being allocated to the constant term.

Equation (5.9) clearly shows the wage-push effects included in the extended model to be complementary with Webb's (1985) fiscalist explanation of the money-supply process. For example, under the wage push approach, higher expected inflation caused a bigger portion of the credit demands necessitated by money wage growth to be channelled toward the Reichsbank — especially given the adverse effect of a higher EXP on the private banks' deposits. There is certainly nothing in the wage-push argument which contradicts Webb's (1984, 1985) hypothesis that rising inflation expectations increased the monetization of *government* debt at the Reichsbank. Further, the wage-push approach does not preclude a positive effect of expected inflation on private debt monetization *over and above* the use of credit to finance rising wages. Specifically, it was extremely difficult for the Reichsbank to ensure that its private sector loans were actually used by industrial firms to finance wage and other factor payments — since this condition conflicted with the Reichsbank's rather passive accommodation of private credit demands. [13]

The nominal wage term actually included among the explanatory variables in equation (5.9) is the predicted value from a prior regression model of money wage determination. This model extends Dutt's (1987) real wage target approach to incorporate the responses of money wage growth to the unemployment rate (U) and expected inflation:

$$\ln(W_t/W_{t-1}) = f_1(U_t) \cdot \ln(V_t/RW_{t-1}) + f_2(U_t) \cdot EXP_t \qquad (5.10)$$

where V is workers' real wage target, RW is the real wage, and the constant unemployment values of f_1 and f_2 are greater than zero. Here, the positive response to the ratio of the target real wage to the last-period actual real wage — with given unemployment — allows for a 'backward-looking' adjustment of wage demands based on prior information. The hypothesized positive effect of expected inflation (again for a given unemployment rate) meanwhile reflects possible 'forward looking' adjustment by workers, a phenomenon likely to become increasingly important as the inflation process accelerates.[14]

As in Rowthorn (1977) and Burkett and Burdekin (1993), each of these two responses is taken to be interactive with the unemployment rate in order to pick up the dampening effect looser labour market conditions have on workers' ability to push through the desired money wage adjustments:

$$f_{1u} < 0 \ (\Delta\ln(V_t/RW_{t-1}) > 0), \quad f_{1u} > 0 \ (\Delta\ln(V_t/RW_{t-1}) < 0) \qquad (5.11)$$

$$f_{2u} < 0 \ (\Delta EXP_t > 0), \quad f_{2u} > 0 \ (\Delta EXP_t < 0) \qquad (5.12)$$

so that increased unemployment operates to (i) reduce positive money wage adjustments to increases in expected inflation and the 'gap' between the observed real wage and workers' real wage target, and (ii) accentuate the negative impacts of reductions in EXP_t and V_t/RW_{t-1} on nominal wage growth.

The long-run target real wage, V, is treated as a constant in our analysis. While V would generally be expected to vary over time with structural changes in the relative bargaining power of workers and firms — as discussed, for example, by Varoufakis and Sapsford (1990) — the assumption of a fixed V does not seem unreasonable when one considers the short interval (3 years) covered by our analysis. With V constant, substitution of (5.11) and (5.12) into (5.10) and first differencing gives our estimating equation for money wage growth:

$$\Delta^2 \ln W_t = c_0 + c_1 \Delta \ln RW_{t-1} + c_2 \Delta EXP_t + c_3 \Delta U_t + c_4 \Delta U_t \cdot \Delta \ln RW_{t-1}$$

$$+ c_5 \Delta U_t \cdot \Delta EXP_t + \varepsilon_t \qquad (5.13)$$

where the expected signs on the coefficients are: $c_1 < 0$, $c_2 > 0$, $c_3 < 0$, $c_4 < 0$, and $c_5 < 0$.

Constancy of the target real wage (V) implies that the estimated constant term should be insignificant. Note that equation (5.13) is based on the testable assumption that unemployment is a predetermined variable — as would be the case if firms' *current* hiring decisions are based on the profitability of employing additional workers at the end of the preceding period. More generally, since the explanatory variables in the nominal wage model are all plausibly predetermined (see section 5 below for empirical verification), use of the fitted values from regression estimates of equation (5.13) as a right-hand-side variable in the money-supply equation is not subject to spurious correlation problems stemming from current-period effects of inflation on the nominal wage. As shown by Hoffman (1987), the presence of an error term in equation (5.13) does, however, necessitate joint estimation of the money supply and nominal wage equations in order to avoid generated-regressor bias.

4. THE DATA AND TESTS FOR STATIONARITY

A comprehensive measure of the monetary base (MB) is obtained by adding total official notes in circulation (Reichsbank notes plus Loan Bureau notes and private bank notes) to official emergency money in circulation plus non-government deposits at the Reichsbank — using the series provided in Statistiches Reichsamt (1925, pp. 46-52). As with Webb's (1985) analysis, we examine the response of the monetary base to (i) the Reichsbank discount rate (BR), as drawn from Holtfrerich (1986, p. 73) and Webb (1989, pp. 6-7); (ii) total government debt outstanding (DEBT), drawn from Webb (1986, pp. 776-7); and (iii) a measure of expected inflation (EXP) given by the forward exchange discount. The latter variable is employed — in preference over the adaptive expectations operator used in a sub-set of Webb's (1985) regressions — because it is the only available measure of inflationary expectations actually held by private agents during this period.[15] The foreign exchange discount series used here is taken from Webb (1985, pp. 482-3).

In order to examine the additional role played by wage changes and labour market conditions we employ series on hourly nominal wage rates for skilled workers (W, calculated as a weighted average over eight industries), and the unemployment rate (U, given by the percentage of trade union members unemployed for each month). The real wage (RW) is obtained by taking the ratio of W to the wholesale price index of the same month — the wholesale price index being generally accepted as the most reliable inflation measure available for the German case. The nominal wage series is taken from Bry (1960, pp. 446-7), while the wholesale price index is from Statistiches Reichsamt (1925, pp. 16-17), and the unemployment rate is as given by Kuczynski (1925, p. 146) and Bry (1960, p. 432).

As previously noted, Webb's (1985) regression equations include the log of the money supply, the log of total government debt outstanding, the level of the discount rate and the level of the foreign exchange discount. Application of unit root tests shows that none of these series is stationary, however. The null hypothesis of a unit root also cannot be rejected for the remaining series considered here: namely, the log of the nominal and real wage rates and the unemployment rate. These findings are obtained after first removing seasonal means by prior regression on a set of seasonal dummies (except for the discount rate, which is set by the Reichsbank and not plausibly subject to seasonality). The last date for which all series are available is August 1923 as there is no data on the forward exchange discount after this point. Unfortunately, with data through 1923:8 included, not only are the variables non-stationary in the levels, but further investigation reveals that certain of the series remain non-stationary even in second difference form (where the null hypothesis of a unit root still cannot be rejected at the 5 per cent level for the monetary base or nominal wages).

If, however, the sample is curtailed at 1923:5 — as in, for example, Sargent and Wallace (1973)[16] — all series are found to be stationary after second differencing, and in each case the null hypothesis of a unit root can be rejected at the 1 per cent level according to the critical values provided by Fuller (1976, p. 373).[17] The first differences of these same series yield mixed results. Nonetheless, the presence of a unit root is in this case rejected at the 5 per cent level or better for the government debt, forward exchange discount, discount rate, real wage and unemployment series — a group which encompasses the variables specified in first difference form in our regression model for money wage growth (see equation (5.13)). The *levels* of each series continue to evidence non-stationarity even over the curtailed sample, as the null hypothesis of a unit root cannot be rejected for any of the variables — and this is true whether or not a time trend is included in the test regressions.[18]

Given that the series employed in levels by Webb (1985) all exhibit strong evidence of non-stationarity, the high explanatory power as well as the apparent support for the 'debt-expectations' model must be considered at least somewhat questionable. In the analysis below, Webb's monetary base equation is re-estimated in differenced form and the effects of government debt, the Reichsbank rate and the forward exchange discount re-examined. Joint estimates of the two-equation system for money supply and wage growth are also presented, with fitted values from the wage equation entered in the money-supply equation as suggested earlier. Finally, we consider the role played by the two Reichsbank policy interventions in July 1922 and February-April 1923 — the effects of which, while found to be insignificant by Webb, are in fact seen to be highly significant once the equations are estimated in differenced form.

5. REGRESSION RESULTS: MONEY SUPPLY AND WAGE EQUATIONS

Table 5.1 presents the ordinary least squares (OLS) results for Webb's (1985) model in differenced form (column (1)), as well as joint estimates of equations (5.9) and (5.13) by generalized least squares (GLS) that extend the debt-expectations model to incorporate wage pressures (columns (3) and (4)).[19] The sample period begins in 1920:6 due to the inclusion of the second difference of the forward exchange discount, the first data point for which is 1920:4. Eleven seasonal dummies and a lagged dependent variable have been added to each of the equations to correct for seasonal factors and possible adjustment lags. Throughout the analysis, standard errors are obtained using the heteroskedasticity-consistent covariance matrix suggested by White (1980). Note also that the exogeneity of the contemporaneous right-hand-side variables (ΔEXP, Δ^2EXP, ΔBR, Δ^2ln DEBT and ΔU) appearing in these equations was confirmed using the test procedure derived by Hausman (1978).[20]

Column (1) shows a positive influence of inflationary expectations and of government debt on the monetary base as was featured in Webb's (1985) analysis. The discount rate is insignificant in this case, again corresponding to the results obtained by Webb. When fitted values from the wage equation are added to the money-supply model, the picture changes dramatically, however. While the government debt variable remains significant in the modified monetary base equation of column (4), the forward exchange discount becomes insignificant. Wage growth, as predicted on the basis of the specification given in column (3), is positive and significant at the 1 percent level, consistent with the importance of 'wage push' in the inflationary process.

The wage equation itself reveals the expected positive effect of the forward exchange discount — consistent with the hypothesized 'forward-looking' adjustment of money wages to expected inflation. Meanwhile, the negative and significant effect of lagged real wage growth supports the role of 'backward-looking' adjustments to prior deviations of the real wage from workers' target real wage. Furthermore, the significant, negative interaction of unemployment with the lagged real wage suggests that, as posited earlier, this 'backward looking' response of workers' nominal wage demands was damped by increases in unemployment. At the same time, the interaction of unemployment with the forward exchange discount is insignificant (although it at least has the predicted negative sign), while the unemployment rate itself enters with a positive sign but is insignificant at any reasonable confidence level. Finally, the insignificant constant term supports the assumed constancy of workers' real wage target.

Besides the effects of wages on money-supply growth, another issue concerns Webb's (1985, p. 485) own acknowledgement that '[m]ost historical accounts describe Reichsbank policy as more complex and variable than the simple model hypothesized here'. In particular, Webb suggests two dummy variables that might be added to the present framework. First, Reichsbank resumption of discounting commercial bills in July 1922 might have been a factor adding to subsequent rates of monetary expansion, as can be tested with a dummy variable set equal to 1 for 1922:7-1923:5 and zero elsewhere. The rationale for this dummy variable would lie, of course, in the Reichsbank adopting a more accommodative policy response to *given levels* of credit demand. Support for this view arises both from the historical analysis of Feldman (1977, pp. 315-19) and from Schacht (1922, pp. 689-90), who states:

Not until the middle of 1922, when the dearth of money began to assume grotesque forms in consequence of the exchange developments, did the Reichsbank come to the assistance of the private money market by energetically supporting the movement toward the re-introduction of commercial bills of exchange.

A second consideration is the Reichsbank's large-scale intervention in the foreign exchange market between 1 February and 18 April 1923. At this time, the German central bank sought to discourage, using 'sermons and flexible quotas, any speculative or unnecessary credit to firms' (Webb 1985, p. 487). Webb argues that even though this 'intervention lowered

Table 5.1 Monetary Base and Wage Determination in Germany, 1920:6-1923:5

Right-hand-side variable	Monetary Base Growth (1)	Monetary Base Growth (2)[a]	Nominal Wage Growth (3)	Monetary Base Growth (4)	Nominal Wage Growth (5)	Monetary Base Growth (6)
	OLS Results		GLS Results for the Basic Model		GLS Results with Allowance for Policy Intervention Effects	
Constant Term	0.03 (0.03)	0.04** (0.02)	-0.03 (0.03)	0.04 (0.03)	-0.02 (0.02)	0.07* (0.02)
Lagged Dependent Variable	0.31*** (0.15)	0.02 (0.14)	-0.26** (0.10)	0.13 (0.17)	-0.31* (0.10)	-0.33*** (0.17)
Policy Intervention Dummy for 1922:7-1923:5	-	0.06* (0.01)	-	-	-	0.08* (0.01)
Policy Intervention Dummy for 1923:2-1923:4	-	-0.15* (0.02)	-	-	-	-0.19* (0.03)
Change in the Forward Exchange Discount	0.62* (0.21)	0.16 (0.15)	2.95* (0.75)	0.35 (0.23)	3.19* (0.75)	-0.29 (0.23)
Change in the Reichsbank Discount Rate	-0.002 (0.01)	0.02* (0.01)	-	0.002 (0.01)	-	0.03* (0.01)
Government Debt Growth	0.09* (0.02)	0.19* (0.04)	-	0.06** (0.03)	-	0.16* (0.01)
Predicted Value for Nominal Wage Growth	-	-	-	0.17* (0.06)	-	0.16* (0.03)
Lagged Real Wage Growth	-	-	-0.66* (0.11)	--	-0.63* (0.11)	-
Change in the Unemployment Rate	-	-	0.01 (0.02)	-	(0.02)	-
Unemployment-Real Wage Interaction	-	-	-0.41* (0.12)	-	-0.43* (0.13)	-
Unemployment-Expected Inflation Interaction	-	-	-0.95 (0.98)	-	-1.62 (1.03)	-
Summary Statistics[b]						
Durbin's h-statistic	-1.21	-1.95***	-	-	-	-
Durbin's m-statistic	-1.82***	-2.86*	-	-	-	-
$\bar{R}^2$	0.68	0.88	-	-	-	-

Notes:

Monetary base growth is specified as the log second difference of total notes in circulation plus emergency money and non-government deposits at the Reichsbank.

Nominal wage growth is specified as the log second difference of the average hourly wage rate for skilled workers.

The policy intervention dummy for 1922:7-1923:5 covers the period when the Reichsbank renewed its practice of discounting commercial bills, and is set to zero elsewhere.

The policy intervention dummy for 1923:2-1923:4 covers the period when the Reichsbank intervened heavily in the foreign exchange market, and is set to zero elsewhere.

The change in the forward exchange discount is specified in second difference form in columns (1), (2), (4) and (6), but is in first difference form in columns (3) and (5).

The change in the Reichsbank discount rate is specified in second difference form.

Government debt growth is specified in log second difference form.

Predicted values for nominal wage growth are taken from OLS estimation of the specifications given in columns (3) and (5).

Lagged real wage growth is specified in log first difference form.

The change in the unemployment rate is the first difference of the percentage of trade union members unemployed for each month.

The unemployment-real wage interaction is the change in the unemployment rate multiplied by lagged real wage growth.

The unemployment-expected inflation interaction is the change in the unemployment rate multiplied by the first difference of the forward exchange rate.

11 seasonal dummies were included in all regressions alongside the variables listed above.

Standard errors are in parentheses.

*, **, and ***, denote significance at the 1 per cent, 5 per cent, and 10 per cent levels, respectively.

[a]   denotes estimated with the variables in rho-differenced form over 1920:7-1923:5 in order to correct for negative serial correlation.

[b]   denotes not applicable for the case where simultaneous equation estimation is performed. Note, however, that when the equations in columns (3)-(6) were estimated individually, the Durbin's *h* and *m* statistics were never significant at the 5 per cent level.

---

prices and inflationary expectations, which slowed the growth of the money supply ... the Reichsbank's credit and monetary policy remained unchanged' (ibid.). However, to the extent that Reichsbank credit policy *did* become significantly less accommodative during this interval, we have a possible negative effect on credit creation to be tested using a dummy variable set equal to 1 for 1923:2-1923:4 and zero elsewhere. While Webb states that neither of these dummy variables was significant in his analysis with non-differenced data, we find that both are significant when stationary data series are employed — as is shown in columns (2) and (6) of Table 5.1.[21]

The single-equation results in column (2) show that both dummies are significant and have the expected sign when Webb's debt-expectations model is estimated in differenced form. Moreover, although government debt growth remains highly significant with the expected positive sign, the expected inflation measure is now insignificant. Note that the monetary base equation was estimated in this instance using rho-transformed variables to correct for the presence of significant first-order negative serial correlation — a problem that was not found to occur in any of the other equations (as confirmed, in the case of the GLS specifications, on the basis of prior single-equation estimation that showed neither of Durbin's (1970) *h* and *m* test-statistics to ever be significant at the 5 per cent level).

In the GLS results, both dummies exhibit the expected sign and are again significant at the 1 per cent level (column (6)). The forward exchange discount is insignificant under allowance for both wage pressures *and* changes in Reichsbank policy. Interestingly, the inclusion of the dummies *plus* the fitted values from the wage equation appears to increase the statistical significance of the positive effect of government debt growth, compared with the GLS results in column (4) that incorporated wage effects alone. Thus, even though Webb's empirical analysis cannot in itself be considered very convincing (especially given that there is no allowance for serial correlation or adjustment lags in addition to the problems posed by the non-stationary regressors and regressands), the hypothesized effect of government debt growth does receive ample confirmation from the data.

Nonetheless, as indicated by the continued significance (again at the 1 per cent level) of the nominal wage variable included in the money-supply equation in column (6), government debt growth and expected inflation alone cannot provide anything approaching a complete explanation of the German money-supply process over this time period. Indeed, the insignificance of the forward exchange premium in columns (4) and (6) suggests that the influence of this variable may be more indirect, i.e., channelled through the wage equation — where it is significant at the 1 per cent level — than direct. At the same time, column (5) indicates continued significance of 'backward-looking ' wage adjustments and of the dampening effect of unemployment on these adjustments (as reflected in the results for lagged real wage growth — alone and in interaction with unemployment). This again indicates that money wage growth involved factors additional to expected inflation, including the bargaining power of labour as affected by labour market conditions.

6. CONCLUSION AND IMPLICATIONS

The foregoing analysis provides some new evidence of the importance of 'fiscal news' (at least insofar as this news influenced inflation expectations) and of government debt as explanations of the money supply process in Germany over the 1920-23 period. However, the impact of expected inflation appears to have operated primarily *via* rising wage claims and resulting increases in private credit demand, rather than increases in the *fraction* of debt discounted at the Reichsbank as suggested by the pioneering investigation of Webb (1985). In addition, the effects of changes in Reichsbank discounting and exchange rate policies are highly significant once regressions are performed on data that have been differenced sufficiently to obtain stationarity.

Money wage growth — as determined by workers' struggles to achieve a predetermined real wage target in the face of extreme inflation — is found to be an extremely significant contributor to the process of monetary expansion in post-World War I Germany. In conjunction with the significant 'backward-looking' adjustment of money wages to decreases in the lagged real wage, and the significant dampening of this adjustment by higher unemployment, this result suggests that the factors influencing the nominal money supply may not be fully reducible to government debt and expected inflation as determined by adverse 'fiscal news' — so that an underlying class struggle over distributive shares may have also played an important role in the German case. In short, the data strongly indicate that the money supply process cannot be adequately understood under an exclusive focus on fiscal pressures — suggesting the desirability of further research into the interaction of government deficits with distributional conflict in the hyperinflation process, as previously modelled, for example, by Kalecki (1962).[22]

ENDNOTES

* Associate Professor, Claremont McKenna College and Claremont Graduate School; and Associate Professor, Indiana State University. This paper was originally published in *Economic Inquiry*, Vol. 30, July 1992, pp. 479-95, and is reprinted with permission. The authors thank Tom Willett, Evan Tanner, Rodney Smith, Pierre Siklos, Ross Eckert and two anonymous referees for helpful comments on earlier drafts, and are grateful to Ignatius So for research assistance.

1. A thorough review of this literature is provided by Siklos (1990).

2. The results of Evans (1978), Noh (1988) and Casella (1989) also support the hypothesized link from the price level *to* the money supply in the German case, but for a dissenting analysis see Protopapadakis (1983). Some direct evidence on the impact

of the German government's fiscal policies on money growth and inflation is provided by Burdekin (1992) and Burdekin and Langdana (1992, Ch. 2).

3.   See, for example, Sargent (1986).

4.   Subsequent analysis of the US case reported in Burdekin and Burkett (1989a, 1989b) provides further support for the importance of private sector pressure in inducing accommodative monetary and credit expansion.

5.   See, for example, Graham (1930, pp. 60-69) and Feldman (1977, pp. 315-9). Indeed, data from Statistiches Reichsamt (1925, pp. 46-52) show that, during the last 18 months of the hyperinflation (1922:6-1923:12), the ratio of the Reichsbank's private-sector loans (commercial bill discounts, Lombards and Loan Bureau loans) to its total lending activity (private-sector loans plus discounts of Treasury bills) rose to over 40 per cent.

6.   See also Webb (1989, pp. 132-4).

7.   Bry's (1960, pp. 32-5) figures indicate that membership in the three largest trade unions rose from 2.18 million in 1918 to 9.18 million in 1920, and then remained relatively stable at just over half of the German labour force during the hyperinflationary period of 1920-23. The number of strikes and lock-outs due to wage disagreements (for all of Germany) increased from 482 in 1918 to 4,356 during 1922, according to the International Labour Office (1925, p. 58). Although this number fell to 1708 in 1923, the accounts provided by Sitzler (1924, p. 646) and Maier (1975, p. 364) suggest that this can be explained by the continuous renegotiation of wages which developed as the inflation exploded, and by the unions' more selective use of the strike weapon as inflation eroded the real value of union strike funds. The continued operation of wage-push pressures in the last year of the hyperinflation is supported by the 'rash of strikes and rioting [which] swept the Ruhr and unoccupied Germany' in July 1923 (Maier 1975, p. 371), and by the large increases in *real* wages which occurred in late-1923 (Webb 1989, pp. 77-83).

8.   The Reichsbank's accommodative private credit policy might thus be viewed as an attempt to relax firms' credit constraints — in an environment where the private credit supply was shrinking rapidly — in order to prevent a contraction of industrial output and employment due to what Blinder (1987) has termed 'effective supply failure'. Note that this interpretation is consistent with the type of 'real bills doctrine' espoused by Reichsbank General Director Havenstein, who 'came to the view that his primary responsibility was that of a helpless producer of money and credit in order to satisfy the insatiable demand for the paper that was considered necessary to keep the economy going' (Feldman 1977, p. 315).

9.   Hence, the fact that the average real wage for skilled workers fell from 50.1 per cent to 22.1 per cent of its 1913 value during the months 1922:6-1922:11 does not necessarily indicate that wage-push pressures on the money supply were not operating during this interval (see section 4 for data sources). Indeed, such real wage decreases might be expected to accentuate upward pressures on money wages (see section 3 below).

10.   The accommodative stance of the Reichsbank's discount policy is indicated by the fact that the Reichsbank discount rate never exceeded 90 per cent per annum during the hyperinflation. Given that Reichsbank credit represented a tremendous subsidy for private borrowers, some quantity-rationing mechanism was obviously implicit in this policy. In practice, the private agents obtaining credit included large banks and industrial enterprises, as well as '[p]eople who enjoyed the favor of the Reichsbank' (Bresciani-Turroni 1937, p. 77). Indeed, Graham (1930, p. 68) notes that 'the Reichsbank's discount of commercial bills was by no means confined to banks but was also done for approved business concerns and for individuals at a rate far below what the commercial banks were charging'. The quantity-rationing implicit in all this is indicated by Webb (1989, p. 17), who notes that 'small firms' and less well-connected

individuals 'had no access to the Berlin money market or the Reichsbank'. Moreover, the Reichsbank's practice of quantity-rationing extended even to favoured industrial concerns such as the Siemens-Rhein-Elbe-Schuckert Union (SRSU): 'The Reichsbank did set limits to the amounts that could thus be discounted ... and these amounts did not cover the enormous needs of the SRSU, which had to be raised from other quarters' (Feldman 1977, p. 319).

11.   Note also that increases in the fraction of government debt discounted at the Reichsbank may have been due partly to rising private credit demand. Here, Bresciani-Turroni (1937, p. 76) observes that prior to mid-1922, '[t]he increasing needs of trade were satisfied by private banks, who secured the means by discounting at the Reichsbank the Treasury bills in which they had largely invested the money of depositors during and after the war. At the end of 1920, 25% of the total value of Treasury bills was held by the eight great banks of Berlin, which had invested 60 per cent of their deposits in this way.'

12.   This also explains the absence of a variable measuring private debt outstanding in Webb's specification (see equation (5.4) above). In addition, some of the Reichsbank's private lending operations — e.g., Loan Bureau loans, Lombards, and even commercial bill discounts — involved the creation of new debt rather than discounts of *pre-existing* commercial bills. Feldman (1977, p. 318) provides an interesting discussion of this point.

13.   The use of money balances obtained *via* commercial bill discounts and other Reichsbank loans for speculative purposes is fairly well established. Graham (1930, p. 65n), for example, states that a 'good share of the borrowing was for the purpose of buying foreign exchange as an investment'. Bresciani-Turroni (1937, p. 77) similarly notes that agents borrowing from the Reichsbank 'could make sure of purchasing goods and foreign exchange. Speculation against the mark was in such ways financed by bank credits. ... Experience showed that it was not practically possible to apply a rigorous distinction between legitimate and non-legitimate credits'.

14.   On this point, see Blanchard (1986, p. 553) and Helpman and Leiderman (1988, p. 59).

15.   See Frenkel (1977) for further discussion.

16.   Evans (1978) has himself previously cast doubt on the desirability of including later data, finding evidence consistent with instability in money demand after June 1923.

17.   As shown by Dickey, Bell and Miller (1986, Appendix B) the limit distribution of these test statistics is not in any way affected by the aforementioned removal of seasonal means.

18.   Documentation of the unit root test results is provided in the Appendix Table 5A.1.

19.   In the extended model, the fitted values of $\Delta^2 \ln W_t$ are obtained from prior OLS estimation of the wage equation. Plugging these fitted values into the money-supply equation then yields the two-equation system given in columns (3) and (4), estimated using the iterative Zellner-Aitken procedure. The simultaneous estimation combined with the heteroskedasticity-consistent covariance matrix yields unbiased and consistent standard errors.

20.   In these tests, the contemporaneous right-hand-side variables appearing in each of the respective models were regressed on the first and second lags of each variable appearing in the model (excluding the interaction terms), 11 seasonal dummies and a constant term. The fitted values obtained from these regressions were then entered alongside the original variables in the regressions of Table 5.1. In no case did the additional test variables add significantly to the explanatory power of the equation, and the null hypothesis of no specification error could not be rejected. (When the same procedure was followed with respect to the augmented equations in columns (2), (5), and (6), the set of test variables again proved to be insignificant.)

21.   In the case of the dummy variable for 1923:2-1923:4, our results also appear to refute
        Webb's (1985, p. 487) claim that 'monthly data could scarcely identify much less tell
        anything about the statistical significance of a dummy variable for this intervention'.
22.   While the present study has focused on the union-led pressure for accommodation of
        wage claims, another potentially important pressure group comprised fixed-income
        pensioners, who — like the middle class and unorganized labour — were actually the
        ones hardest hit by the inflation. For these pensioners, Fergusson (1975, p. 217)
        indicates that 'the social insurance contributions of years amounted in the end to no
        assurance whatsoever: the public purse in 1923 was paying them at rates which ranged
        upwards from the insulting to the disgraceful: and their numbers, excluding the
        unemployed, were reckoned at the end of the year at more than 5,600,0000'. As
        pointed out to us by an anonymous referee, there was, however, much delay in reacting
        to the pension problem. Indeed, Maier (1975, p. 494) states that revaluation pressure
        groups — encompassing both pensioners and other holders of former paper assets —
        were still actively campaigning as late as 1926.

REFERENCES

Blanchard, O.J. (1986) 'The Wage Price Spiral' *Quarterly Journal of Economics*, 101,
    August, pp. 543-65.
Blinder, A.S. (1987) 'Credit Rationing and Effective Supply Failures' *Economic
    Journal*, 97, June, pp. 327-52.
Bresciani-Turroni, C. (1937) *The Economics of Inflation: A Study of Currency
    Depreciation in Post-War Germany*, Allen & Unwin, London.
Bry, G. (1960) *Wages in Germany, 1871-1945*, Princeton University Press, Princeton,
    NJ.
Burdekin, R.C.K. (1992) 'Government Budget Deficits and Real Money Balances in
    Germany, 1920-1923' *Economic Notes*, 21, pp. 258-64.
_____ and Burkett, P. (1989a) 'Government Budget Deficits, Private Sector Pressure,
    and Federal Reserve Policy, 1961-1985' *Economic Notes*, 18, pp. 229-42.
_____ and _____ (1989b) 'Conflicting Claims as a Source of Inflationary Credit
    Expansion in the U.S. Economy' *Manchester School of Economic and Social Studies*,
    57, September, pp. 213-34.
_____ and Langdana, F.K. (1992) *Budget Deficits and Economic Performance*,
    Routledge, London.
Burkett, P. and Burdekin, R.C.K. (1993) 'Real Wages and Distributional Conflict in the
    German Hyperinflation' *Australian Economic Papers*, 32, June, pp. 73-91.
Cagan, P. (1956) 'The Monetary Dynamics of Hyperinflation' in M. Friedman (ed.),
    Studies in the Quantity Theory of Money, University of Chicago Press, Chicago, IL,
    pp. 25-117.
Casella, A. (1989) 'Testing for Rational Bubbles with Exogenous or Endogenous
    Fundamentals: The German Hyperinflation Once More' *Journal of Monetary
    Economics*, 24, July, pp. 109-22.
Colles, W.M. (1922) 'Wage Movements at Home and Abroad: The High Water Mark'
    The Manchester Guardian Commercial, 6 April, p. 464.
Dickey, D.A.; Bell, W.R. and Miller, R.B. (1986) 'Unit Roots in Time Series Models:
    Tests and Implications' *American Statistician*, 40, February, pp. 12-26.

Durbin, J. (1970) 'Testing for Serial Correlation in Least-Squares Regression When Some of the Regressors are Lagged Dependent Variables' *Econometrica*, 38, May, pp. 410-21.

Dutt, A.K. (1987) 'Alternative Closures Again: A Comment on 'Growth, Distribution and Inflation'' *Cambridge Journal of Economics*, 11, March, pp. 75-82.

Evans, P. (1978) 'Time-Series Analysis of the German Hyperinflation' *International Economic Review*, 19, February, pp. 195-209.

Feldman, G.D. (1977) *Iron and Steel in the German Inflation 1916-1923*, Princeton University Press, Princeton, NJ.

Fergusson, A. (1975) *When Money Dies: The Nightmare of the Weimar Collapse*, William Kimber, London.

Franco, G.H.B. (1990) 'Fiscal Reforms and Stabilisation: Four Hyperinflation Cases.' *Economic Journal*, 100, March, pp. 176-87.

Frenkel, J.A. (1977) 'The Forward Exchange Rate, Expectations, and the Demand for Money: The German Hyperinflation' *American Economic Review*, 67, September, pp. 653-70.

Fuller, W.A. (1976) *Introduction to Statistical Time Series*, John Wiley, New York.

Graham, F.D. (1930) *Exchange, Prices, and Production in Hyper-Inflation: Germany, 1920-1923*, Princeton University Press, Princeton, NJ.

Hausman, J.A. (1978) 'Specification Tests in Econometrics' *Econometrica*, 46, November, pp. 1251-71.

Helpman, E. and Leiderman, L. (1988) 'Stabilization in High Inflation Countries: Analytical Foundations and Recent Experience' in K. Brunner & A.H. Meltzer (eds.), *Stabilization Policies and Labor Markets*, North-Holland, Amsterdam, pp. 9-84.

Hoffman, D.L. (1987) 'Two-Step Generalized Least Squares Estimators in Multi-Equation Generated Regressor Models' *Review of Economics and Statistics*, 69, May, pp. 336-46.

Holtfrerich, C.-L. (1986) *The German Inflation 1914-1923: Causes and Effects in International Perspective*, Walter de Gruyter, New York.

Horsman, G. (1988) *Inflation in the Twentieth Century: Evidence from Europe and North America*, St. Martin's Press, New York.

International Labour Office (1925) 'Workers' Standard of Life in Countries with Depreciated Currency' *Studies and Reports*, Series D, No. 15, Geneva.

Kalecki, M. (1962) 'A Model of Hyperinflation' *Manchester School of Economic and Social Studies*, 30, September, pp. 275-81.

Kuczynski, R.R. (1925) 'Postwar Labor Conditions in Germany' *Bulletin of the United States Bureau of Labor Statistics*, No. 380, March.

Laursen, K. and Pedersen, J. (1964) *The German Inflation 1918-1923*, North-Holland, Amsterdam.

Maier, C.S. (1975) *Recasting Bourgeois Europe: Stabilization in France, Germany, and Italy in the Decade After World War I*, Princeton University Press, Princeton, NJ.

The Manchester Guardian Commercial (1922) 'German Paper Money: Credit Difficulties and the Note Issue' 3 August, p. 126.

Noh, I. (1988) 'Test of Rationality of Adaptive Expectations in the German Hyperinflation' *International Economic Journal*, 2, Spring, pp. 39-52.

Protopapadakis, A. (1983) 'The Endogeneity of Money During the German Hyperinflation: A Reappraisal' *Economic Inquiry*, 21, January, pp. 72-92.

Robinson, J. (1938) 'Review of *The Economics of Inflation* by C. Bresciani-Turroni' *Economic Journal*, 48, September, pp. 507-13.

Rowthorn, R.E. (1977) 'Conflict, Inflation and Money' *Cambridge Journal of Economics*, 1, September, pp. 215-39.

Sargent, T.J. (1986) *Rational Expectations and Inflation*, Harper & Row, New York.

_____ and Wallace, N. (1973) 'Rational Expectations and the Dynamics of Hyperinflation' *International Economic Review*, 14, June, pp. 328-50.

Schacht, H. (1922) 'The Discount Policy of the Reichsbank' *Reconstruction in Europe*, No. 11 (Supplement to *The Manchester Guardian Commercial*, 7 December), pp. 689-90.

Schippel, M. (1922) 'The Standard of Life of the German Working Classes To-Day' *Reconstruction in Europe*, No. 9 (Supplement to *The Manchester Guardian Commercial*, 26 October), pp. 562-4.

Schwert, G.W. (1987) 'Effects of Model Specification on Tests for Unit Roots in Macroeconomic Data' *Journal of Monetary Economics*, 20, July, pp. 73-103.

Siklos, P.L. (1990) 'Hyperinflations: Their Origins, Development and Termination' *Journal of Economic Surveys*, 4, pp. 225-48.

Sitzler, F. (1924) 'The Adaptation of Wages to the Depreciation of the Currency in Germany' *International Labour Review*, 9, May, pp. 643-66.

Statistiches Reichsamt (1925) *Sonderhefte zu Wirtschaft und Statistik: Zahlen zur Geldenwertung in Deutschland 1914 bis 1923*, Reimar Hobbing, Berlin.

Varoufakis, Y. and Sapsford, D. (1990) 'A Real Target Model of Wage Inflation with Variable Union Power: The U.K. Experience 1962-1984' *Applied Economics*, 22, August, pp. 1103-17.

Webb, S.B. (1984) 'The Supply of Money and Reichsbank Financing of Government and Corporate Debt in Germany, 1919-1923' *Journal of Economic History*, 44, June, pp. 499-507.

_____ (1985) 'Government Debt and Inflationary Expectations as Determinants of the Money Supply in Germany, 1919-23' *Journal of Money, Credit, and Banking*, 17, November, pp. 479-92.

_____ (1986) 'Fiscal News and Inflationary Expectations in Germany After World War I' *Journal of Economic History*, 46, September, pp. 769-94.

_____ (1989) *Hyperinflation and Stabilization in Weimar Germany*, Oxford University Press, New York.

White, H. (1980) 'A Heteroskedasticity-Consistent Covariance Matrix Estimator and a Direct Test for Heteroskedasticity' *Econometrica*, 48, May, pp. 817-38.

Willett, T.D. (ed.), (1988) *Political Business Cycles: The Political Economy of Money, Inflation, and Unemployment*, Duke University Press, Durham, NC.

_____, Banaian, K., Laney, L.O., Merzkani, M. and Warga, A.D. (1988) 'Inflation Hypotheses and Monetary Accommodation: Postwar Evidence from the Industrial Countries' in T.D. Willett (ed.), *Political Business Cycles: The Political Economy of Money, Inflation, and Unemployment*, Duke University Press, Durham, NC, pp. 200-36.

_____ and Laney, L.O. (1978) 'Monetarism, Budget Deficits, and Wage Push Inflation: The Cases of Italy and the U.K.' *Banca Nazionale del Lavoro Quarterly Review*, 31, December, pp. 315-31.

Appendix

Table 5A.1 Results of Unit Root Tests

Sample 1921:3-1923:5 (1921:4-1923:5 in second difference form)

| Variable | In Levels | | In First Difference Form | In Second Difference Form |
	Without Time Trend (1)	With Time Trend (2)	Without Time Trend (3)	Without Time Trend (4)
ln *MB*	t = 1.06 (0)	t = 1.18 (0)	t = -0.77 (0)	t = -4.93* (0)
ln *DEBT*	t = -0.39 (1)	t = 0.76 (0)	t = -5.79* (0)	t = -7.37* (0)
EXP	t = 1.21 (3)	t = -1.19 (3)	t = -6.14* (1)	t = -9.58* (1)
BR	t = 1.03 (9)	t = -1.18 (9)	t = -11.12* (0)	t = -19.57* (0)
ln *W*	t = 0.77 (0)	t = 0.72 (0)	t = -1.69***(0)	t = -6.30* (1)
ln *RW*	t = -1.22 (0)	t = -1.88 (0)	t = -11.80* (1)	t = -6.83* (1)
U	t = -1.01 (1)	t = 0.45 (0)	t = -2.39** (0)	t = -5.30* (0)

Notes:

*, **, and *** denote significance at the 1 per cent, 5 per cent, and 10 per cent levels, respectively. Critical values are drawn from Fuller (1976, p. 373).

Figure in parentheses after the t-statistic denotes number of lags included in the regressions — as chosen by successively reducing the lags from a maximum of nine (given by Schwert's, 1987, ℓ_{12} criterion) to three (given by Schwert's, 1987, ℓ_4 criterion), to one and finally zero, until such time as an F-test showed the excluded lags of the dependent variable to be significant at the 5 per cent level or better. All variables except BR have had the seasonal means extracted by prior regression on 11 seasonal dummies plus a constant.

In no case was the time trend significant in the first and second difference regressions, hence, only results without the time trend are reported in these instances. Note that the prior extractions of seasonal means makes a constant term redundant here.

6. The Link Between Money and Prices Under Different Policy Regimes: The Postwar Hungarian Experience[*]

Pierre L. Siklos

1. INTRODUCTION

It has been suggested that if the value of a currency is ultimately determined by how it is introduced into the economy monetary expansions need not necessarily be immediately followed by inflation. This has given rise to what may be called the 'backing' theory of money (Bernholz 1988). By contrast, a 'crude' version of the Quantity Theory (QT hereafter) (Sargent 1993, ch. 5; Sargent and Wallace 1981, 1982, hereafter SW) suggests that all price changes are determined by monetary changes. Consequently, two theories of money have been proposed to explain the link between money and price movements.

Laidler (1987) points out that Wicksell and Fisher, both early quantity theorists, understood the possibility that velocity changes in response to a change in fiscal policy, including the degree to which a currency is backed. Michener (1987) shows that an open economy version of the crude QT has little difficulty in explaining the presence or absence of correlations between money and prices.

The US historical experience has recently been a testing ground for the so-called two theories of money. Calomiris (1988, 1988a), Smith (1985, 1985a) and Wicker (1985), find the evidence relatively more favourable to the backing theory while evidence rehabilitating the QT was presented by Michener (1987, 1988) and Bordo and Marcotte (1987).

In the case of hyperinflations it has always been assumed that the QT works well (e.g., Cagan 1956), in large part because such episodes have typically been regarded as 'laboratories' (Sargent 1993, ch. 3), and because fluctuations in real variables are thought to be negligible. However, the lack of significant co-movement between money and price-level movements after the end of a hyperinflation led Sargent to suggest that the backing doctrine explains what the QT could not (also see SW 1982).

The purpose of this chapter is to investigate the link between money and prices in postwar Hungary. While both theories of money can accommodate high or low correlations between money and prices in the present context, the empirical results suggest that the evidence may be more readily interpreted based on the backing theory of money.

Briefly, correlations between money growth and inflation are shown to be sensitive to restrictions placed on the data such as sample selection, and a proxy for the degree to which the money supply is backed. Thus, money growth-inflation correlations are low for the entire period of hyperinflation. When a sample during which bank deposits were indexed is considered, the same correlations are very high. Therefore, the so-called Lucas (1976) critique of econometric models plays a role in the link between money and prices even within an episode of hyperinflation, at least in the case of Hungary. However, irrespective of the sample chosen, or the restrictions considered, the short-run co-movements in money and prices during the hyperinflation are insignificant. This perhaps explains why policymakers were able to rely almost exclusively on seigniorage for over a year. For the post-hyperinflation sample, a structural break was also detected once the legal restriction on the issue of notes disappears. Siklos (1990a) has already provided empirical evidence, using monthly and weekly data, to the effect that since the hyperinflation and post-hyperinflation samples produce significantly different estimates of the money-prices link, the stabilization itself, not surprisingly, also represents a regime change.

2. THE HUNGARIAN HYPERINFLATION OF 1945-1946

The devastation and economic consequences of the war for Hungary are well known (see Siklos 1991; Bomberger and Makinen 1983, hereafter BM). Economic losses were sizeable, and exceeded in the rest of Europe perhaps only by Belgium and Germany, according to a 1946 UN Relief and Rehabilitation Agency report (United Nations 1947).

After Red Army troops freed Hungary from German occupation in April 1945, the Soviet Union exercised strict control over virtually all aspects of Hungarian life, thereby weakening the effectiveness of any post-liberation government (Mark 1982). Demands for reparation payments, and difficulties in collecting taxes throughout the period of hyperinflation meant that the Hungarian government quickly resorted to seigniorage to finance its expenditures. From July to December 1945, for example, tax revenues represented, on average, 6.5 per cent of government expenditures (BM 1983, Table 1, p. 805).

In January 1946, the government decreed that bank deposits would be indexed to a price index, called the tax pengő price index (hereafter TPPI). When tax receipts rose to a peak of only 15 per cent of expenditures in February 1946, the TP policy was clearly seen to be a failure. Subsequently, the note issue accelerated at ever increasing rates.

By March 1946, the government was completing plans for the introduction of economic reforms to be implemented by August 1946, together with the introduction of a new currency to be called the forint. The stabilization succeeded in ending the worst inflation ever recorded.

3. METHODOLOGY

3.1 Estimation Methods

The non-parametric time-series methods used here involve a weaker set of assumptions relative to classical regression and may be suitable in modelling situations where little a priori knowledge is available about the underlying structural economic model (Howrey 1980, section 2, and references therein). Spectral analysis is chosen as the vehicle for estimating a regression, in the frequency domain, in contrast to the more commonly encountered time domain method of regression analysis. Its principal attraction is that it enables relationships to be investigated by cycles or frequencies, which range from infinity (zero frequency) to two periods (or weeks in the case of weekly data) in length. Hence, long- and short-run relationships may be analysed (see, however, McCallum 1984; Barsky 1987). The statistic to be discussed is the coherence, or correlation, between money and prices. By converting frequency domain estimates into the time domain,[1] one can also evaluate whether the distributed lag relationship between money and prices is one-sided, in a model where a two-sided distributed lag of money is assumed to determine current prices. As a result, the validity of certain restrictions often imposed a priori, such as whether there is feedback (Sims 1972) from, say, prices to money, may be evaluated. The implications of such tests have proved to be important in assessing the behaviour of policymakers under conditions of hyper-inflation (e.g., SW 1981 and Christiano 1987). For further details about the techniques used in this chapter, see Jenkins and Watts (1968).

Consistent estimates of cross-spectral functions are obtained first, and the resulting summary statistics, such as partial coherence, are used to interpret the results. Hannan's (1965) efficient estimates of the coefficients of an infinite (two-sided) distributed lag model are generated by using the spectral approach (Dhrymes 1971). Such an approach is the frequency domain equivalent of the Generalized Least Squares method which is used to mitigate the influence of heteroskedastic errors which may arise when hyperinflation or post-hyperinflation data are used. Finally, other time-series techniques could have been applied, such as the vector auto-regression approach. The spectral approach is selected not because it is necessarily superior in all respects but because it is a relatively non-parametric technique, which is useful in the present context.

Since it is usually assumed that fluctuations in economic time series are stationary, an important issue concerns the appropriate transformation necessary to obtain a series with this property. There is now considerable evidence that a large number of economic series, for a variety of samples, countries and frequency of observations, are best characterized by taking first differences in the time series under investigation. While such a transformation is adequate for the post-hyperinflation sample, the same filter will be inappropriate for hyperinflation data. Evans (1978) found that second log differencing was necessary for money and price data from the German hyperinflation of the 1920s and tests (see Siklos 1991) reveal the same to be true for Hungarian hyperinflation data.[2]

3.2 Estimated Models

The following models are used to examine the link between money and prices. The basic hypothesis of this paper is that the relationship between these series is sample sensitive or a function of the kind of policy regime in place, even within the respective hyperinflation and stabilization samples considered.[3] Accordingly, two reduced-form models were considered:

$$p_t = a + B(L) \, m_t + D(L) \, v_t \tag{6.1a}$$

$$p_t = a' + B(L) \, m_t + C(L) \, f_t + D(L) \, v_t' \tag{6.1b}$$

where $B(L)$, $C(L)$, are two-sided infinite degree polynomials in L, and $D(L)$ is one-sided. m and p are the first or second log differences in the money stock and the price level, depending on whether the data are from the hyperinflation or stabilization samples, which are considered separately. The variable f is a measure of the backing or viability of a particular fiscal policy in place. Finally, the error processes v_t and v_t' are assumed to be independent of the processes of the right hand side variables. Model (6.1a) is estimated by samples which were selected according to what were believed to be significant changes in policy regimes.[4] Thus, for the January to July 1946 period, a proxy for the f series was derived measuring the Hungarian government's commitment to protect deposits through indexation. The extent to which deposits were revalorized depended upon a price index (the TPPI, see section 2) published daily, constructed on the basis of prices for essential foodstuffs in Budapest. Until 1st March 1946, revalorization was based on prices sampled two days before. Thereafter, sampling was conducted the previous day.

Assuming the cost of living index (P) measures true fluctuations in the purchasing power of money, the ratio (TPPI/P), called the real TPPI,[5] may be interpreted as a proxy for the government's commitment to abandon seigniorage as a means of generating tax revenues. The reason is that if the real TPPI exceeds 100 the government is, in effect, subsidizing bank deposit holders while a real TPPI below 100 implies that deposits are not fully indexed. Presumably, since the Hungarian government was facing dire budgetary difficulties, values for the real TPPI below 100 would reflect poorly on the government's commitment to cease debasing the currency. Conversely, real TPPI values at or above 100 would signal the government's intention to protect individuals' real wealth which, at the time, was primarily in the form of bank deposits. Nevertheless, without a simultaneous effort to curb spending, persistently maintaining the real TPPI above 100 would, of course, not be sustainable in the long run. The real TPPI series proved to be stationary in first log differences of the levels.[6] The dashed line in Figure 6.1 plots the real TPPI in levels while the solid line represents the same series in log first differences. Until 15th April 15th (24th observation) the real TPPI is above 100 although the value for the index peaks by 21st March 1946 (21st observation). Thereafter, changes in the TP index fall precipitously behind those for consumer prices. While the TP regime is considered to be a homogeneous one, but distinct from the earlier phase of the hyperinflation, the possibility nevertheless exists of even finer policy regime shifts than the ones considered here (see Siklos 1991, chs 7 and 8, and below).

Figure 6.1   The Real Tax Pengő Price Index

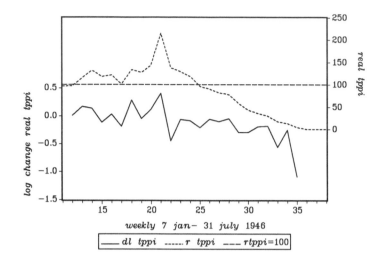

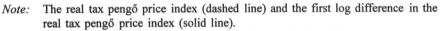

weekly 7 jan– 31 july 1946

Note: The real tax pengő price index (dashed line) and the first log difference in the
real tax pengő price index (solid line).
Source: Siklos (1991). Construction of the index is described in Note 4.

For the post-hyperinflation sample, two proxies for f were considered.
A dummy variable was added to capture the public's potential scepticism
about the government's promise not to issue more than the legal ceiling
of 1 billion forints in notes during the first year of the stabilization, that
is, until August 1947. Also considered is a series representing the rate of
change in government debt (Treasury bills discounted at the central bank).
Under the provisions of the monetary reforms of August 1946 the
Hungarian government was obliged to back almost all of its note issue
using the gold reserves returned by the US, gold and foreign currencies
hoarded by the public during the hyperinflation (Siklos 1991), and
anticipated future government budget surpluses. However, during the first
three months of the stabilization the National Bank of Hungary advanced
sufficient notes to cover an anticipated temporary deficit arising, in part,
from the need to remonetize the economy.

Figure 6.2 plots the logarithm of government debt as well as its growth
rate (log change). During the first year of the stabilization (first 48 weekly
observations) the growth rate in debt tends to hover around zero. One
notable spike in the data occurs in October 1946 when the level of debt
falls by almost 42 per cent, due to larger than expected inflows of gold
from private individuals (see Siklos 1991 for details about the circum-

Figure 6.2 The Level and Growth of Government Debt

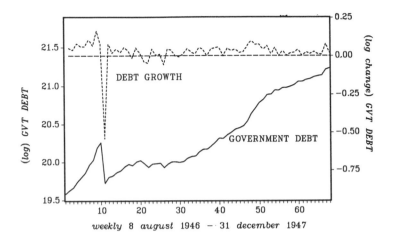

weekly 8 august 1946 – 31 december 1947

Note: Government debt represents the amount (in forint) of Treasury bills discounted at the National Bank of Hungary.

Source: Siklos (1991).

stances under which this event occurred). From all appearances this may be taken as a further indication of the seriousness with which, initially at least, the Hungarian government wished to stabilize inflation. However, as the expiry date for the legal debt ceiling approached and passed no further debt ceiling measures were announced and, as Figure 6.2 reveals, there are more noticeable increases in debt levels and growth rates. Indeed, the growth rate in the debt is, on average, 2.6 per cent for the entire post-hyperinflation sample considered (August 1946-December 1947), 2.3 per cent during the first year when a debt ceiling is in place, 3.0 per cent after that. It seems reasonable to suppose that variations in the amount of government debt outstanding represent a signal of the backing inherent in the note issue and that the period following the imposition of a government debt ceiling may be considered distinct from the earlier post-hyperinflation sample.[7]

Since, in practice, one cannot estimate an infinite distributed lag relationship using a finite sample, the selection of a truncation point and spectral window are important considerations in frequency domain estimation. The truncation point imposes a cutoff in the length of the distributed lag relationship, and, hence, determines the effective degrees of freedom available, while the choice of a window (here the Parzen window) affects the shape of the spectrum of a particular series. Although the choice is to some extent *ad hoc*, selection procedures exist and these were followed in producing the estimates presented in this paper (Jenkins and Watts 1968, chs 9 and 11). Accordingly, truncation points of 4 for the hyperinflation period, and 8 for the post-reform sample, were selected. Estimates were obtained for both aligned[8] and unaligned series. No alignment was necessary for the post-hyperinflation sample, while alignment for the hyperinflation sample was necessary since cross-correlations between m and p showed a peak at the two-week lag of m.

3.3 Data

Weekly data are used. The choice of sample frequency is dictated by requirements of degrees of freedom which is an acute problem, particularly for a typically short event such as a hyperinflation.[9] The entire data set consists of two distinct samples: the period of hyperinflation, following Cagan's (1956) definition, from the week of 23rd October 1945, to 31st July 1946, the last day of hyperinflation (38 observations); and a post-hyperinflation period from 7th August 1946 to 31st December 1947 (68 observations). Money is defined as currency in circulation. Prices represent the cost of living index, including rent, and reflect those in Budapest only.

The data were not seasonally adjusted for two reasons. First, the tremendous growth in the money supply in 1946 masks seasonal variation, while the financial re-intermediation in the post-stabilization period produces the same problem for the August 1946 to December 1947 sample. The sample ends in 1947 because the *coup d'état* by the Communists in early 1948, and the nationalization of the banking system in the same year led to a fundamental change in the construction of both series.[10]

4. EMPIRICAL ESTIMATES

4.1 The Hyperinflationary Period

Figure 6.3 shows the unconditional coherence (correlation) between money and prices. All series are in second log differences of the levels. Statistically significant coherences are those which exceed the approximate critical median level indicated on the figure.[11]

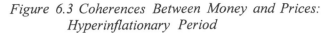

Figure 6.3 Coherences Between Money and Prices:
Hyperinflationary Period

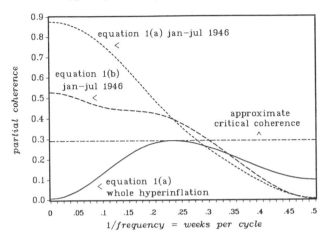

Note: Weekly data on notes in circulation and cost of living index in second log differences for samples indicated in parenthesis. Critical coherence at median level of significance is also shown. A truncation point of 4 and Parzen's window was used.

When the entire hyperinflation is considered, the relationship between money and prices, based on (6.1a), is statistically insignificant at virtually all frequencies.[12] By contrast, when (6.1a) or (6.1b) are estimated for the January to July 1946 period alone there is a significant correlation between money and prices, though not at frequencies of 0.25 (4 weeks) or higher. The absence of any significant correlation between money and prices at the high frequencies may be a reflection of costly adjustment in the desire to reduce money holdings and in the introduction of alternative methods of transacting and banking arrangements (Brunner and Meltzer 1971). Consequently, policymakers had the opportunity to exploit the potential for seigniorage presented by the existence of adjustment lags between money supply and demand (Cukierman 1988 and this volume).

However, another explanation for the results in Figure 6.1 is that the TP experiment was moderately successful in protecting real financial wealth from mid-January to mid-April, almost half the time the policy was in place.[13] In fact, since the real TPPI remained consistently above 100 during this period (see Figure 6.1) the government effectively subsidized bank deposit holders.[14] Demand for money would have risen even if individuals expected the eventual unsustainability of the fiscal policy in place.

Table 6.1 presents the Hannan efficient estimates of equations (6.1a) and (6.1b). Individual coefficient estimates, the cumulative sum of coefficients, their asymptotic standard errors, together with the resulting significance levels, are also given. Estimates of (6.1a) reveal that there is an equiproportionate relationship between p and future and, presumably, expected m over the entire hyperinflation. The hypothesis that lagged m influences current p can be rejected while one cannot reject the hypothesis that current p influences future m. This result is consistent with SW's hypothesis which they could not replicate for Hungary.[15] When equation (6.1b) is estimated, however, both lagged as well as future m significantly affect current p. Note also that both future and lagged real TPPI coefficients are statistically significant though small in magnitude. Hence, as in the German case (Christiano 1987), restrictions on the money supply process have implications for the interpretation of central bank behaviour during the Hungarian hyperinflation.

4.2   The Post-Stabilization Period

Prior to August 1947, the Hungarian government was restricted to issuing no more than 1 billion forints. Thereafter, no new ceilings on the issue of currency were announced. Coherences and partial coherences (not shown) are statistically insignificant at all frequencies whether account of the note issue restriction is taken or not. Indeed, the highest coherence is 0.027.

Table 6.2 presents Hannan efficient estimates of equation (6.1b) for the post-hyperinflation period. Neither lag nor lead terms for money growth are statistically significant, irrespective of whether one considers individual or cumulative effects on inflation. As noted already, this result is consistent with the hypothesis of a regime shift at the end of the hyperinflation, as discussed in Siklos (1990). However, since both proxies for the fiscal policy variable f, the dummy and debt-growth series (d), are statistically significant, there is some indication of the influence of debt growth on inflation. Such a result is consistent with the argument based on the SW framework, that current inflation is explained primarily by the public's perception of the government's ability to generate future surpluses, itself linked in theory to the accumulation of debt (i.e., issue of Treasury bills). In fact, a plot (not shown) of the partial coherence between inflation and debt growth, conditional on money growth, reveals that debt and inflation are significantly correlated with each other during the first year following stabilization at cycles of 20 weeks and longer.

Table 6.1 Hannan Efficient Estimates: Hyperinflationary Period[a]

Variable	23 October 1945 - 31 July 1946		7 January 1946 - 23 July 1946	
	Coefficient	(SE: sig. level)	Coefficient	(SE: sig. level)
Constant	0.033	(0.126;0.797)	3.350*	(1.089;0.022)
m_{t+4}	0.124*	(0.056;0.037)	—	
m_{t+3}	-0.295*	(0.078;0.001)	-0.046	(0.058;0.452)
m_{t+2}	0.166*	(0.078;0.046)	0.302*	(0.095;0.019)
m_{t+1}	0.159*	(0.076;0.048)	-0.027	(0.076;0.732)
m_t	0.781*	(0.086;0.000)	0.094	(0.178;0.615)
m_{t-1}	0.106	(0.109;0.342)	0.560*	(0.125;0.004)
m_{t-2}	-0.085	(0.147;0.568)	0.049	(0.167;0.778)
m_{t-3}	0.310*	(0.159;0.066)	0.111	(0.131;0.430)
m_{t-4}	-0.213	(0.128;0.112)	—	
Σm_{t-i}	0.117	(0.113;0.311)	0.720*	(0.163;0.004)
Σm_{t+j}	0.936*	(0.091;0.000)	0.322*	(0.122;0.038)
TPPI$_{t+3}$			0.000	(0.000;0.897)
TPP1$_{t+2}$			0.001*	(0.000;0.002)
TPPI$_{t+1}$			-0.001*	(0.000;0.004)
TPP1$_t$			-0.001*	(0.000;0.044)
TPPI$_{t-1}$			0.000	(0.000;0.499)
TPP1$_{t-2}$			0.001*	(0.000;0.013)
TPPI$_{t-3}$			-0.000	(0.000;0.339)
Σtp_{t-i}			0.001*	(0.000;0.003)
Σtp_{t+j}			-0.001*	(0.000;0.001)
	$n = 30$, $df = 20$, $R^2 = 0.980$		$n = 21$, $df = 6$, $R^2 = 0.999$	

Notes: TPPI, real tax pengő price index; m, money supply; n, number of observations; df, degrees of freedom; SE, asymptotic standard error; sig. level, significance level R^2, coefficient of multiple determination.

*   Statistically significant at the 10 per cent level. See equations (6.1a) and (6.1b) and subsequent discussion for additional details.

[a] Dependent variable: p_t.

Table 6.2 Hannan Efficient Estimates: Post-Hyperinflation

Variable	15 August 1946 - 31 December 1947	
	Coefficient	(SE: sig. level)
Constant	0.090	(0.068;0.191)
m_{t+4}	-0.033	(0.049;0.501)
m_{t+3}	0.054	(0.050;0.284)
m_{t+2}	0.052	(0.048;0.290)
m_{t+1}	-0.026	(0.047;0.578)
m_t	0.023	(0.048;0.641)
m_{t-1}	-0.049	(0.046;0.291)
m_{t-2}	-0.025	(0.047;0.593)
m_{t-3}	-0.003	(0.049;0.945)
m_{t-4}	0.035	(0.048;0.474)
Σm_{t-i}	-0.043	(0.112;0.701)
Σm_{t+j}	0.122	(0.122;0.325)
d_{t+4}	0.008	(0.062;0.894)
d_{t+3}	-0.026	(0.058;0.652)
d_{t+2}	-0.081	(0.060;0.187)
d_{t+1}	-0.082	(0.060;0.181)
d_t	-0.141*	(0.061;0.027)
d_{t-1}	-0.094	(0.062;0.138)
d_{t-2}	0.085	(0.063;0.189)
d_{t-3}	-0.030	(0.061;0.622)
d_{t-4}	-0.043	(0.061;0.485)
Σd_{t-i}	-0.321*	(0.155;0.045)
Σd_{t+j}	-0.253	(0.155;0.111)
Dummy	0.023*	(0.012;0.065)
	$n = 259, \quad df = 39, \quad R^2 = 0.280$	

Note: d, rate of change in government treasury bills; dummy = 0, 15 August 1946 -31 July 1947; = 1 thereafter.
* Statistically significant at the 10 per cent level.
[a] Dependent variable: inflation. See also note to Table 6.1.

5. CONCLUSIONS

This chapter has investigated the money-prices relationship during and following the Hungarian hyperinflation of 1945-46, using weekly data and time-series methods. It was found that the link between these two variables, as measured by statistical coherence, is significantly different within the pre- and post-hyperinflation samples examined separately. The two series were found to be closely correlated during the hyperinflation only when it became clear that none of the policies could effectively back the Hungarian currency. The post-stabilization period was characterized by the absence of any significant money-prices link. However, while a legally prescribed ceiling on government debt was in place, a statistically significant relationship between debt growth and inflation is found — an indication that fiscal policy influenced inflation.

Thus, unlike previous studies which assume that data from hyperinflation and stabilization samples are generated by two distinct policy regimes only, the evidence presented in this chapter suggests that the data may contain a greater number of distinct samples than previously believed. The viability of the fiscal policy in place was chosen as the vehicle through which money-prices correlations for both the hyperinflation and post-hyperinflation samples can be interpreted.

ENDNOTES

*   Reprinted, with minor changes, with permission from Academic Press, and originally published in *Explorations in Economic History*, vol. 27 (October 1990), pp. 468-82. The financial assistance of the Social Sciences and Humanities Research Council of Canada and the Hungarian Academy of Sciences is gratefully acknowledged. Part of the paper was written while the author was on leave at the Institute of Economics and Statistics, and Senior Associate Member, St. Anthony's College, both in Oxford, U.K., and Visiting Assistant Professor at the University of California at San Diego (UCSD). I am grateful to Dr. Ernő Huszti, former General Manager of the Hungarian National Bank, the late Dr. Gyorgy Ránki of the Hungarian Academy of Sciences, and Dr. Iván Pető, formerly staff member of the New Hungarian Archives. Comments by Bruce Smith, Steven Webb, Michael Bordo, Gail Makinen, Elmus Wicker, David Hendry, three anonymous referees, and the Editor, Larry Neal, are greatly appreciated. Previous versions of this paper were presented at the University of Toronto, the Econometric Society meetings in Chicago, December 1987, UQUAM, Concordia, Nuffield, UCSD and Rutgers.

1.   These are obtained by taking inverse Fourier transforms of the frequency response function, after taking into account the general stationary character of the error process. A regression analogue of what is called Hannan's efficient estimator can be developed, as shown by Amemiya and Fuller (1967).

2.   Siklos (1991a) deals in greater detail with the unit root and cointegration properties of the series under investigation and finds evidence consistent with the conclusions of this paper in the error correction framework.

3.   Michener (1988) criticizes one attempt at marshalling evidence for the backing theory (Calomiris 1988) by pointing out that if inflation expectations reflect the fiscal policy in place these should be negatively correlated with real balances. A plot of real balances and a proxy for inflation expectations (not shown) reveals this to be true for Hungary. See Siklos (1991) for tests. Calomiris (1988a), however, argues that Michener is correct if and only if the other arguments in money demand (i.e., income, wealth, real interest rate) are constant.

4.   Rather than select arbitrarily samples a priori one could estimate models such as (6.1a) and (6.1b) recursively and generate Chow tests (Hendry 1988) for all possible sub-samples. Results (not shown) reveal that the samples selected here are appropriate though one could perhaps wish to exclude observations for July 1946. Overall, the conclusions were unaffected by the omission of the last 4 observations. For more details about problems created by July 1946 data, see Siklos (1991). The Chow F-statistic for a break on 7 January 1946, that is, when the TP policy was introduced is 20.442 (4,20). The Chow statistic for a break on August 1947, one year after stabilization is 2.60 (1,48). Degrees of freedom are shown in parenthesis and both statistics are significant at the 5 per cent level.

5.   To adjust for the built-in bias towards devalorization in the TPPI, caused by the changing delays in its computation and publication, the real TPPI was computed as $TPPI/P_{t-2}$, or $TPPI/P_{t-1}$ where t is the time subscript.

6.   Food prices and the cost of rental accommodation, which essentially define the cost of living index, were also conducted daily but a much wider variety of items were sampled than for the TPPI. It may be, of course, that as inflation accelerated astronomically the timing of the price survey may influence the real TPPI. In computing the data, daily averages were used to construct the weekly real TPPI. I tried a variety of other available price indices with no effect on the conclusions. For more on the construction of this series, see Siklos (1991).

7.   Although other variables may have been omitted from (6.1) residuals were not found to be serially correlated.

8.   Suppose the cross-covariance function (ccf) of two unaligned series has a peak at lag S, which may be positive or negative. Alignment is obtained by lagging or leading one series so that the ccf has a peak at the zero lag. The procedure is recommended to reduce bias in the coherency spectrum. Other truncation points were tried with no qualitative effects on the conclusions.

9.   Normally, a large sample is required to perform cross-spectral analysis, particularly when one is interested in the low frequencies. Raj and Siklos (1988), however, obtained good results using cross-spectral methods for samples even smaller than the ones considered here.

10.   All data are available from the author on request. The MSA programme of Baum, Howrey and Greene (1979) was used to generate cross-spectral estimates, while the RATS programme of Doan and Litterman (1983) produced the Hannan efficient estimates.

11.   See Granger and Hatanaka (1964, p. 79) for a table of critical values. These are essentially a function of sample size and the truncation point.

12.   This result is also sensitive to the selection of the data filter. Thus, if money and prices had instead been expressed in first log differences the resulting coherence plot would have revealed very high correlation between the two series at almost all frequencies. As Jacobs (1977) noted, however, (6.1) in rates of change in a hyperinflation sample amounts to estimating a spurious regression of the kind discussed by Granger and Newbold (1974).

13.   It should be noted that, except perhaps for some valuables (e.g., jewellery or coin), most individuals' wealth was in the form of bank deposits and notes. Peasants outside Budapest owned the land for a time but nationalization was imminent. See Siklos (1991) for additional details.

14.   The motivation to do so was not deliberate. The independent research body, the Hungarian Institute for Economic Research (HIER) was responsible for compiling the index until the end of March 1946 while the Supreme Economic Council (SEC), controlled by the Communist Party, directed economic policy in general. There was conflict between the two groups which eventually led the SEC to exclude the HIER from responsibility for the TPPI. See Siklos (1989, 1990 and this volume) for further details.

15.   SW used a data-saving technique and not the conventional lead-lag type analysis used in this paper. The one-sided money growth-inflation result is obtained even when equation (6.1a) is estimated for the TP sample alone.

REFERENCES

Amemiya, T. and Fuller. W.A. (1967), 'A Comparative Study of Alternative Estimators in a Distributed Lag Model', *Econometrica* 35, pp. 509-29.

Barsky, R.B. (1987), 'The Fisher Hypothesis and the Forecastibility and Persistence of Inflation', *Journal of Monetary Economics* 19, pp. 3-24.

Baum, C.F., Howrey, E.P. and Greene, M.N. (1979), *Multivariate Spectrum Analysis*, University of Michigan, Ann Arbor, Michigan.

Bernholz, P. (1988), 'Inflation, Monetary Regimes and the Financial Asset Theory of Money', *Kyklos* 41, pp. 5-34.

Bomberger, W.A. and Makinen, G.E. (1983), 'The Hungarian Hyperinflation and Stabilization of 1945-1946', *Journal of Political Economy* 91, pp. 801-24.

Bordo, M.D. and Marcotte. I.A. (1987), 'Purchasing Power Parity in North America: Some Evidence For South Carolina 1732-1774', in K. Brunner & A.H. Meltzer (eds.), *Carnegie-Rochester Conference Series on Public Policy*, North-Holland, Amsterdam, pp. 311-24.

Brunner, K., and Meltzer, A.H. (1971), 'The Uses of Money: Money in the Theory of an Exchange Economy', *American Economic Review* 61, pp. 784-805.

Cagan, P. (1956), 'The Monetary Dynamics of Hyperinflation', in M. Friedman (ed.), *Studies in the Quantity Theory of Money*, University of Chicago Press, Chicago, pp. 25-117.

Calomiris, C.W. (1988), 'Institutional Failure, Monetary Scarcity, and the Depreciation of the Continental', *Journal of Economic History* 48, pp. 47-68.

Calomiris, C.W. (1988a), 'The Depreciation of the Continental: A Reply', *Journal of Economic History* 48, pp. 693-99.

Christiano, L.J. (1987) 'Cagan's Model of Hyperinflation Under Rational Expectations', *International Economic Review* 28, pp. 33-49.

Cukierman, A. (1988), 'Rapid Inflation - Deliberate Policy or Miscalculation?', in K. Brunner & A.H. Meltzer (eds.), *Carnegie-Rochester Conference Series on Public Policy*, North-Holland, Amsterdam, pp. 11-76 (reprinted in this volume).

Dhrymes, P.J. (1971), *Distributed Lags: Problems of Estimation and Formulation*, Holden-Day, San Francisco.

Doan, T.A. and Litterman, R.B. (1983), *Regression Analysis of Time Series (RATS)*, version 4.11, VAR Econometrics, Minneapolis.

Evans, P. (1978), 'Time Series Analysis of the German Hyperinflation', *International Economic Review* 19, pp. 195-209.

Granger, C.W.J. and Newbold, P. (1974), 'Spurious Regression in Econometrics', *Journal of Econometrics* 19, pp. 111-120.

Hannan, E.J. (1965), 'The Estimation of Relationships Involving Distributed Lags', *Econometrica* 33, pp. 206-24.

Hendry, D.F. (1988), *PG-GIVE*, version 6.0, Institute of Economics and Statistics, Oxford.

Howrey, E.P. (1980), 'The Role of Time Series in Econometric Model Evaluation', in J. Kmenta & J.B. Ramsey (eds.), *Evaluation of Econometric Models*, Academic Press, New York, pp. 275-321.

Jacobs, R. (1977), 'Hyperinflation and the Supply of Money', *Journal of Money, Credit and Banking* 9, part II, pp. 287-303.

Jenkins, G.M. and Watts, D.G. (1968), *Spectral Analysis and Its Applications*, Holden-Day, San Francisco.

Laidler, D.E.W. (1987), 'Wicksell and Fisher on the 'Backing' of Money and the Quantity Theory', in K. Brunner & A.H. Meltzer (eds.), *Carnegie-Rochester Conference Series on Public Policy*, vol. 27, North-Holland, Amsterdam, pp. 325-34.

Lucas, R.E. Jr. (1976), 'Econometric Policy Evaluation: A Critique', in K. Brunner & A.H. Meltzer (eds.), *Carnegie-Rochester Conference Series on Public Policy*, North-Holland, Amsterdam, pp. 19-46.

Makinen, G.E., and Woodward, G.T. (1988), 'The Transition from Hyperinflation to Stability: Some Evidence', *Eastern Economic Journal* 14, pp. 19-26.

Mark, L. (1982), 'The View From Hungary', in T. Hammond (ed.), *Witnesses to the Origins of the Cold War*, University of Washington Press, Seattle.

McCallum, B.T. (1984), 'On Low Frequency Estimates of Long-Run Relationships in Macroeconomics', *Journal of Monetary Economics* 14, pp. 3-14.

Michener, R. (1987), 'Fixed Exchange Rates and the Quantity Theory in the Colonial Era', in K. Brunner & A.H. Meltzer (eds.), *Carnegie-Rochester Conference Series on Public Policy*, North-Holland, Amsterdam, pp. 233-308.

Michener, R. (1988), 'Banking Theories and the Currencies of 18th Century America: A Comment', *Journal of Economic History* 48, pp. 682-92.

Raj, B. and Siklos, P.L. (1988), 'The Role of Fiscal Policy in the St. Louis Model: Nonparametric Estimates for a Small Open Economy', *Empirical Economics* 13, pp. 169-86.

Sargent, T.J. (1993), *Rational Expectations and Inflation*, Second Edition, Harper-Collins, New York.

Sargent, T.J. and Wallace, N. (1981), 'Rational Expectations and the Dynamics of Hyperinflation', in R.E. Lucas, Jr. & T.J. Sargent (eds.), *Rational Expectations and Econometric Practice*, University of Minnesota Press, Minneapolis, pp. 405-28.

Sargent, T.J. and Wallace, N. (1982), 'The Real Bills Doctrine Versus the Quantity Theory: A Reconsideration', *Journal of Political Economy* 90, pp. 1212-36.

Siklos, P.L. (1989), 'The End of the Hungarian Hyperinflation of 1945-46', *Journal of Money, Credit, and Banking* 21, pp. 135-47 (reprinted in this volume).

Siklos, P.L. (1990), 'The Transition from Hyperinflation to Price Stability: Further Evidence', *Eastern Economic Journal* 16 (Jan.-March), pp. 65-9.

Siklos, P.L. (1991), *War Finance, Restruction, Hyperinflation, and Stabilization in Hungary 1938-1948*, MacMillan and St. Martin's Press, London.

Siklos, P.L. (1991a), 'The Money Growth-Inflation Relationship Under Hyperinflation: An Illustration from Hungary's Postwar Experience', *Applied Economics* 23, pp. 1453-60.

Sims, C. (1972), 'Money, Income, and Causality', *American Economic Review* 52, pp. 540-52.

Smith, B.D. (1985), 'American Colonial Monetary Regimes: The Failure of the Quantity Theory and Some Evidence in Favor of An Alternative View', *Canadian Journal of Economics* 18, pp. 531-65.

Smith, B.D. (1985a), 'Some Colonial Evidence on Two Theories of Money: Maryland and the Carolinas', *Journal of Political Economy* 93, pp. 1178-211.

United Nations, Relief and Rehabilitation Agency (1947), *The Food Situation in Continental Europe*, Operational Analysis Paper no. 41, Geneva.

Wicker, E. (1985) 'Colonial Monetary Standards Contrasted: Evidence from the Seven Years' War', *Journal of Economic History* 45, pp. 869-84.

7. Hyperinflation and Currency Reform in Bolivia: Studied from a General Perspective *

Peter Bernholz

1. INTRODUCTION

Bolivia has been the only country in this generation to experience a hyperinflation and to end it with a successful monetary reform. Following Cagan's (1956) definition, hyperinflation is present from the time at which inflation has reached at least once a monthly rate of 50 per cent or more. The Bolivian inflation showed a monthly average increase of 45.53 per cent in the cost of living index during the year from June 1984 to June 1985. From January to February 1985, the index rose by 182.77 per cent (see Tables 7A.1 and 7A.2), thus fulfilling Cagan's condition. The currency reform took place in August 1985 and after that date the rate of inflation dropped drastically (Table 7.2). It was supposed to reach 'only' 10-14 per cent in 1987.

The present chapter investigates whether the qualitative characteristics, which held during most historical hyperinflations and following successful currency reforms, have also been present in Bolivia. We are thus not primarily interested in the specific causes of the Bolivian hyperinflation nor in the detailed history of the currency reform (see Sachs 1986 and Morales 1987). However, a few words concerning the causes of the hyperinflation and the measures taken to stabilize the currency are appropriate.

As with all earlier hyperinflations (see, e.g., Jaksch 1986), the Bolivian hyperinflation was caused by public budget deficits financed by an inflationary increase of the monetary base. From 1975 onwards, the public budget (including losses of government-owned firms) began to show increasing deficits. According to Morales (1987) (but not to Table 7.1) they fluctuated around 10 per cent of Gross Domestic Product. These deficits were initially covered by foreign credit. Because of the rising foreign debt, the amounts necessary to serve it increased and it became more and more difficult to obtain new foreign credits. In March 1982 a crisis developed in the exchange market which led to a large devaluation of the Peso and reinforced the inflation because of higher import prices. The budget deficit rose and had to be financed by issuing money, since foreign credit was no longer available. Inflation accelerated and the real budget deficit increased because the time lag until public revenues were received and disbursed reduced their real value, whereas public expenditures rose with inflation. Thus in 1984 normal public revenues covered no more than 7.84 per cent of expenditures and the deficit of the government amounted to 30.61 per cent of Gross Domestic Product (Table 7.1).

Table 7.1: Budget Deficit of Bolivia as a Percentage of Total Expenditures and of Gross National Product, 1973-1986

Year	1973	1974	1975	1976	1977	1978	1979
Public Deficit as Percentage of Total Public Expenditures	14.31	8.24	11.05	4.44	16.00	18.92	34.25
Public Deficit as Percentage of Gross National Product	1.55	1.03	1.41	2.02	2.20	2.66	4.44

Year	1980	1981	1982	1983	1984	1985	1986
Public Deficit as Percentage of Total Public Expenditures	40.11	37.46	82.88	87.10	92.16	17.67	-14.71[1]
Public Deficit as Percentage of Gross National Product	6.42	6.65	22.27	17.47	30.61	1.51	

Note: [1] Surplus

Sources: Müller and Machicado, 1987, pp. 90-92.

A currency reform to stabilize the currency was initiated with Presidential Decree No. 21060 on 29 August 1985 by the government of President Paz Estenssoro. Since the Bolivian capital market is very narrow and since it was impossible to get further foreign credit, the main measures of the reform consisted in reducing the fiscal budget deficit as rapidly as possible towards zero. For this purpose it was decided 1) to freeze wages and investments in the public sector, 2) to reduce employment in the public sector by about 10 per cent, 3) to dismantle several public firms, and 4) to increase the price of oil products and of other publicly produced goods and services at least to their international level, thus raising public revenues rapidly. These measures proved to be very successful, as can be seen from Table 7.1. Though the reform took place only at the end of August 1985, the budget deficit for 1985 dropped from 30.61 per cent in 1984 to only 1.51 per cent of gross national product.

Another measure taken consisted in raising the official exchange rate by around 500 per cent (Table 7.2). Note that this also increased public revenues markedly, because of the duties on foreign commerce and of the foreign sales of government-owned firms.

It is also important to mention that all exchange controls were removed and that the indexation of wages was abolished. All goods, credit, capital and labour markets were liberalized.

The measures taken to reduce the public budget deficit implied a similar reduction in the extension of credit by the Bolivian central bank to the government and to publicly-owned firms. Thus money creation to finance public deficits, the source of the hyperinflation, diminished rapidly.

The strict reduction of central bank credit to the public sector was not accompanied by a similar policy concerning private credit. The government wanted to end the real causes of inflation and not to restrict but rather to extend the private sector. In addition, with confidence quickly restored because of the measures taken and executed, some repatriation of flight capital took place. Moreover, with free exchange rates and convertibility, the foreign exchange earnings of the hidden economy (export of cocaine) could now more easily enter normal circulation. It follows that the increase in the real stock of money after the reform (and thus of the nominal stock, given a stable or slowly rising price level), to be discussed later on, was brought about by the Bolivian Central Bank's buying of foreign exchange and extending credit to the private sector.

Let us conclude this short discussion of the currency reform with two remarks. First, the measures contained in the Presidential Decree of 29 August 1985, were soon afterwards complemented by others. Of these, the most important ones were 1) a tax reform, 2) a reform of the tariff system,

3) a national budget, 4) a renegotiation of the foreign debt with the Paris Club of official foreign creditors, and 5) a reform of the state-owned Corporacion Minera de Bolivia, which had shown very big losses.

Second, the combined measures we have denoted by the term 'currency reform' should not be confused with the introduction of a new money, the Boliviano. This new currency unit was introduced legally on 1 January 1987, at a rate of 1 Boliviano = 10,000,000 pesos. Banknotes and coins expressed in the new denomination went into circulation after September 1987. It is important to realize that the Bolivian example shows again that the introduction of a new currency is not a necessary condition for a successful currency reform. Stability of the peso was reached long before the introduction of the new money. A new currency may help to restore confidence but it is not necessary for success.

2. GENERAL CHARACTERISTICS OF HYPERINFLATIONS AND OF SUCCESSFUL CURRENCY REFORMS

Hyperinflations usually show the following general characteristics:

A1. At the beginning of an inflation, the real stock of money, i.e., the nominal stock of money divided by the price level, increases.

A2. If a country embarks on a more expansionary monetary policy than its main trading partners, the corresponding (flexible) exchange rates rise more strongly and quickly than the relative price level. An undervaluation of its currency results and purchasing power parity does not hold. With fixed exchange rates an overvaluation will develop.

A3. When inflation has lasted for some time and accelerates more and more, the real stock of domestic money begins to fall. In the last phase of hyperinflation it reaches a level which is far below the normal stock of the time before inflation.

A4. During the last months of hyperinflation prices rise more strongly than exchange rates. Undervaluation diminishes and the system moves towards purchasing power parity. The same development takes place if the growth of the money supply relative to the corresponding trading partner is stopped.

A5. When a country enters into advanced or hyperinflation, the real budget deficit increases.

These characteristics of hyperinflation have been noted by many observers, mostly without recognizing that they are general characteristics. The cause for A5 has already been stated in the introduction. A3 has been described by many perople, and Cagan (1956) and Allais have given a theoretical explanation of the corresponding empirical facts for several hyperinflations by using a money demand function together with assumptions about the formation of inflationary expectations.

Bernholz (1982) has presented empirical evidence concerning A2 and A4 for 11 cases of inflation and shown that these characteristics were known to several earlier economists, some of whom attempted to provide theoretical explanations for them (e.g., Storch 1823). Bernholz, Gärtner and Heri (1985) pointed out that A1-A4 were valid in 14 historical cases. They used a model of the Dornbusch (1976) type, which had been adapted especially concerning the expectation formation process, to explain these characteristics and to simulate them for several historical cases. Figure 7.1 illustrates A1-A4 for the German hyperinflation of 1914-19.

A few words concerning definitions must be added. It has been mentioned that Cagan calls an inflation a hyperinflation from the month in which a monthly rate of inflation of 50 per cent or more has first been reached. We follow this definition, and define next the term 'advanced inflation'. By 'advanced' inflation we denote an inflation in which the real stock of money has already fallen below its normal pre-inflation level. Moreover, we describe as a creeping inflation one in which the real stock of money is still increasing (apart from minor fluctuations), and a moderate inflation as one in which the real stock of money is decreasing but still above the normal level.

Let us describe now some changes resulting from a successful monetary reform ending hyperinflations. Such a reform is often called a change in monetary regime. It is not necessary to list here the conditions for a successful monetary reform (Sargent 1982; Bernholz 1985). It is enough to state that one necessary condition exists in strongly reducing or eliminating that proportion of public budget deficits (including the deficits of firms owned by the government) which is financed by creating money. The general public, moreover, has to be convinced that the government will follow sound fiscal policies and that the central bank will stick to a noninflationary monetary policy in the future. We will see, however, that the nominal stock of domestic money must increase after the reform has been implemented.

Next, after a successful currency reform, the following general characteristics can be observed:

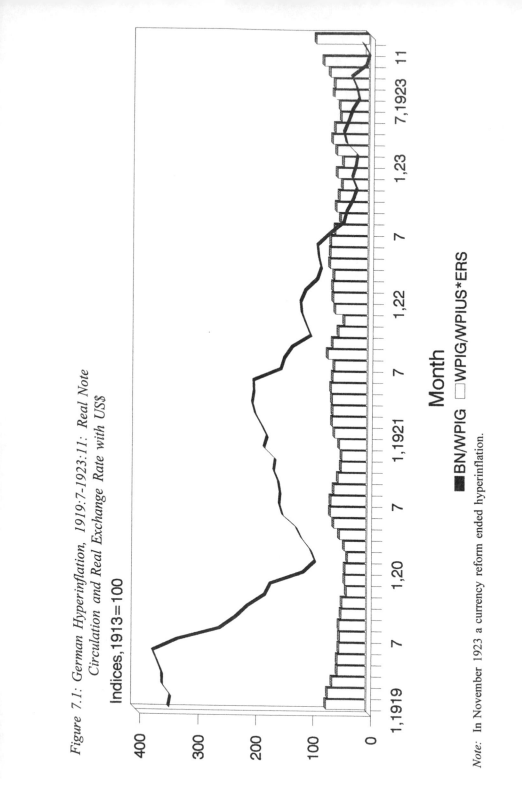

Figure 7.1: German Hyperinflation, 1919:7-1923:11: Real Note
Circulation and Real Exchange Rate with US$

Note: In November 1923 a currency reform ended hyperinflation.

B1.   The real stock of money increases and tends to grow towards its normal level.
B2.   After stabilization, exchange rate and (or) prices tend to move back towards purchasing power parity.
B3.   The real budget deficit falls, even apart from the consequences of measures taken to cut expenditures and (or) to increase taxes.
B4.   The real rate of interest on financial assets denominated in national currency is very high after a currency reform and returns to normal only slowly, i.e., over a period of at least several months.

The causes of characteristic B3 are obvious. The successful currency reform strongly decreases the rate of inflation so that the devaluation of nominal revenue, until it is disbursed for government expenditures, is much less.

Characteristic B1 has been stated as a general characteristic and explained by several economists (Cagan 1956; Sargent 1982; Bernholz 1988). Bernholz (1982, 1988) mentions B2 as a general characteristic. For the question as to whether B2 can be observed after a successful currency reform, it is obviously important whether the currency has still been undervalued or possibly overvalued at the time of the reform, and whether the latter has introduced a fixed or a flexible exchange rate. If a fixed exchange rate has been established, as in most historical cases, then the price level changes until purchasing power parity has been reached. This is usually a slow process taking several years. Note, moreover, that because of domestic political reasons (see Bernholz 1986 for a discussion) fixed exchange rates are usually introduced at a somewhat undervalued rate.

If, on the other hand, no fixed parity has been introduced by the currency reform, then exchange rates move more rapidly and strongly then prices towards purchasing power parity. Some overshooting of this relationship may even occur.

3. GENERAL CHARACTERISTICS OF HYPERINFLATION AND THE BOLIVIAN EXPERIENCE

We want now to check whether the general characteristics of hyper-inflations A1-A5, have been present in the Bolivian case. To do so we have first to decide which year to select as a base for our calculations. It is obvious that we should, if possible, select an inflation-free period, at least with as low a rate of inflation as possible. Secondly, the base year should not be too far distant from the present in order to keep other, especially real, changes within limits.

Let us look at Table 7.2 which contains annual figures for the decades from 1951-86. Two inflationary phases can be distinguished during this period. The first occurred in the fifties and was checked in the early sixties (see Wilkie 1969), the second began slowly in the late sixties and culminated in the hyperinflation starting in April 1984 with a monthly rate of inflation of 92 per cent (see Table 7A.2) as measured by the cost of living index. In between these two bouts of inflation there were a few years of relative stablility, let us say from 1965 to 1969. The annual rates of inflation during these years amounted to 2.86, 6.95, 11.2, 5.84 and 2.22 per cent. The relative money supply, M^B/M_{US}, even declined from 1966 to 1968, and the same happened with the relative price index, CPI^B/CPI^{US}, from 1968 to 1971. The official exchange rate was kept fixed at the same dollar parity from 1959 to 1971 (Table 7.2). Judging from all these developments and considering the importance of relative money supply, we select 1967 as the base year for our calculations. Moreover, this decision biases the developments to be calculated against our hypothesis A2 for later years, since the official exchange rate was kept fixed at the same level until 1971, and since no black market exchange rate was present before 1976.

Let us now turn to Table 7.3 which takes 1967 as a base. If we look at the last column, we find that A1 and A3 are clearly discernible in the Bolivian inflation. Until 1978, the real stock of money M^B/CPI_B grew to about 208 per cent of its 1967 value. This was the period of a slow inflation. Then followed the time of 'moderate inflation' which lasted until the fourth quarter of 1983. The real stock of money fell during these years, but remained above normal. Afterwards the real stock of money decreased to well below normal, i.e., 100 per cent to reach its lowest levels with 36.46 per cent in February and 38.68 per cent in September 1985. That is, it was during this time that Bolivia experienced advanced inflation and hyperinflation.

It is interesting to note that the change from 'creeping' to 'moderate' inflation, as defined by using the development of the real stock of money, corresponded to strong changes of the rate of inflation when the nominal stock of money was still increasing. Whereas from 1977 to 1978 the rate of inflation amounted to 10.36 per cent, it rose to 19.73 per cent in the following year. Similar developments can be observed concerning the quarterly rate of inflation around the time when 'moderate' changed into 'advanced' inflation.

Let us now look at A2. Here we prefer the black market to the official exchange rate since this biases the measure of under- or overvaluation against our hypothesis. The figures in the second to last column of Table 7.3 show that no lasting undervaluation developed until 1981 compared to the base of 1967. $(CPI^B/CPI^{US})/ER_{BM}$ even showed a tendency to move above 100 per cent at least twice, i.e., towards some overvaluation. Now, from Table 7.2, the official exchange rate was kept strictly fixed at different dollar parities until 1981, so that a tendency towards overvaluation would have to be expected according to A2. Until 1975, i.e., before the black market exchange rate became prominent, an undervaluation should be observed only if either a strong depreciation, or a relative stabilization of the money supply, took place (see A4). The latter happened in 1968, with M^B/M^{US} falling below 100 per cent (Table 7.3). According to Table 7.2, the same also happened in 1967. It is thus not surprising that with a fixed exchange rate a certain undervaluation developed in the following years. This development was strengthened by the devaluation in 1973.

The tendency towards overvaluation returned with the accelerating growth of M^B/M^{US} in the early seventies. With a (flexible) black market exchange rate from 1976 and increasing rates of relative monetary expansion, the overvaluation vanished in the first quarter of 1982 and turned into a strong and pronounced undervaluation as predicted by A2. We note that the index of $(CPI^B/CPI^{US})/ER_{BM}$ fluctuated around 30 per cent and reached its lowest point with 23.36 per cent in the third quarter of 1984. In August 1985, i.e., in the month of the currency reform, it was still at 40.19 per cent, but had thus somewhat risen from its lowest position. The latter development seems to confirm the first part of A4, though it is true that the recovery was small compared to other historical experiences.

Finally, it has already been shown in the introduction how strongly the proportion of public expenditures covered by normal revenues (i.e., not by the inflation tax) fell during the process of hyperinflation (Table 7.1), so that A5 is confirmed.

4. CONSEQUENCES OF CURRENCY REFORMS ENDING HYPERINFLATIONS AND THE BOLIVIAN EXPERIENCE

Let us turn now to the consequences of currency reforms, as stated in B1 to B4. Can they also be observed in Bolivia's recent past? We look first

Table 7.2: Relative Money Supply, Price Index and Exchange Rate in Bolivia, 1951-1986

Year	M_1^B [1]	M_1^{US}	M_1^B/M_1^{US}	CPI^B [2]	CPI^{US}	CPI^B/CPI^{US}	ER_{BM} [2]	ER_{OM} [2]
1951	100	100	100	100	100	100		100
1952	150.00	103.69	144.66	124.45	102.07	121.93		100
1953	266.67	105.13	253.66	250.00	102.90	242.95		316.67
1954	450.00	108.42	415.05	560.95	103.31	542.98		316.67
1955	933.33	110.91	841.52	1009.49	103.11	979.04		316.67
1956	3283.33	112.11	2928.67	2814.23	104.55	2691.76		12933
1957	4850.00	111.23	4360.33	6054.74	108.28	5591.74		13883
1958	5016.67	115.72	4335.18	6242.70	111.18	5614.95		16163
1959	6433.33	116.76	5509.87	7509.49	112.22	6691.76		19800
1960	6983.33	117.48	5944.27	8375.91	113.87	7355.68		19800
1961	8266.67	121.41	6808.89	9009.12	115.11	7826.53		19800
1962	9266.67	124.46	7445.50	9538.69	116.36	8197.57		19800
1963	11083	128.47	8626.92	9471.53	117.81	8039.67		19800
1964	13383	134.56	9945.75	10436	119.25	8751.36		19800
1965	15717	141.06	11142	10734	121.33	8846.95		19800
1966	19217	144.43	13305	11480	125.05	9180.33		19800
1967	19867	155.25	12797	12766	128.36	9954.47		19800
1968	21450	167.76	12786	13466	133.75	10068		19800
1969	22683	173.38	13083	13765	140.99	9763		19800
1970	25533	180.83	14120	14305	149.28	9583		19800
1971	29433	192.54	15287	14821	155.69	9520		19800
1972	36833	210.02	17538	15786	160.87	9813		22158
1973	49483	221.89	22301	20768	171.01	12144		33333
1974	70950	228.63	31352	33799	189.65	17822		33333
1975	79317	239.21	33158	36496	207.03	17628		33333
1976	108283	252.85	42825	38138	219.05	17411	35327	33333
1977	130917	274.98	47610	41226	233.33	17669	34983	33333

Table 7.2 (continued)

Year	M_1^B [1]	M_1^{US}	M_1^B/M_1^{US}	CPI^B [2]	CPI^{US}	CPI^B/CPI^{US}	ER_{BM} [2]	ER_{OM} [2]
1978	147183	298.80	49258	45497	250.93	18131	37472	33333
1979	171733	322.61	53232	54475	279.30	19504	38641	33988
1980	246867	340.42	72518	80203	316.98	25302	48474	40850
1981	293117	359.02	81644	105948	349.96	30274	55796	40840
1982	963783	378.99	254303	236920	371.18	63829	282797	106867
1983	2958567	405.77	729124	889772	383.23	232177	1324257	382967
1984	36013319	429.89	8377334	12030450	399.71	3009795	196001650	3629636
1985	3440580725	483.19	712055449	145327836	413.66	35132195	14432343000	736500511
1986	4520956315[3]	562.79	867577337[3]	570644345[4]	421.90	134346860[4]		3203335556

Notes:
[1] End of year.
[2] Annual averages.
[3] End of third quarter.
[4] Average of third quarter.
Sources: International Monetary Fund: International Financial Statistics, Yearbook 1981, August and October 1984, June 1987.
For Black Market exchange rate: World Currency Yearbook 1985, published 1986.
Symbols: see Table 7.3.

Table 7.3: Relative Money Supply, Price Index, Real Stock of Money and Exchange Rate in Bolivia, 1967-1987

Period	M_1^B [1]	M_1^{US} [1]	M_1^B/M_1^{US}	CPI^B [2]	CPI^{US} [3]	CPI^B/CPI^{US}	ER_{BM} [4]	$CPI^B/CPI^{US} \cdot ER_{BM}$	M_1^B/CPI^B
1967	100	100	100	100	100	100	100	100	100
1968	107.97	108.06	99.91	105.48	104.20	101.14	100	101.14	102.36
1969	114.17	111.58	102.23	107.83	109.84	97.81	100	97.81	105.88
1970	128.52	116.48	110.34	112.06	116.30	96.27	100	96.27	114.69
1971	148.15	124.02	119.46	116.10	121.29	95.64	100	95.64	127.61
1972	185.40	135.28	137.05	123.66	125.33	98.58	111.91	88.09	149.93
1973	249.07	142.92	174.27	162.68	133.23	122.00	168.35	72.47	153.10
1974	357.12	147.27	244.99	264.76	147.75	179.04	168.35	106.35	134.88
1975	399.24	154.08	259.11	285.88	161.29	177.08	168.35	105.19	139.65
1976	545.04	162.87	334.65	298.75	170.65	174.91	178.42	98.03	182.44
1977	658.97	177.12	372.04	322.94	181.78	177.50	176.68	100.46	204.05
1978	740.84	192.46	384.92	356.39	195.49	182.14	189.25	96.24	207.87
1979	864.41	207.80	415.97	426.72	217.49	195.93	195.16	100.39	202.57
1980	1,242.60	219.27	566.68	628.25	246.95	254.18	244.82	103.82	197.79
1981	1,475.40	231.25	637.99	829.92	272.64	304.12	281.80	107.92	177.78
1 Q. 1982	1,651.04	219.78	751.22	1,081.62	283.29	381.81	478.08	79.85	152.65
2 Q	2,218.27	221.46	1001.66	1,326.66	287.48	461.48	1,022.59	45.13	167.21
3 Q	3,289.04	225.62	1457.78	2,271.56	292.97	775.36	2,547.65	30.43	144.79
4 Q.	4,851.18	244.11	1987.29	3,332.44	293.71	1134.60	2,806.77	40.42	145.57
1 Q. 1983	5,838.12	238.02	2452.79	4,132.64	293.45	1408.29	4,712.63	29.88	141.27
2 Q:	7,332.09	246.02	2980.28	5,049.46	297.17	1699.18	4,282.94	39.67	145.21
3 Q:	8,811.20	248.35	3547.90	8,147.80	300.63	2710.24	7,547.86	35.91	108.14
4 Q.	15,348	277.79	5525.26	14,279	303.34	4707.26	12,335	38.16	107.49
1 Q. 1984	20,852	273.97	7611.05	23,233	306.56	7653.51	24,365	31.41	89.75
2 Q.	38,563	283.01	13626	58,127	310.01	18750	32,387	57.89	66.34
3 Q.	77,931	283.37	27501	96,547	313.47	30799	131,876	23.36	80.72
4 Q.	288,824	294.78	97980	325,168	315.70	103094	228,665	45.09	88.82

238

Table 7.3 (continued)

Period	M_1^B [1]	M_1^{US} [1]	M_1^B/M_1^{US}	CPI^B [2]	CPI^{US} [3]	CPI^B/CPI^{US}	ER_{BM} [4]	CPI^B/CPI^{US} $\cdot ER_{BM}$	M_1^B/CPI^B
Jan. 1985	405,737	293.70	138,147	548,756	315.44	173,966	541,848	32.11	73.94
Feb.	565,690	288.64	195,985	1,551,725	317.67	488,471	1,231,304	39.67	36.46
March	796,580	291.79	272,998	1,938,737	319.15	642,147	1,197,717	53.61	41.09
April	1,129,228	300.46	375,833	2,167,178	320.39	676,419	1,584,818	42.68	52.11
May	1,867,535	297.62	627,490	2,940,166	321.62	914,174	2,577,937	35.46	63.52
June	2,434,462	305.94	795,732	5,247,073	322.61	1,626,445	4547844	35.76	46.40
July	4,149,063	309.45	1,340,786	8,726,045	323.11	2,700,642	7,896,909	34.20	47.55
Aug.	6,512,317	310.69	2,096,082	14,525,436	323.85	4,485,236	11,158,957	40.19	44.83
Sept.	8,793,816	314.62	2,795,059	22,733,750	324.84	6,998,445	10,783,597	64.90	38.68
4 Q. 1985	16,864,265	330.58	5,101,417	26,890,293	326.81	8,228,112	17,015,397	48.36	62.72
1 Q. 1986	15,444,770	325.67	4,742,460	38,595,731	327.55	11,831,570	19,462,786	60.54	40.02
2 Q.	18,992,335	345.97	5,489,590	42,088,865	326.81	12,878,696	19,303,549	66.72	45.12
3 Q.	20,471,345	357.02	5,733,949	44,103,933	329.28	13,394,052	19,081,637	69.83	46.42
4 Q.	28,200,388	385.59	7,313,568	44,603,397	332.25	13,424,649	19,207,252	69.89	63.22
1 Q. 1987	27,553,619	376.55	7,317,387	46,582,050	334.22	13,937,541	19,739,767	70.61	59.15
2 Q.		387.04							

Notes: [1] End of period
[2] Average of period. For quarterly data average of last month of quarter.
[3] Average of period.
[4] Black market exchange rate for US$.

Sources: International Monetary Fund: International Financial Statistics since 1981. For black market exchange rates until 1981: World Currency Yearbook 1985, published 1986 (formerly Pick's Currency Yearbook). For Bolivian data and black market exchange rates since 1982: Müller and Machicado (1987); Morales (1987).

Symbols: M_1^B, M_1^{US} Banknotes and current deposits held by the public in Bolivia and the USA, respectively according to official definitions.
CPI^B, CPI^{US} Bolivian and US cost of living indices.
ER_{BM} Black market exchange rate for US$.

239

at the real stock of money and see that it increased from 38.68 per cent in September and 44.83 per cent in August 1985 to 62.72 per cent in the fourth quarter of 1985 (Table 7.3). Since the currency reform took place (with a Decree of President Paz Estenssoro) on 29 August 1985, it is not surprising that the real stock of money was still lower in September than in August 1985. The rise afterwards corresponds to B1.

More disturbing is the fact that the real stock of money fell back to rather low levels in the first to the third quarters of 1986 and recovered only afterwards to about 60 per cent. Though the latter fact corresponds to B1, the former appears to contradict it. But this intermittent decline can be explained by specific events threatening the anti-inflationary reforms. To quote Morales (1987, p. 84): 'In December 1985 and January 1986 a revival of inflation happened which put into doubt the continuity of the Nueva Politica Economica. The revival was basically caused by two factors: 1) the somewhat dephased repercussion of the collapse of the tin market in October 1985, which put pressure on foreign exchange reserves and on the exchange rate; 2) an unintended expansion of public expenditures caused partly but not totally by an incorrect calculation of the Christmas wage bonus. From February 1986 the government was able to control the inflation by using even more restrictive fiscal and monetary measures than it had followed before' (my translation). If we look at the monthly rates of inflation we find, indeed, that they rose from 3.2 per cent in November and -1.9 per cent in October to 16.8 per cent in December 1985 and 33 per cent in January 1986. After that they dropped again to 7.9 per cent in February and to 0.1 per cent in March 1986. But it obviously took a somewhat longer time to restore the precarious confidence in the reforms.

If we look next at B2, this is clearly confirmed by the figures for $(CPI^B/CPI^{US})/ER_{BM}$, since they increased from 40.19 per cent in August 1985 to 70.61 per cent in the first quarter of 1987. Thus a tendency towards purchasing power parity can be observed. Only the fourth quarter of 1985 seems to show an interruption of this movement. Was this also caused by the factors mentioned above? This seems in fact to be true, for the exchange rate rose 29.6 per cent in December 1985, much more than the rise of 16.8 per cent in the price level, whereas the exchange rate rose less in January 1986 at 29.5 per cent than the price level at 32.9 per cent, and even decreased in February by 10.8 per cent.

Next, we turn to real interest rates. According to B4 they should be very high after the currency reform and return only slowly to a normal level. This is confirmed for the case of Bolivia. In September 1985 the monthly nominal interest rate amounted to 32 per cent, and fell to 22.5 per cent in October (Table 7.4), corresponding to real *ex post* interest rates of -25.4

per cent and of 24.4 per cent. After that month the real *ex post* interest rate is always positive and rather high, with the exception of January 1986 when it was -12.9 per cent. The reasons for this exception are the same as those already discussed above.

Table 7.4: Nominal and Real (ex post) *Monthly Rates of Interest in Bolivia*

Month	Nominal Rate of Interest (on Bank credits)	Rate of Inflation	Real Rate of Interest
September 1985	32.0	56.5	-24.5
October	22.5	-1.9	24.4
November	21.6	3.2	18.4
December	19.2	16.8	2.4
January 1986	20.0	32.9	-12.9
February	19.8	7.9	11.9
March	18.5	0.1	18.4
April	13.1	3.6	9.5
May	8.5	1.0	7.5
June	8.09	4.3	3.79
July	7.53	1.8	5.73
August	6.79	0.7	6.09
September	6.55	2.2	4.35
October	5.50	0.59	4.91
November	4.34	-0.11	4.45
December	4.49	0.65	3.84
January 1987	4.28	2.45	1.83
February	4.21	1.23	2.98
March	3.25	0.70	3.05
April	3.78	1.59	2.19
May	2.99	0.34	2.65
June	2.49		

Sources: Until September 1986: Morales (1987, p. 85). For monthly inflation from October 1986: Müller and Machicado (1987). The figures for the nominal interest rates since October 1986 were kindly provided by the Swiss Chargé d'Affaires in La Paz.

From 24.4 per cent in October 1985, the real monthly interest rate declined to 7.5 per cent in May 1986 and to 2.65 per cent in May 1987. These figures correspond to annual real interest rates of 1,260 per cent,

138 per cent and 36.87 per cent, figures which confirm that real interest rates were extraordinarily high after the currency reform and that they fell during the following 19 months but were still very high in May 1987. Even on 24 August 1987 the nominal rate of interest for credits (averaged over 12 banks) amounted to 50.51 per cent (see table from the Banco Central in *Ultima Hora*, 19 August 1987) which, for an expected annual rate of inflation of about 10-14 per cent, would still amount to a real rate of 36-40 per cent *ex ante*. We conclude that B4 is confirmed by the Bolivian case.

Let us finally discuss B3, which is also confirmed by the Bolivian figures. Whereas in 1984 ordinary revenue covered only 7.84 per cent of expenditures, this figure increased to 82.33 per cent in 1985 (Table 7.1), a development concentrated in the months after the currency reform. In 1986 the figure rose to 114.71 per cent, so that the budget showed a surplus (Müller and Machicado, 1987, pp. 90-92). It is obvious that this development was only partly due to the decrease in inflation leaving a higher real value of revenues to be spent. Another part was a result of the fiscal measures taken as an ingredient of the reform programme. Still, the rapid growth of real revenues in the first months after the reform of 29 August 1985 shows the importance of the first factor, since it took time before the fiscal measures could be enacted and show up in revenues and expenditures.

5. SOME IMPORTANT DEVIATIONS OF BOLIVIAN DEVELOPMENTS FROM GENERAL PATTERNS

Bolivia is the second poorest country of Latin America and its underdeveloped economy comprises a large sector of self-sufficient Indian peasants scarcely integrated into the monetized economy. In spite of this fact, the general characteristics of hyperinflation corresponding to the experiences of other developed and underdeveloped countries could be observed in Bolivia. We recall that these characteristics could not only be observed in countries like Germany in the early 1920s and Greece in the 1940s, but also during the great French Revolution from 1789-96. In Bolivia they have even taken place in a hyperinflation not related to wars as in these cases. It seems, then, that these characteristics are rather stable ones.

It was stated further that the conditions for and the general consequences of a successful currency reform have been the same in Bolivia as in former historical cases.[1] Having completed this analysis it is advisable to look at some Bolivian developments deviating from the general pattern, for such deviations may draw attention to some problems the country may face in preserving and maintaining the success of the reform of August 1985.

Since the general characteristics of hyperinflation and of the consequences of a successful currency reform held true in the Bolivian case, specific Bolivian developments can be found only as deviations from these characteristics. They must thus be such that the general patterns can still be recognized but that they can themselves be observed since they diverge from the general characteristics in their normal form. These deviations are thus analogous to those of a cannon ball from the flight parabola predicted by the laws of gravity, deviations which are caused by air resistance and strong winds. To measure the importance of the latter factors, one has to know that the flight would, without their influence, follow a parabola. In economics, of course, the general characteristics mentioned can as yet only be stated qualitatively, not quantitatively. The same must thus be true of the specific causes of the deviations for which we have to look.

What, then, are the deviations of Bolivian monetary developments in the early 1980s from regular patterns? In a sense they were already implicitly stated in our earlier analysis. Let us put them together:

1) First, there was only a very weak tendency towards purchasing power parity in the last months of hyperinflation up to August or September 1985. We have noted this fact above, a fact which is in strong contrast to other historical experiences (Bernholz 1982, pp. 28-33). Since the development of $(CPI^B/CPI^{US})/ER_{BM}$ from 23.36 per cent in the third quarter of 1984 to 40.19 per cent in August 1985 is not very pronounced and also very irregular, some doubts are even possible whether A4 was really present.

2) The real stock of money decreased strongly during the hyperinflation but remained at levels which seem still to be too high if we compare them with those reached in other hyperinflations.

3) After the currency reform the real stock of money M^B/CPI^B rose to 60per cent of its 1967 value in the first quarter of 1987. This figure seems to be rather low for a time one and a half years after the currency reform.

4) The high real interest rates after the currency reform are normal. But real interest rates of about 37 per cent in May and August 1987, nearly two years after the currency reforms, do not correspond to normal developments. In Germany the real interest

rate had returned to normal levels in about one year after the
currency reform of November 1923 (Bernholz 1988).

5)   Inflation has not been fully defeated two years after the currency
reform. For 1987 a rate of 10-14 per cent has to be expected from
the development of the first five months of that year. This does
not correspond to the experiences made, say, in Germany and
Austria in the 1920s, though similar events happened in Poland in
the 1920s and in Greece after World War II.

Next, let us look at possible reasons for these deviations. Concerning 1)
and 2) it is not possible at the moment to give a definite answer. Both
may have to do with the underdevelopment of the economy in the sense
that people and markets did not respond as rapidly and as strongly to
hyperinflationary developments by purchasing as much and as rapidly as
possible and thus driving up prices more quickly. The less efficient and
less developed market institutions, the less developed information and
transportation systems and the lack of an adequate education of broad
segments of the population may all be factors causing weaker and less
rapid reactions to inflation. Only a study looking at the time paths of real
exchange rate and real stock of money in many inflations in countries in
different stages of development may permit the correctness of this
hypothesis to be tested.

It might be wondered, however, whether the insufficient fall of the real
stock of money is not caused by our neglect of the growth of real gross
domestic product. But as can be seen from Table 7.5 this does not change
the overall picture. The real stock of money adjusted for GDP growth, i.e.,
$(M^B/CPI^B)/GDP$ does not increase as much from 1970 to 1980 as M^B/CPI^B.
But the lowest level is even higher than that of $M^{B'}/CPI^B$ (see e.g.,
February 1985). On the other hand, it is true, a higher level is reached
after the currency reform of 1985, and $(M^B/CPI^B)/GDP$ rises to 74.24 per
cent in the fourth quarter of 1986 instead of the 63.22 per cent to which
M^B/CPI^B increases. So the deviation mentioned under 3) becomes weaker.
Still, the overall picture discussed above remains true.

Next, let us turn to the possible causes of the low level of the real stock
of money 19 months after the currency reform. Here, several reasons can
be responsible and have been put forward by experts in Bolivia in
personal conversations with the author. First, it is supposed that the export
value of cocaine amounts to about one half of total exports. This illegal
export is paid for in cash, i.e., in dollar bills, and it is possible that the
farmers cultivating the respective crops and the workers on the farms, in
the processing plants and in the transport of cocaine are also paid in dollar
bills. Moreover, part of the proceeds are used to buy durable consumption

Table 7.5: Unemployment, Real Stock of Money and Gross Domestic Product in Bolivia 1970-1987

Period	Unemployed as Percentage of Total Labour Force	Gross Domestic Product, GDP (in prices of 1980)	M_1^B/CPI^B (1967 = 100, from Table 7.3)	M_1^B/CPI^B GDP
1970		100	114.69	114.69
1971		102.39	127.61	124.64
1972		105.70	149.93	141.84
1973		109.97	153.10	139.22
1974		112.83	134.88	119.54
1975		117.28	139.65	119.07
1976		121.29	182.44	150.42
1977		123.20	204.05	165.62
1978		124.08	207.87	167.53
1979		120.88	202.57	167.58
1980	4.77	117.08	197.79	168.94
1981	9.68	114.41	177.78	155.39
4Q 1982	10.89	108.27[1]	145.57	134.45
4Q 1983	13.04	98.50[1]	107.49	109.12
4Q 1984	15.41	95.02[1]	88.82	93.47
Feb.1985		95.02[2]	36.46	38.37
Aug.1985		90.84[1]	44.83	49.35
Sept.1985		90.84[1]	38.68	42.58
4Q 1985	19.24	90.84[1]	62.72	69.04
2Q 1986		90.84[2]	45.12	49.67
4Q 1986	20.50	85.151	63.22	74.24

Notes:
[1] Annual figures
[2] Annual figures of preceding year
Sources: For percentage of unemployed and Gross Domestic Product: Müller and Machicado 1987, pp. 16-17, 28-29. For other figures see Table 7.3.

goods in the USA. These are imported into Bolivia and may also partly be sold for dollar bills. If these reports are correct, the dollar circulation caused by the illegal cocaine traffic may be partly responsible for the low real demand for national money.

We suspect, however, that the weak real demand for national money is mainly caused by the still lingering distrust in the long-term stability of monetary policy. This suspicion is nourished by deviation 4), the very high real interest rates of credits denominated in national money two years after the currency reform. With the success of the reform in defeating hyperinflation real interest rates can still amount to about 37 per cent only if a strong revival of inflation and/or a strong devaluation of the Boliviano are expected. The inflation which persists may support such doubts.

Even this, however, is probably only part of the story. Until now we have not yet mentioned that credits denominated in national money but with a value maintenance clause showed a nominal interest rate of 30.20 per cent (average) on 19 August 1987 (*Ultima Hora*, La Paz, 24 August 1987). Moreover, credits denominated in dollars had an average interest rate of 34.32 per cent at the same date. Now these interest rates were lower than the 50.51 per cent nominal interest charged on credits denominated in Bolivianos, but they are still extraordinarily high compared to the interest rates in world markets. In Germany after the currency reform, interest rates for credits denominated in gold, rye or coal corresponded much more closely to world market rates in contrast to the interest rates on credits denominated in marks. Also, they fluctuated from the beginning, and without any tendency, between 8 and 13 per cent (Bernholz 1988).

These additional facts seem to support the assumption of a general mistrust in Bolivian political institutions and in the stability of property rights. Such mistrust seems to be justified if one looks at Bolivian historical political instability and the present situation. On average, Bolivian presidents have remained in office for less than a year. The present President, Paz Estenssoro, on whose backing the reform Cabinet and its reforms depended, is already eighty years old. Note that the reforms were usually only undertaken with presidential decrees and not with the help of laws. In Parliament the presidential party, the MNR, has only a relative majority, so that the President had and has to rely on the support of the party of former President Banzer. Moreover, even the MNR has wings strongly opposing the present stabilization policies. Finally, Bolivia has a history of exchange controls, which makes it doubtful whether deposits and credits denominated in dollars will not be changed into assets denominated in national money by a new government, as happened a few years ago.

Now, if the institutional instability of the political system and thus of property rights should be the main cause of deviations 3) and 4) then it may also be responsible for deviation 5), the remaining inflation. For if the real stock of national money had grown to 100 per cent instead of 60per cent or 70 per cent because of more confident expectations concerning long-term stability, then the remaining inflation would have been wiped out as in the German and Austrian cases of the early 1920s.

Before concluding this section, some additional points have to be mentioned. First, it has been said that the high real interest rates may be at least partially a consequence of lack of competition in the Bolivian banking system, of its inefficient organization and of the very fact of the insufficient growth of the nominal money supply leading to a real stock of money that is too small. The last point seems to be rather doubtful, given the above institutional explanation, the remaining rate of inflation and the high interest rates on dollar-denominated credits. The first two points may, however, be more readily accepted as possible partial explanations. Both factors would tend to keep all kinds of interest rates high. Moreover, the spread between interest rates on credits and on deposits of banks has been very high indeed. For national money denominated credits and time deposits, it amounted on 19 August 1987 on average to not less than 22 per cent (*Ultima Hora*, 24 August 1987). And according to private communications, the accounting system of Bolivian banks is so bad that they are not able to determine whether additional deposits and credits with an interest spread of 5 per cent would lower or increase their profits.

The remaining Bolivian inflation causes additional worries to authorities and to outside observers. Such worries concern first the exchange rate of the dollar. Here it is necessary to point out that the Banco Central has followed a policy of dirty floating since the currency reform and has let the exchange rate rise less than the price level. Though the exchange rate was clearly undervalued immediately after the currency reform, this undervaluation has in time been slowly eroded by the remaining inflation. This was caused by the reluctance of the authorities to devalue the Bolivar more strongly, since they are afraid that otherwise inflationary expectations might be rekindled. It has even been calculated that, at the end of 1987, there may be an overvaluation of the Boliviano compared to the US$ of about 13-20 per cent. According to our figures in Table 7.3, taking 1967 as a base, this is not true. The index of $(CPI^B/CPI^{US})/ER_{BM}$ may move up to around 80 until the end of 1987. But it has to be conceded that things look different if a base period immediately before the beginning of hyperinflation is taken (say 1982). Even our figures show a strong reduction of undervaluation since September 1985 which means a sizeable deterioration of the competitive position of export and of import-competing sectors of the economy. This has taken place at a time in which inflation and currency reform have reduced economic activity and led to unemployment figures of 20-30 per cent of the total labour force (see Table 7.5). Finally, it must be taken into account that the world market price of tin, traditionally Bolivia's most important export good (now replaced by cocaine), collapsed at the end of 1985. Taking all these factors into account, the rise of the real exchange rate must indeed be a threat for the future if the remaining inflation cannot be brought under control. The situation would become even more dangerous if the US dollar should recover against the other major currencies.

6. CONCLUSION

Bolivia is the second poorest country in South America. Because of inflation, the fall in tin prices and domestic factors, its gross domestic product has been falling since 1979 (Table 7.5). The successful currency reform has brought another, though smaller fall, as had to be expected from historical experience. At the end of 1986, GDP was about 15 per cent lower than in 1970. Unemployment also rose very strongly, as usual, during the final stage of hyperinflation. The reform led to a further increase. It follows that the success of the currency reform does not yet imply an end to the very bad real situation. This understandably engenders political pressures, labour unrest and strikes to change the monetary and fiscal policies which were so successful in fighting inflation.

The above monetary analysis of the Bolivian hyperinflation, of the reform and its consequences has confirmed that they followed the general qualitative characteristics found in other historical cases. But the study of the deviations from these patterns and of their possible causes has led, by necessity, to the real problems faced by Bolivia and to the political and institutional factors probably responsible for them. It seems that only a building-up of long-term confidence can restore the stability of the Bolivian economy. The real stock of money must rise and real interest rates prohibiting sound real investments in a time of a deep depression must fall to a normal level. The remaining inflation must be finally defeated and an adequate exchange rate be found and maintained without destroying the confidence in a sound monetary and fiscal policy. To accomplish these tasks the safety of the property rights of individuals and the reliability of stable monetary and fiscal policy in the future must be established without doubt.

How could these ambitious aims be reached? Only by institutional changes preventing often changing political majorities and new presidents from altering economic policies and property rights from one day to the other. What institutions could help to attain such stability? One ingredient would be an independent central bank required by law or constitution to follow a sound monetary policy, e.g., by prescribing the stability of the exchange rate of the Boliviano with a fixed currency basket containing the currencies of the major industrial countries. Constitutional requirements forbidding fiscal deficits, exchange controls and the confiscation of private property without due compensation in stable money would be further institutional measures. Such articles in the constitution would, of course, be helpful only if they could be changed by (say) a three-quarters or two-thirds majority in parliament.

These are, of course, not the only institutional changes that could be thought of. Nor are they complete. Bolivia does not enjoy a strong tradition of institutional and constitutional thinking. In the present situation a change of prevalent doctrines seems, however, to be necessary for a long-term improvement of economic and political conditions. It is thus at least encouraging that some weak plants of institutional thinking are beginning to take root in Bolivia.

ENDNOTES

* First published in Journal of *Institutional and Theoretical Economics (JITE)* 144, 1988, pp. 747-771. I am grateful to many persons in Bolivia who generously provided facts and were prepared to offer their views and insights and to discuss my own hypotheses. The comments of an unknown referee were helpful in improving the chapter. The Volkswagen Foundation's financial support allowed the author to become personally acquainted with the Bolivian situation.
1. We call the Bolivian currency reform 'successful', since it has succeeded in removing hyperinflation and in defending a rather low rate of inflation for more than two years. As will be argued in this section, however, this does not imply that monetary stability will be maintained in the future.

REFERENCES

Allais, M. (1966), 'A Restatement of the Quantity Theory of Money' *American Economic Review* 56, pp. 1123-56.
Bernholz, P. (1982), 'Flexible Exchange Rates in Historical Perspective' *Princeton Studies in International Finance*, No. 49, July.

Bernholz, P. (1985), 'Hyperinflation and Monetary Reform' *Schweizerischer Bankverein: Prospects*, February 1985, 1, pp. 1-6.

Bernholz, P. (1986), 'The Implementation and Maintenance of a Monetary Constitution' *Cato Journal* 6, pp. 477-511. Reprinted in Dorn, J.A. and Schwartz, A.J. (eds.), *The Search for Stable Money*, The University of Chicago Press, Chicago and London.

Bernholz, P. (1988), 'Inflation, Monetary Regime and the Financial Asset Theory of Money' *Kyklos*, 41.

Bernholz, P., Gärtner, M. and Heri, E. (1985), 'Historical Experiences with Flexible Exchange Rates' *Journal of International Economics* 19, pp. 21-45.

Cagan, P. (1956), 'The Monetary Dynamics of Hyperinflation', in Friedman, M. (ed.), *Studies in the Quantity Theory of Money*, The University of Chicago Press, Chicago.

Dornbusch, R. (1976), 'Expectations and Exchange Rate Dynamics' *Journal of Political Economy* 84, pp. 1161-76.

Jaksch, H.J. (1986), 'Kleine ökonometrische Modelle für sich rasch entwertende Währungen' *Ifo-Studien* 32, pp. 241-47.

Morales, A. (1987), *Estudio, Diagnostico, Debate, Precios, Salarios y Politica Economica durante la Alta Inflacion Boliviana de 1982 a 1985*, Ildis, La Paz, without date.

Müller, H. and Machicado (1987), *Estadisticas Economicas*, Idea, La Paz, without date.

Sachs, J. (1986), *The Bolivian Hyperinflation and Stabilization*, Mimeo, Cambridge, Mass.

Sargent, T.J. (1982), 'The Ends of Four Big Inflations' in R.E. Hall (ed.), *Inflation: Causes and Effects*, The University of Chicago Press, Chicago.

Storch, H. (1823), *Cours d'Economie Politique*, 4 vols, Paris.

Ultima Hora. (1987), Newspaper, La Paz, 19 August.

Wilkie, J.W. (1969), *The Bolivian Revolution and U.S. Aid since 1952*, University of California, Los Angeles.

Table 7A.1: Relative Money Supply, Real Stock of Money, Relative Price Index and Exchange Rate in Bolivia, 1982-1987

Month	M_1^B	M_1^{US}	M_1^B/M_1^{US}	CPI^B	CPI^{US}	CPI^B/CPI^{US}	M_1^B/CPI^B	ER_{BM}	ER_{OM}/CPI^{US}
Jan. 1982	100	100[1]	100	100	100[2]	100	100	100	100
Feb.	108.41			116.05			93.42	104.76	175.97
March	121.52			125.52			96.81	114.29	175.97
April	137.40			141.37			97.19	188.10	175.97
May	149.06			147.04			101.37	209.52	175.97
June	170.15			153.96	106.07[3]	145.15	110.52	245.24	175.97
July	214.62			187.19			114.65	354.76	175.97
Aug.	237.94			220.66			107.83	438.10	175.97
Sept.	273.19			263.62			103.63	611.90	175.97
Oct.	316.05			302.20			104.58	519.04	175.97
Nov.	329.58			358.88			91.84	550.00	799.67
Dec.	393.47	105.50	372.60	386.74			101.74	673.81	799.67
Jan. 1983	372.78			398.04			93.65	811.90	799.67
Feb.	402.80			428.92			93.91	1026.19	799.67
March	460.17			479.60			95.95	1130.95	799.67
April	501.88			519.73			96.57	954.24	799.67
May	537.96			567.83			94.74	869.05	799.67
June	525.33			586.00	109.51[3]	535.11	98.18	1028.57	799.67
July	632.87			644.99			98.12	1211.90	799.67
Aug.	652.86			812.29			80.37	1709.92	799.67
Sept.	696.66			945.57			73.68	1811.90	799.67
Oct.	765.79			1054.66			72.61	2061.90	799.67
Nov.	858.39			1316.02			65.23	2888.10	2039.98
Dec.	1248.81	115.69	1079.45	1657.12			75.36	2961.90	2039.98
Jan. 1984	1309.55			1815.58			72.13	5476.19	2039.98
Feb.	1427.71			2233.29			63.93	5000.00	2039.93

251

Table 7A.1 (continued)

Month	M_1^B	M_1^{US}	M_1^B/M_1^{US}	CPI^B	CPI^{US}	CPI^B/CPI^{US}	M_1^B/CPI^B	ER_{BM}	ER_{OM}/CPI^{US}
March	1,792.32			2,296.28			78.05	6,666.67	2,039.98
April	2,141.75			4,408.98			48.58	7,142.86	8,159.93
May	2,672.51			6,482.05			41.23	8,095.24	8,159.93
June	3,405.76			6,745.80	114.22[3]	5,905.97	50.49	7,738.10	8,159.93
July	4,897.73			7,094.99			69.03	10,357	8,159.93
Aug.	5,586.94			8,158.96			68.48	15,476	8,159.93
Sept.	6,946.94			11,204			62.00	34,762	8,159.93
Oct.	9,571.99			17,829			53.69	35,714	8,159.93
Nov.	12,445			23,456			53.06	40,690	34,969
Dec.	28,832	122.57	23,523	37,736			76.40	52,676	34,969
Jan. 1985	40,065			63,684			62.91	150,571	34,969
Feb.	54,031			180,081			30.00	269,262	183,599
March	78,602			224,995			34.93	286,200	183,599
April	110,952			251,506			44.12	380,514	183,599
May	184,723			341,213			54.14	618,962	273,358
June	248502			608,934	118.20[3]	515,173	40.81	1,091,936	273,358
July	418,300			1,012,677			41.31	1980,793	273,358
Aug.	665,621			1,685,709			39.49	2,679,269	305,998
Sept.	898,812			2,638,302			34.07	2,589,145	4,397,744
Oct.	1,155,204			2,588,967			44.62	2,667,157	4,496,389
Nov.	1,183,684			2,671,814			44.30	3,254,093	4,885,218
Dec.	1,723,689	137.76	1,251,226	3,120,678			55.23	4,085,402	6,481,489
Jan. 1986	1,520,515			4,149,254			36.65	5,333,848	8,395,124
Feb.	1,574,012			4,479,119			35.14	4,564,002	7,507,621
March	1,578,603			4,479,120			35.24	4,673,021	7,705,426
April	1,717,961			4,639,921			37.02	4,590,860	7,770,706
May	1,885,025			4,684,928			40.24	4,605,543	7,769,482
June	1,941,198			4,884,506	120.56[3]	4,051,515	39.74	4,634,788	7,771,754

Table 7A.1 (continued)

Month	M_1^B	M_1^{US}	M_1^B/M_1^{US}	CPI^B	CPI^{US}	CPI^B/CPI^{US}	M_1^B/CPI^B	ER_{BM}	ER_{OM}/CPI^{US}
July	2,036,306			4,971,450			40.96	4,602,726	7,768,654
Aug.	2,085,522			5,004,262			41.67	4,605,607	7,790,902
Sept.	2,092,367			5,118,359			40.88	4,581,507	7,813,505
Oct.	2,323,303			5,148,557			45.13	4,607,412	7,838,148
Nov.	2,283,100			5,142,894			44.39	4,613,690	7,854,141
Dec.	2,882,349	160.56	1,795,185	5,176,323			55.68	4,611,667	7,849,449
Jan. 1987	2,556,736			5,303,143			48.12	4,633,571	7,859,649
Feb.	2,916,947			5,368,372			54.34	4,630,476	7,922,481
March	2,816,243			5,405,950			52.10	4,739,524	8,107,303
April	2,935,547			5,488,661			53.48	4,826,524	8,179,600
May	2,887,776			5,507,323					

Notes:
1 December 1981
2 1981
3 Annual average

Sources: Müller and Machicado (1987), Morales (1987). For US dates: International Monetary Fund, International Financial Statistics, Yearbook 1983, July 1987.

Symbols:
M_1^B/M_1^{US} Banknotes and current deposits held by the public in Bolivia and the USA, respectively, according to official definitions.
CPI^B/CPI^{US} Bolivian and US cost of living indices.
ER_{BM} Black market exchange rate of the US$
ER_{OM} Official market exchange rate of the US$.

Table 7A.2: Monthly Rate of Inflation for Bolivia, 1982-1987

Date of Inflation	Monthly Rate of Inflation	Date of Inflation	Monthly Rate of Inflation
Jan-82	NA	Sep-84	37.3%
Feb-82	16.1%	Oct-84	59.1%
March-82	8.2%	Nov-84	31.6%
April-82	12.6%	Dec-84	60.9%
May-82	4.0%	Jan-85	68.8%
June-82	4.7%	Feb-85	182.8%
July-82	21.6%	March-85	24.9%
Aug-82	17.9%	April-85	11.8%
Sep-82	19.5%	May-85	35.7%
Oct-82	14.6%	June-85	78.5%
Nov-82	18.8%	July-85	66.3%
Dec-82	7.8%	Aug-85	66.5%
Jan-83	2.9%	Sep-85	56.5%
Feb-83	7.8%	Oct-85	-1.9%
March-83	11.8%	Nov-85	3.2%
April-83	8.4%	Dec-85	16.8%
May-83	9.3%	Jan-86	33.0%
June-83	3.2%	Feb-86	7.9%
July-83	10.1%	March-86	0.1%
Aug-83	25.9%	April-86	3.6%
Sep-83	16.4%	May-86	1.0%
Oct-83	11.5%	June-86	4.3%
Nov-83	24.8%	July-86	1.8%
Dec-83	25.9%	Aug-86	0.7%
Jan-84	9.6%	Sep-86	2.3%
Feb-84	23.0%	Oct-86	0.6%
March-84	2.8%	Nov-86	-0.1%
April-84	92.0%	Dec-86	0.7%
May-84	47.0%	Jan-87	2.5%
June-84	4.1%	Feb-87	1.2%
July-84	5.2%	March-87	0.7%
Aug-84	15.0%	April-87	1.5%
		May-87	0.3%

Source: See Table 7.3.

PART IV

The Ending of Hyperinflation

8. Necessary and Sufficient Conditions to End Hyperinflations[*]

Peter Bernholz

1. INTRODUCTION

In the social sciences it is often difficult to formulate necessary or sufficient conditions for certain events to happen or for the success of given measures. Necessary *and* sufficient conditions may be impossible to formulate. We know, for instance, that deficits of government are necessary for hyperinflations to happen. But they are certainly not sufficient since they may be financed out of savings. Also a continuous increase of the stock of money is necessary for an inflationary development. Such a development is, however, not sufficient if real gross national product increases as strongly or more rapidly than the stock of money.

In this chapter we intend to discuss necessary and sufficient conditions to end hyperinflations. For this purpose we are going to look at eleven hyperinflations and at some advanced inflations. Until now thirteen hyperinflations have, as far as is known to us, happened in the sense of Cagan's work (1956). According to this definition we speak of a hyperinflation from the month in which for the first time an inflation of at least 50 per cent is observed. Two of these hyperinflations, namely in Argentina and Nicaragua, were not finished at the time of completion of this chapter, January 1990. A fourteenth hyperinflation may just be developing in Peru, two others possibly very soon in Brazil and Yugoslavia. The latter hyperinflations are not considered since there has not yet been any real reform. The final reform of the hyperinflation in mainland China 1937-50 is also excluded since no material is available concerning the circumstances in which the hyperinflation was ended by the Communist government after the defeat of the National government in 1949. The very first hyperinflation occurred in France from 1789 to 1796. This hyperinflation was not ended by governmental measures but by natural substitution of the bad inflation money by good money. However, in France as in China in 1948, currency reform was tried in 1796. Both reforms will be discussed in this chapter.

Another successful currency reform was engineered in the free city of Danzig. Danzig had been created as a free state by the Treaty of Versailles. Since this city belonged, until this currency reform, to the German currency region it followed German inflationary developments up to the reform. Because of insufficient material about this reform it cannot be discussed in this chapter.

We therefore have a total of eleven hyperinflations to discuss (Table 8.1) from which we can draw conclusions as to the success or failure of currency reforms. These conclusions will allow us to get a picture about necessary and sufficient conditions to end hyperinflations. Besides these reforms we will consider the recent reforms to end advanced inflations in Argentina (Plan Austral, June 1985), Brazil (Plan Cruzado, February 1986) and Israel (June 1985).

2. POLITICAL ECONOMIC PRECONDITIONS FOR SUCCESSFUL REFORMS

Monetary regimes, not binding government and/or central bank and leaving them room for discretionary decisions, have always shown an inflationary tendency. This tendency is caused by the fact that politicians competing for votes with other parties to gain governmental power, have to use discretionary policies available to them to support groups of voters and specific interests to maximize their chances to be elected or reelected. Even independent central banks are not in a position to withstand fully the political pressures exerted on them. Since we have discussed these relationships in an earlier paper (Bernholz 1986) it is not necessary to revert to them here.

But if government and politicians are, in this way, interested to have room for monetary discretion, then we have to ask why they are prepared to undertake reforms to end or to lower inflation, for such measures will necessarily limit their discretionary leeway. Or to put the same question in a somewhat different way, what are the necessary conditions to make such reforms politically feasible?

In the paper mentioned, we have tried to answer this question for moderate and for hyperinflations. Concerning the latter, it has been said: 'First it has to be stated that the return to a stable monetary regime is inescapable as soon as the system has entered the phase of hyperinflation. For continuous hyperinflation has to end in a collapse so that either a reform or the substitution of the inflating currency by a stable money or by barter has to follow. In highly organized modern states usually the path of reform has been chosen.'

It is well known that during hyperinflation or already during a phase of advanced inflation, the public restricts more and more its use of the inflating currency. First, money is no longer used as a unit of account. Moreover, the decreasing real stock of money leads to liquidity problems and furthers the substitution of the national currency by foreign currencies or by other stable stores of value. As a consequence, the real revenue received by the government from the inflation tax, decreases more and more. At the same time normal revenue from ordinary taxes diminishes because of the misallocation of resources resulting from inflation and because of the time lag between declaration of taxes and their expenditure. Since the population has meanwhile learned about the mechanisms of inflation, any expansionary effect of increasing rates of inflation is limited. The demand for labour decreases and the misallocation of resources even leads to increasing unemployment. In such a situation government parties or opposition can gain a broad majority of voters if they propose a monetary reform. But in such a situation scarcely anybody believes in proposals made by the government or monetary institutions to change the inflationary situation. As a consequence, the introduction of a new monetary regime, which seems to be a credible safeguard against further inflation, is inescapable. Without the introduction of such a stable regime the reform would falter as it did in the cases of the substitution of the French *assignats* by the *mandats* in 1796 or as in the Chinese Currency Reform of 1948. If this analysis is correct then we have to expect that each hyperinflation leads to attempts at currency reform. Historically this has been true for all hyperinflations until 1985. A reform was also tried in Argentina in 1989. Only the future will show whether reforms will also be attempted in Nicaragua where hyperinflation has taken place since December 1988 and possibly in Peru.

For a currency reform to be successful to end hyperinflation, certain necessary conditions have to be fulfilled which will be discussed later on.

Table 8.1: Hyperinflations: Characteristics of Attempted Currency Reforms

Country	Date of Reform(s)	New Currency Unit?	Reform Credits		Institutional Safeguards		Exchange Rate Regime
			Domestic	Foreign	Central Bank	Budget	
Austria 1914-22	9.11.1922 (4.10.1922) (18.11.1922)	1 Schilling = 15,000 Kr. (after success)	yes	yes	yes (League of Nations)	yes	100 Kr = 0.0014$ (9,1922) (Exchange Controls)
Bolivia 1967-85		1 Boliviano = 10 Mill.Pesos (after success)	no	negligible	no. Management & 2/3 Personnel changed	no	Controlled Floating
China, Mainland 1937-49	August 1947	1 Gold Yuan = 1 Mill. Fapi	no	yes, not related to reform	note issue limited (controlled by government commission)	no	1 $ = 4 Gold Yuan (given up 11,48)
Germany 1914-23	15.- 20.11.1923	1 Rentenmark = 1 Bill. Mark (20.11.1923)	no (Credit limit of 1.2 Bill. at Rentenbank)	yes (but after success)	yes. (Rentenbank decree)	no	1$ = 4.2 Rentenmark (20.11.1923)
France 1789-86	15.3.1796	1 Mandat = 30,000 Assignats	Forced loan (before)	no	no. (no central bank existing)	no	Fixed exchange rate with real estate
Greece 1939-46	11.11.1944 25. 1.1946	1 New Drachma = 50,000,000 Dr.	no (Credit limit of 2 Bill. N Dr. at Central Bank)	Support through grants in kind	By law (violated). Treaty and Control with and by UK and USA	no	1£ = 500 N Dr. Devaluation by 68.75%, gold convertibility, 14.10.47 Bonus Certificate System

Table 8.1 (continued)

Country	Date of Reform(s)	New Currency Unit?	Reform Credits		Institutional Safeguards		Exchange Rate Regime
			Domestic	Foreign	Central Bank	Budget	
Hungary 1 1914-24	June 1924	1 Pengoe = 12,500 Kr. (after success)	yes?	yes	yes (League of Nations)	yes	Fixed Exch. Rate with £. 3,800 Pengoe = 1 Kg fine gold, 9/10 fine
Hungary 2 1939-46	1.8.1946	1 forint = $4*10^{29}$ Pengoe = $2*10^{8}$ Tax Pengoe	yes (Credit limit 300 Mill. forint at Central Bank)	yes	yes Article 50 of Central Bank Statutes revalidated	no	1$ = 11.74 Forint. Required gold reserve, no convertibility
Poland 1914-27	11.1.1924 7,1926	1 Zloty = 1.8 Mill. PMark	yes (Credit limit 50 Mill.Z. 1927 at Central Bank)	no	yes	partly	1$ = 8.91 Zloty 1$ = 5.1826 Zloty
Soviet Union 1914-24	2,1924 (from end of 1922 Tchervonetz)	1 Gold Rubel = 10^{9} Sovt. R. = 10^{11}New R. = 10^{15}Old R.	yes?	no	yes (by decree)	partly (by decree)	1$ = 5.14 Tchervonetz = 51.4 Gold Rubels (Foreign Trade Monopoly of State)
Taiwan 1937-52	15.6.1949	1 New Taiwan $ = 40,000 TaipiYuan	no	no	Note issue limited (Limits later extended)	no	1 US$ = 5 NT$

It follows from this statement that a currency reform need not be successful even if the political conditions for a reform are present. The political preconditions for successful reform are thus necessary but not sufficient conditions. But what will be the consequences if a reform ends in failure? In this case, the bad money is substituted by a 'natural' substitution by good money (Bernholz 1989). If this happens the government has to legalize the good money to get tax revenues again. For revenues out of ordinary taxes are always decreasing because of the devaluation of tax income by inflation during the time between the receipt of the revenues and the moment of the expenditure.

In the later course of the hyperinflation, even the revenue from the inflation tax usually diminishes. This happens since the basis of the inflation tax, that is the real stock of the inflating money, decreases because of the substitution of the bad through the good money. In this way the real value of the tax revenue shrinks in spite of the increase of the tax rate which is the rate of inflation. In Table 8.2, four cases of advanced inflations (among them one hyperinflation) are enumerated in which the bad money has been perfectly substituted by good money.

Table 8.2: Advanced Inflations Ending in Total Natural Substitutions of Bad Through Good Money

Country	Period	Earlier Currency Reforms that Failed[1]	Kind of Good Money	Source
USA	1776-81	March 1780: new dollar bills 1:20	specie and state paper money	Phillips 1972, p. 170ff. Bezanson 1951, pp. 325ff.
France	1789-96	February 1796: mandats terri-toriaux 1:30	gold and silver specie	Thiers 1840,
Peru	1875-87	September 1880[2]: incas 1:8	silver coins	Garland 1908, pp. 58ff.
Mexico	1913-17	June 1916: infalsificable currency 10:1	gold and silver specie	Banyai 1976, pp. 73ff. Kemmerer 1940, pp. 114-15

Notes: [1] By a currency reform, we understand a change of the monetary regime with the *intention* to produce a new stable money. The mere removal of zeros or introduction of newly denominated paper notes is not considered to be a currency reform.

[2] From the report given by Garland it is doubtful whether a currency reform was seriously intended.

We can draw one important conclusion from the fact that bad money is replaced by good money, in the case of a sufficiently high and longlasting inflation. The event of a hyperinflation seems, in itself, a sufficient condition for ending it either through a successful currency reform or through natural currency substitution.

3. SOME CHARACTERISTICS OF HYPERINFLATION

Before formulating the economic conditions for successful reforms it seems advisable to recall some characteristics of hyperinflations which are important for finding the necessary measures to end them:

1. The real stock of the inflating money, i.e., the nominal stock of money divided by the price level has decreased to a small fraction of the normal amount (see Table 8.3, Figure 8.1).
2. This fact corresponds apart from a higher velocity of the inflating money to a substitution by value-stable money (Bernholz 1989). Thus it is estimated that in August 1923, 2-3 billion gold marks in foreign currency were circulating in Germany (Beusch 1928, p. 8), whereas total circulation had amounted to 6 billion gold marks in 1914. To this amount had to be added shortly before the currency reform, 1.2 billion gold marks in value stable emergency money. By contrast the value of the inflating money amounted only to 80-800 million gold marks in the month before the currency reform (Lansburgh 1929, p. 43f.; Holtfrerich 1980, p. 209f).
3. The consolidated budget deficit of all government agencies including state-owned firms, amounts to a high fraction of total government expenditures (Table 8.4) and is mainly financed by money creation.
4. A substantial part of the deficit is caused by the inflation itself, since tax receipts out of ordinary taxes devalue before they have been expended by the government.
5. Apart from a few exceptions which can be explained, an under-valuation of the currency develops if the rate of inflation is higher than in the main trading partners. This means that the value of the domestic price level divided by the exchange rate times foreign price level falls below its normal value, i.e., below relative purchasing power parity. This undervaluation tends to diminish towards the end of hyperinflation, but this process is usually not finished at the time of the currency reform (Table 8.4, Figure 8.2).

Table 8.3: Characteristics Before and After Attempted Currency Reforms

Country	dCPI/CPI		BN/CPI		Real Rate of Interest
	before	after	before	after	%
Austria 1914-22	m90.58 (9,22)	m-8.87 (10.22) a3.83 (-9,23)	min37.72 (9,22) 53.99 (10,22)	104.83 (8,32) 110.12 (11,23)	
Bolivia 1967-85	m66.46 (8,85) m56.51 (9,85)	m-1.87 (10,85) a19.4 (-9,86) a17.55 (-5,87)	min 36.45 (1,85) (M1/CPI)	38.38 (9,85) 55.66 (10,85) 61.69 (2,86)	1273.55 (10,85) 66.67 (9,86) 36.87 (5,87)
China 1937-49	m94.26 (8,48)	m5.74 (9,48) m11.88 (10,48) 11248955 (31.8.48-25.4.49) (WPI)	min19.09 (31.8.48)	15.1. (11,48) 1.16 (25.4.49)	
Germany 1914-23	m10128.62 (11,23) m29525.71 (10,23) (WPI)	m1.43 (12,23) (WPI) a-1.68 (-12,24) (CPI)	min 4.93 (15.11.23)	16.56 (30.11.23) 44.5 (12,23)	113.18 (12,23) 11.13 (12,24)
France 1789-96	m103.4 (3,96) m21.83 (ER) (3,96) a5295.83 LPT (-3.96)	m-27.6 (ER) (4,1796) m43.04 (ER) (5,96) 235.44 (ER) (3-9,1796)	min4.41 (3,96)		
Greece 1939-46	m8895.82 (10,44) m11288 (10.11.1944) m32.86 (1,46)	m43.95 (12,44) m-8.05 (1,45) a1117,76 (-12,45) m-13.59 (2,46) a1.27 (-1,47)	min0.3 (10.11.44) 110.86 (1,46)	20.15 (12,44) 188.9 (11,45) 242.86 (2,46)	

Table 8.3 *(continued)*

Country	dCPI/CPI		BN/CPI		Real Rate of Interest
	before	after	before	after	%
Hungary 1 1914-24	m79.14 (2,24) m4.45 (5,24) (WPI)	m-0.89 (6,24) a-6.33 (-7,24)	min18.41 (8,23) 30.27 (5,24)	35.57 (6,24) 60.15 (6,25)	20.87 (1924)
Hungary 2 1939-46	m1.295*10^{16} (7,46)	m2.21 (8,46) a40.91 (-7,47) a-7.72 (-6,48)			-15.2 (10,46- 7,47) (Planned rates & credit rationing)
Poland 1914-27	m157.7 (12,23) m51.19 (1,24) a13.86 (-1,26) a24.36 (-5,26)	m5.73 (2,24) m-0.86 (3,24) a24.48 (-1,25) a11.52 (-6,27)	min104.12 (12,23) (1,1 = 100) 920 min18.9 (12,23) (6,1 926 100 (6,26)	172.12 (1,24) 31.27 (1,24) = 100) 122.78 (6,27)	
Soviet Union 1914-24	m213.19 (2,24) a55.47 (-2,24 in Tcher- wonetz)	m3.52 (3,24) a0.6 (-0,5 for 10 months)			
Taiwan 1937-52	m102 (5,1949) 729 (1-5,1949) (WPI)	82 (15.6.-12,1949) a89 (1950) a53 (1951) a 3.4 (1952) (WPI)	3.85 (5,1949)	40 (12,1950)	positive

Symbols:

BN	Banknotes in circulation	m	monthly
M1	BN and deposits of the public in checking accounts	a	annually
		d	change of ...
CPI	Cost of Living Index	min	Minimum
LPT	Local Price Tables (Price Index)	(10,22) means October, 1922	
WPI	Wholesale Price Index	(-5,87) means year from June 1986 until	
ER	Exchange Rate	May 1987	

Table 8.4: Characteristics Before and After Attempted Currency Reforms

Country	Deficit/Expenditure %		CPI/(CPIA*ER)		dU/U (Before=100)
	before	after	before	after	after
Austria 1914-22	51.36 (7-12,22) 39.64 (1922)	15.6 (1923) 1.11 (1924)	min14.97 (9,21) 45.29 (9,22)	44.09 (9,23) 55.11 (5,25)	540.63 (3,23) 248.04 (11,23) 409.26 (3,24)
Bolivia 1967-85	92.16 (1984)	17.67 (1985) -14.71 (1986)	min24.53 (9,84) 46.53 (8,85)	75.13 (9,85) 80.96 (9,86) 82.96 (2,87)	124.05 (IV 85) 133.03 (IV 86) (IV 84=100)
China 1937-49	66.67 (1-6,48)	78.25 (9-12,48)			
Germany 1914-23	88.86 (1923)	-12.19 (1924) (Only Reich)	min30.78 (2,20) 77.06 (10,23)	91.45 (30.11.23) 79.68 (12,24)	130.23 (1924)
France 1789-96	91 (1795)				
Greece 1939-46	99 (1.4.- 10.11.46) 45 (1,46)	71.1 (11.11.44- 31.3.45) 50 (3,46)	min26.19 (6,41) 49.45 (8,44) 82.34 (10,44) min35.71 (7,45) 65.79 (1,46)	127.45 (9,44) 467 (10.11.44) 175.65 (11.11.44) 191.03 (12,44) 77.69 (5,47)	91.93 (31.12.47) (7,46=100)
			CPI/ER for Gold Sovereign		
Hungary 1 1914-24	At least 27.28 (1-6,24)	8.45 (7,24-6,25)	min46.68 (1,20) 94,24 (5,25)	94.31 (6,24) 100.24 (3,25)	117.65 (1925) 137.68 (6,25)
Hungary 2 1939-46	Between m83.53- 93.22 (7,45-5,46)	21.89 (1946/47) 4.02 (1947/48)	min0.08 (23.6.46) 42.11 (30.6.46)	71.29 (8.8.46) 80.73 (31.5.47)	248.57 (8,47)

Table 8.4 (continued)

Country	Deficit/Expenditure %		CPI/(CPIA*ER)		dU/U (Before=100)
	before	after	before	after	after
Poland 1914-27	61.92 (2,1923-1,1924)	12.49 (1924)	min.14.98 (9,21) 47.03 (12,24) 46.05 (5,25)	41.3 (3,24) 47.02	174.26 (1,25)
Soviet Union 1914-24	84.12 (1921) 33.33 (1,22-9,22) 26.93 (10,22-9,23)	5.5 (10,23-9,24)	min57.14 (12,22) 97629.14 (2,24)		
Taiwan 1937-52	high	19 (1950) 13 (1951) 2(1952) -2.72 (1953)			

Symbols:
CPI   Domestic Cost of Living Index
CPIA   Foreign Cost of Living Index
ER   Exchange Rate
U   Unemployment
m   monthly
a   annually
d   Change
min   Minimum
(9,22) means September, 1922
(IV,86) means fourth quarter of 1986

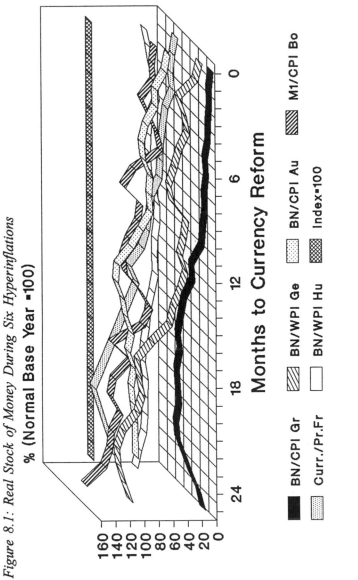

Figure 8.1: *Real Stock of Money During Six Hyperinflations*
% (Normal Base Year =100)

Local Price Tables France. Bo:Bolivia
Gr:Greece,Ge:Germany,Au:Austria,Fr:
France 1794-96,Hu:Hungary 1922-24.

Figure 8.2: Bolivian, German and Greek Hyperinflations: Real Exchange Rates 60 Months Before Attempted Currency Reforms

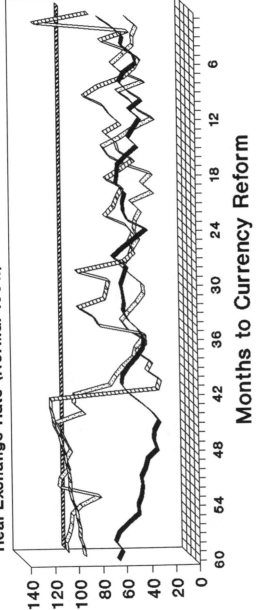

Real Exchange Rate (Normal=100%)

Months to Currency Reform

WPI/WPIUS•ER$ Germ.

CPI/CPIUS•ER$ Bolĺv.

CPI/ERGold£ Greece

Index=100

Greece: ERGold£: Exchange Rate for Gold Sovereigns

6. The population has lost all belief in government and central bank. Or
    as a Brazilian expressed it in 1984: 'If our ministers express some
    opinion we just believe the contrary'.

The characteristics of hyperinflations just mentioned suggest already
certain conclusions for promising reforms. In contrast to moderate
inflation the nominal stock of money has to be increased strongly to bring
the real stock of the national money back to its normal level. The
alternative would be a substantial fall of the price level at a constant
nominal stock of money. This would, however, lead to such a severe
depression and to such pronounced unemployment that the measures
would soon have to be repealed because of political reasons. It is because
of this that one has to be critical concerning recommendations of the
International Monetary Fund to reduce the rate of money creation and to
diminish the budget deficit *gradually* for countries experiencing advanced
inflation.

Secondly, the higher nominal stock of the national money should be
reached, at least partly, by causing the public to exchange its balances of
foreign exchange (see point 2) for buying national currency.

Thirdly, to reach the two ends just mentioned it is necessary to restore
the confidence of the population in the stability of the national currency
with the help of adequate reforms.

Fourthly the reforms have to take into account the level of the real
exchange rate.

Finally, we have to mention that because of point 2, the deficit will
already be diminished due to success in stabilizing the price level.

4. SUFFICIENT ECONOMIC AND INSTITUTIONAL CONDITIONS FOR A SUCCESSFUL CURRENCY REFORM

Today it is relatively well known which bundle of measures is sufficient
to end a hyperinflation through a successful currency reform. This fact has
recently been proved again by the successful currency reform in Bolivia
in 1985 (Bernholz 1988, Morales 1988). On the other hand, we are
scarcely able to state which measures are necessary *and* sufficient for
success. Let us first present a bundle of measures which are together
sufficient to end a hyperinflation (see Bernholz 1985):

1. Absolute limitation of the amount of credit which can be extended by the central bank to the government in the future to cover its budget deficit, or the losses of government-owned enterprises. This rule has to be anchored either in international treaties or in a constitution which can only be changed by a qualified majority of parliament. Independence of the central bank from other governmental agencies should be introduced.

    a. To realize point 1 the budget deficit of the government has to be reduced either by cutting expenditures and/or by tax increases, to a level which can be covered by taking up normal credits in the capital market. A limitation of the budget deficit by constitutional rule is advisable.

    b. In order to realize point 1a it may be necessary to reduce the domestic debt by a certain percentage, to bring down expenditures for interest to a feasible amount.

    c. The same may be true for the foreign debt. In this case, however, a moratorium on repayments and on interest payments of 8-10 years is preferable to maintain future credit worthinesss.

2. If the problem of maintaining foreign credit worthiness can be solved according to point 1c, it will be possible to receive a foreign bridging credit, which can be used to finance short-term balance of payments and budget deficits, until the balance of payments situation has improved and the budgret reforms (point 1b) become felt.

3. The real stock of money has to be increased to a normal level after it fell during the hyperinflation to a very low level. To prevent a depression in reaching this aim, the nominal stock of money has to grow adequately. Otherwise the price level would have to fall substantially. It is obvious that these aims can only be reached together if it is possible to remove inflationary expectations as much as possible, once and for all, by the reforms. For this purpose the following measures are helpful, besides those mentioned already under points 1 and 1b:

    a. A new government implementing the measures;

    b. A new directory of the central bank or even better a new central bank with different personnel;

    c. A new currency unit.

4. To make the reform socially more acceptable all private long-term credits which lost their value through the inflation should be revalued partially at the cost of debtors.

5. Confidence in the reforms would be gained by removing, as soon as possible, exchange controls and obstacles to imports. Excessive import duties and subsidies for exports should slowly be removed. During a

limited period, adequate import duties could be introduced for goods which have been sheltered until now by exchange controls.

It is obvious that certain of these conditions are not necessary for a successful currency reform. For instance, it is certainly not necessary to introduce a new currency unit even though this is helpful to change inflationary expectations. An independent central bank is only necessary if it is expected that the government would not be able, after the currency reform, to resist political pressures to finance part of government expenditures by money creation.

It follows from these short deliberations that hypotheses concerning the necessity or sufficiency of certain conditions for successful currency reforms can be empirically tested. Because of this we now turn to the empirical material concerning the success or failure of historical currency reforms.

5. DISCUSSION OF FACTORS DECISIVE FOR THE SUCCESS OF CURRENCY REFORMS

In Tables 8.3 and 8.4 we have put together some characteristics which are important for judging the consequences of currency reforms (see Table 8.1 for these reforms). Let us look first at the monthly rates of inflation before and after the currency reform (Table 8.3). It is obvious from these figures that the monthly rates of inflation are very low or even negative, immediately after the reform. In the month before the reform, however, all these rates amounted to very substantial figures. For annual rates of inflation for the year after the reform a more differentiated picture emerges. Whereas the rate remained below 3.9 per cent in Germany, Austria, Hungary 1 and the Soviet Union (10 months), it amounted to figures between 19.4 and 40.91 per cent for Bolivia, Poland and Hungary 2. In Taiwan it even reached 82 per cent for six and a half months in 1949 and 89 per cent in 1950. Finally, the annual rate of inflation amounted to 235.44 per cent in France for six months (exchange rate), in Greece to about 1,118 per cent and in China for scarcely eight months to 11,248,955 per cent.

Though the last mentioned figures, except for China, were much lower than before the currency reform, one has to conclude that the reform faltered, especially in the cases of France, Greece and China. We have thus to ask which causes could be responsible for this development. Even the reforms in Poland, Hungary 2 and Bolivia seem not to have been a full success compared to Germany, Austria, Hungary 1 and the Soviet Union and should therefore be critically analysed. We have already mentioned, moreover, that in France bad money was substituted for good money after a reform which turned out to be a failure. The same happened in 1949 in southern China where the inflating currency was replaced by the Hongkong dollar and specie coins before the Communists defeated the Kuomintang government and drove them from the mainland (Chou 1963, p. 172).

Let us first look at the budget deficits after the reform (Table 8.4) to analyse the causes of these different developments. We find that the deficit amounted to 78.25 per cent of expenditures in China from September to December 1948. In Greece the deficit reached 71.1 per cent of expenditures in the four and a half months after the reform, in the year after that date it was still 50 per cent. In France, no reduction of the deficit took place (Thiers 1840, pp. 61-64, 11-113), which in 1795 had amounted to 91 per cent of expenditures. These developments contrast with those in Germany, Hungary 1 and the Soviet Union. In these countries a budget surplus of 12.19 per cent was reached in Germany, and of 8.45 per cent in Hungary 1 in the first year after the currency reform, whereas the Soviet deficit was lowered to 5.5 per cent of expenditures. With the exception of Bolivia and Austria it seems, therefore, that the reduction of the budget deficit has been responsible for the different results of the reforms.

If one looks more closely at the different cases, this impression is strengthened and Austria can be eliminated as a different case (see below). We state further that the first currency reforms in Poland and Greece of January 1924 and November 1944, were followed by second reforms in July 1926 and January 1946. In both cases the success of the first reform was thus considered to be insufficient, though in Poland only a moderate inflation happened after the first reform. This moderate inflation came about because of the following reasons. Though the reform had ended the financing of the budget deficit by money creation through the central bank, the treasury made full use of its still remaining right to issue small change to finance the budget deficit. By the second reform this money creation by the treasury was ended and the budget deficit reduced (Heilperin 1931). As a consequence the annual rate of inflation fell from 24.48 per cent to 11.52 per cent after the second reform (Table 8.3).

In Greece the situation was less favourable. In fact, the government had not taken decisive measures to reduce or to eliminate the budget deficit in November 1944. The reduction of the deficit from 99 to 71.1 per cent happened only as a consequence of the reduction of the rate of inflation. This reduction was caused by the fact that the public increased its real stock of the inflating money from 0.3 per cent of the normal level on 10 November 1944 to 20.15 per cent in December 1944 and 188.9 per cent in November 1945. It seems that the dominant public impression was that a sincere currency reform was attempted. This impression was strengthened by the fact that monetary authorities sold gold sovereigns for several months to stabilize the exchange rate. Obviously, however, this was not a stable state of affairs. The monthly rate of inflation which still amounted to -8.05 per cent in January 1945, rose again to 1,117.76 per cent for 1945. We conclude that the first currency reform had failed since the problem of the budget deficit had not been solved. The return to hyperinflation was threatening in January 1946 when the second reform took place with substantial help from England (Delivanis and Cleveland 1949). The rate of inflation during this month already amounted to 32.86 per cent. The second reform was more successful, since it took stronger measures to reduce the deficit and to finance it, at least partially, with the help of foreign credits. The annual rate of inflation was lowered to 1.27 per cent in the first year after the reform. Complete stability, however, was not reached even then and additional measures had to be taken to fight reviving inflation during the next years, since the problems of the budget deficit had not been completely resolved even by the second reform (Delivanis and Cleveland 1949, Eliades 1954/55).

Events in Taiwan were similar to those in Greece, though the rate of inflation remained lower after the first currency reform and no second reform became necessary. But additional measures to increase price stability also became necessary in the years after the currency reform. As can be seen from Table 8.3, the rate of inflation amounted to 82 per cent in the six and a half months after the reform. It fell to an annual rate of 89 per cent in 1950, to 53 per cent in 1951 and finally to 3.4 per cent in 1952. How could this slow stabilization be reached after a currency reform which had not been very successful in the beginning? To answer this question we look at Table 8.4 again and take note that the budget deficit was successively reduced from 19 per cent in 1950 to 2 per cent of expenditures in 1952 and that in 1953 even the surplus of 2.72 per cent of total expenditures could be reached.

We have already seen that no sufficient measures to reduce the budget deficit were taken in Taiwan immediately during the currency reform. But now the government succeeded in financing part of the budget deficit by using deposits of the public and thus reducing the amount of money creation (our analysis of the Taiwanese developments is based on Makinen and Woodward 1989). Already the reform program of 15 June 1949 contained a programme for savings deposits denominated in gold. This programme allowed individuals to save the New Taiwan dollars in accounts which were convertible into gold at maturity. In May 1950, moreover, a programme was created which allowed deposits with the Bank of Taiwan and with other commercial banks which earned a positive real rate of interest. Both programmes were very successful. The first programme, however, had the disadvantage that it led to a substantial reduction of the gold reserves of the Bank of Taiwan. As a consequence, it had to be terminated in June 1950 since the currency reserves were nearing exhaustion. The deposits of the public with the banks, especially following the second programme, were partly used to extend credits to the government by way of the Bank of Taiwan. In this way a substantial part of the budget deficit was financed.

In spite of this partial success the situation just mentioned would probably have been unstable in the long run since the real indebtedness of the government increased too much. Only the outbreak of the Korean War in June 1950 secured the final success of the stabilization. The United States initiated a support programme which amounted to 10 per cent of GNP at the end of 1950. A substantial part of the programme consisted of consumption goods and raw materials which were sold by the government and strongly increased its revenue. Even then, high one digit or, exceptionally, even two digit rates of inflation remained the rule until 1961.

The example of Taiwan shows that not only the amount of the budget deficit but also the way in which it is financed is important. The reduction of the rate of inflation in the first years after the currency reform was not reached only by increasing the real stock of national money. As important was the selling of currency reserves (as in Greece) and the direct or indirect extension of value stable credits to the government by the public. But even here it is obvious that the partial failure of the currency reform was caused by an a insufficient reform of government finances and that only the elimination of the budget deficit led to the permanent success of stabilization.

It remains to discuss the cases of Austria, Hungary 2 and Bolivia. Developments in Hungary 2 (compare also Bomberger and Makinen 1983, Siklos 1989) can be completely explained by the changes of the budget deficit. After the reform in 1946/47, this deficit still amounted to 21.89 per cent of government expenditures, but fell to 4.02 per cent in 1947/48. Correspondingly, the annual rate of inflation decreased from 40.91 per cent in the first year after the currency reform to minus 7.72 per cent in the second year.

Things seemed to be different for Austria. The budget deficit still amounted to 15.6 per cent of expenditures in 1923. In 1924 it decreased to 1.11 per cent, whereas the rate of inflation had already decreased in the first year after the currency reform to 3.83 per cent. But it has to be taken into account also in this case that not only the size of the budget deficit but also the way of its financing is important for the success of the reform. In the Austrian case the government was able to finance the budget deficit by selling foreign exchange to the new Austrian National Bank. The foreign exchange stemmed mainly from foreign credits which, therefore, were finally used to cover the deficit (League of Nations 1946; de Bordes 1924).

The case of Bolivia seems to be more difficult to explain. Since the currency reform took place only at the end of August 1985, the reduction of the budget deficit in 1985 to 17.67 per cent of government expenditures implies that during the last four months of this year the budget deficit turned into a surplus. In 1986 even a surplus of 14.71 per cent of expenditures was reached. The annual rate of inflation of 19.4 per cent in the first year after the currency reform and of 17.55 per cent until May 1987 seems not to correspond to these figures. Even the decrease of the rate of inflation to about 10 per cent in 1987/88 cannot remove these problems. I have tried to show in another paper (Bernholz 1988a) that a persistent doubt in the permanent success of the reforms taken was probably the cause of these developments. These doubts in the permanent success of the reforms were probably caused by the political instability of Bolivia and the absolutely insufficient institutional safeguards for the reforms. The lack of confidence caused by these factors can also be seen in the extraordinarily high real rates of interest and in the rather small increase of the real stock of money after the currency reform, at least if we compare it with the increase of the real stock of money in other countries after the reforms (Table 8.4; Sachs 1987). Moreover, in contrast to the other successful currency reforms, the exchange rate of the Bolivian currency was not fixed, but after a first strong devaluation slowly lowered in its value to the dollar in a process of controlled floating. This fact may also have contributed to more inflationary expectations and thus finally to a higher rate of inflation.

6. CURRENCY REFORMS DURING ADVANCED INFLATION

To round off our conclusions let us look at the attempted currency reforms in Argentina, Brazil and Israel during 1985/86 (Table 8.5). We will, however, not discuss the so-called heterodox measures contained in the reform packages (compare the respective papers in Bruno et al. 1988). In these cases an attempt was made to end advanced inflations. Let us note that we speak of an advanced inflation whenever the real stock of the inflating money has fallen below its normal level. Thus hyperinflations are extreme cases of advanced inflations. Advanced inflations, even if they are not yet hyperinflations, show many of the same qualitative characteristics as the latter. Successful currency reforms have therefore to fulfil corresponding preconditions. From the deliberations of section 2, it should, however, be less probable that in this phase of an inflation, successful currency reforms can be decided on and completed. The economic conditions are not yet as difficult as has been depicted in section 2 as necessary for energetic reform attempts. It is perhaps not surprising then that in five of the six cases mentioned in this chapter, the reform measures taken have turned out to be insufficient to be successful. These are the three cases (without France) from Table 8.2 and two cases from Table 8.5, namely Argentina and Brazil. Only the Israeli reform proved to be successful.

If we look at the figures in Table 8.5 we observe that inflation in Argentina and Brazil for the year after the reform had already reached an annual rate of 50.9 and 69.8 per cent in spite of remarkable initial successes. In the years to follow, inflation increased drastically. Argentina entered with a monthly rate of 78.5 per cent hyperinflation in May 1989, and the Brazilian rate of inflation should have reached at least 1,000 per cent in 1989. In contrast to these developments, Israel showed in the year after the reform a rate of inflation of 'only' 15.8 per cent.

What are the reasons for these developments? Again the budget deficit seems to be decisive. Brazil reduced its deficit (central state, states and government-owned enterprises) from 14.7 (with central bank 27.5) to 7.37 per cent (10.8 per cent) of GNP in 1986 compared to 1985. Such a reduction should be too small to lead to a permanent success, especially since a big part of it is just a consequence of the initial decrease of the rate of inflation. The reduction of the budget deficits of Argentina and especially of Israel was much larger (Table 8.5).

The figures for Argentina are, however, probably somewhat misleading. It has to be suspected that they do not comprise all credits extended by the central bank at negative real interest rates to private and state-owned enterprises and to the provinces by way of the provincial banks. Machinea and Fanelli (1988) assert, on the other hand: 'The fiscal deficit cannot be blamed for the increase of the inflation rate. Renewed inflation was mainly caused by wage push in June and July of 1986 and a passive

Table 8.5: Advanced Inflations: Characteristics Before and After
Attempted Currency Reforms

Country		Argentina	Brazil	Israel
Date of Reform		14.6.1985	27.2.1986	1.7.1985
New Currency Unit		1 Austral = 1000 Pesos Arg.	1 Cruzado = 1000 Cruzeiros	
dCPI/CPI	before	m30.53 (6,85) a1036.17 (-6,85)	m22.4 (2,86) a289,3 (-2,86)	a500 (1984) 350 (1-5,85)
	after	m6.19 (7,85) a50.9 (-7,86) a116.6 (-7,87)	m-0.9 (3,86) a69.8 (-3,87)	m27.5 (7,85) a15.8 (-6,86)
Deficit/GNP (Arg.:GDP)	before	11.9 (3-6,85)	14.7 (1985) wo. CB 27.5 (1985) w. CB	12.5 (1-6,85)
	after	3.2 (7,85-3,86)	7.37 (1986) wo. CB 10.8 (1986) w. CB	2.5. (1-6,86) 3.5 (7,85-6,86)
Unemployment after Reform			125 (II,1986) 108 (III, 1986) (1-6,85=100)	76.82 (2,1987) (2,1986=100)
Credits Domestic		no	no	no
f. Reforms Foreign		no	yes	yes
Real Interest Rate after Reform		107 (IV, 1985) (for Firms)	194.27 (3,87) (Over Night Money)	168.3 (7-12,85) 35.3 (1-6,86) 25.6 (7-12,86)

Sources: Banco Central do Brasil, Relatorios 1986 and 1987; International Monetary Fund, International Financial Statistics; Fischer (1987).

Symbols:

dCPI/CPI	Rate of Inflation (Cost of Living Index)
GNP	Gross National Product
GDP	Gross Domestic Product
m	monthly
a	annually
wo.CB	without Central Bank
w. CB	with Central Bank
(6,85)	means June 1986
(-2,86)	means year from March 1985 until February 1986

monetary policy from April onward. Nominal interest rates lagged behind inflation, and in some months real rates turned negative' (p. 142). It has to be asked, however, why the central bank extended credit at negative rates of interest in spite of its 'passive policy'.

And, in fact, the following quotations from Canavese and di Tella (1988) seem rather to show that at least from April 1986 a hidden financing of public deficits took place: 'Even so, the money supply kept growing around 5per cent per month after April 1986. The commitment not to finance fiscal deficits by printing money was held, but some enterprises failed to collect enough revenues to pay interest on their external debts, forcing the central bank to take care of those external payments using reserves without a corresponding absorption of money, a covert way to bypass the original commitment. Moreover, the central bank rediscounted paper of official financial institutions, which were financing debts of the provinces, even if it was quite unlikely that they would be repaid' (pp. 163f.).

It seems to follow that the total budget deficit including this covered financing has been a decisive factor for the again accelerating inflation (de Pablo 1988 reaches similar conclusions).

In Israel things developed more favourably. The country received substantial American financial contributions, which were larger than the budget deficit remaining after the reform. Thus no money creation was necessary to finance the budget deficit (Fischer 1987; p. 277, Bruno and Piterman 1988).

The above discussion of sixteen attempted currency reforms during advanced inflations (among them thirteen hyperinflations) has demonstrated the decisive importance for successful reforms of removing or drastically reducing the budget deficit. We could, however, also convince ourselves of the importance of how the remaining deficit was financed and that the public believed in the adequacy and permanency of the measures taken. This means that the political institutional changes implied by the reform should be such that people believe in the permanent stability of the new monetary regime.

7. THE IMPORTANCE OF INSTITUTIONAL REFORMS

During a longlasting advanced inflation or a hyperinflation, government and central bank lose any public credibility. For a currency reform to succeed it is, however, of decisive importance that the measures taken restore at once and as much as possible, the confidence in the currency. Only then will the public be prepared to expect a low rate of inflation or even a total end to it. And only then are people ready to maintain increased real cash holdings of the national currency. If this is the case, then a strong transitory increase of the nominal stock of money will be possible, together with a stable or very slowly rising price level so that the rate of inflation and the budget deficit decrease as a consequence only of the dramatic fall of inflationary expectations. A relatively stable level of prices and a strongly rising nominal and real stock of money are, however, necessary on their part to prevent a strong recession or even a depression implying a substantial growth of unemployment. The latter has, however, to be prevented because otherwise it might politically not be feasible to maintain the measures taken, at least in democracies. Moreover, a reduction of the budget deficit is inescapable, as we have seen, to prevent future inflationary money creation to finance it and thus for the permanent success of the currency reform.

A fundamental change in the expectations of the population is thus a necessary ingredient of any currency reform in an advanced inflation or hyperinflation. Or to quote Thomas Sargent (1982): the reforms have to imply an abrupt change of 'the policy regime' and 'the fiscal regime' in the sense of 'setting deficits now and in the future [in such a way] that is sufficiently binding as to be widely believed' (p. 42).

From the point of view of public choice theory however, we have to ask ourselves how the credibility of government and central bank can be restored, given the fact that it has been absolutely eroded. Certainly, the taking of office by a new government and/or of a new central bank directory may help. But did not many changes of governing parties or changes in the directory of the central bank happen before without a substantive change of economic policy and without a notable change in the inflationary situation?

A solution to this problem lies in binding the hands of the central bank and/or government in such a way that by changing the institutions ministers and central bank directors are no longer capable of financing the government budget deficit partially or completely by creating new money. To quote Sargent (1982) again: 'The essential measures that ended hyperinflation in each of Germany, Austria, Hungary (1), and Poland were, first, the creation of an independent central bank that was legally committed to refuse the governmment's demand for additional ... credit and, second, a simultaneous alteration in the fiscal policy regime' (p. 89).

With the help of Table 8.1, let us now discuss the importance of the institutional safeguards. The success of the reforms, measured in terms of the rate of inflation during the year after them, was greatest in Austria, Germany and Hungary 1. In all these cases a new independent central bank was created which was not allowed to extend to the government more than a strictly limited amount of credit or only credit sufficiently covered, for instance, by gold and foreign exchange. Austria and Hungary signed protocols of agreement with the League of Nations in which they were obliged to balance their budget and agreed that a commissioner of the League of Nations should monitor whether these measures had been adequately taken (League of Nations 1946; de Bordes 1924; Sargent 1982; Heilperin 1931).

In Poland things did not develop as advantageously in the first year after the reform since the rate of inflation still amounted to 24.48 per cent. But even here, as mentioned by Sargent, a new independent central bank was created which was not allowed to extend credit to the government for more than 50 million zloty. We have already seen, however, that the Ministry of Finance could still issue small change and that it used this right to finance a remaining budget deficit. This means that the institutional reforms had been insufficient, a fact not discussed by Sargent. Neither does Sargent mention the second reform after moderate inflation which closed this gap and led to the final stabilization.

The reforms in France, China, Greece in 1944 and Taiwan in 1949 led to failures. In all these cases institutional safeguards were either insufficient or were totally absent. An independent central bank was not instituted in any of these cases. In Greece, China and Taiwan a limit for the issue of banknotes was decreed. But in the first two cases this limit was soon surpassed, whereas Taiwan increased the limit during the following years. In China the committee charged with the responsibility of monitoring whether the limitation of the note issue had been observed, consisted mainly of members of the government. It is obvious that such a committee is more interested in financing the budget deficit than in limiting the creation of money.

The second Greek currency reform which succeeded in stabilizing the currency was based on the Anglo-Hellenic Convention of 24 January 1946. Under this convention a currency committee was established which had the statutory right to decide, by unanimous vote, about an increase of the volume of banknotes. Besides three members of the government an Englishman and an American also belonged to the committee. As a consequence a real control of the money in circulation and thus indirectly of the budget deficit had been institutionalized. Similar to the cases of Germany, Austria and Hungary 1, where the reintroduction of the gold (exchange standard) was a main ingredient of the reform, Greece, too, introduced gold convertibility of the new drachma at a fixed parity (Delivanis and Cleveland 1949; Makinen 1989). One should recall that a gold (exchange) standard also limits strongly the possibility of the central bank creating money, if free convertibility and a fixed gold parity are present. This helped also in the case of Greece though exchange controls were not absent. The institutional safeguards taken by the second Greek currency reform explain why the rate of inflation fell to 1.27 per cent in the year after the 1946 currency reform. Note that this happened though the budget deficit decreased only slowly.

Let us now discuss the cases of Bolivia, Hungary 2 and the Soviet Union. In Bolivia, as has already been mentioned, no sufficient institutional safeguards were introduced. It is true that a new government instituted the reforms, but this fact was not very important considering the political instability characteristic of Bolivia for decades. Also the exchange of most of the personnel of the central bank could not compensate for the dependence of the latter from the government. It has to be suspected that the remaining inflation of 10-19 per cent, in spite of a balanced budget or even of a budget surplus, can be explained only by the insufficient institutional changes guaranteeing the stability of the new monetary regime (Bernholz 1988).

By contrast, in the cases of Hungary 2 and of the Soviet Union, institutional changes to safeguard the reforms were undertaken. In Hungary, article 50 of the statutes of the central bank was revalidated. Under this article any granting of credit to the government was strictly limited. But how credible was this measure, given the threat of a total Communist takeover of the government? Should this political instability, together with the remaining budget deficit of 21.89 per cent of expenditures for 1946-47, provide an explanation for the remaining high rate of inflation of 40.91 per cent in the first year after the reform (for another explanation see Bomberger and Makinen 1983, pp. 819-21)?

In the Soviet Union, too, institutional safeguards were not missing but they were not very credible, for in a dictatorship or oligarchy institutional safeguards are basically not possible, since power holders can remove or transgress them at their discretion at any time. Nevertheless they were probably believed, for in spite of the remaining budget deficit of 5.5 per cent of expenditures, the rate of inflation dropped to minus 0.5 per cent for the ten months after the reform.

The case of Russia makes it quite clear that an institutional safeguarding of reforms to stabilize expectations is, in a true sense, only possible in a constitutional state with division of power. However, in such a system, certain oligarchies or even simple parliamentary majorities cannot change or remove any time institutional rules limiting their discretionary powers. There must exist institutions or agencies holding certain rights to make public decisions, which are independent of the government to limit its discretionary powers. Moreover, independent institutions like constitutional and administrative courts, which have the right to control whether the different governmental agencies have observed the institutional rules and which can force them to do so have to be present. The example of the Soviet Union, however, also shows that the population may even trust a dictatorial regime.

Finally we have to stress that institutional safeguards are not necessary for the success of currency reforms. This is proved by the examples of Taiwan and Bolivia. These cases show, however, that currency reforms which are not secured by institutional changes, take more time to be successful and imply even higher real interest rates after the reform (Table 8.3), a fact which hinders real economic development. It is well known, however, that even in the long run, discretionary monetary regimes show a tendency towards inflation, since they are not bound by institutionalized limits (Bernholz 1986, pp. 83-5). This tendency towards inflation is even more pronounced if, additionally, there is no independence of the central bank, so that no institutional safeguarding of the monetary regime is present (Parkin and Bade 1978).

8. THE IMPORTANCE OF INCOMPLETE INFORMATION FOR THE CONSEQUENCES OF REFORMS

It follows from Tables 8.3 and 8.4 that the rate of inflation fell drastically and that the real stock of the national money increased immediately after currency reforms. Note that this happened even during currency reforms which failed. The same is true for the three reforms during advanced inflations described in Table 8.5.

This fact can be explained only by assuming that most economic agents had no clear picture about the kind and about the chances of success of the measures taken, or about the nature of the change of the monetary regime. The majority of the public must have assumed, even in the cases of the unsuccessful reforms, that with a certain probability, they would lead to success. Or, as expressed by Makinen and Woodward (1989) 'In Taiwan the public appears to have believed in a nonexistent regime change — based on the kind of evidence used by Sargent. And Taiwan is not an isolated instance. Makinen (1984) has shown that in Greece the public reacted favorably to two reforms [one of them we have not included as a reform in Tables 8.1, 8.3 and 8.4] that failed to contain elements necessary to stabilize prices. Thus, the public may have difficulties in distinguishing regime changes from superficial changes in economic policy' (p. 103).

From our tables we can add France 1796, China 1949, Argentina 1985 and Brazil 1986 as additional evidence to prove this hypothesis. The wrong interpretation of events by a majority of economic agents can be easily understood. A vast majority of the public is not versed in monetary theory or consists of inflation specialists. As a result most citizens could not correctly judge the consequences to be expected from the measures taken, even if they had all necessary information about the kind and nature of these measures and about the institutional safeguards taken. But even this cannot be expected. It follows then, also, that the vast majority of the public cannot be sure whether sufficient measures for a successful currency reform will lead, in fact, to a success. Similarly, they cannot know whether insufficient measures might not be successful. The difference between the two cases may be only that a greater number of citizens believe with a higher subjective probability in the success of reforms containing sufficient ingredients for a success.

The very high real interest rate which usually prevails for about one year after the currency reform (compare Germany and Hungary 1 in Table 8.3) and the fact that the real stock of the national money remains for months below its normal level (Table 8.3), seem to be an indication for the correctness of this hypothesis. For note that in these cases, the budget deficit had been successfully reduced or even turned into a budget surplus and that the reforms had been institutionally safeguarded. For Austria, de Bordes (1924) explains: 'The interest on mortgage credit is still so high ... that farmers cannot get sufficient credit for intensive cultivation' (p. 226) 'The [National] Bank is attempting to bring down the extremely high rate of interest, which forms a severe handicap on Austrian industries' (p. 227).

It has to be admitted that a different interpretation of the reasons for the subnormal real stock of money and the very high real interest rates can be made. According to this other hypothesis, the phenomena mentioned were caused by the fact that, by a too restrictive monetary policy, the central bank prevented the real stock of money reaching the normal level (Dornbusch and Cardoso 1987). It seems, however, that such a hypothesis about the policy of the central bank, which would certainly be feasible, does not describe the relationships correctly in the cases discussed in this chapter. For if the public is generally not able to discriminate between sufficient and insufficient measures for a successful currency reform, then the opposite must also be true. Secondly, we know, for instance, for Germany that the interest rate on bonds denominated in units of wheat, coal or gold showed a normal level. How can the 7.87-13.34 per cent of nominal interest rates on bonds denominated in gold be explained in comparison to interest rates reaching from 30-26.32 per cent for monthly money between January and June 1924, if not by remaining inflationary expectations (Bernholz 1988b, pp. 13-15)? Finally, it has to be mentioned that unemployment increased substantially, even in the three most successful cases of currency reforms (Table 8.4 compare also Wicker 1986).

Taking the evidence together, one can agree with Sargent (1982) that a change of the monetary and fiscal regime taken at one stroke will change expectations much more rapidly and much more strongly than gradual economic measures. It will thus lead to a smaller recession and to a smaller increase of unemployment than the latter. But it contradicts the empirical evidence to asssume that currency reforms can bring about an immediate and complete change of inflationary expectations.

ENDNOTE

*   With a few minor corrections, reprinted with kind permission of Rodopi Publishers, from G. Radnitzky and H. Bouillon (eds.), *Government: Servant or Master?*, Amsterdam and Atlanta 1993, pp. 141-70. The original paper was completed in 1988.

REFERENCES

Banyai, R.A. (1976), *Money and Finance in Mexico During the Constitutionalist Revolution 1913-17*, Tai Wan Enterprises, Taipei.

Bernholz, P. (1985), 'Hyperinflation and Monetary Reform', *Swiss Bank Corporation*: *Prospects* 1, February, pp. 1-6.

Bernholz, P. (1986), 'The Implementation and Maintenance of a Monetary Constitution', *Cato Journal* 6, pp. 477-511.

Bernholz, P. (1988a), 'Hyperinflation and Currency Reform in Bolivia: Studied from a General Perspective', *Journal of Institutional and Theoretical Economics* 144, pp. 747-71.

Bernholz, P. (1988b), 'Inflation, Monetary Regime and the Financial Asset Theory of Money' *Kyklos* 41, pp. 5-34.

Bernholz, P. (1989), 'Currency Competition, Inflation, Gresham's Law and Exchange Rate', *Journal of Institutional and Theoretical Economics* 145, pp. 465-88.

Beusch, P. (1928), *Währungszerfall und Währungsstabilisierung*, Julius Springer, Berlin.

Bezanson, A. (1951), *Prices and Inflation During the American Revolution, Pennsylvania, 1770-90*, University of Pennsylvania Press, Philadelphia.

Bomberger, W.E. and Makinen, G.A. (1983), 'The Hungarian Hyperinflation and Stabilization of 1945-46', *Journal of Political Economy* 91, pp. 801-24.

Bordes, J. van Walré de (1924), *The Austrian Crown*, P.S. King & Son, Westminster.

Bruno, M. et al. (eds.) (1988), *Inflation Stabilization. The Experience of Israel, Argentina, Brazil, Bolivia and Mexico*, The MIT Press, Cambridge, Mass. and London.

Bruno, M. and Piterman, S. (1988), 'Israel's Stabilization: A Two-Year Review', in M. Bruno, et al. (eds.), *Inflation Stabilization. The Experience of Israel, Argentina, Brazil, Bolivia and Mexico*, pp. 3-47.

Canavese, A.J. and di Tella, G. (1988), 'Inflation Stabilization or Hyperinflation Avoidance? The Case of the Austral Plan in Argentina, 1985-87', in M. Bruno et al. (eds.), *Inflation Stabilization. The Experience of Israel, Argentina, Brazil, Bolivia and Mexico*, pp. 153-90.

Chou, S.H. (1963), *The Chinese Inflation, 1939-1949*, Columbia University Press, New York and London.

Delivanis, D. and Cleveland, W.C. (1949), *Greek Monetary Developments 1939-48*, Indiana University, Bloomington, Indiana.

Dornbusch, R. and Cardoso, E.A. (1987), 'Brazil's Tropical Plan', *The American Economic Review* 77, Papers and Proceedings, pp. 288-92.

Eliades, E.A. (1954/55), 'Stabilization of the Greek Economy and the 1953 Devaluation of the Drachma', *IMF Staff Papers* 4, pp. 22-72.

Fischer, S. (1987), 'The Israeli Stabilization Program, 1985-86', *The American Economic Review* 77, Papers and Proceedings, pp. 275-8.

Garland, A. (1908), *Estudio sobre los Medios Circulantes Usados en el Peru*, Imprenta la Industria, Lima.

Heilperin, M.A. (1931), *Le Problème monétaire d'après-guerre et sa solution en Pologne, en Autriche et en Tchecoslovaquie*, Recueil Sirey, Paris.

Holtfrerich, C.-L. (1980), *Die deutsche Inflation*, de Gruyter, Berlin and New York.

Kemmerer, E.W. (1940), *Inflation and Revolution*, Princeton University Press, Princeton, NJ.

Lansburgh, A. (1929), 'Artikel Banken (Notenbanken)', in L. Elster & and A. Weber (eds.), *Handwörterbuch der Staatswissenschaften*, Ergänzungsband, Gustav Fischer, Jena, 35ff.

League of Nations (1946), *The Course and Control of Inflation. A Review of Monetary Experience in Europe After World War I*, Economic, Financial and Transit Department, League of Nations, Geneva.

Machinea, J.L. and Fanelli, J.M. (1988), 'Stopping Inflation: The Case of the Austral Plan in Argentina, 1985-87', in M. Bruno et al. (eds.), *Inflation Stabilization. The Experience of Israel, Argentina, Brazil, Bolivia and Mexico*, pp. 111-52.

Makinen, G.E. (1984a), 'The Greek Stabilization of 1943-46', *American Economic Review* 74, pp. 1067-74.

Makinen, G.E. (1984b), 'The Greek Hyperinflation and Stabilization of 1943-1946', *Journal of Economic History* XLVI, pp. 795-805.

Makinen, G.E. and Woodward, T.G. (1989), 'The Taiwanese Hyperinflation and Stabilization of 1945-1952', *Journal of Money, Credit and Banking* 21, pp. 90-105.

Morales, J.A. (1988), 'Inflation Stabilization in Bolivia', in M. Bruno et al. (eds.), *Inflation Stabilization. The Experience of Israel, Argentina, Brazil, Bolivia and Mexico*, 307-346.

Pablo, J.C. de (1988), 'Comment' in M. Bruno et al. (eds.), *Inflation Stabilization. The Experience of Israel, Argentina, Brazil, Bolivia and Mexico*, pp. 195-201.

Paldam, M. (1985), *Inflation and Political Instability in Eight Latin American Countries*, Institut of Economics, Aarhus Universitet, Denmark, Memo No. 3, pp. 1946-83.

Parkin, M. and Bade, R. (1978), 'Central Bank Laws and Monetary Policies: A Preliminary Investigation', in M.A. Porter (ed.), *The Australian Monetary System in the 1970s*, Monash University, Melbourne, pp. 24-39.

Philipps, H. Jr. (1972), *Continental Paper Money*, Augustus M. Kelley, Clifton. First. Ed. 1865.

Sachs, J. (1987), 'The Bolivian Hyperinflation and Stabilization', *The American Economic Review* 77, Papers and Proceedings, pp. 279-83.

Sargent, T. (1982), 'The Ends of Four Big Inflations', in R.E. Hall (ed.), *Inflation: Causes and Effects*, University of Chicago Press, Chicago and London.

Siklos, P.L. (1989), 'The End of the Hungarian Hyperinflation of 1945-1946', *Journal of Money, Credit and Banking* 21, pp. 135-47.

Thiers, L.A. (1840), *History of the French Revolution*, Translated by Frederick Shoberl, 3 vols, Carey & Hart, Philadelphia. First French edn 1825.

Wicker, E. (1986), 'Terminating Hyperinflation in the Dismembered Habsburg Monarchy', *The American Economic Review* 76, pp. 350-61.

9. The End of the Hungarian Hyperinflation of 1945-1946 *

Pierre L. Siklos

1. INTRODUCTION

Hyperinflation has been described as a laboratory for the study of the effects of a change in the rules under which fiscal and monetary policies are conducted (Sargent 1993, ch. 3). The rational expectations approach to macroeconomics concludes that a hyperinflation may be ended abruptly without resulting in significant output or unemployment costs. In order for the no transition costs hypothesis to be applicable, however, credible economic reforms must be introduced. In other words, agents' perceptions about the kind of fiscal and monetary policies in place must have changed.

There are now several papers disputing the above interpretation of the end of hyperinflations this century (Garber 1982; Wicker 1986; Dornbusch and Fischer 1986). Garber (1982), for example, argues that significant negative real effects appeared approximately one and a half years after the end of the German hyperinflation, even though economic agents apparently correctly perceived a change in policy regime signalling price stability. The reason is that the capital goods industry was the recipient of subsidies financed by the inflation tax. The resulting distortion in relative prices produced transition costs when the policy of subsidies was terminated after the end of the hyperinflation, despite credible announcements of a change in regime leading to price stability. Garber's argument illuminates the need to explore possible changes in the 'natural rate' of unemployment (the unemployment rate at a stable inflation rate) following a hyperinflation. By contrast, Sargent (1993, ch. 3), Bomberger and Makinen (1983, hereafter BM) and Wicker (1986) did not account for possible changes in the natural rate of unemployment in their studies of hyperinflation, though they devoted some attention to possible sources of change in the unemployment rate. More generally, Garber's evidence underlines the need to consider the widest possible range of evidence to assess not only the credibility of economic policies but also the magnitude of economic costs — the so-called transition costs — in achieving price stability. A similar point was made by Eichengreen (1986).

The purpose of this chapter is to assess the significance of the no transition costs hypothesis in the case of the Hungarian hyperinflation of 1945-46. In doing so, new evidence is presented of the kind favourable to Sargent's (1993, ch.3) viewpoint by extending BM's (1983) earlier study of the Hungarian experience.

The evidence suggests that, by the end of 1946, the state of Hungary's economy compared favourably with that before the outbreak of World War II. Nevertheless, the extreme inflation experienced in Hungary did lead to conditions that would not likely arise in an episode of milder inflation, and it is argued that these may account for the transition costs to price stability.

The chapter is organized as follows. Section 2 addresses the question of credibility in the reforms leading to price stability. Section 3 deals with the transition costs following the end of hyperinflation. Section 4 presents a summary and some concluding remarks.

2. PREWAR POLICIES AND THE CREDIBILITY OF THE AUGUST 1946 REFORMS

By the late 1930s Hungary allied itself with Germany, which had decided to put its economy on a war footing. Since Hungary was essentially an agrarian economy (Berend and Ránki 1979), the prospect of assisting Germany's war preparations presented Hungary with the opportunity to industrialize more rapidly than would otherwise be possible. However, as policymakers were concerned about excess demand inflation, they sought to implement industrialization in a gradual fashion.[1] After war was declared in Europe, spending on the industrialization programme was accelerated. Thus, Ausch (1958, p. 41) calculates that, until 1942, changes in government debt financed approximately half of the spending for the war. In 1944, this figure reached 91 per cent.[2] As the war dragged on Germany increasingly was unable or refused outright to pay for goods imported from Hungary.

The devastation and economic consequences of the war are well known and, hence, need not be repeated here (e.g., see BM 1983). Suffice it to say that losses in national wealth were significant, and perhaps greater than that suffered by any other Western European nation, with the exception of Belgium or Germany.[3]

By March 1946, the Supreme Economic Council (SEC)[4] was completing plans for the introduction of a new currency, as well as other economic reforms, to be implemented sometime in mid-summer.[5] The introduction of a new currency, called the forint (florin), was planned for the second half of July. Also during this period, the SEC began stockpiling foodstuffs, in particular, to ensure an adequate supply in the weeks following stabilization.[6] At the same time, a political decision had been made not to end inflation through foreign credits.

Although some of the factors contributing to the credibility of the reforms of August 1946 have been noted elsewhere (BM 1983; Siklos 1987a), some new evidence is available to reaffirm the notion of a credible regime change leading to price stability.

A decision in late spring 1946 on a system of taxation, as well as on a policy of rapid nationalization, meant that taxes could be readily collected from what would become state enterprises. It was expected, however, that during the first three months following stabilization, budget deficits would have to be tolerated (Siklos 1987a). Moreover, the planners of the stabilization were determined to set the quantity of new currency to be issued in line with their estimates of the postwar output of the Hungarian economy (Ausch 1958). Other details of the package of reforms were gradually announced in newspapers (see *Szabad Nép* [Free People]), beginning in April 1946, thereby enabling policymakers to gauge society's mood about the viability of the stabilization plan prior to its implementation. Finally, the SEC deliberately set a high value for the forint in terms of gold and the US dollar to ensure that demand for the new currency would be relatively strong and thereby, in part, further ensure its general acceptability. As a result, the additional reserves subsequently purchased from individuals by the central bank were to prove larger than expected.[7] This was to have some bearing on the quantity of notes to be issued during the first year following stabilization.[8]

Estimates of velocity of circulation for the entire hyperinflationary period, with the exception of the last month of the inflation (July 1946), and for several months following stabilization, are available and may be used in assessing the path of expected inflation. They are shown in Table 9.1. If we use a demand for money function of the type formulated by Cagan (1956), based on the Cambridge version of the quantity theory (Laidler 1993, pp. 49-51), in which the reciprocal of velocity is inversely related to expected inflation, the data suggest that expected inflation rose very rapidly during the first half of 1946.[9] By the end of September 1946, two months following stabilization, the data suggest a sharp fall in velocity which continued until April 1947, consistent with a rapid fall in expected inflation. The above scenario is indicative of the phenomenon

Table 9.1 Estimates of Velocity of Circulation

Month	Velocity (1945 July =1)
August 1945	1.4
September	1.5
October	3.3
November	5.3
December	7.9
January 1946	6.0
February	16.0
March	83.7
April	130.4
May	192.0
June	315.2

Month	Velocity (1946 Aug. =1)
August 1946	1.00
September	0.59
October	0.49
November	0.45
December	0.38
January 1947	0.38
February	N.A.
March	N.A.
April	0.27
May	0.28

Sources: Ausch (1958, p. 124). Using the Quantity theory equation ($MV=Py$, where M = money supply, V = velocity, P = Price level, y = real output) Ausch substitutes the volume of goods (principally foodstuffs) produced for y, and consumer prices for P, to estimate V. M is defined as notes in circulation. Data are end of month figures. Figures for the Aug. 1946 to May 1947, were calculated from data in *Gazdaságstatisztikai Tájekoztato* (Economic Statistics Bulletin), 1946-1947, pp. 39, 335, using a measure almost identical to the one used by Ausch.

that led Sargent to suggest that hyperinflation may be ended abruptly.

The stabilization plan, however, could also be interpreted as being akin to a real bills policy of the kind discussed by Sargent and Wallace (1982).[10] Thus, except initially, the central bank did not resort to the discounting of government debt, unlike during the period of hyperinflation, but accommodated 'private' borrowers (these were all to become state owned enterprises) by advancing loans to finance their debt. Thus, on 1 August 1946, advances by the central bank to borrowers, other than the government, stood at 0.054 million forint. By 31 December 1947, the same total stood at 1,651.8 million forint while advances to the government reached 124.8 million forint. (See *Magyar Nemzeti Bank Havi Közleményei* [Monthly Bulletins of the National Bank of Hungary] 1947, p. 568.) By contrast, between July 1945 and August 1946, private borrowers were able to obtain up to 100 million pengő from the government (*Szabad Nép* [Free People] 31 July 1945). Based on BM's (1983) figures, this represented a very small proportion of total advances by the central bank. This would explain why money growth produced dramatically different implications for inflation before and after August 1946, though this fact need not necessarily surprise someone using the quantity theory (Laidler 1987).

3. THE TRANSITION COSTS OF STABILIZATION

The reforms leading to price stability appear to have been credible. Yet, as will be seen below, transition costs following hyperinflation did occur. It seems useful to describe them in order to highlight distinctions between an economy emerging from a hyperinflation and one experiencing milder inflation as well as because the real effects following the Hungarian hyperinflation cannot be fully explained by the transition to a peacetime economy.

3.1 Price Distortions

Garber (1982) argued that hyperinflation in Germany produced a bias in favour of investment goods over consumer goods. As prices for capital goods are unavailable, Figure 9.1 plots the ratio of wholesale prices (mostly for industrial goods) to consumer prices in Hungary for the period 1938 to 1948. Data for 1938 to 1942, inclusive, are annual. Thereafter, with the exception of the December 1944 to December 1945 figures, for which ratio data are unavailable, the data are monthly.[11] Since a large

Figure 9.1 Ratio of Wholesale to Consumer Prices

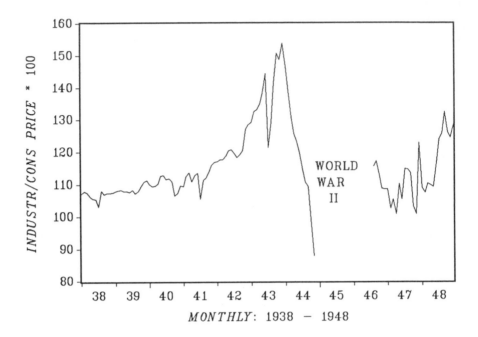

MONTHLY: 1938 − 1948

Note: December 1944-1945 data not available.
Sources: Wholesale Price Index: *Magyar Statisztikai Évkőnyv.* [Hungarian Statistical Yearbook],
(1943-46), p. 167, column IV, except for January to July 1946, which is from *The State of the
Hungarian Currency.* Budapest: Hungarian General Credit Bank 1946, p. 18, Table V.
Consumer Price Index: *Atszámitas a Pengőtol a Forintig.* [Conversion from the Pengő to the
Forint.] Budapest: National Bank of Hungary 1946.

proportion of capital was imported (Berend 1966; Ausch 1958; Basch 1943), Figure 9.1 suggests how resources may have moved away from consumer goods towards investment goods. Wholesale prices rose steadily relative to consumer prices until 1944, only to fall to below the prewar level after August 1946. In fact, the ratio of prices was not, on average, much higher during the January to July 1946 period, that is, during hyperinflation, than during the last prewar year (1938), the ratio being 95.8 in the latter year, and averaging 107.8 in the period of high inflation. To be sure, the pattern of relative prices reflects the bias introduced because of the war effort but the levels did not reach anywhere near those reported by Garber for Germany (1982, p. 16). More importantly, the peak in the relative price of investment goods, in late 1943 and early 1944, occurred well before hyperinflationary levels were reached. Also, the resources which flowed into industry because of war preparations were simply converted after the war into heavy industry in peacetime, a common development in Eastern European countries (Spulber 1957), and not into consumer goods as in Germany. Moreover, employment in investment goods industries, which were capital intensive, does not appear to have risen significantly in Hungary during the early 1940s, as it did in the German case, primarily because of a shortage of skilled labour (Ausch 1958, ch. 2), and also, in part, due to the legacy of German economic policies of the 1930s outlined briefly in section 2. Finally, as alluded to above, the proceeds of the inflation tax were not extensively shared with private borrowers during the hyperinflation. Hence, relative price movements shown in Figure 9.1 did not result from any massive subsidies to the private sector, unlike the earlier German experience.

Although price distortions of the kind suggested by Garber did not arise in Hungary, the SEC's decision in mid-1946, about how to set prices at the beginning of August 1946, may have produced price distortions of a kind that led to real economic effects following stabilization.[12]

Industrial prices were initially set high relative to agricultural prices (Siklos 1987a).[13] This may be seen in Figure 9.1, which shows a sharp increase in the ratio of wholesale prices to consumer prices in August 1946, relative to the 1938 figure. The SEC's reasoning was that, since reconstruction was being achieved relatively more rapidly in agriculture than in industry, a greater price incentive was necessary for the latter to redevelop quickly. Yet, prices set by the government did not prevent continued black markets in several commodities (principally food), despite severe legal restrictions on their existence. The SEC reluctantly relaxed price regulations. The result can be seen in Figure 9.1 which shows a drop in wholesale prices relative to consumer prices into 1947.[14] Combined with severe credit constraints imposed by the government, the sole source of credit in an economy increasingly nationalized, the drop in wholesale prices led to a drop in output and an increase in unemployment. Similar difficulties affected the production of raw materials, which also experienced falling output in 1947. The above policy, perhaps more than any other, produced a recession in 1947. Whether or not the resulting economic effects should be labelled transition costs is debatable. If not, the impact of the SEC's pricing policy actually reinforces Sargent's scenario for a potential abrupt end to even a mild inflation, assuming that credible policies are introduced.

3.2 Unemployment

Data (see Siklos 1991 for additional details), reveals rapid progress in employment between July 1945, the postwar low, and December of the same year, in many key industries. It is clear that the effects of reconstruction began to show up early in some industries. Steel, leather, rubber and textile industries, were recovering quickly from the effects of the war. Other industries, however, were still lagging. By mid-1946, total industrial employment was above the prewar level (see *MNBHK* [Monthly Bulletins of the National Bank of Hungary] 1948). Yet, a policy introduced by the government in late 1945, and later reversed again by the end of 1946, would also have a significant impact on employment and unemployment.

The Hungarian government created a Reconstruction Ministry (see *Magyar Közlöny* 1946 [Hungarian Gazette]), and its first task was to hire for the reconstruction effort all those who were not otherwise employed.[15] This effort was aimed primarily at repairing roads, bridges and railway links, and the harvesting of crops. However, once the stabilization plan was put in place, the Reconstruction Ministry was wound down and it ceased operations by the end of 1946. One reason is that much of the destroyed infrastructure had, by then, been repaired. Moreover, the agricultural sector essentially was restored to its prewar state. Clearly then, such policies affected the natural rate of unemployment, as it is generally interpreted, which would have risen following stabilization, particularly in early 1947.

It is not surprising, therefore, that unemployment figures appear to show steady increases during 1947, as shown in Table 9.2. The data are not seasonally adjusted. However, since the figures exclude the agricultural sector, there should be little bias in interpreting them as shown.[16] By 1949 continued growth in employment, together with the drop in unemployment, meant a lower unemployment rate. However, nationalization

Table 9.2 Labour Force Data After Stabilization

Year	Month	Unemployment[a]			Industrial Employment (thousands)		
		Industry	Percent of Total[b]	Rate[c]	Total	Percent of Total	(1938=100)
1946	Aug.	24,024	77.2	5.0	457.7	58.8	66.4
	Sept.	25,209	73.0	—[d]	—	—	—
	Oct.	28,212	69.6	—	—	—	—
	Nov.	26,506	63.0	—	526.5	62.0	76.4
	Dec.	27,849	62.2	5.0	—	—	—
1947	Jan.	35,995	65.8	—	—	—	—
	Feb.	39,260	65.5	—	554.9	62.4	80.6
	Mar.	47,708	67.2	7.9	—	—	—
	Apr.	50,031	66.4	—	—	—	—
	May	54,074	66.9	—	609.6	63.5	88.5
	June	—	—	—	—	—	—
	July	53,990	66.1	—	633.7	64.1	92.0
	Aug.	59,716	65.1	8.6	—	—	—
	Sept.	64,189	64.1	—	—	—	—
	Oct.	69,962	65.8	—	—	—	—
	Nov.	74,202	68.0	—	636.8	63.9	92.5
	Dec.	82,813	71.6	11.5	—	—	—
1948[e]	Jan.	110,589	—	—	—	—	—
	Feb.	114,182	—	—	—	—	—
1949	Jan.	96,000	—	—	—	—	—
	Feb.	103,000	—	—	—	—	—
	Mar.	102,000	—	—	—	—	—
	Apr.	95,000	—	—	—	—	—
	May	83,000	—	—	—	—	—
	June	77,000	—	—	—	—	—

Notes:
[a] Union members only.
[b] Unemployment in the remaining unionized sectors are for apprentices, clerical workers, caretakers, and unionized workers in the trade industry.
[c] Unemployed industrial union members, as a percent of industrial labour force.
[d] Signifies not available.
[e] In March 1948, all firms with 100 employees or more were nationalized. In October 1948, the first 3-year plan was introduced.
Sources: Magyar Gazdaságkutató Intézet Helyzetjelentései, 1945-47. [Situation Reports of the HIER], pp. 107-8; *MNBHK*, 1948, for Jan. and Feb. 1948 data; Baksay (1983, p. 117, table 17) for Jan. to June 1949 figures.

of all sectors of the economy, largely completed by the end of 1948 (Pető and Szakács 1985), as well as laws requiring that all able-bodied individuals possess some employment, meant that unemployment statistics are biased past March 1948.[17]

Since the unemployment data after stabilization reflect the policies of the Hungarian government after the end of the war, it is not clear that they shed much light on the possible existence of real effects after the abrupt end to hyperinflation, as has been attempted elsewhere though with some caution (BM 1983), since the natural rate of unemployment did not remain constant.

3.3 Output

Table 9.3 shows estimates of National Income (NI) for Hungary between 1938/39 and 1946/47. Thereafter, as the economy became almost completely nationalized, the data are not readily comparable with the earlier figures. However, indications are that, by 1948, NI had essentially attained its 1938 level (Pető and Szakács 1985, ch. 4).[18]

Table 9.3 National Income

Year	in millions of pengő	in 1938/30 pengő
1938/39	5,192	5,192
1939/40	5,940	5,506
1940/41	6,743	5,312
1941/42	8,311	5,171
1942/43	10,348	5,467
1943/44	10,543	5,214
1944	22,298[a]	7,097[a]
1945/46	9,274[b]	2,541[c]-2,576[d]
1946/47	11,816[d]	3,137[c]-3,202[d]

Notes:
[a] Estimate for 1944 available for Jan. to Dec. period only. See Ausch (1958), pp. 31 and 41.
[b] See Ausch (1958), p. 154.
[c] See 'Magyarország' and Pető and Szakács (1985), p. 20.
[d] All other estimates from *Magyar.*
Sources: Magyar nemzeti Jövedelem. [Hungary's National Income], Budapest, March 1947, no. 31; Ausch (1958); 'Magyarorszag Várhato Nemzeti Jövedelme az 1945/46 és az 1946/47 Gazdasági Évben.' [Hungary's Anticipated National Income for the Fiscal Years 1945/46, and 1946/47], HIER, Budapest, 5 June 1946; Pető and Szakács (1985).

The economic effects of the war were small until 1944 when the entire economy was geared to servicing the German war effort. The destruction from the war, which took place in large part during late 1944 and early 1945, shows up in the 1945/46 NI figures.[19] It is important to note, however, that expenditures on the war effort affected 1938/39 figures due to the Győri programme (see n.1). Hence, the most conservative estimate of real NI for 1946/47 does not fare badly with peacetime NI (60.4 per cent of the 1938/39 figure; 65 per cent, according to Spulber (1973, p 218)), if one accounts for the effect of war preparations on the prewar results.[20] In fact, internal studies by the HIER reveal that gross domestic production in 1946/47 was only 0.1 per cent lower relative to the business cycle peak of 1928/29, and 50 per cent greater relative to the business cycle through the year of 1932/33. (HIER, 'Adatok a Magyar Gyáripar Konjunkturális Helyzeténck Megélhéséhez' [Data on the Cyclical State and Needs of Hungarian Industry] no. 6, 25 Nov. 1947, p. 18).[21]

Of course, in examining these figures, account should also be taken of the severe burden of war reparation payments on the postwar data, as well as the postwar reconstruction policies of the Hungarian government described above. Pető and Szakács (1985, p. 23) have calculated that war reparation payments amounted to 33 per cent of government expenditures during the period January to March 1946, 30 per cent of the same figure for the July to December 1946 period, and 39 per cent during the 1946/47 fiscal year.

Since annual data may be a somewhat incomplete guide to the events of 1945-46, Table 9.4 provides some monthly manufacturing production data. Production was, by January 1946, approximately 60 per cent of prewar production (Ausch 1958, p. 77). At the time of stabilization, manufacturing production rose to approximately 80 per cent of the 1938 figure. Production data for coal and steel, two vital raw materials, likewise show a dramatic increase in early 1946, especially the second half of 1946. By August 1947, one year after stabilization, production averaged over 90 per cent of the prewar level.[22] Finally, evidence about the performance of the agricultural sector is also available. It reveals that by the summer of 1947 production of the most important agricultural commodities compared favorably with production for the 1931-40 period.[23]

3.4 Other Factors

Finally, a few other factors are sometimes thought to produce transition costs, such as territorial changes, large foreign trade deficits, and high real

Table 9.4 Hungarian Production Data

Year	Month	Index of Production[a] (1946 January = 100)	Average daily production of: coal (1937-1938=100)	steel
1945	June	—[b]	43.9	—
	July	—	43.1	10.2
	Aug.	—	52.7	9.6
	Sept.	—	56.8	6.2
	Oct.	—	53.0	—
	Nov.	—	54.1	—
	Dec.	—	65.2	—
1946	Jan.	100.0	61.9	15.3
	Feb.	103.0	68.6	16.1
	Mar.	104.7	69.5	17.1
	Apr.	111.2	67.4	25.4
	May	134.8	66.7	43.2
	June	115.1	65.0	50.1
	July	128.7	58.2	51.9
	Aug.	136.5	68.3	57.5
	Sept.	136.5	68.8	62.5
	Oct.	154.2	77.1	66.4
	Nov.	157.2	79.6	74.6
	Dec.	141.5	76.7	58.0
1947	Jan.	141.3	86.8	53.0
	Feb.	—	85.1	64.8
	Mar.	—	92.8	74.8
	Apr.	114.7	91.2	89.4
	May	122.3	89.1	97.4
	June	125.8	88.8	94.9
	July	125.7	83.8	90.9
	Aug.	130.8	87.5	102.3
	Sept.	151.5	92.2	112.1
	Oct.	173.8	95.9	91.6
	Nov.	—	101.1	87.3

Notes:
[a] Index of average production in sixteen manufacturing industries.
[b] Signifies not available.
Sources: Gazdaságstatisztikai Tájékoztató [Economic Statistics Bulletin] 1947, pp. 101, 683, 694 and *Magyar Gazdaságkutató Intézet Helyzetjelentései* [Situation Reports of the HIER] 1945-47, no. 54, p. 144.

interest rates. It is doubtful that any of the above considerations were particularly important in the Hungarian case.

Territorial changes took some time to be determined by treaty and, in any event, Hungary ended up with borders virtually identical to the prewar boundaries. In the case of foreign trade, the volume of exports exceeded the volume of imports (at 1938 prices) for the first 4 months following stabilization. Thereafter, a foreign trade deficit appeared but, based on a monthly average of figures for August 1946 to July 1947, the foreign trade deficit represented only 0.44 per cent of 1946/47 NI.

Real interest rates appear to have been negative throughout the first year of the stabilization. Hence, only quantity constraints on credit, which were severe as noted earlier, were effective. Discount rates at large and small banks were fixed at 12 and 13 per cent, respectively, while inflation in consumer prices between October 1946 and July 1947 was approximately 28.2 per cent in black markets during the same period.

4. CONCLUSIONS

There is perhaps justification for the use of the term 'Hungarian Currency Miracle' (Varga 1946) in describing the end of that country's hyper-inflation in 1946. Yet, this chapter has shown that transition costs did follow the end of the Hungarian hyperinflation. These costs resulted from the extreme nature of the inflation, the introduction and subsequent dismantling of massive reconstruction projects, as well as the process of economy-wide nationalization. More importantly, the price-setting behaviour of policymakers following stabilization was particularly significant in producing real effects in the Hungarian case. Therefore, the Hungarian experience, like the German one which preceded it, raises the possibility that an easy escape from hyperinflation may not be readily obtained. However, the fact that the price-setting problems experienced in Hungary in 1946 would not generally arise in milder inflations, actually reinforces Sargent's case for a no transition cost to lower inflation. In reaching such a conclusion, however, it is crucial to recognize the differences that are likely to arise between an economy emerging from a hyperinflation and one experiencing milder inflation. Finally, the chapter attempted to show that output data following the end of hyperinflation do not conceal much in the way of effects resulting from adjustment to a peacetime economy.

ENDNOTES

*.   Reprinted, with minor changes, with permission from the Ohio State University Press, and originally published in the *Journal of Money, Credit and Banking*, vol. 21 (May 1989), pp. 135-147. Financial assistance from the Social Sciences and Humanities Research Council of Canada (SSHRC), the Hungarian Academy of Sciences, under a Bilateral Exchange Grant, and Wilfrid Laurier University, is gratefully acknowledged. I am grateful to Dr. Ernő Huszti, former general manager of the National Bank of Hungary, the late Dr. György Ránki of the Hungarian Academy of Sciences, and Dr. Iván Pető then a staff member of the New Hungarian Archives, for their help. The hospitality of St. Antony's College and the Institute of Economics and Statistics, University of Oxford, where the final version of this paper was completed, is also appreciated. A large literature in Hungarian exists in the National Archives consisting mainly of economic studies of the 1945-1948 period conducted by the Hungarian Institute for Economic Research (HIER). Considerable difficulties in researching Hungarian sources, however, existed at the time the research was carried out (Siklos 1988). Finally, Michael Bordo, Gail Makinen, Elmus Wicker and three anonymous referees, offered helpful criticisms on earlier versions of this paper.

1.   The policy, known as the Győri programme, stipulated that 1 billion pengő (US $185.2 million US at 1938 exchange rates) were to be spent over a period of 5 years on industries directly or indirectly connected with German war preparations. See Siklos (1991) for fuller details.

2.   Spending figures for war purposes include armaments, clothing for troops, their transportation, as well as other commodities (including food) related to or to be used for war purposes.

3.   According to a UN Relief and Rehabilitation Agency report, *The Food Situation in Continental Europe* (operational analysis paper no. 41), 1947.

4.   The SEC was formed in December 1945 to monitor and plan the reconstruction and eventual stabilization, and was endowed with quasidictatorial powers.

5.   It is widely believed that the architect of the reforms was Eugene Varga (BM 1983, p. 814). In fact, he did not plan the reforms at all, reluctantly returning to Hungary after the war to lend credibility to them. Individuals in charge of implementing the stabilization of the pengő were not fully aware of his opinions on the subject, though their actions did, to some extent, reflect his ideas on inflation control. See J. Varga (1981), and Vas (1977).

6.   This policy resulted in the interesting phenomenon whereby official prices occasionally rose faster than black market prices (Huszti 1986).

7.   By the end of August 1946, 350 million forint notes were issued instead of the planned 240 million (Ausch 1958). Overvaluation of a stabilized currency is not, however, an unusual phenomenon (Bordo 1986).

8.   Berend (1966), and Vas (1977), stress that money supply was to be introduced at a rate slower than required by the anticipated needs of trade during the first year following price stability. Also in J. Varga (1981). The negative real economic effects experienced by Hungary may thus, in part, also be explained by Sargent's (1986) concern that excessive monetary control after a hyperinflation should be avoided to prevent a recession.

9.   Velocity moves with expected inflation in the manner described only if there are no changes in the other arguments of money demand. Data on the Hungarian experience with indexation in early 1946 also suggest a dramatic rise in expected inflation in the months leading up to stabilization (Siklos 1987b).

10.   Also see Chapter 6 in this volume for empirical evidence.

11.   It should be noted that the relative prices in Figure 9.1 were determined by the SEC for the beginning of August 1946. Thereafter, price regulations were relaxed. Food prices dominate the construction of consumer prices.

12.   The consumer price index on 31 July 1946 stood at 399,623 x 10^{24} (26 Aug. 1939=1), and so any relative price ceased to have much meaning at the end of the hyperinflation.

13.   BM (1983, p. 819) also mention this fact but fail to consider the output effects of the resulting price distortions, nor did they explore fully the rationale for the SEC's decision.

14.   As a result, official inflation during the first year following stabilization, was not significantly different from inflation in black markets, a further indication of the success of the stabilization. In Budapest, it stood at 27 per cent between 25 October 1946, and 7 September 1947, and 28.4 per cent in black markets, during he same period. Thereafter, the differential is apparently greater, which is one reason why such data ceased to be reported (see *Gazdaságstatisztikai Tájékoztató* [Economic Statistics Bulletin], September 1947, p. 14). However, between 25 October and 20 December 1947, official inflation in food prices was 4.7 per cent while, in black markets, the inflation rate during the same period was 22.4 per cent, based on the source listed above. No other data are available.

15.   There were some exceptions to this rule which affected, for example, those returning from prisoner-of-war camps.

16.   Detailed monthly figures for unemployment in the agricultural sector are unavailable, but what evidence there is suggests that unemployment was minimal in that sector. One source (Baksay 1983) suggests that agricultural unemployment was high after stabilization, for a short period, especially in 1947, as a consequence of poor weather experienced in 1946. The author does not mention the role of collectivization in this sector, begun in 1945, which no doubt also had some employment effects, as well as the government policy change indicated in the text, which also had repercussions in the agricultural sector. The data in Table 9.2 are for unemployment in the unionized sector which represents approximately 85 per cent of total unemployment. Union contracts were not such that union workers were laid off last.

17.   Available unemployment data for the March to December 1948 period are incomplete, and appear to be unreliable, and were therefore not included in the table. The absence of unemployment data for this period, during which time the programme for nationalization progressed rapidly, suggests perhaps that the immediate impact of this policy on labour markets was greater than policymakers were willing to admit, especially on the eve of national elections. I must add, however, that I have no formal evidence to support this contention.

18.   Because Hungary was essentially an agrarian nation its fiscal year was not on a calendar year basis. Spulber (1957, p. 218) presents different estimates from mine. His 1938 estimates appear to be on a calendar year basis. The figures in Table 9.1 are based on the 'new' system of National Accounting (1947). It is unclear, however, how this system differs from North American standards of the time.

19.   Possibly because much of the destruction resulting from the war occurred in 1945, Ausch (1958, pp. 30-1, 41) presents NI figures for the calendar year 1944. See Berend (1966).

20.   Expenditures on the war effort represented 20.7 per cent of real NI of 1941, 30.5 per cent of the 1942 figure, 35.7 per cent of 1943 real NI, and 47 per cent of 1944 real NI.

21.   Mark (1947), an economist at the US Legation in Budapest in 1945-46, cites UN Rehabilitation Agency reports in 1946 which place Hungary's rate of recovery as fastest among all the European nations along with Belgium. Further indications of the dramatic recovery of Hungary in the space of a few months is provided by the

following data. In May of 1945, only 3.3 per cent of total vehicles, relative to the 1938 total, operated in Hungary. By December of 1946, this rose to 80.8 per cent. Furthermore, 65.7 per cent of bridges, and 53.8 per cent of railway bridges across the two main rivers in Hungary (Danube and Tisza), and 87.7 per cent of other bridges were reconstructed by the time of stabilization. See *Magyarország Háborus Kárai: A Pénzugy Minisztérium Béketárgyalási Anyagok Összefoglalása II rész* [Hungary's War Damages: A Synthesis of the Finance Ministry's Materials Used in the Peace Talks, Part II], Budapest: Hungarian State Printers, 1946.

22.   Also, average production in 21 major industries reached 104.3 per cent of 1938 output by October of 1947 (Pető and Szakács 1985, p. 121). Also, see discussion in HIER, 'Magyarország Gazdasági Helyzete Stabilizáció Kezdetén' [The State of Hungary's Economy at the Beginning of Stabilization], Budapest, 30 Nov. 1946.

23.   Land reforms begun in March 1945 must also have had some influence on production data. The number of small property holders (250 acres or less) increased by roughly 54 per cent while the number of large holders decreased by approximately 43 per cent (Pető and Szakács 1985, p. 39).

REFERENCES

Ausch, S. (1958), *Az 1945-1946 Évi Infláció és Stabilizácio*, [The 1945-1946 Inflation and Stabilization], Kossuth, Budapest.

Baksay, Z. (1983), *A Munkaerőhelyzet Alakulása és a Munkanélkuliség Felszámolasá Magyarországon (1945-1949)*, [The Development of Employment and the Elimination of Unemployment in Hungary (1945-1949)], Akadémiai Kiadó, Budapest.

Basch, A. (1943), *The Danube Basin and the German Economic Sphere*, Columbia University Press, New York.

Berend, T.I. (1966), 'Az 1946 Évi Stabilizáció', [The 1946 Stabilization], *Közgazdasági Szemle* 13 (July/Aug.), pp. 890-98.

Berend, T.I. and Ránki, G. (1979), *Underdevelopment and Economic Growth*, Akadémiai Kiadó, Budapest.

Bomberger, W.A. and Makinen, G.E. (1983), 'The Hungarian Hyperinflation and Stabilization of 1945-46', *Journal of Political Economy* 91 (October), pp. 801-24.

Bordo, M.D. (1986), 'Explorations in Monetary History: A Survey of the Literature', *Explorations in Economic History* 23, pp. 339-415.

Cagan, P. (1956), 'The Monetary Dynamics of Hyperinflation', in M. Friedman (ed.), *Studies in the Quantity Theory of Money*, pp. 25-117, University of Chicago Press, Chicago.

Dornbusch, R. and Fischer, S. (1986), 'Stopping Hyperinflations Past and Present', *Weltwirtschaftlichtes Archiv* 122, pp. 1-47.

Eichengreen, B. (1986), 'Book Reviews', *Journal of Economic Literature* 24 (December), pp. 1812-15.

Garber, P.M. (1982), 'Transition from Inflation to Price Stability', in K. Brunner & A.H. Meltzer (eds.), *Carnegie-Rochester Conference Series on Public Policy*, vol. 16, pp. 11-42, North-Holland, Amsterdam.

Huszti, E. (1986), 'Hiperinfláció és Stabilizáció 1945-46: Negyven Éves a Forint.' ['Hyperinflation and Stabilization 1945-46: The Forint is Forty Years Old'], National Bank of Hungary, Budapest.

Laidler, D.E.W. (1993), *The Demand for Money*, 4th edn, Harper-Collins, New York.

Laidler, D.E.W. (1987), 'Wicksell and Fischer on the "Backing" of Money and the Quantity Theory', in K. Brunner & A.H. Meltzer (eds.), *Carnegie-Rochester Conference Series on Public Policy*, vol. 27, pp. 325-34, North-Holland, Amsterdam.

Mark, L. Jr. (1947), 'Post-War Inflation in Hungary', M.A. University of California.

Pető, I. and Szakács, S. (1985), *A Hazai Gazdaság Négy Évtizedének Története: 1945-1985 (I)*, [Four Decades National Economic History: 1945-1985 (I)], Közgazdasági es Jogi Könyvkiadó, Budapest.

Sargent, T.J. (1993), *Rational Expectations and Inflation*, 2nd edn, Harper-Collins College Publishers, New York.

Sargent, T.J. and Wallace, N. (1982), 'The Real Bills Doctrine Versus the Quantity Theory: A Reconsideration', *Journal of Political Economy* (December), pp. 1212-36.

Siklos, P.L. (1991), *War Finance, Reconstruction, Hyperinflation and Stabilization in Hungary, 1938-48*, Macmillan & St. Martin's Press, London and New York.

Siklos, P.L. (1988), *The Hungarian Hyperinflation and Stabilization of 1945 and 1946: A Bibliography (with an Introduction)*, unpublished.

Siklos, P.L. (1987a), 'Hyperinflation and Stabilization: Hungary, 1945-1946', *The New Hungarian Quarterly* (Fall), pp. 137-42(a).

Siklos, P.L. (1987b), 'Additional Thoughts on the Hungarian Hyperinflation of 1945-46', *South African Journal of Economics* 55 (March 1987), pp. 83-5.

Spulber, N. (1973), 'National Income and its Distribution', in E. Helmreich (ed.), *Hungary*, pp. 214-28, Greenwood Press. Westport, Conn.

Spulber, N. (1957), *The Economics of Communist Eastern Europe*, MIT and John Wiley & Sons, New York.

Varga, I. (1964), *Az Ujjab Magyarpénztörténet és Egyes Elméleti Tanulságai*, [The New Hungarian Monetary History and Some of its Theoretical Lessons], Közgazdasági is Jogi Könyvkiadó, Budapest.

Varga, I. (1946), 'A Magyar Valutacsoda', [The Hungarian Currency Miracle], HIER, Budapest.

Varga, J. (1981), 'Jó a Forint, de Kevés Van Belőle', [The Forint is Good but there are Too Few of Them], in *A Tőkés Gazdaság a II. Világháború után: Válogatott Irások (1945-1954)* [The Capitalist Economy after World War II: Selected Writings (1945-1954)], pp. 43-46, Kossuth, Budapest.

Vas, Z. (1977), *30-Éves as Forint*, [The Forint is 30 Years Old], National Bank of Hungary, Budapest.

Wicker, E. (1986), 'Terminating Hyperinflations in the Dismembered Hapsburg Monarchy', *American Economic Review* 76 (June), pp. 350-64.

Index